Luminos is the Open Access monograph publishing program
from UC Press. Luminos provides a framework for preserving and
reinvigorating monograph publishing for the future and increases
the reach and visibility of important scholarly work. Titles published
in the UC Press Luminos model are published with the same high
standards for selection, peer review, production, and marketing as
those in our traditional program. www.luminosoa.org

Life at the Center

Life at the Center

Haitians and Corporate Catholicism in Boston

Erica Caple James

UNIVERSITY OF CALIFORNIA PRESS

University of California Press
Oakland, California

Suggested citation: James, E. C., *Life at the Center: Haitians and Corporate Catholicism in Boston*. Oakland: University of California Press, 2024.
DOI: https://doi.org/10.1525/luminos.188

Cataloging-in-Publication Data is on file at the Library of Congress.

ISBN 978-0-520-40054-2 (pbk. : alk. paper)
ISBN 978-0-520-40055-9 (ebook)

33 32 31 30 29 28 27 26 25 24
10 9 8 7 6 5 4 3 2 1

CONTENTS

ACKNOWLEDGMENTS

This book about the Haitian Multi-Service Center in Boston centers the contemporary lives of people and places that developed on unceded land once stewarded by the Massachusett peoples (among others). As an African American scholar who received and later researched my own multiracial heritage—including enslaved, Indigenous, and occupying peoples—I am aware how challenging, poignant, and sensitive the process of uncovering, verifying, and preserving undocumented histories can be. I have not been able to trace fully the genealogies of the edifices, places, and spaces in which this story unfolded (and was written). I acknowledge all those known and unknown persons who once cared for and embodied these sites, the complexities of their histories, and their enduring ties to these geographies. Any mistakes, oversights, or omissions are unintended.

I am tremendously grateful for the support I've received over the many years I've worked on this project. I have been as much a recipient of the care, welcome, compassion, and advocacy the Haitian Multi-Service Center staff and advisory board members offered as were their clients. I wish I could name them all, but instead I hold them in highest esteem. I am deeply indebted to Catholic Charities and the Archdiocese of Boston for allowing me to document the work done on site and for the willingness of many staff members to discuss their mission and charitable practices in everyday life. My hope is that my interpretation will permit further discernment regarding the role of "works of mercy" in civic engagement. The Center's story offers opportunities to reflect on how best to promote and protect "life," and through what kinds of institutional partnerships. It also provides a necessary window through which to understand better Haitian history and the experiences of Haitians. Thank you to Jean Richard Anthenor, Serginio Sylvain, and Brittany Peters for assisting me with translating and transcribing a few sensitive interviews.

I have also received encouraging feedback from many colleagues—undergraduate students, graduate students, faculty, and staff—at Harvard University, Harvard Divinity School, Georgetown University, Washington University in St. Louis, Teachers College, Columbia University, UVA, Wellesley College, Brown University, the University of Chicago School of Social Services Administration, and MIT, among others. I am grateful for support from Arthur Kleinman, Mary-Jo DelVecchio Good, and Byron Good, especially for awarding me the NIMH Postdoctoral Fellowship at the Department of Social Medicine, Harvard Medical School. During the fellowship I trained at the University of Miami Department of Anthropology, and I thank them for hosting me. I am especially thankful for my time as a fellow at the Radcliffe Institute for Advanced Study and for assistance from the NIH Health Disparities Research Program. Without the expert assistance of Chris Walley and Chris Boebel at MIT, the documentary film *Doing Anthropology* would not have captured a pivotal moment in the Center's history. I also appreciate early support from fellow scholars in MIT Anthropology, and in particular for the manuscript workshop. Receiving feedback from Regine Jackson, Margarita Mooney, Elisabeth McAlister, and Linda Barnes—and in another context, from Michael Fischer (and his students) —was critical and helpful in thinking through this history. Discussions with Yehuda Goodman helped me to consider how faith-based organizations and the state coproduce charity and affect each other's forms of governance. Conversations with Amy Moran-Thomas about mercy aided me in discerning what to reveal and what to leave unsaid.

My colleagues in DUSP have offered new ways of thinking about charity, humanitarianism, and development, and their respective roles in "worldmaking." I am especially appreciative of the "homeplace" the department aspires to create within and outside MIT. DUSP's mission to improve racial justice, multiracial democratic governance, the climate crisis, and the wealth gap by means of our collective work has been tremendously inspiring. I am especially grateful to former students Laurie Denyer-Willis, Darien Williams, and Bridget Burns for their research assistance, and to many others in my courses for providing me invaluable feedback as I completed this work.

At the University of California Press, I thank Kate Marshall, Kevin O'Neill, Stephanie Summerhays, Chad Attenborough, and the production team, plus the Atelier series authors. They have assembled a wonderful community of writers. I thank the anonymous reviewers for their feedback on the manuscript, particularly the reader whose comments reflected a close reading and deep commitment to placing this work in the context of sociomoral struggles. The work is better for their time and feedback. I thank MIT for funding the open access version of this book.

No words can express my gratitude to Michele David, Michelle Jacobs, Thabele Leslie-Mazwi, Dean Donahue, Dana Kotler, William Caddoo, Elaine Cao, and their respective staff members for enabling me to reach this milestone (and to be able to continue writing).

To Sheri Weiser, Dale Gadsden, Merina Corby, and Yvette Scudder: thank you for your friendship and for reminding me to have fun.

To my parents June Cargile and Raymond James: thank you for instilling in me a deep curiosity about religion and the unseen, and respect for a life of scholarship. Mom, your reminders to "stop"—whether regarding the length of my sentences, my doubts, or overburdening myself—will ring in my ears forever. Dad, I promise one day we will sail together. To my siblings—Lori James, Ray James, and Kalle James-Wintjen—to cousins Khadija James-Keating, Linda McMurdock, and Diane Sammons, and to all of our families: your reading has improved the work, your care and encouragement have been priceless, and your love makes it all worthwhile.

Finally, to my immediate family, who have been with me throughout this journey: Kieren, you are always in my heart. Ayanna and Faisal, you were both with me daily at the Center and you bring me joy each day. Malick, your support and love have made traveling this road a vocation. Rocky, you are our four-legged member (and cannot read—yet), but your spirit and love are indomitable!

My family, I look forward to our next adventures.

1

———

Life at the Center

A corporation is an artificial being, invisible, intangible, and existing only in contemplation of law. . . . By these means, a perpetual succession of individuals are capable of acting for the promotion of the particular object, like one immortal being.
—CHIEF JUSTICE JOHN MARSHALL,
   DARTMOUTH COLLEGE V. WOODWARD, 1819

Though we laud charity as a Christian virtue we know that it wounds.
—MARY DOUGLAS

Toute vérité n'est pas bonne à dire. (Some things are better left unsaid.)
—FRANTZ PÉRALTE MONESTIME,
   FOUNDER AND FIRST HMSC EXECUTIVE DIRECTOR

"I didn't want to talk to you."

"I know," I responded, relieved at completing an intense interview with Frantz Monestime about his life and reasons for cofounding the Haitian Multi-Service Center (the Center).[1] The conversation was difficult to arrange and almost didn't take place. I had heard about Monestime, the Center's first executive director (ca. 1982–86), from several stakeholders, but I'd had difficulty finding him. Some who united to establish the Center were no longer in Greater Boston. A few pioneers, as one founder called this group, had died. Others refused to talk about these early years or did not respond to my requests for information. Perhaps they were reluctant to revisit this history and had chosen to move on and not look back.

We met one evening in spring 2011 at Monestime's office suite in a commercial area of suburban Boston. At first he was hesitant to sign a consent form indicating whether I could use his name, title, or direct quotations from the interview. To my surprise, his hesitation was neither solely about signing, nor telling his story, but rather about the institutions or persons I represented and my intentions: "Did you ever work for Catholic Charities? Who are you again? Why are you writing this book?" I was unsure whether Monestime's concerns stemmed from nervousness about the consent process, deeper ambivalence and, perhaps, antipathy toward the Roman Catholic Archdiocese of Boston (the Church) and area Catholic institutions, or a desire to control the interview process (maybe all three). I repeated much of my initial phone introduction, saying that I was not and had never been an employee of Catholic Charities (the Charity), but I had served on the HMSC Advisory Board, between 2005 and 2010 roughly, and was now writing the Center's biography.

I told him I wanted to present the history as accurately as possible, but I needed these permissions in writing for clarity and to protect us both. His story, I said, was one of the most important pieces of a complicated organizational puzzle I had been attempting to assemble about the Church, the Charity, and the Center. He deliberated, pen poised in the air. Without his story in his own words, I said, the book would be inaccurate and incomplete. I knew there were disputes regarding how, when, and by whom the Center was founded. I wanted to uncover why there were discrepancies regarding these events.

With a deep sigh, he put pen to paper, releasing me to record his words, to identify him by name, and to quote directly from his speech. He told me he'd been asked many times before to do audio or visual interviews on his tenure at the Center, but he had never done so.[2] He was tremendously frustrated to hear and see the Center's history reported incorrectly on the radio or in the newspaper, but had maintained silence, feeling he shouldn't or couldn't speak out.

"There are things maybe I should not tell you, too," he said with heaviness. "There is a saying we have in Haiti: 'Toute vérité n'est pas bonne à dire' [Some things are better left unsaid—literally, Every truth is not good to say]." I affirmed it was up to him what he wanted to disclose, and he should just tell me as much as was comfortable. My job would be to tell the story as best I could.

"Ok. Let's go."

THE CHURCH, THE CHARITY, AND THE CENTER

Monestime was not present when, on September 25, 2003, nearly one hundred people gathered on a vacant, grassy Boston lot for a sign-unveiling ceremony announcing the site as the "Future Home of the Dorchester Community Service Center: A center responding to the needs and interests of our diverse community." Located near the intersection of Columbia Road and Geneva Avenue, an area with high concentrations of racial and ethnic minorities and much smaller percentages of European Americans, the land had been described as "empty" and "unused" (Forry 2003).[3] For many neighborhood residents the parcel symbolized Boston's neglect of its most vulnerable populations. The billboard listed a cast of characters involved in the service center project and diagrammed visually some of the intricate connections among Haitians, the Church, and affiliated Catholic

FIGURE 1. Sign unveiling for the Dorchester Community Service Center. Photo credit: Catholic Charities Archdiocese of Boston, Inc.

charitable institutions, city, state, and federal government, public and private donors, and, through the charities, countless volunteers.

A Charity media photo capturing the sign and celebration participants further maps some of these public and private stakeholders (see Figure 1). Although the sign did not acknowledge Jean Yawkey (1909–92)—one of the former owners of the Boston Red Sox baseball team, whose foundation pledged five million dollars to complete the new ten million dollar building[4]—the names of local dignitaries were prominently displayed. Standing at the sign's left, Mayor Thomas M. Menino (1942–2014) was listed across from his counterpart in the Church, Archbishop Séan Patrick O'Malley, who stood at the billboard's immediate right.[5]

Established as a diocese in 1808 and attaining status as an archdiocese in 1875, by the early 2000s the Roman Catholic Archdiocese of Boston (RCAB—the Church) served nearly two million ethnically diverse Catholics in 290 parishes across 144 communities in eastern Massachusetts.[6] The archdiocese had educated approximately 42,000 students annually in its Catholic schools and 156,000 in religious education classes. Through pastoral and social service outreach, the Church had ministered to two hundred thousand individuals.[7] In addition, the archdiocese had aided nearly one million patients annually through its "health care ministry."[8] Although Protestants have increasingly attracted Haitians in Haiti and the diaspora (Brodwin 1996, 2003; Conway 1978; Louis 2014; Richman 2005),

Haitians remain predominantly Catholic and send many children to Catholic schools (Jackson 2007).

Underneath the names of these state and church executives were those of their respective cabinet members: the African American civic leader, Charlotte Golar Richie, chief [of Housing] and director of neighborhood development in the mayor's office (not pictured), and South Boston native, Dr. Joseph Doolin, the first layperson to serve as archdiocesan cabinet secretary for social services (pictured next to Archbishop O'Malley).

Dr. Doolin also served as president of the Charity. Since its founding as a child welfare agency in 1903, the Catholic Charitable Bureau of the Archdiocese of Boston, Inc. had been a clearinghouse for Catholic social welfare in eastern Massachusetts. In the sign's lower left corner, the Charity's own trademark, a bright red heart enclosing a smaller black cross, was one of two color images. Catholic Charities USA (CCUSA) reports that in 2009, 163 Catholic charities agencies in the United States served 9,164,981 (unduplicated) people through "food services" (food banks and pantries, soup kitchens, home delivered meals, etc.), "services that strengthen families" (counseling and mental health, immigration, refugee, pregnancy, addiction, and adoption programs), "services that build strong communities" (social support, education and enrichment, socialization and neighborhood services, and health-related services, especially to at-risk populations), "housing-related services" (temporary shelter, counseling and assistance, supervised living, permanent housing, and transitional housing), "basic assistance" (clothing, basic needs, utilities, emergency financial, and prescription assistance), and "disaster services."[9]

At the time, approximately 165 national Catholic charitable organizations offered humanitarian relief, economic development, and social services through a federation the Holy See authorizes called Caritas Internationalis.[10] The Church and affiliated Catholic social service agencies around the world presented their work as promoting life and providing support to persons in need "from cradle to grave."

At the heart of the sign was a striking architectural rendering of the proposed red and gold brick Yawkey Center through which the Church and the Charity would offer several social services. Listed at the sign's base, the childcare, adult education, employment and education, family services, and AIDS programs buttressed the church, state, and private sector actors named above them. An onlooker would not assume the Church had pledged funding for a new Haitian social service center. Most Haitians thought the new Dorchester building would be theirs, in the way the Archdiocese of Miami—in concert with Haitian civic leaders, volunteers, and parishioners—inaugurated the ten-acre Notre Dame d'Haiti Catholic Church and the Pierre Toussaint Center in 1981 to offer Haitian newcomers economic, educational, legal, social, and spiritual support (Mooney 2009: 1–13).

In very small print, between the church and private sector stakeholders on the right of the sign, were names of two Charity programs that would occupy the new building. Since its birth, the Haitian Multi-Service Center (HMSC—the Center), established "by Haitians, for Haitians," had helped refugees, immigrants, and the American-born poor to rebuild new lives. In 1978, Haitians founded the Center in Boston's St. Leo Parish. Between 1986 and 1992, the Charity gradually assumed supervision when Cardinal Bernard Francis Law transferred the Center from direct administration by the Chancery, the archdiocese's administrative offices (CCAB 1995: 19). In merging with the Charity, the Center was incorporated into the largest private social service network in Massachusetts with an annual operating budget of approximately forty million dollars spread across 140 social service programs.[11] Through the Charity, the Center became an affiliate of Catholic Charities USA (CCUSA), the largest private human services network in the United States, with an operating budget of approximately $4.275 billion dollars, 67 percent of which was funded by government agencies.[12]

FINDING THE CENTER

I became invested in the lives of Boston Haitians when, in spring 2005, "Dr. Taylor Smith," a friend, mentor, and social scientist, nominated me to the Center's advisory board, which she had served (unbeknownst to me) for nearly ten years. She offered to discuss with Pierre Imbert, its longest serving executive director, the new ethnographic research I hoped to conduct, and she thought an opportunity might open in Boston or with the Center with his support. Imbert and the HMSC Advisory Board approved my membership at their April meeting. My first board experience occurred at its June 2005 annual retreat. The staff and board members communicated hope, enthusiasm, and accomplishment as they prepared for the move into the new Yawkey Center. At the retreat I was appointed liaison between the board and other Boston Haitian nonprofits working to reduce racial and ethnic health disparities in the Haitian community. In December 2005, the HMSC began moving into the new building.

After five months circulating between the board and the Haitian social service network, I developed the strong sense that the Center epitomized an American success whose story should be told. In February 2006, with Imbert's backing, I requested permission from the advisory board, Charity administrators, and Center staff to conduct ethnographic research onsite and to write the Center's history. In June 2006, I received authorization and commenced volunteering. Between 2006 and 2007, I spent nearly fifteen months participating daily in programs, collecting staff members' life histories, and conducting archival research. I volunteered in the adult education and elder psychosocial support programs and documented other health programs—an HIV/AIDS prevention program, Sante Manman Se Sante Pitit (Healthy Mother Healthy Child, SMSSP), and general education and health promotion activities. I interviewed more than sixty current and former stakeholders: Church leaders in the archdiocese of Boston, Charity employees and members of its board of trustees, Center staff and advisory board members, as well as other community leaders. Between 2007 and fall 2010, I continued service on the advisory board (albeit less frequently), until an out-of-state move made participation unfeasible. From 2011 to 2016, I interviewed additional stakeholders, as I located them, about the Center's identity, culture, and connections to Catholic institutions.

Toward the end of my research, the hopefulness and pride shared collectively at the 2003 sign unveiling had taken a dramatic turn. By 2009, most long-term Center staff members had either been fired or had resigned. Many advisory board members left or limited their participation. Although archdiocesan community outreach intensified following the 2008 hurricanes and the devastating 2010 earthquake in Haiti, the Center no longer had its own executive director and was neither predominantly Haitian-managed nor independent. In 2017, Haitians publicly protested the closure of the last Center program prioritizing their community. At this writing, the former hub of the Massachusetts Haitian American community is a shell of itself and fully managed by Catholic Charities. What happened?

• • •

This book describes how public and private actors with distinct but complementary missions collaborated to help Haitian refugees and immigrants gain economic independence, health, security, and citizenship in the United States.[13] Beginning in the 1970s, Haitian professionals mobilized volunteers and resources to tackle their compatriots' challenges in the Boston area. From the 1980s to the late 1990s, their efforts, supported by Catholic institutions, produced a social service program offering new Haitian arrivals and long-standing impoverished residents various modes of social and civic incorporation. By the early 2000s, these same successes anchored an archdiocesan fundraising campaign for the establishment of a new Dorchester community service center. The interaction between the secular and religious stakeholders strengthened,[14] but also eroded, the independent organizational gains Haitians had made in response to their community's social, political, legal, economic, and health crises.

Thus, this ethnographic history also offers a postmortem assessment of the factors leading to the Center's apparent death. My use of clinical language is intentional and aims to unravel interwoven questions. Was the decline of the Center's corporate body "natural"—as in the life course of an organization—unintended, or deliberate? Does its fate reflect the psychosocial legacies of Haiti's turbulent past or other political and economic factors? Did the institution change too drastically from its founding mission, causing its constituents to rescind their support? Or has the Center transcended the limitations of its initial material form to become something else—fully incorporated within the Church's charity network?

It is important to acknowledge deeply held disputes whether the Center has, in fact, died. If I search for "Haitian Multi-Service Center" on the internet, the agency appears under education programs on the Charity website.[15] The archdiocesan weekly newspaper, the *Boston Pilot*, advertised the Center in 2022.[16] Although the HMSC name remains on the Yawkey Center building, the Center is no longer semi-autonomous. Despite hopes for a new era in a new building, something has irrevocably changed. Many long-standing stakeholders argue what remains of the program now serving the Charity has lost its soul.

In telling this story, the book explores several paradoxes of aid relevant beyond this case: despite the best of intentions, and whether in the form of religious charity, humanitarian relief, sustainable development, or corporate social responsibility initiatives, charitable actors may inadvertently reproduce the social inequalities and power disparities between donors and recipients. A second paradox arises from the empirical investigation underlying this study: giving practices can generate power and social capital for the donor, even while the recipient benefits from aid. Third, the power and trust generated by aiding others—through bodily care, material support, education, and pastoral care, and so on—can create good will and loyalty but may deepen aid recipients' dependence. Finally, inequity in parties to charitable transactions can lead to resistance to organized benevolence, conflicts, and even abuse. Nevertheless, the same modes of charity or philanthropy that previously caused harm can be redeployed or promoted visibly to repair damage and rebuild "charitable brands."

This book suggests scholars, policymakers, and planners ask why, in the face of such paradoxes, do stakeholders remain faithful to or depart from mission-driven institutions perceived to have betrayed or harmed them? What processes sustain or wound stakeholders' faith in, and loyalty to, an organization? I refer to the constellation of such paradoxes using the concept of "corporate Catholicism."

CORPORATE CATHOLICISM

> **Corporate,** *adj.* and *adv.* /ˈkɔːpərət/
> a. United into one body. Embodied. Corpulent. Having a body. Material. Pertaining to or affecting the body. Of or belonging to a body politic, or corporation, or to a body of persons.
> *n.* A large company, a corporation.
> *v.* To form into a corporation or body politic; to incorporate.
> **Corporate culture,** *n.* the ethos of a particular company, or that of large businesses in general; the approach a company takes towards the working environment of its staff.
> **Corporate identity,** *n.* (a) *U.S.* status as a legally distinct incorporated company; (b) *orig. U.S.* a company's public image, esp. the use of a distinctive logo and coordinated packaging, etc., to aid product recognition.
> —*OXFORD ENGLISH DICTIONARY*

The Center's biography suggests three main concepts to be developed across this book: corporate Catholicism, pastoral power, and the compassion economy (James 2010, 2012, 2019). Corporate Catholicism indexes the historical ways the Church and affiliated Catholic institutions have integrated others into the Church's "mystical body." The concept also signifies how religious bodies may construct legal entities or facsimiles to engage the state, such as for property ownership. Corporate Catholicism is rooted in a faith-based vision of economy and society enacted in local moral worlds (Kleinman and Kleinman 1991). Nonetheless, Catholicism possesses a hierarchical corporate governance structure and a mobile regulatory system to (1) ensure compliance with canon law, (2) manage conflicts, (3) monitor the movement of people, finances, symbols, and information, and (4) administer property throughout its global network (Laguerre 2011: 24–28, 64–91). But as social theorist Michel S. Laguerre (2011: 22) argues, "Transglobal network government is not simply the public administration of a transnational organization, but it is also management of religious and moral values."

The chapters of this book expand Laguerre's notion of corporate network governance and draw on various definitions of the word "corporate" (from the Latin root *corpus, corporis* [body]) to inform the meanings of corporate Catholicism. "Corporate" refers to assemblages of persons united into one body, like a corporation; members of a body politic who are incorporated into, forced from, or excluded from a political body; the fleshly, corporal (or corporeal) and carnal nature of embodiment, which becomes an object of pastoral care; processes of legal incorporation (and the working conditions under which charity is enacted); and finally, the representational images associated with a corporation—its brand. In corporate Catholicism, charity, typically divided into corporal and spiritual "works of mercy" (Delany 1911), addresses the care needs of embodied individuals, but offers both donors and recipients opportunities to coproduce pastoral power.

"Pastoral power," a power of care (Albahari 2015, 2019; Foucault 1982, 2007), facilitates corporate Catholic processes. Michel Foucault argues pastoral power is a "Christian" form of governance preceding (and undergirding) sovereign power, discipline, biopower, and governmentality in modern secular states (Foucault 1991, 2007). Although Foucault affirms, "Where there is power there is resistance" (1990: 95), he does not analyze resistances to pastoral power and presumes "pastors" hold greater power to compel obedience than may occur in practice. As this ethnographic history will later show, pastors confront corporeality and carnality in their flock (and in themselves) and may violate the ideals of the Catholic charitable brand.

SANCTUARY

The Center's natal home at St. Leo's was roughly a mile south of the Columbia Road lot in Franklin Field—a Greater Boston neighborhood often depicted as a "hot spot" for gang violence, crime, drugs, sex work, and other social ills. The historic Victorian buildings the Center shared with the parish were dilapidated. Still, the site provided some shelter from environmental dangers and moral risks. In addition, the Center's programs shielded clients from racial discrimination, economic and legal insecurities, educational and linguistic barriers, and hunger and ill health. These conditions greatly hampered their path to social and political incorporation in Boston, in Massachusetts, and in the United States (see Figure 2).

FIGURE 2. Haitian Multi-Service Center, main building, ca. 2004. Photo credit: Robert L. Powell.

The Center was an oasis for Haitian migrants establishing new lives in the United States. Haitians in Greater Boston likened it to Plymouth Rock (Forry 2006), Ellis Island (Manly 1994) and the Citadel (Stockman 2003), "the symbol of Haitian nationhood" (Bellegarde-Smith 2004: 44). King Henri Christophe built the citadel fort in northern Haiti between 1806 and 1820. The structure enabled the newly independent Republic of Hayti (1804) to ward off military incursions by foreign powers in the nineteenth century (Trouillot 1995). Haitians also compared the Center to the *lakou*, a spatial compound in Haiti where an extended family—including ancestral spirits and family Vodou spirits (*lwa* in Haitian Creole)—live, work together, and maintain cultural traditions across seen and unseen worlds.

Comparisons of the Center to iconic edifices, historic events, and complex sociocultural institutions indicate its importance to Haitians across Greater Boston and other transnational communities. Much like Alexis de Tocqueville's nineteenth-century observations of civic associations, democracy, and citizenship in the United States,[17] the Center embodied an American ideal. Its spirit of tolerance, self-help, voluntarism, hospitality, reciprocity, and justice brought together populations from diverse class, racial, and ethnic backgrounds whose paths might not ordinarily have crossed.

Once the largest of a handful of Haitian social service organizations, the Center offered food and emergency relief, childcare and language classes, educational and health programs, refugee and immigration services, legal counseling, employment assistance, and other aid across Greater Boston. Like many programs sited in the national Catholic Charities "movement"—an assemblage "committed to social transformation" whose mission stems from "roots in the Gospel and its Catholic identity and tradition" (Snyder 2010: 13)—its mandate has been to support families, promote community development, and assist immigrants in the struggle for social and economic self-sufficiency.

The Center embraced numerous stakeholders, including current and former clients, staff, and advisory board members; current and former Charity staff members and members of the Charity's board of trustees; Catholic clergy, Haitian civic leaders, and the Greater Boston Haitian communities. Throughout my research there, its staff members asserted that the embattled former archbishop of Boston, Cardinal Bernard Francis Law, also found refuge at the Center.[18] The HMSC's connection to the controversial cardinal was profound at times of crisis—whether in Haiti or in the archdiocese. The ultimate benefit of the Center's connection to the cardinal remains in question and returns this analysis to the concept of pastoral power.

Pastoral power is produced and reproduced not only in the sacramental encounters between priests and the laity, but also through acts of caregiving (Kleinman 2009). In contemporary institutionalized charity, pastoral power is deployed not only toward the material and corporal, and moral and spiritual dimensions of life, but also to save the "secular soul"—an entity conjured through modern bureaucratic procedures (Foucault 1979; Fassin 2018; Povinelli 2006, 2011; Rose 1999). Pastoral care has been extended, and sometimes exchanged, between the Charity, the Center, and their respective staff members and clients, as well as between these organizations and the Greater Boston Haitian community (among others). I aim to show in this book how pastoral power occurs along a continuum: ranging from compassionate care, correction, and discipline to troubling situations producing what I call "negative charisma," including exploitation and abuse. Pastoral power emerges, is reinforced, and resisted in corporate Catholic settings.

Corporate Catholicism also interacts with the compassion economy: finite flows of beneficent material resources, knowledge and expertise, technologies, therapies, and other forms of aid circulating between an aid apparatus and its clients and between the aid apparatus and donors (James 2010, 2019). This apparatus, a powerful transnational network of mobile humanitarian and development actors, "governs" clients through social services provided in place or on behalf of fragile or failing states (James 2010, 2011, 2012, 2019). Such an economy aims to mitigate crises, promote sustainable development, and empower populations identified as in need of intervention. Although the temporal, structural, and political contexts undergirding corporate Catholicism and the compassion economy may differ, there are similarities between the secular aid I observed in Haiti and the faith-based practices I witnessed in the United States, including disputes regarding how (and to whom) benevolence circulates.

How do individuals and institutions confront suffering, offer social rehabilitation, and facilitate migrant incorporation through faith-based charity? In addition to incorporation models based on ethnic or national identity, there are other possibilities of inclusion as members of "networks of social relations through which an individual or an organized group of individuals becomes linked to an institution recognized by one or more nation-states" (Glick Schiller, Çağlar, and Guldbrandsen 2006: 614; see also O'Neill 2010; Ong 1999 and 2003). The Church, one such network of social relations, also operates as a nation-state. Within Catholic theology, charity comprises "merciful" spiritual and corporal works intended to shelter, feed, heal, educate, administer, and even "save" diverse bodies, minds, and souls (Delany 1911).[19] As a human services network, public and private grants, material resources, technical expertise, social and political capital, and individual acts of pastoral care also flow through the Catholic compassion economy.

Because neoliberal secular states continue to retrench entitlements and social welfare, affiliation with faith-based organizations (FBOs) offering services on behalf of the government can provide alternative paths to persons seeking civic inclusion. Territorial institutions like the Vatican City-State, the Holy See, and the universal Church, and hybrid public-private charitable entities like the Charity and the Center, operate through forms of "network governance" (Laguerre 2011) offering their members opportunities for sociopolitical incorporation. These institutions can ease paths to citizenship in nation-states. In focusing on a primary location, the Center, I follow Çağlar and Glick Schiller's (2018: 11) work on migrants, city-making, and a multiscalar method that "situates urban actors within various networks of power." An ethnographic focus on a single site requires multiscalar scholarship to acknowledge that "no site can be understood apart from its interconnections through time and space, and these interconnections can be studied in a single site."

A postmortem assessment of the Center shows how a Catholic compassion economy provides means of migrant incorporation in partnership with, but at times, in opposition to, the state.[20] Over its history the Center's engagements with entities like the Church, the Charity, and the City, as well as public and private donors, compelled staff members to improvise continually to best serve their clients. In documenting the charitable practices of everyday life (Certeau 1984), I emphasize the historical and global heterogeneity of Catholic compassion economies. In part, following Max Weber's *The Protestant Ethic and the Spirit of Capitalism* (1930), this book documents what could be called "*A Catholic Ethic and the Spirit of Capitalism*." In the Archdiocese of Boston, the charity extended to Haitians has been symbolically rich as an index of the Church's institutional accountability. The story of the Center is not only an allegory about how power flows in Catholic and faith-based institutions; it also offers a cautionary tale for other voluntary and private sector corporations seeking to preserve their brands during processes of institutional transformation.

But what happens when faith-based organizations (FBOs) lose pastoral power or moral legitimacy? The Center's history parallels events occurring in the American Catholic Church—namely, a decline in laity and clergy attrition, especially in response to institutional betrayals. "Secularization" processes and the bureau-cratization of everyday charitable life have fomented disenchantment with both Church and Center practices (Asad 1993, 2003; Certeau 1984; Hirschkind and Scherer 2011; Norris and Inglehart 2004; Taylor 2007; Weber 1946). However, this "corporate ethnography" of the Center (Benson and Kirsch 2010) offers a parable not only for Catholic but also religious *and* secular nonprofit corporate entities espousing a principled mission (i.e., those advocating for human rights, civil rights, women's rights, humanitarianism, etc.). The Center may even symbolize how external actors have treated Haiti itself.

CENTERING LIFE

At the unveiling ceremony, most stakeholders considered the barren field a "promised land." Deliverance from the decaying but beloved St. Leo buildings was imminent. Although many Haitians felt the modern building would represent the community's social and political recognition, the proposed move caused considerable debate—even reopening superficially healed psychosocial wounds inflicted previously in Haiti, endured on journeys to America, and received in Massachusetts.

Relocating required the Center to share the new building. The Charity's largest community service program, Greater Boston Catholic Charities (GBCC, also known as Catholic Charities/Greater Boston), was the second program listed on the sign. GBCC linked historically to the Charity's founding a century earlier. In 1999, GBCC established the Greater Boston Community Service Center in Uphams Corner, about a mile north. The satellite program offered adoption and counseling services to pregnant women and families seeking to adopt, psychosocial support to people living with HIV/AIDS and their families, at-risk youth services, a food pantry, and other assistance.

The Charity hoped to consolidate services offered by the Haitian Multi-Service Center and Uphams Corner programs in the new building (Robinson and Stephen Kurkjian 2002). Although a faith-linked position strengthened the Center's fiscal and infrastructural stability, when Center stakeholders attempted to address Haitians' complex needs in previous years, the Church, the Charity, and the Center clashed regarding how best to do so. Archdiocesan attempts to combat HIV/AIDS (and high maternal and infant mortality rates) by advocating sexual abstinence rather than contraceptive use provoked contentious public conflicts among these institutions. The Charity even sought to reduce the Center's autonomy. These disagreements, prioritizing differing conceptions and practices of "life," suggested Haitian pragmatism in promoting livelihoods, human rights, health, and dignity deliberately challenged Catholic theologies of life, sex, and the body.

By documenting another sense of life, the Center's biographical history and everyday life, I witnessed a community-based advocacy organization undergoing changes to its corporate identity. Could the Center uphold Catholic moral tenets while meeting the requirements of public and private donors "outside" the Church—funders who expected programs to promote best practices in medicine and public health? Was it primarily intended to serve Haitians or a broader client base? At the heart of these questions were recurrent struggles over whether the Center was primarily "Catholic" and fully incorporated into the Church's mystical body, or secular, "Haitian," and only affiliated with Catholic institutions until it became self-sustaining. In short, how would the Center promote life, and whose lives mattered?

CARDINAL LAW AND CHURCH CONTRADICTIONS

The sign-unveiling celebration highlighted the entangled relationships among religious and governmental agencies, voluntary and private sector corporations, and the communities the new Dorchester service center would support. Although the building project demonstrated accountability to their respective (and sometimes overlapping) constituents, a shared religious identity as Catholics linked many participants. Corporate Catholicism had played a positive historical role by aiding migrants and the poor in establishing new lives in the United States. In so doing, the Church and Catholic charities had accumulated tremendous religious and civic power.

Under a large white tent near a towering maple tree, the ceremony's mood was initially formal and solemn, but then celebratory, resembling a wedding or other occasions bringing families and friends together. This union was between church and state, private businesses, and nonprofit actors representing local communities. Behind a wooden podium bearing Boston's blue and white seal stood Mayor Menino, State Senator Jack Hart, State Representative Martin ("Marty") J. Walsh—a future Boston mayor and U.S. secretary of labor—and the first Haitian state representative in Massachusetts, Marie St. Fleur.

Around the pavilion perimeter were prominent Catholics who played significant roles in this story: Archbishop O'Malley stood next to Dr. Doolin and members of the CCAB Board of Trustees. Dr. Roger Jean-Charles, a Haitian physician who once served as chairman of the HMSC Advisory Board, had worked with the archdiocese to aid his compatriots in the United States and abroad. Close to the trustees stood a charismatic Haitian American who had shepherded the building project from conception to fruition, Center executive director Pierre Imbert. Both Jean-Charles and Imbert were present in November 2000 when Cardinal Law made an impactful pastoral visit to the Center to assess its needs (see Figure 3). An observer of the meeting reported:

> [Cardinal Law] had come to the Haitian Center himself and shared bread with us and lunch . . . to sort of bear witness to the conditions of the buildings and engage with the brothers and sisters, clients of the Haitian Center. . . . This is a cardinal that

FIGURE 3. Cardinal Law visits St. Leo Parish. Photo credit: Robert L. Powell.

did good things for the immigrant population [that] enhanced the strong support that he'd received until the end from the immigrant community of Boston, and particularly from the Haitian community, with which he engaged as a Church leader so closely and so much. I think it was a, it was a very positive relationship.

Law's encounter with the Haitian children in the daycare was particularly moving. Another witness said: "I was really touched . . . when he visited the daycare . . . it was some time in November . . . the kids, they were kind of amazed to see . . . a man with a robe . . . black with the red [sash] . . . and then with the royal cap. He was sitting in those little chairs with the kids." That a "prince" of the Church treated Haitian children with kind regard and equality was considered remarkable. Cardinals were only subject to a pope's authority. The witness continued,

and there was one thing that happened. . . . One of the kids was playing with the [Cardinal's] ring . . . and one of the kids said to him, "Do you have a mother?" And that was on the anniversary of the death of the Cardinal's mother. . . . The people from the . . . Elder Program had a special program for him. They sung . . . for him and [gave] him food—this was the . . . national [dish]—the rice and beans . . . with . . . *griyo* [fried pork], and *banann peze* [fried plantains]—so he sat down and ate with everyone, and he had a tour of the building, and he saw the conditions.

A former Center employee present at the time said, "At the end he pledged then and there that . . . he *will* rebuild, he will help rebuild the Haitian Center because the conditions of the building were so miserable. . . . the Cardinal had a transformation that happened to him right then and there and he made that pledge."

Cardinal Law next attended the February 2001 Charity board of trustees meeting to propose a new building for the Haitian community. In May 2001, the Center was featured in the archdiocese's $325 million capital campaign. The same Center employee said:

> Cardinal Law very soon thereafter built a case for the entire archdiocese which . . . which directly included the Haitian Center. . . . The Haitian Center and the Labouré Center [a Charity social service center in South Boston] happened to be perhaps the only two centers directly named in . . . the subsequent launch of a $325 million capital campaign. And the Haitian Center—a case was built for the Haitian Center for five million dollars from the capital campaign.

When Law's role in the clergy sexual abuse scandal emerged early the following year, the news provoked widespread calls for his ouster and severely hampered the capital campaign. But among Haitian Catholics there remained overwhelming support for Law and loyalty to the Church, perhaps for which the new space was a reward.

Throughout this project I was continually surprised to hear from Haitians (and others) about Cardinal Law's support to their community at critical junctures. Repeatedly I had to reconcile the duality of what I learned. Stories of his public benevolence and solidarity with Afro-Caribbean and Latin American populations, especially their children, contrasted with revelations of private actions he had taken to conceal (and therefore enable) the clerical abuse of other youths. Such negative disclosures sometimes coincided temporally with his public advocacy for vulnerable children. Cardinal Law was not the only leader in a Catholic institution to embody this paradox.

I also sought to understand how conceptions of race and racism may have influenced the extension or denial of charity toward Haitians (and others). But another set of questions connects to "whose lives matter?" How are we to understand individuals (and institutions) whose practices are both benevolent and merciful—fostering economic empowerment, social incorporation, political recognition, and justice—while these same individuals (and institutions) act in ways that strip others of their innocence, dignity, and bodily integrity, all in the name of charity? Are such contradictions embedded in all institutions or are mission-driven organizations particularly vulnerable to the erosion of their moral and ethical cultures?

THE CHURCH AND THE CITY

Other steadfast Center stakeholders spoke at the 2003 sign unveiling. Next to Imbert were members of the HMSC Advisory Board, including the ceremony's final speaker, Mr. Robert L. Powell, an African American Catholic and one of Boston's first Black firefighters. Powell had aided the organization since its founding. On either side of a center aisle sat Center staff members and clients, municipal employees, Charity social service program representatives, and neighborhood residents. Sitting in the first row were four beautiful Haitian children who were acknowledged in speeches several times and became the subject of media photos (see Figure 1).

The assemblage resembled a political rally. Civic leaders jubilantly called out the names of staff and other politicians using the cadences of campaign speech. Reminiscent of religious services to consecrate a space or bless a new endeavor, some speakers proclaimed their religious identity and motives for service. Above the clamor of delivery trucks, municipal sirens, and car horns, Charlotte Golar Richie emceed with a resounding voice. The former state representative proclaimed, "This is a special day, a very, very special day for Dorchester and for the City of Boston! . . . Change is coming! Change is coming to this long vacant property. That's a really good thing. Where we're gathered right now, it's going to be a different place a year from now and we're all here to celebrate the future development of this site." Golar Richie next introduced Archbishop O'Malley and lauded his facility with Dorchester's numerous languages and cultures.

After thanking the mayor and Charity president, O'Malley praised the Center in his renowned sonorous voice: "We know the . . . great needs of this neighborhood, and we know that this new center will house the Haitian Center and be available for all the needs of the community, for the various and diverse communities that are here—the Cape Verdeans, the Hispanics, Vietnamese, African Americans, everybody in this neighborhood." As the congregation bowed their heads, O'Malley's prayed the first section of Psalm 127 in his benediction, "If the Lord does not build the house, in vain do its builders labor." Although unspoken, the completing verse, "if the Lord does not watch over the city, in vain does the watchman keep vigil," implicitly reminded participants that God's blessing was required for the building's success and the City's security. O'Malley petitioned, "We pray for the help of God that this project will be brought to successful completion, that all who will work here will be kept safe, and that we will gather together again to celebrate the new gift to the people of this city and this neighborhood. And we ask this and all prayer through Christ our Lord. Amen."

Subsequent speakers underscored the historical roles of Catholic charities in public and private development and in incorporating migrants into the city, state, and nation. Calling the land and future community service center "an oasis for the new people in our city . . . looking for hope and opportunity," Mayor Menino acknowledged Boston's debt to the Church. After crediting the Charity for launching the initiative, he likened the proposed building to "a settlement house for people coming for services—ESL programs, afterschool programs, services that are needed [for] . . . 'the new Bostonians' . . . people who represent the diversity of our communities." The mayor continued:

This has to be the multi-service center for the community—especially for the Haitian community. . . . As we have the new population come to Boston, we have to make sure that we welcome you and give you the services [for you to feel that] "Boston is the city [where] we want to stay and bring up [our] children," [like those] we have right here in front of me [referring to the four Haitian children seated in the front row of the audience]. This will be part of the renaissance of this neighborhood.

After mentioning other recent municipal projects to "renew" the surrounding vicinity—two senior housing units and a brand-new middle school a few blocks north on Columbia Road—the mayor's final remarks to O'Malley drew thunderous applause: "I just want to say to the archbishop, thank you for being in Boston. Thank you for [what you are doing] for our Church. That means so much to so many of us." Others thanked O'Malley for "bringing our Catholic community together," and, implicitly, for beginning to heal its corporate wounds.

WOUNDS OF CHARITY

Catholics still reel from the disclosure of Cardinal Law's direct involvement in clergy sex abuse cases in previous decades. Although, in the 1990s, the local media covered reports of pedophile priests, the January 2002 *Boston Globe* exposé charged Law with concealing such cases, transferring pedophile priests to other parishes, and denying knowledge of their egregious acts. The scandal shattered the trust and legitimacy the Church had earned in Massachusetts and eroded the legal immunity its officials had previously enjoyed internationally. In May 2002, Law became the first American cardinal "compelled to testify under oath in a lawsuit in which he was a named defendant" (Lawler 2010: 179). Lay and clerical groups repeatedly called for his resignation. On December 13, 2002, after consulting with Pope John Paul II, Law became the first cardinal to resign for his role in abuse cases. When similar crimes were acknowledged in multiple North American dioceses, as well as internationally, Boston became the epicenter of sexual scandal in the universal Church—a disaster still traumatizing victims globally that may have damaged the Catholic charitable brand irreparably.

In the wake of the ongoing scandal and resulting membership retrenchment, the Dorchester land acquisition and construction plan symbolized the Boston Church's partial emergence from disgrace. The ecclesial real estate holding expansion was also significant because the archdiocese suffered long-standing decreases in both parishioners and men and women religious—the priests and religious sisters who originally staffed parishes and other Catholic institutions.[21] Such losses contributed to the closure and divestiture of Catholic schools, hospitals, and other archdiocesan properties. The aging of the clergy, and the conversion of many Catholics to Evangelical Protestantism (or away from organized religion altogether), were additional factors contributing to the Roman Catholic Church's decline in the United States (O'Connor 1998; Seitz 2011).

Boston's Haitian Catholics were already deeply aware of these attrition processes. In 1999, the archdiocese "suppressed" (decommissioned) St. Leo Church and merged the faithful into Dorchester's St. Matthew Parish. Although the community lost a focal point of Haitian piety, St. Leo's buildings were "relegated to profane use" and given to the Center for its growing programs. And as is now known, Haitian children were among those wounded by clergy sexual abuse. In June 2002, publicized legal documents showed the Church received numerous complaints against one specific priest, Rev. Paul J. Mahan. Mahan reputedly had "kissed and molested Haitian boys" while serving at St. Matthew's (Cardinal Law removed him from the priesthood in 1998).[22] After this revelation, the prominent focus placed on Haitian children at the sign-unveiling ceremony was dense with additional meaning. To them was given a promise of care and protection, and perhaps, institutional reparations.

CHURCH AND STATE

Given these fissures in the Church's moral, social, and material foundations, the unveiling celebration was a civic achievement. In exchange for the land, the new community service center gift fulfilled Catholics' religious obligation to perform charity as individuals and as a corporate body. The building represented philanthropic capital and, perhaps, an act of corporate penance demonstrating to the city and community the Church's contrition, continued relevance, and moral legitimacy. Dr. Doolin, who was scheduled to retire at the end of 2003 (Abel 2003), spoke about the building's significance:

> In closing, just, just a couple of words about one aspect of why this building is important. . . . This project is a sign of the Church's *will* to continue to be a presence in Boston's neighborhoods. . . . You cannot judge an institution solely by its mistakes—you really have to look at the whole record—and the whole record of the Church in Boston is the tradition . . . of including service to people, helping waves of newcomers acculturate and become part of society, educate people, provide social services, [and] provide healthcare.

Although tacitly acknowledging the ethics scandals, his words invoked the Church's historical role as a force for good. Doolin's stress on the Catholic "will" to serve highlighted the state's dependence on Church missions to incorporate people, and perhaps, "to 'manage' or 'pacify' . . . populations" through care or "a pedagogy of conversion intended to transform 'unruly subjects' into lawful subjects" (Das and Poole 2004: 9).

The relationships between care, conversion, discipline, and governance emerge throughout this book. Although contemporary Catholic charities do not proselytize clients explicitly, the Church's caring mission enlivens adherents' shared Catholic identity. State Representative St. Fleur stated, "As a Roman Catholic who truly believes in the work of the Church . . . I celebrate Catholic Charities. . . . Second to the state, Catholic Charities is the largest provider of assistance to low-income families in the state and that is something to be really recognized and supported."

The final speaker, Mr. Powell (as he was commonly called), first acknowledged the Charity as an agent of community development then affirmed the Center as a partner in the labor to care for Greater Boston's souls. After describing the new building as the culmination of a dream, he pledged Center staff and advisory board members to working with the Charity to serve a broader client base than Haitians:

> The Haitian Center, in concert with Catholic Charities, anticipates a substantially expanded program base at the new building, serving Haitians and welcoming the diverse community in the surrounding neighborhoods. . . . The Haitian Center will continue to offer childcare, adult education, including ESL, employment and job development services, health and life skills education, and prenatal care. But we will also offer new programs which will appeal to our broader service population.

Not all Center supporters agreed. Some prominent Haitian activists speculated publicly that the proposed move was a corporate takeover: "Apparently people were led to believe this is their project, and they later found out, no, it is a Catholic Charities project." Instead of the pride Haitians felt in having their freestanding Center, this individual continued, "where their language is understood and their culture respected," the move to the new building was "the difference . . . between owning and renting their own home, and they fear Catholic Charities will be more likely to take the lead in programs and services" (Paige 2003).

Some fears appeared justified (and time seems to have borne out the truth of these statements). After the September 2003 unveiling ceremony, the derelict St. Leo's rectory was condemned. The Charity attempted to shift some Center programs to the Greater Boston Uphams Corner space (and management) and to transfer Pierre Imbert to a fundraising position in Charity headquarters. Fearing such a move would erode their institutional identity and autonomy, Center staff opted to consolidate most programs in the Victorian home (see Figure 2) until the Yawkey Center's completion. These would not be the only struggles to preserve the Center's independence, identity, and mission. But in 2003, these difficulties lay in the future.

SEARCHING FOR LIFE

From previous work, I knew the Center's critical importance to Haitians seeking to *chèche lavi* (Haitian Creole for "search for life or a livelihood"). Recurrent political repression had provoked waves of citizens to flee their homeland. Under the repressive dictator François ("Papa Doc") Duvalier (1957–71), some middle-class Haitians had sought safety and economic opportunity in the United States. Years of egregious human rights abuses perpetrated under "President-for-Life" Jean-Claude ("Baby Doc") Duvalier (1971–86), compelled thousands of disadvantaged Haitians to flee. Many of these asylum seekers were detained in prison-like facilities while their legal claims were pending. The majority were ultimately repatriated to Haiti.

The largest exodus commenced in the early 1990s. On September 30, 1991, a military apparatus still loyal to the Duvaliers ousted former priest, Jean-Bertrand Aristide, the first democratically elected president, then brutally subjugated the poor pro-democracy sector until an international military intervention in October 1994. Through therapeutic and ethnographic work with survivors of political violence (1995–2000), I learned how the military regime, civilian attachés, and local gangs collaborated to disappear, torture, rape, and murder men and women *militan* (activists) struggling for democracy, human rights and health, education, and economic justice.

More than three hundred thousand Haitians went into hiding inside their nation. Thousands escaped on foot to the Dominican Republic and were subjected to racial discrimination and exploitative labor conditions (Martinez 1995). Others chartered rickety boats across perilous seas pursuing sanctuary. U.S. Coast Guard cutters interdicted tens of thousands at sea then incarcerated them in camps on Guantánamo Bay, Cuba. Again, the majority were repatriated, much as their compatriots had been in the 1980s (see Chapter 3). A small minority of returnees would join select *militan* in becoming "beneficiaries" of a few "victim rehabilitation" assistance programs operating in the aid apparatus.

During this early fieldwork, I wondered whether Haiti's experience as the "Republic of NGOs" represented a global phenomenon—namely, the privatization of social welfare. How had Haitians coped with the psychosocial aftermath of trauma in the diaspora? Had they been able to find political, economic, social, and spiritual security in the United States? If they were subjected to political persecution prior to leaving, would their psychosocial experiences resemble those of individuals who either were not able to leave Haiti or who chose to remain and necessarily endured cycles of *ensekirite* (Haitian Creole for insecurity) in subsequent years?[23] What forms of insecurity existed for Haitians in the United States, especially in the post-9/11 era?

FAITH-BASED CHARITY AND THE SECURITY STATE

Alongside anthropologies of the practice of Christianity (Cannell 2006) and Catholicism (Norget, Napolitano, and Mayblin 2017), there has been increased interest in religious philanthropy in recent years (Albahari 2015, 2019; Besteman 2016, 2019; Bornstein 2005, 2012; Bornstein and Redfield 2010; Caldwell 2004, 2017; Clark 2004; Elisha 2011; Ghodsee 2010; Huang 2009; James 2011, 2019; McAlister 2013;

Muehlebach 2012, 2013; Zigon 2011). Many studies document the role of religion in aiding immigrants to maintain transnational social networks and become incorporated into receiving nation-states (Alba, Raboteau, and DeWind 2009; Ebaugh and Chafetz 2002; Mooney 2009; Napolitano 2016). Contemporary literature on U.S.-based religious nonprofits has focused on their advocacy for immigrant rights (Çağlar and Glick Schiller 2018; Coutin 1995; Stepick, Rey, and Mahler 2009) and the creation of "cultural citizenship" for immigrant Others (Ong 1996; Rosaldo 1994). Other studies interpret donors' or volunteers' motivations to labor charitably as processes of "moral selving" (Allahyari 2000), efforts to "save" both donors and recipients, and to reenchant capitalism (Weber 1930; see also James 2019).

Although social theories of secularization posit a decline in the temporal power of religious institutions in the modern West, Catholic corporate entities have partnered with federal, state, and municipal government for centuries, raising questions about whether there has been a fully secular moment (particularly in the United States). In this light, recent debates about the so-called "resurgence" of public religion in the current "postsecular" moment must be reconsidered (Beaumont and Baker 2011; Berger 1999; Calhoun, Juergensmeyer, and VanAntwerpen 2011; Cloke and Williams 2018: 42–44; Greed 2020). Regardless of recent temporal characterizations of (organized) civic piety, there are few analyses examining the practices of everyday charitable life in American Catholic agencies or how their practices have changed over time.

The example of the Church, Charity, and Center shows how religious nonprofit corporations can be inextricably linked to secular government, especially when the welfare state declines. In the contemporary United States, Catholic influence on domains ranging from social services to education, healthcare, and immigration grew over the twentieth century, in part because of foundational principles in Catholic social teachings. J. Bryan Hehir (2000: 102–8), Jesuit scholar and current secretary of health and social services in the Archdiocese of Boston, identifies solidarity, socialization, and subsidiarity as fundamental concepts informing the relationships among economy, society, and state. The moral principle of solidarity defines personhood as social and entails mutual obligations to ensure the "common good" through care, concern, and protection of others. Citing Pope John XXIII's encyclical *Mater et Magistra*, Hehir (2000: 104) defines socialization as "the multiplication of social relationships, that is, a daily more complex interdependence of citizens, introducing into their lives and activities many and varied forms of associations, recognized for the most part in private and even in public law." As social relationships increase in complexity and interconnectivity, there are moral consequences from the interpersonal to the international levels.

Although public intervention may be required to fulfill socioeconomic needs and protect human rights and dignity, the subsidiarity principle promotes private, interpersonal, or local responses to preserve "freedom," whether of individuals or corporate persons. Only if necessary should more complex private and then public interventions commence. A 2011 interview with an archdiocesan leader further clarified Catholic perspectives on private charity and public entitlements:

> *ECJ:* One of the questions that I'm wondering about is . . . this term, "subsidiarity" . . . I'm still not getting it.
>
> *AL:* . . . It's based on the Latin word "subsidium," which means help. . . . And . . . the principle begins by saying that when you have a social question, you should start at the most local level to solve it. Another way to say it is don't go to the state first. . . . But if you find that the nature of the problem is larger than you can solve at the lowest level, you keep going up the social ladder to get to the point where you can hit the right balance between the state and civil society. . . . So, it starts as a conservative statement but in fact it moves from that to an argument that the state has a positive role.

Andrea Muehlebach's (2013) ethnographic work on neoliberalism in Italy offers an example of a more "conservative" approach. She argues the neoliberal "Catholicization" of public policy has encouraged the privatization of social welfare and state conscription of NGOs to provide social services. At the same time, the Italian state promotes individual giving as an ethos of civic participation—especially citizen voluntarism grounded in Catholic theologies of love, and giving without an expected return gift (Muehlebach 2013: 459).

Under such conditions, the relationship between aid providers' and recipients' ethical statuses is critical to analyze. Muehlebach (2013: 461) argues, "Contemporary neoliberalism's moral style, like Catholicism's . . . consists of 'cycle[s] of sin, repentance, atonement, release, followed by renewed sin.'" Volunteers are compelled to give freely as a component of solidarity with the exploited and dispossessed but also to expiate their own sins "through worldwide commitments to charity and philanthropy" (462). However, "these acts of redemption . . . require an Other dependent on and willing to receive our gifts and thus capable of operating as a vehicle for consolation"; thus, the vulnerable poor become "objects of love, not subjects of justice" (462). Whether charity as love is necessarily in opposition to justice is explored throughout this book.

The role of Catholic charity in mediating between racial, ethnic, and impoverished Others and states, and between charity recipients and Catholics, has been political, even biopolitical. Charitable labor not only fulfills religious obligations to care for and potentially transform others, it may also be a form of individual and institutional penance. Providing charity to stigmatized populations may also balance or mitigate negative perceptions of an individual's or institution's self-presentation, of their brand. As this ethnographic history of Haitians and corporate Catholicism progresses, I explore whether redemptive charity requires a dependent and receptive Other.

"[A] POPULATION THAT MOST PEOPLE DON'T WANT TO TOUCH"

A May 2007 interview with a Charity employee illustrates how the perceived worth of recipients influences the practice of charity, and how giving can confer merit on the charitable donor, whether individual or organizational. This individual asserted that the tragic events of September 11, 2001, provoked donor reluctance to contribute to institutions serving migrants, especially those of African descent. Stereotypes about charity recipients as unworthy or threatening deepened institutional and individual reticence to aid the "stranger among us" (NCCB/USCC 2000), regardless of background (see also Besteman 2016, 2019):

> It's gotten so much worse after 9/11 and people don't take the time to listen and to want to be educated. . . . I mean it's tough. I mean, we used to, during the Kosovo refugee crisis, we raised like a million dollars, but see, those are White refugees, right? We go to conferences, and the lone Sudanese person stands up and says, "Why aren't you fighting for my people? Why isn't [anybody] listening to us? But there's a lack of will, you know. "Oh, that's Africa—leave them be." You know? I mean you hear some of the most horrific things, and you know it's not right . . . and it's racism. . . . You know, it's so difficult, like even within our own network. Some Catholic . . . Charities agencies are resisting . . . resettling Africans!

As we spoke, the disjuncture between the brands organizations and corporations promote publicly and their "off-stage" practices was brought into relief (Shryock 2004).

The staff person affirmed the Charity mission aligned with their personal sense of vocation and then emphasized the obligation to support the Catholic mission to welcome the stranger and incorporate those deemed "undesirable," regardless of required sacrifices (Agier 2011):

> This is one part of my faith that I am really proud of. I'm proud that we do this. I'm proud that Catholic Charities, especially in Boston, and I can't stress enough how supportive this archdiocese is with immigrants and refugees . . . Because after 9/11, a lot of dioceses said "Nope. We don't want this. It's too difficult. It's too hot. We don't want it. It bleeds money. We don't want it." But, you know, time and again, even as . . . every year [we] come in with a budget that's, WELL, not balanced! [laughing], [we're] reminded that this is the mission, simple as that, this is the mission.

This strong sense of personal and institutional vocation and identity relates directly to theologies of solidarity and care for society's neediest through local and private action before involving governmental intervention.

Charity permits Catholics to demonstrate their vocation or "charism" (a spiritual gift or talent from God that is also a sign of grace). Such work implicitly influences the "economy of salvation" and, as Foucault puts it, the "economy of merits and faults" (1982, 2007). The term "economy" connotes management of exchanges among obligated parties, whether in social, material, financial, or spiritual realms. The Catholic sense of a salvation economy or a "divine economy" reflects a covenantal relationship between God and members of God's household through Jesus Christ, the Holy Spirit, and the sacramental practices of the corporate Church. Offering charity to certain populations yields salvific merit or reward. Populations considered "the least of these" (Mt 25:40)—the poor, the vulnerable migrant, the orphan, the widow, the homeless, the sick—are in many ways the select (Mt 20:16, "So the last shall be first, and the first last: for many are called, but few chosen."). By caring for them, one "encounters" Jesus Christ and may come closer to salvation (Mt 25:40: "Inasmuch as ye have done it to one of the least of these my brethren, ye have done it to me.").

We continued discussing the Charity's challenges, especially how large donors withheld support from Catholic institutions to protest the clergy sex abuse crisis. The proposed solution to reenchant donors showed how charity donors and recipients' identities and moral statuses influence the ebbs and flows in compassion economies:

> Just by sharing our experiences helps a lot. . . . Sharing the rich history that this particular diocese has with the Haitian population is going to speak volumes for us. We need to highlight the great work that happened many, many years ago, *to reach out to a population that most people don't want to touch.* I mean, how many charities have a Haitian Center?

Advertising charity provided to outcast or marginalized groups was a strategy to counter the negative image Catholicism had earned after the scandal. However, it was not clear if "touch" meant physical or social contact, material aid, or organized management. I argue these actions (and others) circulate pastoral power in the Catholic compassion economy.

Fundamentally, Catholic charity involves willingness to contact directly, even physically, the "woundedness" of so-called Others, especially when such populations embody what is feared, denigrated, or maligned. Interpreting the significance of touch requires a deeper analysis of corporality. In a "Catholic sensorium" individuals can "perceive extraordinary presence that inheres in the material environment" (Mitchell 2017, 213). In this sensorium, the body can be porous and "pick up the presence of the Holy, as distributed in the environment" (Mitchell 2017, 213). Touching sacred relics and religious icons may impart "grace." Grace is a free gift of a benevolent "otherworldly force or originary substance that sets things in motion [and] bears a family resemblance to ethnographic concepts like *mana* or *hau*"

(Pitt-Rivers [1992] 2017, 52–53).[24] But majority populations have not always perceived raced and gendered persons as having equal capacity to embody, merit, receive, or impart grace. Valentina Napolitano's (2017, 244) work on Latin American migrants in Rome describes how participation in a lay Catholic brotherhood enables "gendered migrant bodies [to be] invested with a *Catholic officium* (in the sense of being invested with an office related to liturgy)." An outcast man conscripted to help carry the Lord of Miracles statue was transformed by physical contact with the emblem of grace and by inclusion among the faithful. Physical contact with the sacred can convey mercy, worthiness, and uplift migrants' moral statuses.

A Catholic sensorium can regulate licit and illicit touch. Jon P. Mitchell (2017, 213), an anthropologist of Catholicism and politics in Malta, provides another understanding relevant for this analysis: "In Catholicism, the body can also be entered by the forces of good or evil, but this porousness extends beyond the straightforward vulnerability of the body to spiritual incursion." While contact with sacred persons or objects can confer mercy and healing, persons or objects considered either materially or spiritually threatening may harm. I suggest this spiritual "porosity" influences how some Catholics understood charitable work with the most marginal populations: when contact is potentially harmful, risking interaction through works of mercy can convey greater social, spiritual, and organizational merit (see also Benton 2016).

The willingness to touch (and manage) the Other through charity may counteract the negative impact of clerical abuse on the corporate Catholic brand. The Charity staff person continued:

> I know . . . that [the president of the Charity] really works to, to highlight Charities, I mean [the executive director] will say "we're the best kept secret in Boston," that's what he likes to say. But you know it is kind of true, 'cause people are like, "Oh, I didn't know Catholic Charities did refugee and immigration work. Oh, I didn't know you have a Haitian Center!" . . . So, we need to do a much better job at marketing ourselves, which is why they have this whole marketing campaign now. We've actually started to invest money in positive advertising, and we need to get [it] out there.

Advertising charity to enhance Catholic institutional images was a formal Charity promotion strategy. On February 21, 2007, the agency intranet announced a campaign "[targeting] those with little or no knowledge of Catholic Charities, specifically those 35–54 years of age." The "overall communications strategy" recommended:

- Use current communications vehicles to convey clear, consistent messages regarding the breadth and scope of our services.
- Plan new communication activities and use new tools to introduce new audiences to the agency.
- Leverage central and regional development activities to convey messages.
- Develop client profiles from a variety of programs for a variety of uses.

- Use client profiles to demonstrate the significance of services provided.
- Define *Catholic Charities' brand* and use it consistently across the entire agency (my emphasis).
- Implement external communications policy-guidelines, procedures, and accountability for the external communications representing the agency.

Although advertising such activities could be fruitful in capturing the thirty-five- to fifty-four-year-olds' market, the instructions were ambiguous about whether the target market was future service users or potential donors (a subsequent interview suggested donors). Developing client profiles to "demonstrate the significance of services provided" resembled how aid agencies in Haiti circulated to funders "trauma portfolios"—dossiers (re)presenting the suffering of their clients—as tangible evidence of the agency's successful achievement of results (James 2004, 2010). Using commercial business strategies to promote anti-poverty work suggests faith-based charities are hybrid religious and secular corporations seeking to "Catholicize" social welfare and to weight the balance of merits and faults for every individual, and arguably the corporate body of the Church, toward salvation.

Institutions like the Charity have become integral civic actors managing migrants and other vulnerable populations in partnership with the state. That religious nonprofits provide social welfare with relatively minimal public oversight suggests greater attention must be paid to how these institutions operate in everyday life. The historical ties between the Center, the Church, and the Haitian communities of Greater Boston, as well as between the Center, the Charity, and public and private donors, offer a compelling portrait of these partnerships. But this work suggests Catholic corporate philanthropy has been extended to exceptionally marginal groups like Haitians, not simply from compassion, political solidarity, and opposition to structural inequities and injustice, but also to promote (and rehabilitate) the Catholic charitable brand.

A STATEMENT ON METHODS AND ETHICS

In mapping the Church's, the Charity's, and the Center's respective work in Greater Boston there were numerous challenges. Several key stakeholders could not be reached, declined participation, or did not respond to requests for information. Others who agreed to participate subsequently withdrew.[25] As concerns for privacy, especially for Center health services clients, prevented my speaking directly with most, typical encounters occurred in public instructional settings. Given these limitations, I consulted with Center staff and redesigned the project to focus on their challenges serving Haitian immigrant and refugees. As some were former clients, I learned much about the early history from them. I witnessed how staff and advisory board members composed the Center's "heart," resembling the "keepers of the flame" Stephen Hopgood (2006) described in his book on Amnesty

International. As individuals who protect and safeguard an organization's mission, keepers make personal and professional sacrifices to ensure institutional security. Those keepers participating in this project entrusted me with stories of the trials, disappointments, and joys of supporting the Center.

The story of the Haitian Multi-Service Center asks crucial questions about the Catholic Church, its teachings, and Catholic institutional relationships with Haitian immigrants, refugees, and others in need. Although the clergy sex abuse scandal marks one legitimacy crisis,[26] there are other issues warranting increased attention explored throughout this book: What is the practice of Catholic charity in everyday life? How has it changed over time? Have clerical sex scandals affected Catholic institutions' ability to fulfill their evangelical and charitable missions? How do Catholic charities approach contemporary political issues—foreign policy, economic and social welfare, abortion and contraception, same-sex marriage, health disparities, migration, and national security—in local settings? What does organized care for the poor, the homeless, the sick, and strangers among us, have to do with the Catholic brand, especially in Boston?

The following postmortem assessment moves from analyzing historically distal events shaping the Center's life to assessing proximal and acute "symptoms" of irreparable change. The chapters are roughly chronological, analyzing select encounters between Haitians, religion, and the state, ranging from colonial Saint-Domingue to the present, and the roles of Catholic charities in refugee resettlement (Chapter 2). Chapter 3 traces the paths of Haitian refugees through a variety of "purgatorial spaces" on their journeys to reach the Center. Using the mnemonic method of the "memory palace," the heart of the book portrays Haitians' quests for security and "life" and the Samaritans who aided them in establishing new social institutions in the diaspora. Chapters 4 through 9 offer an overview of the Center's birth, development, maturity, and, as some allege, decline—including intense institutional struggles over its identity and mission—preceding and succeeding the move into the Yawkey Center. Like many organizations, corporations, and even families, this story contains critical events reflecting each stakeholders' labors to balance charity, pragmatic mercy, and justice as each interpreted these concepts. I am grateful to have been allowed to witness these struggles with race, religion, and rights in a globalizing world.

2

Building the Brand

Migrants and Roman Catholic Charity

The poor belong to us. . . . We will not let them be taken from us!
—BISHOP ALOISIUS MUENCH, AT THE NATIONAL CONFERENCE
OF CATHOLIC CHARITIES ANNUAL MEETING, 1935

On March 8, 2007, the Charity launched a print marketing campaign, "Discover the Work of Catholic Charities," to advertise aiding more than "200,000 people in need throughout Eastern Massachusetts each year" (Reidy 2007). Announced by Charity intranet in February 2007, the campaign sought to display visually the "Catholic charitable brand":

The three primary messages you will see to explain the Catholic Charities brand are:

- As an anti-poverty agency, Catholic Charities responds to the needs of the poor and working poor in our communities. This is accomplished by providing or helping them access emergency food, fuel, utility, rental, and mortgage assistance.
- Catholic Charities provides a variety of support services for children and families in order to strengthen and preserve families and provide children with the opportunities they deserve.
- With a variety of multicultural and multilingual services for immigrants and refugees, Catholic Charities is working to help these populations adjust to their new surroundings and become active participants in their communities.[1]

The advertisements adapted Church stained-glass imagery (typically illustrating the lives of Jesus, his disciples, and Catholic saints) for the *Boston Globe* business section. Each image of charitable works "encrypted in a subtle stained-glass window" implicitly encodes conceptions of race, gender, ethnicity, and vulnerability. The March 8 food pantries advertisement "features a working mom looking through her full kitchen cabinets, which may not be full if it were not for Catholic Charities" (see Figure 4).[2] The March 21, 2007, *Boston Globe* panel

FIGURE 4.
Food pantries
advertisement, 2007.
Image credit: Hill
Holliday/Catholic
Charities Archdiocese
of Boston, Inc.

depicts "services we provide to children and families through our many childcare programs. The image of a child and her teacher are encrypted in a subtle stained-glass window" (see Figure 5).[3] An early April image of a mother reading to her child "focuses on the many parenting services we provide to families" (see Figure 6).[4]

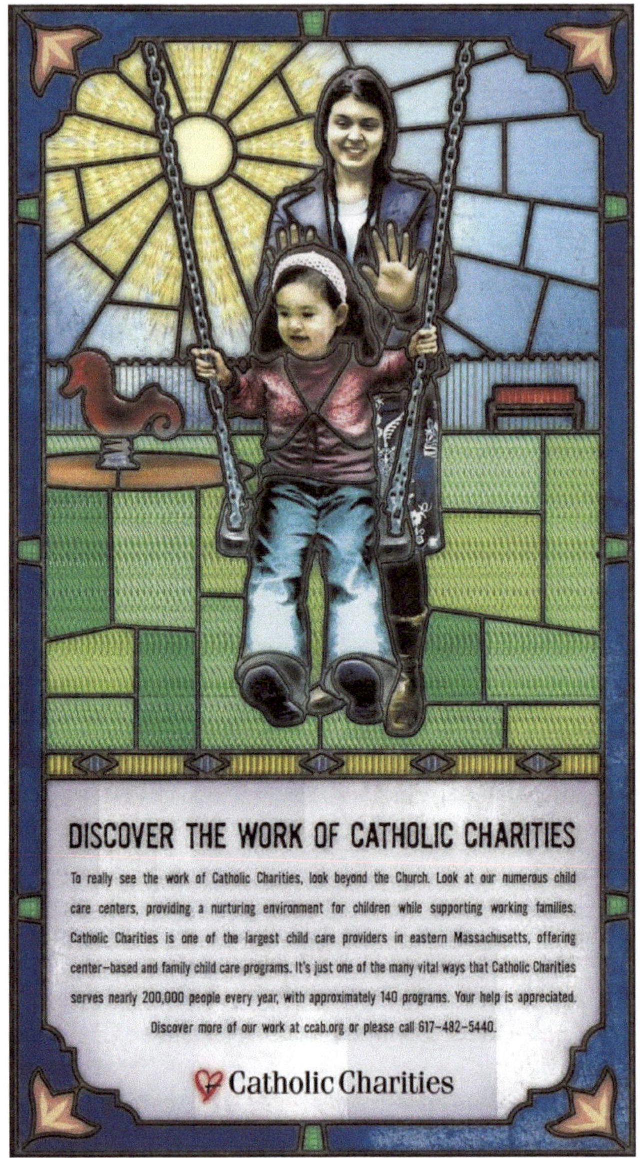

FIGURE 5. Child care advertisement, 2007. Image credit: Hill Holliday/ Catholic Charities Archdiocese of Boston, Inc.

A fourth image, showing two men of African descent—one appearing to instruct the other with trust and even intimacy—represents "refugee and immigration services" (see Figure 7). However, the Charity announcement did not discuss this ad; it does not seem to have been promoted publicly.

The campaign's modern yet nostalgic aesthetic humanizes "multicultural" social welfare providers and recipients. In their iconography, the images

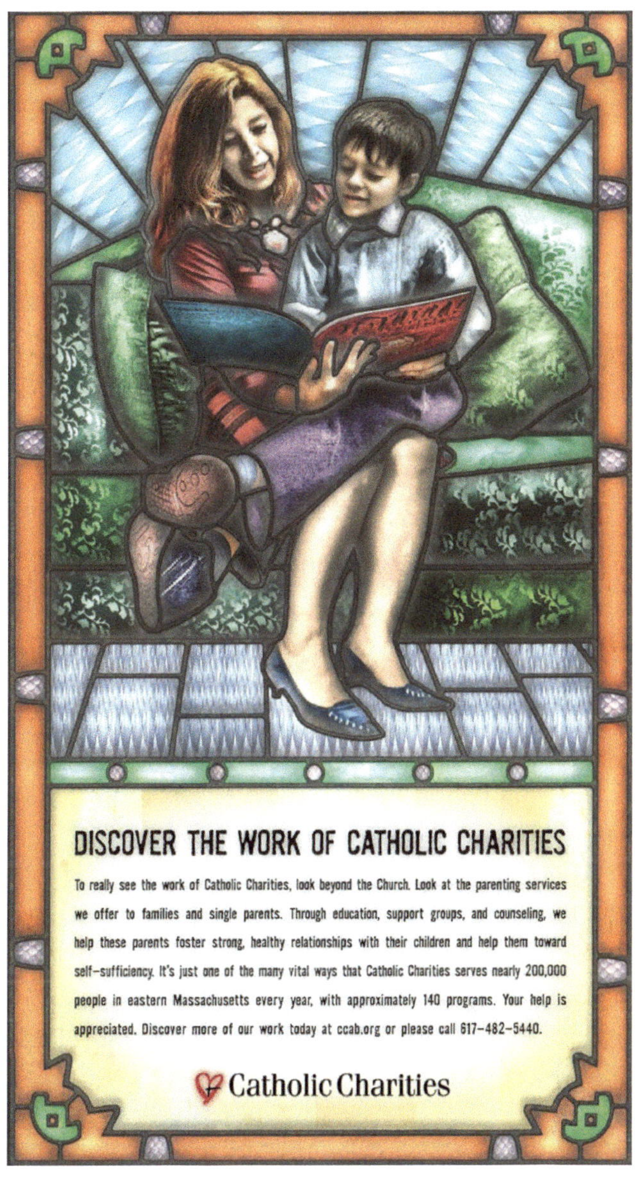

FIGURE 6. Parenting advertisement, 2007. Image credit: Hill Holliday/Catholic Charities Archdiocese of Boston, Inc.

emphasize caring acts in familial or instructional settings and render such exchanges sacred. Each image's caption, "To really see the work of Catholic Charities, look beyond the Church," evokes Dr. Doolin's unveiling ceremony statement on the continued relevance of Church traditions of social support. The statement proposes interpersonal and organizational charity as the true heart of Catholicism, rather than ecclesial sex scandals, the male clerical

FIGURE 7. Refugee and immigration advertisement, 2007. Image credit: Hill Holliday/Catholic Charities Archdiocese of Boston, Inc.

hierarchy, and colonial and imperial histories troubling the faithful, the faithful departed, and others outside the Church.

It is important to trace how the Church defines and promotes the "Catholic charitable brand" and whether orthodox ideology is transformed when practiced in local settings over time. Catholic interpretations of religious doctrines influence how charity is practiced in everyday life. As such, Catholicism in Haiti has been a tool of colonial and postcolonial repression but also a way of humanizing the enslaved and repressed. In more recent times the Church's social teachings have propelled community organizing and campaigns for social, political, and economic liberation. In analyzing secular and religious interventions against HIV/AIDS, physicians Paul Farmer and David Walton (2000: 109) argue progressive Church forces in Latin America emphasized "social and economic rights for the poor" over and against the sovereign power of authoritarian states. In the secular modern West, however, "progressive forces in the church . . . have been more concerned with individual liberties and with sexual freedoms of one sort or another" (109). Thus, in recent years, the Church in Haiti has focused on "repression against the poor" but "has had little to say" about sex, sexuality, and contraception (109).

Local doctrinal differences on promoting "life" may correlate with the Church's historical struggles for incorporation, organizational "citizenship," and sovereignty in nation-states. Similar to other migrants seeking sanctuary and citizenship in North America, the Church and its members have struggled to build a corporate caring brand. As Catholics became established American civic actors in the nineteenth and twentieth centuries, they founded charitable institutions to facilitate migrant incorporation into both church and state. Religious charity was a "work of mercy" providing not only pastoral care but also means of integrating marginal persons into institutions offering membership, even the state. Eventually Catholics performed such work on behalf of government, but not without some loss of autonomy, and even accruing—as a few people have argued—some harm to its charitable brand.[5] Although partnering with secular authorities has posed ethical challenges and double binds, Catholic actors have attempted to retain moral authority by advocating for just public policies.

One cannot fully interpret the Center's incorporation into the Charity and, as some have put it, its demise, without understanding the specific models of charity each institution advocated along different paths of migrant incorporation. Because the Church's standing varies in relation to historical nation-states, it may emphasize different doctrines locally. As such, this chapter sketches the role of Catholic charity in Haiti and North America, with select episodes highlighting different approaches to civic action that reflect the Church's relation to the nation-state. From an overview of the Church's structure, communications, and conception of its "charitable brand," the roles of Catholicism and corporate charity in Haiti and the United States are examined from colonial to contemporary times. Racial, gender, and ethnic conceptions influence the biopolitics of charity in each context, and contribute to later conflicts arising between the Church, the Charity, and the Center over how best to promote life.

. . .

The Roman Catholic Church, one of the "oldest and largest transnational actors," has been a powerful, mobile agent in civil and political affairs. Catholic institutions range from "the smallest level of sub-parochial units . . . to missionary religious orders, such as the Jesuits, that can claim to be prototypes of globalization" (Ryall 2001: 41). The Church and affiliated Catholic organizations have influenced (and even governed) more than one billion Catholics through "schools, universities, newspapers, radio stations and political parties . . . to . . . development agencies and the so-called 'new movements'"[6] (Ryall 2001: 41). The Church uses a transnational communication network and the secular media to disseminate its "articulation of collective ideas, promotion of collective norms, and . . . representation of symbolic ideas" (Hanson 1987: 5–6). Not only do these activities generate "expressive power" (Ryall 2001: 46); liturgical and sacramental practices coproduced by a diverse network of individuals, institutions, and the laity, generate "pastoral power" (Foucault 1982, 2007). The Church deploys pastoral power through policy initiatives instituted at the highest levels of governance to interpersonal sacramental encounters in local settings around the world.

The diversity, complexity, and scope of Catholic organizations can produce tensions within and outside its faith community. Contemporary relationships between the Holy See—the Church's central governing body in the Vatican City State—and transnational Catholic actors, whether clerics, organizations, or members of the laity, have been polarizing, particularly over issues of autonomy and interpretive authority (Reese 1996: 246–63; Ryall 2001: 42).[7] The relationships between Catholic institutions and "secular" governments, nongovernmental agencies, and non-Catholics can also be contentious, in part because the Church's "network governance" precedes the formation of the modern nation-state (Laguerre 2011).

Diplomatic disputes between church and state have concerned the power of the papacy in civic and political affairs. The Church's territorial, organizational, and moral positioning—as a state and as an international private network—enables critiques of secular national policies, economy and society, charity and justice, and public and private realms. For theological and instrumental reasons, Catholics have challenged and shaped governmental policies toward "the poor." With expertise supporting mobile populations, the Church and related charitable social service institutions have become forces governing vulnerable populations on the state's behalf (Maurutto 2003). These diverse arenas of Catholic activity—missionization and conversion, celebration of the sacraments, education, advocacy, and governance—are components of corporate Catholicism with long histories. But how does "the Church" define Catholic charity?

A CATHOLIC ETHIC AND THE SPIRIT OF CHARITY

On January 26, 2006, Pope Benedict XVI released his first encyclical, *Deus Caritas Est* (God Is Love), a treatise outlining the Catholic charitable brand. The letter, a form typically circulated to bishops in the Catholic hierarchy, was addressed "to the bishops, priests, and deacons, men and women religious, and all the lay faithful" and it comments on the "political, social, and economic order" (Hehir 2000: 99).[8]

Affectionately called the "Grand Inquisitor" by Cardinal John O'Connor and considered "the enforcer" of orthodoxy before his election to the papacy (Allen 1999), between 1981 and 2005 Cardinal Joseph Ratzinger was prefect of the Vatican's "Congregation for the Doctrine of the Faith" (CDF).[9] In the 1980s, the CDF—the congregation possessing the duty "to promote and safeguard the doctrine on faith and morals in the whole Catholic world"[10]—pronounced on the threat of biomedical technologies to "human rights, human life and the institution of the family,"[11] the pastoral care of homosexuals, the administration of the sacraments, and other liturgical matters. Between 1986 and 1992, Ratzinger presided over the first revision of the Catholic catechism since the sixteenth-century Protestant Reformation prompted the first catalogue of Roman Catholic beliefs, practices, and prohibitions.[12] In the 2000s, the CDF reaffirmed Catholicism as the only mediator of salvation,[13] banned definitively women's ordination and same-sex marriage, and pronounced on Catholic political participation.

The CDF also disciplined clerics whose work challenged orthodox theology and the pope's central interpretive authority.[14] In 1985 Ratzinger silenced the Brazilian Franciscan friar Leonardo Boff for his reputedly "Marxist-inspired" promotion of democracy, human rights, and economic justice as "liberation theology."[15] Ratzinger's 1984 and 1986 statements on liberation theology warned that "atheism and the denial of the human person, his liberty and his rights are at the core of Marxist theory."[16] In 1986, Ratzinger revoked the American priest Father Charles E. Curran's license to teach Catholic theology for the latter's publicly criticizing the Church's position on sexuality, contraception, and divorce (Reese 1996: 254–56).[17] Ratzinger labeled any dissent from orthodox theology a divisive force: "one who dissents from the Magisterium as you do is not suitable nor eligible to teach Catholic theology."[18] These censures concerned the Holy See's capacity to exercise pastoral power over global Catholics, whether in the religious hierarchy or laity, and as institutions or individuals.

Although Cardinal Ratzinger's CDF role suggested his first encyclical as Pope Benedict XVI might carry a disciplinary tone, *Deus Caritas Est* "did not mention abortion, homosexuality, contraception or divorce" but rather how sex "should mature into unselfish concern for the other, creating a love that leads to working for charity and justice for others."[19] This call to love through charity was presented as the original impetus propelling Christian activity in the world. Also absent was any discussion of the controversial roles the Church has played during the development and expansion of Christendom.[20]

Deus Caritas Est (Benedict XVI 2005) links Catholic tenets on the body, sex, love, and marriage to the Church's historical missionary activities. After presenting ancient Greek and Hebrew concepts of love, Benedict XVI defines "Christian" love as the culmination of a process: "being Christian is not the result of an ethical choice or a lofty idea, but the encounter with an event, a person, which gives life a new horizon and decisive direction" (par. 1). Encountering Jesus, the second person of the "Trinity" (God the Father, God the Son, and God the Holy Spirit), enables Christians to reorient their lives toward salvation through acts of charity. Benedict XVI describes charity (*caritas*) as the "practice of love" and exhorts Christians to evangelize others, observe required liturgical rituals, and "do good," for others within and especially "beyond the frontiers of the Church . . . whoever they may be." The encyclical presents pastoral power and the Catholic charitable brand in the form of a genealogy.

GENEALOGIES OF CATHOLIC CHARITY

Deus Caritas Est reframes the Catholic charitable mission (or brand), tracing its lineage through inspired charismatic individuals, social institutions, and partnerships with government. In the early Church, "All who believed were together and had all things in common; and they sold their possessions and goods and distributed them to all, as any had need" (Acts 2:44–45, cited in par. 20). Benedict XVI next calls the *diaconia*, a fourth-century Egyptian monastic institution, "the earliest legal structures associated with the service of charity in the Church" (par. 23). The *diaconia* later developed "into a corporation with full juridical standing, which the civil authorities . . . entrusted with part of the grain for public distribution" (par. 23). The partnership between Catholics and government to provide social support would become a component of its brand.

The encyclical names founding genealogical ancestors (to whom supplication is possible in prayer)—from monastic and mendicant order leaders (i.e., Francis of Assisi, Ignatius of Loyola, Vincent de Paul, Louise de Marillac, Teresa of Calcutta, etc.) to "Mary, Mother of the Lord," to whom Benedict XVI devotes a concluding prayer.[21] The encyclical does not discuss how evangelical, sacramental, and charitable acts expanded and secured Christendom. Nor does it discuss the punitive, oppressive, abusive, and imperial forms of Catholic pastoral power. The roles of Catholicism in Haiti and the United States provide a complicated portrait of these dynamics.

THE CATHOLIC CHURCH IN HAITI

Haitian Catholic history challenges the charitable brand promoted in *Deus Caritas Est*. Catholicism arrived in Haiti in 1492, when "Indians of the island of Ayti (as they called it) discovered Columbus strolling with some of his men on their beaches" (Nicholls 1996: 19). In 1493, Pope Alexander VI issued a papal bull granting to the Catholic monarchs of Spain the rights to all lands discovered in the New World on the condition that "inhabitants found there would be instructed in the principles of Catholicism" (Greene 1993: 74). That indigenous (and later enslaved persons) were forcibly converted justified colonial imperialism and human exploitation (Angrosino 1994: 824–25). In 1501, by royal decree, enslaved "Christian" Africans were exported from Spain to Hispaniola to supply needed labor; "around 1517, the massive importation of slaves from Africa to Saint-Domingue [Hispaniola] began" (Laguerre 1973: 36). From the sixteenth to the seventeenth century, the British, French, and Dutch sought to break the Spanish monopoly over trade, mining, agriculture, and the control of the slave trade in the Caribbean (Williams 1970: 69–95). In 1697, Spain ceded control of the western part of Hispaniola (Saint-Domingue) to France (Leger 1907: 34–35; Nicholls 1996: 19; Williams 1970: 81).

Roman Catholicism made deep inroads in Saint-Domingue under French monarchical rule. In 1685, King Louis XIV enshrined the spiritual authority of Catholicism in the Code Noir (the Black Code or Negro Code), the "King's Edict for the Governance and Administration of Justice and the Policing of the French Islands of America and for the Discipline and Commerce in Negroes and Slaves."[22] In addition to saving souls, church-state partnerships sponsored charities to manage the health and welfare of colonists. In 1694, the French king funded the Sisters of Charity "to operate hospitals in the two largest colonial towns: Léogâne and the capital of Cap François" (Brodwin 1996: 26). The hospitals combined elements of three French pastoral institutions: the "*hôpital* established by a church for parish residents would take in not only the sick, but also abandoned children, invalids, and the elderly, and it also distributed food and clothing to the poor" (Brodwin 1996: 26); the *hôtel Dieu*, in which surgeons provided only medical care and served area parishes; and the *hôpital général*, which housed the poor, but also confined the insane, the homeless, and other "threatening" populations (Brodwin 1996: 26–27; see also Foucault 2006). In the Cap François hospital, the king's physician and surgeon supervised the Sisters of Charity, who provided medical care and social support to French settlers, the French poor, sailors, and members of the royal militia (Brodwin 1996: 27). The ambiguity of enslaved persons, as subjects with souls and as heritable "objects" like movable goods, sparked little religious debate regarding the moral status of slavery in the colonies. Indeed, when European philosophers and scientists pondered whether Africans were human or whether their dark complexion was a sign of a divine affliction stemming from God's ancient curse against Ham (Eze 1997; Jordan 1968: 3–20), Jesuits and other Catholic religious orders in Saint-Domingue owned Africans (Greene 1993; Laguerre 1973; Swarns 2023; Williams 2022). However, some Jesuit priests taught the enslaved the Catholic catechism, educated them, and advocated for their humane treatment (Laguerre 1973: 39; Peabody 2002). In response, the proslavery plantocracy accused Jesuits of fund mismanagement, distorting Catholicism "to suit their purposes" and being the "corruptor of slaves," leading to the order's expulsion from Saint-Domingue in 1763 (Breathett 1962: 284; Ramsey 2011: 37).[23]

VODOU, REVOLUTION, AND CATHOLICISM
IN POSTINDEPENDENCE HAITI

Although possessing legal authority, Catholicism developed in Saint-Domingue alongside Vodou (Desmangles 1992), the enslaved majority's spiritual practice, which combined African traditional religions, the Catholic symbolic tradition, Freemasonry, and Indigenous spiritual practices to which Africans were introduced. Vodou adherents recognized as spiritual community members the individual, ancestors, *lwa* (literally, "law" or "spirit" in Haitian Creole), and the monotheistic God (perceived as less accessible in day-to-day life). While the enslaved venerated Catholic saints publicly, each saint also symbolized an African or Amerindian spirit with parallel attributes. Various legally permissible "dances"—in the evenings, on Sundays, and on Catholic religious holidays—concealed Vodou celebrations (Moreau de Saint-Méry 1958: 63–64; Fick 1990: 39).

The Vodou faith empowered escaped persons in maroon communities to organize against their colonizers. Médéric-Louis-Elie Moreau de Saint-Méry, a Martinican French Creole lawyer who settled in Cap Français, described fearfully the Vodou priest's or priestess's charisma: "To disobey them, to resist them, is to resist god himself. . . . In short it means to expose oneself to very serious dangers. . . . One would not credit to what extent the Voodoo chiefs keep other members in dependence on them . . . It can be made into a terrible weapon—this extravagant idea that the ministers of this alleged god know all and can do anything" (Spencer 1985: 1–2, 6–7; Moreau de Saint-Méry 1958: 64–65, 68–69).

Because Vodou became an instrument for generating racial solidarity and political consciousness, throughout the eighteenth century "the church worked assiduously toward the eradication of these African 'superstitious' practices in the colony" through "a series of police rulings that curtailed the movements of the slaves and controlled the use of objects that might be of use in Vodou rituals" (Desmangles 1992: 26). In August 1791, in the same Cap François region from which the Jesuits had been expelled, escaped Africans reportedly held a large Vodou ceremony launching a revolutionary wave of violence across the territory. The revolution culminated in the defeat and expulsion of the French from Saint-Domingue and the declaration of independence on January 1, 1804 (Dubois 2004; Fick 1990).

THE CHURCH IN HAITI FROM 1804 TO 1860

As in France following its tumultuous revolution, the new "Republic of Hayti" restrained Catholic pastoral power following independence in 1804. During the revolution Haitians had destroyed Church properties and murdered priests, leading to a rupture with Rome (Laguerre 1973: 45). The Church also objected to state restrictions on its authority. Although revolutionary leader Toussaint Louverture's 1801 constitution proclaimed "the Catholic religion was to be the only publicly professed religion in the colony," it permitted state administration of the clergy, prohibited the Church from forming an association, and ensured "government would assign priests and determine the length of their service" (Greene 1993: 80–81). Jean-Jacques Dessalines's 1805 constitution later abolished the Church's official status, by "admitting of no predominant religion," advocating religious toleration, and in Article 52 asserting "the state does not provide for the mainte-nance of any religious institution, nor or any minister."

The Church objected to its subservience to the secular state. Constitutional laws bringing marriage under civil authority also undermined Church author-ity over and promotion of the nuclear family. Furthermore, the 1805 constitu-tion "allowed divorce, required civil marriage ceremonies, and gave inheritance benefits to illegitimate children" (Greene 1993: 86–87; see Articles 14, 15, and 16, respectively). The new republic would not have formal diplomatic relation-ships with the Holy See until the signing of a concordat with Rome in 1860. In subsequent decades, Roman Catholicism had varying degrees of official status but always under strict separation of church and state, and with state appoint-ment and payment of priests (Greene 1993: 84–85; Nicholls 1996: 34–35, 70). The moral and cultural hegemony the Church hoped to establish in the territory was further challenged when President Boyer (1818–43) permitted Protestant mission-aries to evangelize in Haiti (Greene 1993: 85). In addition, Freemasonry and Vodou continued competing with and limiting Church power. However, in 1898, with state support, the Church launched an antisuperstition campaign that targeted Vodou and secret societies practicing sorcery to eradicate "fetishism" (Greene 1993: 101; see also Ramsey 2011: 101–16).

Political, economic, and cultural threats to both church and state increased when the United States occupied Haiti in 1915 to protect American business inter-ests (Renda 2001). After World War I commenced the United States was concerned about German merchants' influence in Haiti, some of whom financed Haitian political groups and "had established strong links with the urban elites" (Trouillot 1990: 100). Under occupation, Protestantism expanded exponentially as a result of American missionary activity. The Church protested "the occupation force should not get involved with Church-State matters" (Greene 1993: 105).

After the end of the occupation in 1934, the Catholic leadership and newly sovereign, pro-Catholic Haitian state (Nicholls 1996: 181–83) sought to eradicate Vodou using another antisuperstition campaign (1941–42). In subsequent years, the Catholic stance toward Vodou softened, with Bishop Paul Robert of Gonaïves affirming that Vodou contained "authentic values" and "practices which are able to assist us wonderfully in understanding the sense of the Christian calling and even of the priestly and religious vocation" (Nicholls 1996: 198, citing Robert 1952: 1, 4, 19, 20). Nevertheless, Bishop Robert would castigate Vodou's "African" origins, claiming the "church must demand a total abandonment of paganism among its people" (Nicholls 1996: 198, citing Robert 1955: 3, 9, 21). Between 1860 and 1953, the Church ordained only 103 Haitian priests (Greene 1993: 110).

Internal tensions between the Church and government escalated between Dr. François Duvalier's election to the presidency in 1957 and his death in 1971, during which time he attempted to usurp Catholic pastoral power and suppress civil society. Duvalier introduced a *Catechism of the Revolution*, which burlesqued "the Holy Trinity, substituting Haitian heroes for the saints, and portraying himself as the embodiment of all of them. The *Catechism* even include[d] an adaptation of the Lord's Prayer, which begins, 'Our Doc who art in the National Palace for Life'" (Greene 1993: 111). Although Duvalier was ultimately excommunicated, the Holy See eventually accepted his control over the Church, including the appointment of archbishops and bishops (with Church assent). A few Haitian priests even accepted political appointments in his repressive administration (Greene 1993: 111, 114; Trouillot 1990: 159–60).

LIBERATION THEOLOGY IN HAITI, 1968–91

Despite Duvalier's suppression of civil society and control over the Catholic hierarchy, churches became "the only place where people could gather and share experiences, and progressive Catholics began to use this space to put their ideas into practice" (Arthur and Dash 1999: 141). Following Vatican II (1962–65) and the 1968 meeting of Catholic bishops in Medellín—where the Church articulated a "preferential option for the poor" and adopted Freirian concepts of consciousness raising—Catholicism became a potent force for human rights, economic justice, and democracy in Haiti.

This vernacularization process enabled "indigenous and non-indigenous clergy and religious, and committed laymen and laywomen" to reorient the Haitian church toward a grassroots path of "evangelisation, social justice, and defence of the poor" (Maguire 1999: 152). St. Leo Parish's Father Leandre Jeannot, an activist in Haiti and cofounder of the Haitian Multi-Service Center, accepted his religious vocation while in exile in Colombia during these years. Under President Jean-Claude Duvalier (1971–86), a network of Catholic actors provided a framework for a politically active liberation theology movement promoting human rights, democracy, and justice (Wilentz 1989). In 1983, Pope Jean Paul II visited Haiti and "explicitly attacked injustice, inequality, oppression," and pleaded for social transformation, saying, "Something must change here" (Lawless 1992: 103). The papal endorsement aided Haitians who were empowering themselves through the *ti kominote legliz* (base ecclesial groups) to demand representative government.

The pro-democracy movement formed from grassroots religious activism produced Duvalier's ouster in 1986, then the formation of the Lavalas (flood) party, and culminated in the election to the presidency of a former Salesian priest, Jean-Bertrand Aristide, on December 16, 1990. While in Haiti I observed how lay Haitian Catholics and priests, as well as international priests who were persecuted for defying Haiti's dictators, tirelessly promoted human rights, citizenship, and economic justice. Nevertheless, the Church hierarchy was largely aligned with reactionary forces and opposed the *ti legliz* movement. After Aristide was ousted on September 30, 1991, the Vatican "was the only foreign state to recognize the new regime diplomatically" (Dupuy 2007: 132).

THE ROMAN CATHOLIC CHURCH
IN COLONIAL AMERICA

Church and state alliances sponsoring missions to "Christianize" Native Americans and enslaved African populations justified British, Spanish, Portuguese, Dutch, and French colonization of the "New World" (Raboteau 1978: 96–98). For Spanish settler colonists, monarchical edicts sanctioned religious missionization and conquest of Indigenous populations. But state control influenced religious actors' capacity to deploy "charity." According to historian Jay P. Dolan (1985: 18–19), under the Spanish Crown, "civil control of the church was so thorough that the very smallest aspect of ecclesiastical life was subject to the scrutiny of civil authorities." Both church and state aligned, however, in instituting an oppressive system of labor exploitation (the *encomienda*) that only few clerics protested, such as the Dominican friar Antonio de Montesinos in Hispaniola in 1511 or Bartolomé de Las Casas. The latter's advocacy for justice toward the Indigenous contributed to the legal abolition of the labor system in 1542 (24–25). Under the ongoing Spanish mission system, quasi-racial assumptions of Native inferiority and savagery justified "reducing the Indians from a dispersed, sometimes nomadic, existence into a more disciplined, settled way of life" through forced conversion and spatial containment in towns (25; see also Nemser 2017: 1–65). Although in Canadian North America colonial French Catholicism was considered "antipapal"—averse to Vatican governance—church and state were allied to such a degree that "up until 1663 the 'church was the practical master of Canada'" (Dolan 1985: 34). Jesuit missionaries in New France desired to convert indigenous populations but the decline of state power and papal suppression of the Jesuit order in 1773 diminished evangelization in Canada (37–42).

In the English colonies, however, the Roman Catholic Church's path of arrival, incorporation, and assimilation unfolded from relative sociopolitical and economic weakness. Following Puritan settler persecution of Catholics, in April 1649, the governor of Maryland, Lord Baltimore, issued the "Act Concerning Religion," a statement of religious toleration (Massa and Osborne 2017: 14–15). In 1785, Catholics numbered roughly 15,800 (in Maryland), "of whom more than three thousand were 'slaves of all ages of African origin, called Negroes,' and ... in Pennsylvania there were about seven thousand Catholics, 'very few of whom are negroes'" (Raboteau 1978: 112).[24] The free Protestant majority perceived Catholics as "aliens" whose religious practices were aberrant, barbaric, and superstitious (see Figure 8).

Historian Thomas H. O'Connor (1998: 3–40) traces the hostility toward Catholics, particularly in New England, to the English Puritans' antipathy toward

FIGURE 8. Illustration from Samuel B. Smith (1836), *Flight of Popery from Rome to the West.*

individuals loyal to the Roman Church (see also Daniels 2004: 9–12). In the seventeenth century, believing Irish Catholics were considered dangerous, and French Jesuits were perceived as threats to the English colonies, accused of being "a particularly subversive brand of secret agents doing the bidding of the Vatican" (O'Connor 1998: 7). Catholic priests were banned from Massachusetts's territory "under penalty of life imprisonment." If they escaped the territory and were recaptured, they were subject to execution (O'Connor 1998: 8).

In contrast with the 1805 Haitian constitution enshrining religious toleration, a young John Adams espoused antipapist views, claiming "popery was incompatible with liberty, and . . . that Catholicism had no right to recognition or toleration" (O'Connor 1998: 11). Adams's beliefs sharpened John Locke's, whose 1689 *A Letter Concerning Toleration* established the principle of separation of church and state: government should neither establish religion nor possess "concernment for the interest of men's souls," but rather procure, preserve, and advance the civil "interests" of society—"life, liberty, health, and indolency of body; and the possession of outward things, such as money, lands, houses, furniture, and the like" (Locke 1689). The prevailing anti-Catholic sentiment remained virulent until the American Revolution, when revolutionary forces allied with the French in the war against the British (Farrelly 2018: 70–71), then resurged in the early-nineteenth century when "the large influx of Catholic foreigners . . . threatened the homogeneity of the Anglo-Saxon Protestant culture of the United States" (Dolan 1985: 201). Although in the eighteenth century Jesuit missionaries ministered to

Catholics (including Native Americans) in the eastern states, formal organization of the Church and its benevolent institutions began only after independence from Britain (Oates 1995: 1).

ORGANIZED CHARITY IN COLONIAL AMERICA

The institutionalization of Catholic charity occurred alongside the growth of Catholicism in a nation still hostile to the Church (Oates 1995).[25] Catholics founded charities not only to aid their own religious communities but also to evangelize external populations. In this "economy of salvation," conceptions of gender, race, and nationality (among others) influenced ideas about who should give and receive charity. Such conceptions also shaped the divisions of charitable labor among religious and lay actors.

Religious sisters and nuns in colonial America, for example, made vows of poverty, chastity, and dedication to the poor—establishing orphanages, schools, residences for the destitute, hospitals, and hospices—and cared for and disciplined persons under their direction. In the commemoration of Catholic Charities USA's hundredth anniversary, Larry J. Snyder traces CCUSA's genealogy to the "arrival of the Ursuline sisters in New Orleans in 1727" (CCUSA 2010: 11; see also Kammer 2009: 34–35).[26] Despite women's challenges administering colonial institutions, as well as any moral ambivalence they may have had about owning enslaved human beings, the Ursulines managed an orphanage, a school instructing young French women, a chapel, and a hospital (Clark 2007; Lachance 1988), and evangelized "black and Indian girls and women" (Davis 1990: 72; Clark 2007). Although they reportedly "played a crucial role in the formation of an Afro-creole majority in the Catholic Church of New Orleans" (Clark 2007: 5), the slaveholding Ursuline sisters, Shannon Dee Williams (2022: 25) argues, "refused to admit African American candidates into their ranks." The exclusion of Black women candidates provoked the later establishment of separate Black Catholic religious orders.

Saint-Domingue refugees resettling in New Orleans and other American cities were among the earliest Catholic charity recipients; however, their presence exacerbated tensions regarding to and from whom charity should be extended. In three large movements during and after the Haitian Revolution (1793, 1798, and 1809), plantation owners fled with their families and some enslaved Blacks to the United States, Jamaica, and Cuba (Lachance 1988). Black Saint-Domingue refugees were suspected of being vectors of the "cancer of black liberty," possessing the potential to incite enslaved populations to revolt (Bolster 1998; Jordan 1968; Lachance 1988). These refugees eventually found social support from Catholics (and other humanitarians) in New Orleans, Baltimore, Charleston, Philadelphia, New York, and other cities. They also helped establish churches (Laguerre 1998;

White 2010). New York would become the home of the venerable Pierre Toussaint, an enslaved Saint-Domingue refugee brought with the French Catholic family that "owned" him.[27] Toussaint eventually ran a successful hairstyling business, the earnings of which helped him to cofound (with Elizabeth Seton) one of the first orphanages in New York City (Zéphir 2004: 13). In Philadelphia, Saint-Domingue "refugees were welcomed by the three Catholic churches in the city, St. Joseph's, St. Mary's and Holy Trinity, all near to where the French were living. White, mulatto and black Saint-Dominguans worshiped there, although not always together" (Branson and Patrick 2001: 202). In Baltimore, racial tensions and general ambivalence toward Black Saint-Domingue refugees also arose from fears "the black refugees might influence the native blacks to revolt against their masters" (Laguerre 1998: 38). In response to Baltimore's Black Catholics' needs, women of Haitian descent established the Oblate Sisters of Providence in 1829 (Williams 2022: 29–34). Composed of "virgins and widows of color" (O'Grady 1930: 17), the Oblates, the first congregation of women religious of African descent, chose the education of children of color as their charism.[28] Although there would not be another major influx of Haitian refugees until the late 1970s, contemporary Haitian arrivals would encounter Catholic charities radically altered in character from those encountered in the nineteenth century.

RACE, GENDER, AND CHARITABLE LABOR

Waves of European migrants to America from the mid-nineteenth to the mid-twentieth centuries sparked the proliferation, professionalization, and bureaucratization of Catholic charities. In the early nineteenth century, local parishes encouraged charitable giving and volunteerism among working class communities to support their churches. By the 1830s, immigration from Germany, France, and Ireland had begun to expand Catholic populations in the United States; however, these economically poorer communities needed charitable aid themselves and were unused or unable to respond to the Church's solicitations for assistance (Oates 1995: 5). Throughout the nineteenth century, wealthier benevolent societies in Europe aided these "New World" missions "not only in monetary gifts, but also in the large numbers of clergy and religious who emigrated to work in American dioceses" (Oates 1995: 4).

Benevolent institutions managed by religious societies answered the call for funding and volunteer labor; however, the gendered division of charitable labor typically cast women religious as providers of direct care. In 1808, Catholic convert and widow, Elizabeth Seton, established the Sisters of Charity (SOC) "under the authority of the first American bishop, John Carroll, Bishop of Baltimore," an order dedicated to aiding poor and orphaned children.[29] Orders like the SOC gained particular expertise in providing institutionally based care because "priests in religious orders certainly did not see direct personal charity work as part of their responsibilities, a stand that aroused some criticism in poor city parishes of the 1850s" (Oates 1995: 24).

In the nineteenth century, conflicts over the gendered division of compassionate care continued to emerge. Male clerics who resisted direct labor in soup kitchens or food pantries claimed women were better suited to these works, as "this duty has devolved especially on the female sex, because it is better gifted than the male for the ministry of compassion."[30] Lay fraternal benevolent societies like the Society of Saint Vincent de Paul responded to crises in their natal countries and locally with fundraising for buildings, hospitals, and orphanages, but not direct care for the needy (Oates 1995: 25–29). Furthermore, "bishops pressured communities like the Sisters of Mercy and the Sisters of Charity to divert sisters from orphanages, hospitals, and social welfare agencies to parochial schools" because they "were willing to accept lower salaries than teaching brothers and, of course, lay teachers. . . . Pastors by the 1930s were in general agreement that brothers had become an expendable 'luxury' to be replaced whenever possible with less expensive sisters" (Oates 1995: 154). Disputes regarding the sexual division of charitable labor and the expanding role of a professional laity would recur as Catholic charities began to partner with government to offer social services to the American poor and to incorporate refugees into the United States. Similar conflicts about gender and pastoral power would arise in the 1980s at the Haitian Center as the institution began to professionalize.

Prevailing understandings of gender, race, and ethnicity produced and reproduced stratified paths of piety upon which Catholics were differentially able to accumulate salvific merit through charity. Nonetheless, charitable work enabled women (and persons of color) to acquire civic power outside the spheres in which societal norms would ordinarily confine them. In so doing, they accrued pastoral power, but a power considerably limited by the religious structures and local communities in which it was deployed. In 1832, during a cholera epidemic in Baltimore, Fr. Jacques Joubert, co-founder of the Oblate Sisters of Providence (OSP), asked the Black sisters to aid the SOC as demonstration of their equal capacity for charity (Davis 1990: 101). Joubert argued their labor could generate additional merit:

> I addressed a few words to them on the good work they were about to undertake, on the merits attached to the sacrifice they were making to God of the life He had given them. I pointed out to them the dangers to which they were obliged to expose themselves in thus devoting themselves to the service of the sick poor . . . I told them that if God permitted that they should be victims of their zeal, they would die martyrs of charity. (Davis 1990: 102)[31]

As Black Catholics were prevented from joining established religious orders, perhaps the Oblates had to demonstrate extraordinary piety and dedication. Indeed, one of the Oblate sisters became infected and died. There were other risks than managing schools, maintaining their devotional practices, or nursing the

FIGURE 9. Burning of the Ursuline Convent in Charlestown, Massachusetts, 1834.

sick (Davis 1990: 101). "[A]fter the Oblate Sisters had established their convent in Baltimore, there were threats from extremist whites to burn the place. On one occasion, the Haitian American nuns were so upset that three priests, one of them from Saint Domingue, came to sleep at the convent to provide protection to the sisters after they had informed the local city authorities of the threats" (Laguerre 1998: 38).

In Charlestown, Massachusetts, in 1834, erroneous rumors of nuns being held against their will at the Ursuline convent sparked a mob dressed as monks with painted faces to destroy the property and burn it to the ground (see Figure 9).[32] A contemporary attack against Haitian nuns at St. Leo Parish shows how interpersonal and institutional resistances to Catholic women's pastoral power remain.[33]

Early American Catholic charities permitted religious authorities and the laity to incorporate marginal populations into the Church and receive limited political recognition or quasi-citizenship in the nation-state. Women religious and religious of color were partially able to transcend conventional norms of gender, race, and the sexual division of (charitable) labor to gain management expertise; however, not without substantial risk. Nonetheless, the political economy of salvation remained gendered and raced.

MIGRATION AND THE (BIO)POLITICS OF CHARITY IN BOSTON

From the late nineteenth to the mid-twentieth century, Catholic charity was not only enmeshed in local politics; it increasingly reflected a biopolitics involving production and reproduction, and race, gender, and ethnicity. Migrants, the poor, the sick, and others perceived as living "sinfully" (i.e., the wayward, juvenile offenders, sex workers, etc.) became objects of institutional rehabilitation and reintegration programs. Like the predominantly Protestant majority, Boston Catholics' apprehensions about destitute and newly arriving immigrants also implicated public health and security. In the 1820s, the first of several waves of Irish immigrants began arriving to labor on construction projects (O'Connor 1998: 55). The influx revived earlier fears according to which Catholics were considered "enemy aliens" loyal to a "foreign prince": "Protestant associations struck out at Roman Catholics in their communities with even greater determination." These Protestants ascribed the rapid growth in Catholic numbers "less to adverse economic conditions than to a deliberate, worldwide papal conspiracy to reestablish the menacing power of the Roman Catholic Church in the New World" (O'Connor 1998: 57).

For the mid-nineteenth-century, majority Protestant, Massachusetts population, the Irish influx posed what could now be called a "biosecurity" threat. Having fled hunger and disease in Europe, the economically poor and unskilled peasants packed Boston's slums. Irish Catholics were stigmatized as "alien" for their reputed criminality and their cultural differences, and for competing for employment against the already existing working poor:

> The physical realities of overcrowded slum districts, the high morbidity and mortality rates, and the crushing poverty of the mass of immigrants appalled the native-born middle and upper classes, while the working classes viewed the foreigners as economic competitors. Yankee leaders bemoaned the strain on municipal services and the drain on the public treasury which resulted from the disproportionate numbers of Irish in the city's almshouses and jails. (Walton 1993: 11)

Although the Irish were the largest ethnic immigrant group in Boston by the close of the nineteenth century, after 1880, eastern and southern Europeans began arriving in large numbers. While many were Catholic (Italians, Poles, Lithuanians, and Portuguese), "large numbers of Polish and Russian Jews crowded into the West End," creating a sense of alarm for *both* Yankees and Irish Catholics (Walton 1993: 13; see also McLellan 1984).

Native-born Bostonians tended to view new ethnic arrivals as vectors of danger, urban decay, immorality, and inherent disease (Walton 1993: 14). Charitable interventions aimed at ameliorating urban poverty by reforming, controlling, and "Americanizing" new immigrants and their children (Walton 1993: 14):

> Reformers equated Americanization and uplift with Protestantism and feared the immigrants' Catholicism or Judaism would be a permanent barrier to their full assimilation. . . . The varied [Protestant] postbellum philanthropies, the "benevolent empire," did not deal exclusively with the immigrant, but the Irish, Italians and Jews were of special concern. (Walton 1993: 18, citing Schneider 1980: 136)

Anxieties about "their" poor propelled Catholics to use charities "to protect themselves against the threat of infidelity and attempts by Protestants to rob Catholics of their faith" while "gaining respectability and proving the worthiness of Catholics in the greater social community" (Walton 1993: 88–89).

Promoting Catholic respectability, loyalty, and civic inclusion was of paramount importance. Protestant missionaries attempted to capture the hearts and minds of poor Catholic families who "were ashamed of their poverty" or who "ignored the Church's moral teaching and lapsed into a dissolute and sinful life" (Walton 1993: 89). Catholics perceived such interventions as attempts to "force them to barter their souls and the souls of their children for the present need of food or fuel" (Walton 1993: 89). One 1892 charity study called Protestant missionization an "unchristian traffic in souls."[34] The theological dimensions of this economy of salvation were well known. Distressed families seeking assistance from Boston's Catholic Charitable Bureau (discussed below) "openly threatened 'that if they cannot receive help in the way they demand from Catholic authorities, they will immediately apply to Protestant societies or institutions for aid'" (Walton 1993: 131, citing CCB Annual Report 1908: 16. See CCAB 1908). By accepting Protestant philanthropy, these families could deny other Catholics the opportunity to give; charitable exchanges offered participants opportunities to accrue merit in the economy of merits and faults.

Catholic charity demonstrated the diverse community's capacity to reduce the so-called "burden" of poor and "deviant" Catholics on public monies. Indeed, charity "became a primary emblem of Catholic identity in American culture and the chief means by which the church established a public voice" (Brown and McKeown 1997: 1). In other words, the provision of charity had become the public face or "brand" of corporate Catholicism.

After the Great Depression, Catholics entered debates about public welfare from concerns about losing the "terrain" of Catholic souls to state control. During the National Conference of Catholic Charities 1935 meeting on New Deal social security, "a Catholic bishop rose to the floor to mark the territory. 'The poor belong to us,' Bishop Aloisius Muench defiantly reminded his colleagues. 'We will not let them be taken from us!'" (Brown and McKeown 1997: 1, 193).

Apprehensions about retaining Catholics related to pastoral obligations to monitor and regulate the religious community's "economy of salvation." From the late nineteenth to the early twentieth century, the St. Vincent de Paul Society viewed charity as a means to redistribute material wealth between rich and poor, and to encourage devotions and prayer among them (Skok 1998: 21–23). For Boston's Vincentians, "Personal piety and religious conviction intertwined with the realities of class, politics, and ethnicity." However, "the shared bond of religion would cut across the differences of social and economic status between the middle-class Vincentians and the poor; all were equal in the eyes of God, and the act of worshipping together symbolized that equality" (Walton 1993: 95, 98).

By giving alms and sharing religious faith, St. Vincent de Paul members participated in the "spiritual economy of merits and satisfactions," a "celestial exchange bank offering rewards for good behavior. Individuals could make deposits by performing 'good works,' which the Church taught were essential to their salvation" (Skok 1998: 23). Just as the Oblate Sisters of Providence were told risking their lives to care for the infectious poor would be meritorious spiritually, "the Society told its members that their good works would 'accumulate . . . and mingle to form an immense return on the day of remuneration—cannot one say that they are like the savings-bank of eternity?'" (Skok 1998: 23).[35]

Performing charitable labor earned Catholics the "modern" equivalent of an "indulgence." Prior to the sixteenth century, when reformists began criticizing this component of the compassion economy, Catholics could "purchase" indulgences to improve their chances at attaining salvation after death: "Granted only by the pope, the indulgence released an individual from some of the punishment due in the afterlife for his sins, after confession and absolution had removed his guilt" (Skok 1998: 23). The Church changed this practice during the Counter-Reformation: "Instead, the faithful could earn them by reciting certain prayers or performing acts of charity" (Skok 1998: 23). By participating in the spiritual economy of charity for indulgences, not only could the wealthy benefit, poor charity recipients could earn indulgences praying specific prayers for others, especially their benefactors (Skok 1998: 24).

Religious charity was undoubtedly motivated by compassion, mercy, and concern for charity recipients' souls. In competing with Protestant missionary efforts, Catholics attempted to retain control over, and even broker, this intangible economy of salvation. Efforts to retain the Catholic poor in the Church's corporate body were critical because the "least of these" represented a spiritual capital reservoir. Extending charity toward them generated and circulated merit in the Catholic compassion economy. Because of their multiple, historical afflictions, impoverished Haitians have offered a "rich" territory, enabling religious and secular Samaritans to accumulate merit in compassion economies.

SCIENTIFIC CHARITY

Love is therefore the service that the Church carries out in order to attend constantly to man's sufferings and his needs, including material needs. And this is the aspect, this service of charity, on which I want to focus in the second part of the Encyclical.

—BENEDICT XVI 2006: PAR. 19; EMPHASIS IN THE ORIGINAL

In *Deus Caritas Est*, Benedict XVI offers "service of charity" best practices guidelines, stating such work "needs to be organized if it is to be an ordered service to the community" (par. 20). Although organized charity is currently performed at diocesan, national, and international levels under the *Caritas* umbrella network (par. 31a), practitioners should be "professionally competent: they should be properly trained in what to do and how to do it, and committed to continuing care." Caregivers must also be compassionate: "We are dealing with human beings, and human beings always need something more than technically proper care. They need humanity. They need heartfelt concern" (par. 31a).

This contemporary papal exhortation to care humanely and professionally recalls late-nineteenth- to early twentieth-century dilemmas over charitable best practices. A movement to promote "scientific charity" in administrative bureaus conflicted with Vincentian theologies of compassionate interpersonal spiritual exchanges with the poor. Concerns for social and economic justice offered compelling justification for incorporating the new social work methods into Catholic agencies (Conrad and Joseph 2010: 49). Other tensions arose from transforming charity from a private realm of pastoral exchange to a semipublic activity increasingly performed in partnership with other religious and secular institutions. While professionalizing charitable organizations in their communities, Catholics "began to experiment with 'cooperation' in welfare work," joining "local charity federations" and becoming members of the "National Conference of Charities and Corrections" (Brown and McKeown 1997: 5).[36] With the support of American Catholic universities, these Samaritans "publicly accepted a program of 'scientific charity' in 1910 with the founding of their own NCCC, the National Conference of Catholic Charities" (Brown and McKeown 1997: 6).

The intent of the NCCC was to "help Catholic social workers adapt to the emerging social service profession" (Yankowski 2010: 89). In so doing, the Catholic conference and charity workers in dioceses across the United States revisited disputes concerning gender, vocation, and pastoral power. The NCCC's predominantly female membership "took up the task of making their practices more acceptably 'scientific'" by becoming "informed on non-Catholic and private welfare initiatives (mothers' pensions and community chest funding, for instance)" and adopting "the methods and standards of non-Catholic social work and social reform" (Brown and McKeown 1997: 6). Although "these Catholic activists continued to use the language of charity to characterize Catholic social provision" (Brown and McKeown 1997: 6), at the diocesan level, the professionalization, bureaucratization, and laicization of charity challenged both "masculine" and "feminine" pastoral power:

> Lacking the cachet of consecrated religious women and often stigmatized for earning a living by serving the poor, the social workers displaced traditional volunteers, challenged the pre-eminence of religious women and of institutional charities, and

created considerable animosity among pastors accustomed to having the sole authority in matters pertaining to the welfare of dependent children and needy families in their parishes. (Brown and McKeown 1997: 6–7)

Conflicts concerning the legitimate exercise of pastoral power reflected broader ambivalence whether professionalized and bureaucratized charity was sufficiently "Catholic." From the 1920s until the 1930s, Catholic lay women continued offering charity, but increasingly with diocesan bureau clergymen as directors.

As Brown and McKeown (1997: 63–64) document, several approaches to social service clashed during these years: the traditional Catholic model viewing charity as a "right to life," propelled by "a believer's love of God as its highest motive and expressed itself in daily and sustained attention to human needs," and a second "rights" position, arguing social welfare should not require the benevolent impulses of the "advantaged classes." Public care should be an entitlement reflecting social and economic justice—"fair wages, child labor laws, public health measures, and social insurance against industrial accidents." In removing lay volunteers and replacing them with professionals, Rev. John O'Grady, a priest with doctoral training in sociology and labor economics, instituted a third way that modernized and expanded the NCCC. The reorganization enabled priests who directed diocesan charitable bureaus to craft NCCC policy and expand the influence of Catholic charities on secular public policy in Washington, DC. (Brown and McKeown 1997: 64–65). Catholic charities shifted from a separatist, voluntary mode of giving eschewing government involvement in the Church's terrain to promoting the "Catholic charitable brand" to both non-Catholics and government as an alternative social care model. As a result, Catholic charitable leaders became influential in crafting American public welfare (Brown and McKeown 1997: 6).

When social welfare was federated under the New Deal, Catholics became increasingly concerned about the "growing involvement of state and federal government in the lives of individuals and families" (Brown and McKeown 1997: 6–7). Catholic leaders lobbied for their agencies to play a strong role in the new welfare state using federated funding. By presenting their "charism" as service to the poor and the brand of Catholic charities as the "protector of the religious rights of Catholic welfare recipients" (Brown and McKeown 1997: 7), American Catholic charities agencies were classified as "public," thereby becoming Federal Emergency Relief Administration fund managers (Brown and McKeown 1997: 7–8; see Chapter 7). Catholic charities leaders influenced the FDR administration to "shape the provisions of Aid to Dependent Children and Child Welfare Services" and to eliminate mandated state participation, because it "would have threatened the established local patterns of funding for Catholic child-care where state laws prohibited the allocation of state funds to private institutions" (Brown and McKeown 1997: 8). At municipal, state, and national levels, Catholic charities continued advocating for the poor and providing social welfare, but with increased reliance on public funding. Such dependency would pose problems for the Charity in the 2000s, when state laws required the agency to choose between aiding children and complying with nondiscrimination laws.

SCIENTIFIC CHARITY AND BOSTON'S CATHOLIC CHARITABLE BUREAU

The institution I call "the Charity"—the Catholic Charitable Bureau of the Archdiocese of Boston, Inc. (also called Catholic Charities Archdiocese of Boston, CCAB)—has evolved during its long history. In some respects, recent friction between the Church, the Charity, and the Center originates in the early organization and bureaucratization of Catholic charity in Boston.[37] In response to Protestant missionary threats to the security of the Church's corporate body, on January 1, 1903, the Charity was established in Boston as the "Central Bureau of Information," with a Greater Boston parish priest committee serving as officers (McLellan 1984: 29–33). When Massachusetts mandated the deinstitutionalization of public almshouses, Catholic clerics and laypersons worried about Protestant charities working with the state to transfer "delinquent" and "dependent or neglected children"—many born of immigrant Catholics (Hewitt 1940: 20)—into Protestant families' care. In 1892, Father Frederic Gigault, the Tewksbury almshouse chaplain, reported to Archbishop John Williams how "minor wards of the state placed out in foster homes from state institutions were being placed out with little or no regard to their spiritual well-being" (McLellan 1984: 6). As private asylums like the New England Home for Little Wanderers released Catholic children to Protestant foster homes, and the Unitarian-managed Pine Farm in Newton was accused of "deliberately evading Catholic interests in its handling of Catholic childrens' cases" (McLellan 1984: 7), Father Gigault "pleaded for an effort to 'save the faith of the Catholic infants in the almshouses and provide for orphans and [abandoned children] in some Catholic asylum'" (McLellan 1984: 6).[38]

Although Catholics had established residential "asylums" in Boston and other Massachusetts towns since the 1830s—orphan asylums, homes for children from single parent families, residences for working girls, childcare facilities (for mothers who could not remain at home), homes for the elderly, and hospices—Catholic children were still becoming wards of the state (McLellan 1984: 20–28). Heightened fears for their welfare provoked Catholic leaders to begin counting immigrant and indigent populations to ensure no child of "theirs" was lost. In 1901, a committee of priests adopted plans to "safeguard the religious rights of Catholic children" through the "supervision of every Catholic child in the care of the State, Municipal or private charity" and the creation of an office "where a catalogue of all these children shall be kept as to their location, family history and religious duties and where also a directory of homes suitable for placing Catholic children shall be kept" (Hewitt 1940: 9, citing *Annual Report of the Catholic Charitable Bureau*, 1902; see also McLellan 1984: 29–31).

In 1908, Archbishop William J. O'Connell restructured the archdiocese and centralized oversight of Catholic charities. The Central Bureau of Information became known as the Catholic Charitable Bureau (CCB). The CCB's reports documented "religious welfare" work—pastoral care, discipline, and correction of individuals—and assessed the moral and health status of persons receiving care. These practices constituted charitable biopolitics, a professional compassion economy intertwined with the religious economy of merits and faults. In terms of pastoral care (and power), one of the bureau's purposes was to record the frequency of a ward's attendance at Catholic Mass and confession, ensuring local clergy examined the child's inner conscience and, by extension, the state of their souls. Early reports tabulated the following: numbers of neglected children and juvenile offenders reported to the bureau; children placed in Catholic families or discharged to relatives; children to be transferred from Protestant to Catholic families; numbers of Catholic homes made available to the state for fosterage; numbers of cases reported and settled, letters on file, and numbers of Catholic wards of the city (CCAB 1904). From 1912 to 1921, summaries of the bureau's general services record exponentially increasing numbers of home visits, telephone calls, cases recorded, letters received, and letters sent out on clients' behalf (Hewitt 1940: 74). In effect, successful efforts to "resettle" Catholic children would prefigure and mirror later refugee resettlement work.

For those outside the Church, the CCB's annual reports became evidence demonstrating Catholics' performance of their civic duty. To further document the bureau's growing expertise, in the 1910s the CCB's scope of work expanded to include programs involving the "protection and correction of delinquent Catholic youths," a summer vacation camp for underprivileged and "sickly" children, an emergency fund for elders in distress, and public health measures to combat an influenza epidemic (Hewitt 1940: 34–35). In 1912, in alignment with the growing national movement toward social work professionalization, a charity column was added to the *Pilot*, the weekly Catholic news bulletin, to "[explain] in a scientific and professional manner the nature and motives of Catholic charities" and provide "the public with the opportunity of learning more of the works of the charitable societies and institutions of the Archdiocese" (Hewitt 1940: 42).

CCB statistical and documentary procedures enumerated acts potentially influencing the economy of merits and faults. By 1946, the Archdiocese of Boston and a newly legally incorporated CCB were under Archbishop Richard J. Cushing's pastoral care. The CCB annual report classified individual "services" according to four categories: "spiritual works"—baptisms arranged (238), marriages validated (54), referrals to pastors for counsel (878), and other spiritual works (795)—and "corporal works"—persons referred for medical care (1,057), placement in homes and hospitals (1,266), court cases (874), situations obtained (167), burials (26), and other corporal works (3,550). Two final categories were also tabulated: the "children's department" counted 3,072 "infants and children under care during the year" and 103 "children adopted during the year," as well as the "maternity cases," which enumerated the "total number of applications during the year" of both married and unmarried mothers (CCAB 1946). In this fascinating cataloguing of "works of mercy," some acts appear to target the corporal, the "body," and the spiritual works, the "soul."

According to Joseph Delany (1911), works of mercy are obligations imposed by religious law that "demand more than a humanitarian basis if they are to serve as instruments in bringing about our salvation. The proper motive is indispensable." Catholic theologians have considered the virtue of mercy as similar to justice, as it "controls relations between distinct persons" (Delany 1911). As such, "the traditional enumeration of corporal works of mercy is as follows: to feed the hungry; to give drink to the thirsty; to clothe the naked; to harbour the harbourless; to visit the sick; to ransom the captive; [and] to bury the dead. The spiritual works of mercy are: to instruct the ignorant; to counsel the doubtful; to admonish sinners; to bear wrongs patiently; to forgive offences willingly; to comfort the afflicted; [and] to pray for the living and the dead" (Delany 1911).

Delany also notes how men's and women's religious orders were founded to perform particular works. For example, the charism (or brand) of both the Trinitarians and the Order of Our Lady of Ransom was the "recovery of Christians who were held captive by the infidels." According to the anthropologist Patrick Gaffney (personal communication, February 2, 2012), individuals could give finances and resources to religious orders founded to carry out specific works. The merit these men and women religious generated would accrue to the donor, by proxy, as if the donor had carried out the work personally.

Through its documentation, one can argue the CCB not only demonstrated to non-Catholics the community's capacity to take care of their own, but the bureau and its publications implicitly notified readers of works performed to protect public health and public security, and, by extension, corporate Catholic spiritual health. The *First Annual Report* (1908) enumerated Carney Hospital's care for dying consumptives, St. Elizabeth's support for "poor housewives, domestics, and working girls" with noncommunicable diseases or in need of "gynecological" treatment, and St. Mary's Infant Asylum's sheltering of "children abandoned, neglected, or abused by ill-human parents." The same report documented Daly Industrial School's "industrial education of deserving poor girls over fourteen years of age," the House of the Angel Guardian's education and training of "orphans, destitute, neglected and wayward boys age 7 to 15," and the House of the Good Shepherd's reclamation of wayward girls, fallen women, and a "protectory and preservation class" of girls who "receive a good education and are taught such branches of industry as will enable them to earn an honest livelihood when discharged from the home." These children were separately housed in order that they "not come in contact with the other inmates of the other department," and suitable positions were found for them upon completion of their training. It is not clear how the so-called deserving and unworthy poor were distinguished or by whom, but a moral economy of healthcare and education is explicit and spiritual benefit of Catholics providing care and protection to their brethren implicit in such reports.

In deploying Catholic pastoral power for the correction of delinquents—physical surveillance and moral regulation combined with disciplinary practices—an early form of "private policing" (Maurutto 2003: 83) was enacted as a surrogate for the state. In 1913, the CCB established the first training program for social workers joining charitable and correctional work (Hewitt 1940: 44). The bureau's social work resembled rehabilitative, reform, and training activities occurring in other North American dioceses. In response to a growing prison reform movement in Canada in the late nineteenth century, for example, the Archdiocese of Toronto began to play a direct role in the juvenile justice system (Maurutto 2003: 103–5). The archdiocese began operating the St. John's Industrial School for boys (1895), administered by the Christian Brothers, and St. Mary's Industrial School for girls (1900), administered by the Sisters of the Good Shepherd. Like the Good Shepherd sisters in Boston, the Sisters of the Good Shepherd in Toronto had, by 1900, accumulated extensive expertise in private policing:

> The Sisters of the Good Shepherd had been involved in prison work since 1875, when they founded the Good Shepherd Female Refuge for Fallen Women, an asylum for adult female prisoners and prostitutes. In the early 1900s the asylum also housed a number of young female delinquents sentenced by the courts, particularly when overcrowding became a problem at St. Mary's. (Maurutto 2003: 105)

As a result of their historical expertise reforming juvenile delinquent girls, Boston's Good Shepherds eventually received state subcontracts continuing their early moral reform and policing work. In 1992, the Archdiocese of Boston drew on the Good Shepherds' experience to help resettle Haitian unaccompanied minors paroled from detention camps in Guantánamo Bay, Cuba (see Chapter 3). In facilitating juvenile justice work, Catholic charitable institutions indirectly acted as apparatuses of security. But such acts can also be interpreted as sacrifices made by proxy to implement virtuous works for both church and state.

Like other agencies in the national Catholic charities movement (Brown and McKeown 1997: 65–67), the CCB advocated for immigrants and refugees and took public stances against national migration policies. In 1921, the Boston bureau began to combat federal legislation (1917) imposing a literacy test on prospective immigrants and critiqued subsequent restrictive measures establishing quotas for certain ethnic nationals. According to former NCCC director, Rev. John O'Grady (1930: 284), this literacy requirement attempted to prevent "undesirable classes such as paupers, criminals, anarchists, and diseased and immoral persons" from entering the United States. In response, Cardinal William O'Connell established the Immigrant Welfare Department of the Catholic Charitable Bureau with an advisory board that included the bureau's director and "priests of nationalities most concerned with the problem of immigration" (Hewitt 1940: 50). The department coordinated with state and federal immigration offices and the National Catholic Welfare Conference to provide services prefiguring the Charity's contemporary refugee and immigration services.

From the 1920s to the 1930s, tensions grew in the Archdiocese of Boston regarding "Catholic" charity identity, values, and links to the public sphere. Some Catholics felt the CCB's engagement in public charity had begun to accommodate, rather than critique, the onslaught of modernity, science, and secularism. As "an immigrant community eager to [participate] in the larger society" when discrimination against them remained (i.e., "classified ads still listed 'Protestant' as a necessary qualification for many jobs"), Catholic fulfillment of charitable acts that served the general public gave "evidence of [these Catholics'] civic responsibility, demonstrated by shouldering a fair share of the city's welfare load" (Walton 1993: 166, 145, 167).

A solution to dilemmas about whether organized charity was too modern, secular, and insufficiently Catholic was to identify examples of "scientific charity" in Catholic history. Early twentieth-century Boston Catholic leaders traced the genealogy of professional charity to ancient and early modern religious actors: "The deacons and deaconesses appointed by Pope Fabian in ancient Rome were the first friendly visitors, attending the sick and the poor and distributing alms. Later the English monasteries, according to Charitable Bureau director Anderson, were the 'settlement houses . . . of those days'" (Walton 1993: 165). By reframing Catholic charity as the epitome of modernity, the Bureau developed a "parallel system of charities" that "reached from the cradle to the grave" and "paradoxically demonstrated both their separateness from the non-Catholic world and their similarities to it" (Walton 1993: 166–67).

Nevertheless, the brand of charity that Boston Catholics practiced was not the only issue impeding the institutional "conversion to modernity" (van der Veer 1996). Of paramount concern, especially to the Catholic leadership, was the mode and organization of charity. During his tenure (1907–44), Cardinal O'Connell sought not only to expand the archdiocese's work but also to ensure its efficiency and fiscal responsibility. After his installation as archbishop, O'Connell inaugurated "a reorganization process that brought all phases of diocesan life under the supervision of the archbishop who exercised control through a cadre of newly created bureau directors answerable to him" (McLellan 1984: 47). The loose network of Catholic charitable institutions would also be reorganized, but the rationale for such institutional restructuring was deemed pastoral: "So important are these various charities in the eyes of the Archbishop that not only has he directed and outlined the work of the new office, but in a special manner has shown particular interest in these charitable institutions by frequent visits, personal observation, and the establishment of means and methods for their general welfare and management" (CCAB 1908: 1).

In addition to the pastoral care with which the Cardinal surveyed his "flock," both Catholic institutions and individual caregivers and recipients were subjected to his discipline. O'Connell viewed Catholic charity as both a virtue and a "business," albeit one often "mismanaged and in deplorable financial conditions"

(McLellan 1984: 49).[39] According to Daniel McLellan (1984: 46), a Franciscan historian studying the CCB's first eighty years, "O'Connell implemented Roman Curial bureaucracy at a time in American history when such corporate arrangements were looked upon as conditions for success." This business model required a modern, "rational" approach:

> An agency such as a diocesan charitable bureau must have, then, as its chief aim, under episcopal direction, to bring all charitable and social institutions within the diocese to as high a state of effective service as possible. . . . they are under very definite obligation to accept, within reason, suggestions emanating from proper authority which are intended to advance the general cause of religion and charity throughout the diocese. (McClellan 1984: 49)[40]

As McLellan (1984: 50) reports, O'Connell's strategy to implement this approach was to secure "a position within the corporate structure of each institution from which he could control policy, personnel, and finances." However, these attempts to consolidate, regulate, and improve diocesan social service agencies would be resisted, especially by the superiors of the men's religious order managing the House of the Angel Guardian and of the women's order administering Carney Hospital (McLellan 1984: 50–53). Up until the 1970s, when the CCB once again underwent reorganization, conflicts would recur between diocesan leaders advocating a more traditional, pastoral style of charity and those who gave primacy to the professional, scientific, social work model.

. . .

American Catholic benevolent institutions have been conduits through which migrants, the poor, and other vulnerable populations are incorporated into and retained within Catholic communities. Catholic charities offered material support, vocational training, education, and care, as well as moral rehabilitation and correction for "delinquents." By engaging in correctional work on behalf of the government, these institutions deployed both compassionate and disciplinary modes of pastoral power to reduce the fiscal burden the poor posed to the state, but also to reduce the public health and security threat the sick and "deviant" presented to the body politic. Catholic charitable initiatives actively participated in a compassion economy in which the moral stakes of charity were high: an essential component of organized care, *caritas*, has been achieving the salvation of both the "donors" and the "recipients" of charity.

During these early years of national brand building (or nation-building), and throughout the twentieth century, Boston's Catholic social service agencies would grapple with many similar ethical challenges. Conceptions of race, gender, and ethnicity (among other factors) influenced whether actors involved in such exchanges could deploy pastoral power and (hopefully) accumulate merit in the divine economy of salvation. Debates regarding the centralization or decentralization of the Charity network, clerical versus lay agency administration, and professional and scientific, versus traditional and pastoral, care would become particularly contested, especially as Catholic Charities' role as a provider of private welfare in Massachusetts increased. Finally, concerns regarding the increasing partnerships with government and the eventual dependence on public funding would affect the Catholic charitable brand and pose a crisis to it at the national level. As the next chapter recounts, the journeys of Haitian refugees to the United States traveled through a variety of asylums, including some managed by Catholic charities, and would test conceptions of the corporal and spiritual works of mercy.

3

Life in Purgatorial Spaces

Haitian Migrants between Church, State, and Law

From birth to mourning after death, law "takes hold of" bodies in order to make them its text. Through all sorts of initiations (in rituals, at schools, etc.) it transforms them into tables of the law, into living tableaus of rules and customs, into actors in the drama organized by a social order.

—MICHEL DE CERTEAU

It's not a whole lot of difference between the Catholic structure and the penal structure.

—MARTIN CONROY, ADULT EDUCATION INSTRUCTOR
  AT THE HAITIAN MULTI-SERVICE CENTER (CA. 2003–8)

In 1998, I met "Jean-Robert Paul" at the Human Rights Fund (II) Victim Assistance and Rehabilitation Program in Haiti (informally called the Rehab Program; see James 2010). At twenty-one, the pleasant young man had a mischievous grin and greeted me with a smile each day. Although he worked informally as a grounds caretaker, he had been a Rehab Program beneficiary since April 1997 when another agency, Médecins du Monde (Doctors of the World), ceased operations.

Jean-Robert was considered an "indirect" victim of organized violence. Although not assaulted directly, in June 1994 a program psychologist said soldiers had beheaded his parents in front of him. After the killings, Jean-Robert fled by boat with hopes of attaining asylum in the United States.[1] Such hazardous journeys frequently resulted in interdiction, immediate repatriation, or death by starvation or drowning.

Although fortunate to land in South Florida, Jean-Robert was apprehended, then detained at the Krome Service Processing Center, the notorious adult detention facility in Miami, while his asylum request was pending. Krome was established in a former Nike missile base that was converted into a processing center for Cuban refugees in 1980. In the 1980s, Krome was likened to a "theater of the absurd" and a concentration camp (Nachman 1993: 251, 254). But, as an unaccompanied minor, he did not remain in Krome for long. According to his medical file, he was granted asylum in September 1994, and was then moved to an unnamed program for "unaccompanied refugee minors" (URMs) in Boston, Massachusetts. While in Boston, recalling his parents' murder provoked visual and auditory hallucinations, paranoid thinking, and violence toward others. Psychiatrists diagnosed him with "subchronic schizophrenia" and prescribed antipsychotics and antidepressants.

In October 1996, despite receiving political asylum, Jean-Robert was repatriated. His reported chronic psychosis represented a "state of exception," rescinding a legal status of political asylum (Agamben 1998, 2005). Back in Haiti, Médecins du Monde rediagnosed him as schizophrenic, then prescribed psychotherapy and a new course of anti-anxiety and antipsychotic medications. But Jean-Robert had not asked for treatment. He desired social assistance to return to America.

· · ·

Jean-Robert's life story has remained with me. In part, this chapter reflects my attempts to understand his experience, as well as those of other Haitians who fled their country and were apprehended. Although I searched for traces of his passage from Haiti to Boston and back, I have been unsuccessful in finding records of him or persons who knew him in the United States. The fragments of his case exemplify the powerful forces compelling Haitians to risk death or incarceration to seek asylum, sanctuary, and security elsewhere. His story shows the arbitrariness of legal regimes impeding Haitians' pursuit of freedom, safety, and simply, "life."

Jean-Robert is one of thousands of Haitians moving through institutions subjecting them to "compassionate repression" (Fassin 2005: 366), modes of humanitarian governance "oscillating between sentiments of sympathy on the one hand and concern for order on the other hand, between a politics of pity and policies of control." Humanitarian, human rights, medical, and religious groups have all played "pastoral" roles to intercede on behalf of vulnerable populations living in contexts of political, economic, and social insecurity. Although these institutions have provided care, they have also operated as apparatuses of national security to manage, contain, and incorporate, as well as exclude, liminal or "disordered" persons on behalf of nation-states.

Jean-Robert's story demonstrates how such processes may exacerbate (and release) the traumatic memories refugees and migrants may embody. By beginning in Haiti, moving to Miami, and ending in Boston, not only does this chapter analyze the histories, moral economies, and (bio)politics of migration, it also chronicles some ways Haiti's "poorest" citizens journeyed to the United States.[2]

On another level, this chapter presents the path by which both they and I ultimately found the Haitian Multi-Service Center. Although contemporary legal regimes require a distinction, the *ensekirite* (insecurity) driving Haitians' exodus from Haiti blurs the artificial boundaries between economic and political roots of migration, migrant and refugee status, and perhaps the moral and legal dimensions of their status—especially because the Haitian state remains fragile (and is often thought of as having failed). Once distinctions are applied, asylum seekers traverse paths of incorporation or exclusion and routinely sojourn through *purgatorial spaces*. Purgatorial spaces are "outside" the social order (i.e., displaced persons camps, detention facilities, mental asylums, orphan asylums, and others). Third parties often manage these bureaucratic spaces, and those who govern them conceive of their work as caring. Implicit in my use of the purgatory concept is the idea that containment is temporary: a variety of technical and technological procedures (legal, medical, educational, vocational, etc.) permit detainees to transition from one social status to another. Such spaces also blur the boundaries between compassionate and repressive pastoral power.

I analyze the roles of both secular and faith-based NGOs working on behalf of government to care for, house, and police migrant lives. Both nonprofit and for-profit corporations are among the institutions mediating the relationships between undocumented Haitian migrants and the nation-state. As my analysis progresses, I extend the concept of corporate Catholicism by examining Catholic charitable actors' labor to incorporate refugees into both church and state, especially through their management of detention centers (and through other intercessory acts made on the detainees' behalf). I describe the social, political, and economic forces (among others) propelling Haitians to leave their nation "unlawfully" and the bureaucratic webs capturing them in purgatorial spaces while their legal statuses and future fates are determined.

My 2004 visit with the delegation to the Krome adult detention facility demonstrates how the physical plant and its disciplinary practices inscribe inmates into a political order from which they will be incorporated or expelled. Our visit to another site, then called "Boys Town"—a Miami residential facility Catholic Charities managed for unaccompanied refugees—presents what was called a "softer" form of detention and incorporation processes for children. Although Catholic organizations have opposed discriminatory federal migration policies, they have also regulated, detained, and contained migrants for government. A third case, one of compassionate asylum, analyzes Cardinal Bernard Francis Law's 1992 intercession to liberate Haitian children from Guantánamo Bay, Cuba. His pastoral power produced exemptions from conventional (secular) national security and migration policies. A final anecdote follows a Haitian Multi-Service Center staff person, "Rénald St. Jacques," from Haiti through Krome to Boston in the late 1980s. His story highlights the Haitian liberation theology tradition and shows the strategies and tactics (Certeau 1984) Haitian asylum seekers deployed using their own bodies to protest detention. Even under orders of imminent deportation, migrants may resist expulsion from the body politic to remain in the United States as undocumented persons.

THEORIZING ASYLUMS

The concept of "asylum" carries at least two connotations (James 2011): the first, from contemporary human rights law, refers to a refugee—someone who, because of a "well-founded fear of being persecuted for reasons of race, religion, nationality, membership of a particular social group or political opinion" (UNHCR 1979: 11, 81), has fled their country seeking safety and security across the borders of a sovereign nation-state with prior authorization. Legal refugee status may confer eligibility for social welfare entitlements and other assistance, and, in some countries, the capacity to work lawfully. For those applying for asylum after entering another country "unlawfully," receiving asylee status often generates institutional and interpersonal compassion and care.

In the institutional sense, the term "asylum" describes a space of safety, seclusion, and sanctuary for persons categorized as vulnerable or liminal—those unprotected by (and even victims of) a moral, political, legal, or social order. Historical asylums, some of which were previously described (i.e., infant and orphan asylums, hospice centers, industrial schools, etc.), have offered therapies, treatment, moral training, and respite from the exigencies of corporeal existence. The term also indexes spaces of confinement, containment, and even punishment of those deemed threats to the moral, legal, and social order—because of their bodily afflictions, past misfortunes, or personal "transgressions" (i.e., lazar houses for persons with leprosy, mental asylums, maternity houses for women facing unplanned pregnancies, detention centers for juvenile delinquents, and other prisons; see also Foucault 1979, 2006).

These spaces resemble "total institutions," overwhelmingly encompassing social establishments in which "barriers to social intercourse with the outside world" are "built right into the physical plant, such as locked doors, high walls, barbed wire, cliffs, water, forests, or moors" (Goffman 1961: 4). Erving Goffman characterizes total institutions according to types providing "care for persons felt to be both incapable and harmless"—such as the "homes for the blind, the aged, the orphaned, and the indigent"—or offering "care for persons felt to be both incapable of looking after themselves" but who pose an unintended threat to the community—such as "TB sanitaria, mental hospitals, and leprosaria" (Goffman 1961: 4). In contrast to these more pastoral spaces is another category: this includes structures or programs "organized to protect the community against what are felt to be intentional dangers to it, with the welfare of the persons thus sequestered not the immediate issue" (Goffman 1961: 4–5). In further examining total institutions, however, the distinction between benevolent care and repressive protection begins to fade. All are sites of surveillance, restricted freedom, discipline, and social control (Goffman 1961: 6–13).

The spaces containing asylum seekers are characterized by temporal indeterminacy. The labor of external actors determines detainees' future fate. That external intercessors may assist immigration detainees to make the transition from so-called "unlawful entrant" to lawful asylee recalls Catholic theological conceptions of purgatory.

PURGATORY

In Roman Catholic theology, the idea of purgatory refers to a temporary space or condition of spiritual cleansing in which the souls of the dead undergo purification. Prior to entering heaven, the souls in waiting must complete payment of the "satisfaction" owed for unforgiven sins (Hanna 1911). According to the Catechism of the Catholic Church, "the Church gives the name *Purgatory* to this final purification of the elect, which is entirely different from the punishment of the damned" (Catholic Church 1995: 1031). Catholics also believe the living may intercede on behalf of souls in purgatory by praying for their salvation: "This teaching is also based on the practice of prayer for the dead already mentioned in the Sacred Scripture. . . . The Church also commends almsgiving, indulgences, and works of penance undertaken on behalf of the dead" (Catholic Church 1995: 1032).

Anthropologists have used the concept of purgatory to characterize interstitial places in which "patient-prisoners" engage in moral reflection on life beyond the clinic's walls while undergoing detoxification from drug addiction (Garcia 2010: 51–53). Others apply the concept to characterize "zones of practice" in which secular modern scientists debate the impact of biotechnology on "life," as well as the moral and political economies that such technologies generate (Rabinow 1999: 17–23). Some social theorists have employed another Catholic concept, "limbo,"[3] to characterize how "asylum applicants occupy positions precariously in-between undocumented, paperless illegality and 'refugee' status" (Cabot 2012: 17; see also Butler 2006).

My use of the purgatory concept builds on the multiple connotations of "asylum" as physical and moral spaces containing embodied persons who are "outside," but also incorporated within, a social order, as well as on a second meaning of the word referring to a legal status granted to persons. By focusing on detainees, I show how some purgatorial spaces inculcate routines directed toward the corporeal body and disciplinary practices intended to instill in the migrant a set of normative moral dispositions.[4] At the same time, other inscription practices render migrants "legible" to the state as subjects who are either worthy or unworthy of incorporation (Certeau 1984). But these are not solely conditions of objectification and subjugation. Adult Haitians detained at Krome were able to deploy the corporal nature of their bodies in protest while working with external intercessors who mobilized administratively on their behalf.

The purgatorial spaces examined in this chapter also illustrate the intercessory roles of Catholics (and other nongovernmental actors) on behalf of detained migrants and, if "paroled" as asylees, in the resettlement process. Purgatorial spaces therefore render visible or bring into relief the indeterminate "zones of indistinction" (Agamben 1998: 6) between the political life of individuals included in sovereign states and the bare lives of excluded populations categorized in terms of their biology. Purgatorial spaces may also emerge in the indeterminate realms of governance among voluntary and private sector organizations and government.

But let me be clear—in using the concept of purgatory I am not suggesting detainees are imprisoned because of the unforgiven "sin" or crime of unlawful entry for which they must atone. Nor am I suggesting repatriated detainees are being consigned to eternal damnation in their countries of origin. Rather, my goal is to analyze slippages between logics and practices of compassion, discipline, and repression embedded in such spaces. Indeed, the rules and regulations regarding how refugees may apply for asylee status—a form of secular salvation, so to speak—are not universal or static. For Haitians such rules are often suspended.

STATES OF INSECURITY

Over its history, the government of Haiti has been characterized as incompetent, corrupt, failed, fragile, and even predatory (Fatton 2002; Glick Schiller and Fouron 2001; Lawless 1992; Rotberg 1971; St. John 1884; Trouillot 1990). With the recurrence of human-authored and "natural" disasters, and frequent states of emergency, the government of Haiti has been deemed incapable of protecting its citizens. Conversely, scholars have described the Haitian state as "apparent"—possessing only a fiction or shadow of sovereignty—when in truth "political actions as well as all . . . financial activities are monitored and constrained from abroad to such an extent that national leaders are left with no domain from which to take any action that will benefit the majority of their people" (Glick Schiller and Fouron 2001).

Haitians have not usually controlled the discourses circulating about their government, cultural practices, and people. For complex reasons, the Haitian government has brokered imported humanitarian relief and development programs— what could be called an insourcing of aid—with little power to oversee or control how external actors implement programs throughout the country (James 2010). As a result, international governmental and nongovernmental actors, as well as their partners in Haitian civil society, have offered social services to Haitians their state has yet to provide, especially to its poor majority. When Haitians conclude their country cannot support life, many have chosen to *chèche lavi* (literally, "seek life"; figuratively, "search for a way to make a living") outside the nation's borders, in hopes of obtaining security, sanctuary, and even citizenship elsewhere.

But, as the Haitian case demonstrates, when migrants flee without prior legal authorization and recognition as political refugees, they can be subjected to governance by public and private agencies and agents. When the causes of flight are difficult to distinguish under conventional human rights law categories, other statuses may influence whether such populations are perceived as eligible or deserving of incorporation or as risks to the security of the host nation-state—thereby initiating processes of detention and exclusion. When perceptions of undocumented migrants shift from worthiness of humanitarian sanctuary to posing a threat, protection may blur into containment, repression, and expulsion (Fassin 2005). The example of Haitian refugees and immigrants offers troubling cases for analyzing further the roles of religious and secular nongovernmental institutions in the governance of humanity and life (Feldman and Ticktin 2010; Fassin 2018; James 2019).

THE "HAITIAN PROBLEM"
AND THE HAITIAN PROGRAM

In the mid-1970s, in response to deteriorating political, economic, and environmental conditions at home (see James 2010; Trouillot 1990), Haitians began entering the United States "illegally" in larger numbers. In 1980, the World Bank estimated Haitian life expectancy at fifty-one years, the lowest in Latin America, and ranked Haitian infant mortality the highest.[5] Between 1965 and 1980, Haiti had the lowest rate of increase in daily caloric intake and protein consumption, the lowest rate of literacy (approximately 23 percent), and the lowest GDP per capita of Latin America ($267 in 1980), with even lower figures in rural areas.[6]

At the end of the 1970s, an exponential increase in Haitian attempts to enter South Florida by boat created both a local and a national crisis, resulting in these Haitians' detention under the United States Immigration and Naturalization Service's (INS) "Haitian Program." Prior to 1978, there were 1,926 Haitians who awaited either exclusion or deportation hearings to determine if they would be granted political asylum. Entrants apprehended at the time of arrival in the United States were "entered and processed immediately" (EPI) and faced exclusion proceedings. Those who "entered without an inspection" (EWI) faced deportation hearings (Miller 1984: xii). In 1978, there were nearly two thousand new entrants, culminating in an influx of 22,499 in 1980. By the end of 1981, the INS reported that nearly forty thousand Haitians awaited processing (Miller 1984: xii).[7] In response to the influx, the INS developed the "Haitian Program," which categorized Haitians as a burgeoning problem or threat to be contained by systematically denying them opportunities to present claims to refugee status.

Cold War politics influenced the disparate legal treatment between Haitians and migrants of other national origins. Haitians were distinguished from other ethnic entrants because their country was neither "war-torn" nor "Communist-controlled," a categorization enabling government officials to label Haitians solely as economic rather than political refugees (Conway and Buchanan 1985: 95). Their exclusion from political recognition recalls Giorgio Agamben's (1998: 11) discussion of the exception and the ban. In his analysis of sovereign power and bare life, Agamben states, "Bare life remains included in politics in the form of the exception, that is, as something that is included solely through an exclusion." In the example of Haitian asylum seekers, the overwhelming tendency to designate them as economic migrants includes them within customary international human rights law by means of a virtual exclusion or denial of legitimate status as political refugees.

Furthermore, representing Haitians as a menace in political discourse justified and routinized their unjust categorization as economic migrants. Evidence of the differential impact of Cold War politics on migrant incorporation policies and practices is found in the massive acceptance of more than 322,500 Indochinese refugees between 1975 and 1980, and the inclusion and resettlement of 125,000 Cuban exiles who joined over 600,000 others in 1980.[8] According to Aihwa Ong (2003: 53, 58–59), however, the screening process for Cambodian refugees in camps in the Thai border zone—and in Thailand, the Philippines, and Indonesia—was also discriminatory, culturally insensitive, and subjugating: "transform[ing] refugees into viable migrants entailed a system of symbols through which dependency was thoroughly institutionalized."[9] The majority of Haitian entrants did not receive an opportunity for such symbolic transformation.

Discourses of economic burden and indolence emerging in South Florida local politics offered additional justification for the disparate legal treatment of Haitians. In the 1970s, anthropologist Alex Stepick conducted field research in the region and found mixed reaction to Haitians:

> Some were struck by the desperation and courage motivating a 700-mile sea journey in overcrowded, barely seaworthy boats. Others believed that the Haitians were a disruptive force, destroying the community and draining public resources. While Miami's economy may have been rejuvenated by Cubans, the black Haitians without skills or capital were viewed as an unwanted burden. (Stepick 1986: 11)

In contrast to perceptions of Haitians as malingering, unskilled, and unsuccessful, Stepick affirms most were so hard-working they had conflicts with Mexicans, other migrants, and native-born African Americans competing for employment.[10] As I would later learn, similar interethnic tensions had materialized in Greater Boston.

In addition to discourses casting Haitians as national security threats and public burdens, federal public health institutions represented Haitians as "disease carriers."[11] This stereotype had some limited factual basis, as a few Haitians entered the United States afflicted with tuberculosis and typhoid; however, a Dade County Health Department study stated malnutrition and starvation were their most severe health problems (Stepick 1986: 11). Nevertheless, some health officials reinforced perceptions of Haitians posing what could be called "biosecurity" risks to South Florida (Nachman 1993: 228), a stereotype resonating profoundly in the local media.[12] On October 27, 1979, a *Miami News* article titled "Haitian Health Crisis Hits Dade," asked the governor to declare sections of northwest Miami a "special health emergency zone":

> State and county health officials said yesterday that local resources are over strained in meeting the widespread medical problems among the estimated 15,000 Haitian refugees in Dade County. . . . The refugees suffer from such communicable diseases as tuberculosis and venereal infections, as well as from malnutrition, anemia, dysentery, diarrhea, intestinal parasites, skin disorders, and complicated pregnancies. (Cited in Farmer 1992: 236)

By emphasizing the communicable nature of Haitians' diseases and the economic burden of caring for the sick, these health officials shifted attention away from the structural dimensions of suffering—the social, political, and economic roots of Haitians' illnesses—to the immediate threat that such suffering posed to the Dade County public. By way of contrast, Ong (2003: 95) states how Southeast Asian refugees received extraordinary medical benefits in California: "although more than seven hundred thousand Southeast Asian refugees have settled in the United States since 1975, they never became a threat to public health. . . . Today, the perception of polluting immigrants is reserved mainly for refugees and peoples from poor regions and sites like Haiti and Africa, whose populations are widely considered to be carriers of HIV."

This process of classifying Haitians as a biosecurity threat was compounded by discourses on AIDS: in late 1981, the Centers for Disease Control and Prevention (CDC) began to list Haitians as a population at high risk for contracting AIDS. Negative stereotypes contributed to Haitians being included in the high-risk category as an ethnic and national group:

> Some US researchers proposed that AIDS began with an outbreak of African Swine fever in Haitian pigs, and that the swine virus had been passed to humans. . . . Another idea was that animal sacrifice and other voodoo rituals could explain the origins of human infection. Others proposed that Haitians might have contracted the virus from monkeys as part of bizarre sexual practices in Haitian brothels. (Sabatier 1988: 45)

The specter of AIDS and aberrant cultural practices only intensified the extent to which Haitians were stigmatized as dangerous disease carriers.

Not only did these discourses justify discrimination against Haitians in places of employment, schools, and hospitals, such forms of rhetoric also justified their quarantine in detention centers and their eventual exclusion from the United States. In 1981, after determining that "illegal" immigration by sea—in particular Haitian migration—had become a "serious national problem detrimental to the interests of the United States,"[13] President Ronald Reagan's administration devised a policy to stop the flow of Haitian boat people to the United States altogether (Stepick 1986). On September 29, 1981, Reagan established the Haitian Migrant Interdiction Program through Proclamation 4865 and Executive Order 12324. The proclamation claimed waves of Haitian migrants "'severely strained the law enforcement resources of the Immigration and Naturalization Service' and 'threatened the welfare and safety of communities' in the southeastern United States" (LCHR 1990: 10). Executive Order 12324, issued the same day, permitted the secretary of state to "enter into, on behalf of the United States, cooperative arrangements with appropriate foreign governments for the purpose of preventing illegal migration to the United States by sea" (Miller 1984: 73; LCHR 1990: 10).[14]

After the INS guidelines for interdiction at sea were established, the first interdiction took place on October 12, 1981. By intercepting Haitians at sea before they entered US territory—an intervention in a zone of indistinction—the Reagan administration was able to circumvent laws requiring that refugees be given due process in a judicial arena. Thus, the president's orders solved the so-called "Haitian Problem" before it ever reached US territory. From that time until 1990, 364 boats were intercepted carrying nearly 21,461 Haitians. All but six were returned to Haiti (LCHR 1990: 4, 10).[15]

Regardless of this interdiction policy, refugees from the 1991 to 1994 coup period still sought liberty in the United States by sea, especially after the violence in Haiti escalated between 1993 and 1994.[16] During this time the exodus peaked at nearly forty thousand ill-named "boat people" in one year. When the number of interdicted persons exceeded the capacity of the US Coast Guard to process them at sea, Haitians were interned in another purgatorial space, the GTMO camps at the US naval base in Guantánamo Bay, Cuba (Farmer 2003; Smith 2000; Kahn 2019). At the time, GTMO was not considered US territory and was outside the jurisdiction of customary international human rights law. Thus, long before the indefinite detention of suspected architects of terrorist jihad against the United States, Haitians and other nationals were confined at Guantánamo through logics justifying apprehension, containment, exclusion, and expulsion in the name of security.

In more recent years, the United States has framed its interdiction policy as a benevolent practice of efficient "humanitarianism"—a form of protection or security, rather than coercion, threat, or punishment—that relieves taxpayers of a burden of care:

> As the United States' primary maritime law enforcement agency, the Coast Guard is tasked with enforcing immigration law at sea. . . . When successful, illegal immigration can potentially cost U.S. taxpayers billions of dollars each year in social services. In addition to relieving this financial burden on our citizens, the Coast Guard's efforts help to support legal migration systems. Primarily, the Coast Guard maintains its humanitarian responsibility to prevent the loss of life at sea, since the majority of migrant vessels are dangerously overloaded, unseaworthy or otherwise unsafe.[17]

In practice, Guantánamo was and continues to be a space where civil law has been suspended and the state of exception is the rule. Portraying interdiction (and containment) as benevolent echoes the concept of compassionate repression (Fassin 2005). Such paradoxes of humanitarian detention emerged in the contemporary purgatorial spaces containing Haitians.

HAITIAN MIGRANTS IN DETENTION

In the early hours of February 29, 2004, after a rapid acceleration of insecurity, President Jean-Bertrand Aristide was once again forced to flee Haiti. I watched these events unfold while conducting postdoctoral research with Miami Haitian refugee and immigrant communities between 2003 and 2004. Observers and long-time advocates for Haitian democracy and human rights exclaimed, "It's déjà vu all over again!" (Maguire 2004; Cheryl Little, personal communication, March 2004). In the days following Aristide's expulsion, it was unclear what had happened. A pervasive feeling of confusion, frustration, and anger was expressed through social unrest in Little Haiti, North Miami, Homestead, and other areas with high Haitian resident concentrations. In the local and national media, the events surrounding Aristide's ouster and initial exile to the Central African Republic were contested.

On March 10, 2004, I joined a delegation formed to evaluate the status of Haitian detainees in several South Florida detention centers. TransAfrica Forum, a Washington, DC advocacy organization tracking how US policy affects Africa and the African diaspora, sponsored the delegation (TransAfrica Forum 2004). Haitians were detained in four locations. The Krome Service Processing Center held Haitians and other "illegal entrants" (Nachman 1993: 231). In the 1980s, the notoriously understaffed facility lacked sufficient Creole interpreters, running water, sanitation, supplies, and telephones, and had only limited shelter apart from hangars and tents. Toward the end of 1980 some improvements were made to provide more permanent structures. One year later, Krome had expanded to include a men's and women's dormitories, a juvenile facility, a cafeteria, and an administration building (Nachman 1993: 231–32; Dow 2004: 48–77). After public protests against its unsanitary conditions, additional improvements were made.

Regardless of the improvements to Krome's physical infrastructure, for many inhabitants it was a space of vulnerability rather than humanitarian protection. In 2000, reports surfaced documenting the "widespread sexual, physical, emotional, and verbal abuse of women detainees by Krome officers." Women were subsequently transferred to another detention center, the Turner Guilford Knight Correction Center (Women's Commission for Refugee Women and Children June 2001: 1). By 2004, under Department of Homeland Security oversight, Krome only housed adult males and was considered a model detention center.

At the time of our delegation, sixty-five Haitian women were detained at a second location north of Miami, the Broward County Transitional Center, a facility managed by the Wackenhut Corrections Corporation. This multinational corrections and residential treatment company had changed its name to the GEO Group Inc. after a series of scandals.[18] Haitian women and children were confined at a third location, a southwest Miami Comfort Suites Hotel leased by the US government. Our delegation was denied access to this location. Finally, Catholic Charities of the Archdiocese of Miami, Inc. (CCAM) managed another detention center for the federal government, "Boys Town," a facility for "unaccompanied refugee minors." Although different in intent and practices, our visits to Krome and Boys Town revealed several similarities between secular correctional or penal institutions and religiously based reformatories. Protection and penitential confinement were two sides of the same coin.

As our vans approached Krome's peri-rural location, dry trees and grasses surrounded us. Tall, rusted fences topped with razor wire enclosed the landscape. We drove through two sets of gates to a checkpoint where we presented identification and received visitor passes marked "Escort Required" in red print. After parking next to an unremarkable cream-colored building with green trim, Officer George Hernandez came to greet us and gave us copies of the detainee handbook. As we approached the building, I recalled I was approaching where Jean-Robert Paul was detained before his parole to Boston.

After passing through an X-ray security checkpoint we were escorted through another set of doors and we viewed rooms where detainees spoke to visitors by phone through double-paned glass. Internees were visible around us. Officer Hernandez next led us to an outdoor area to observe detainees in a grassy courtyard completely fenced in with barbwire. In a straightforward style, he said detainees were given a "Know Your Rights" presentation on arrival and Haitian Creole presentations were given several times a week. At the time Krome housed 127 Haitian men, 102 Cubans, and individuals from other nations to form a population of 505. After observing these inmates, I noticed a color-coded uniform system and asked Officer Hernandez what the colors signified. A strict schedule kept each color-coded detainee group in its proper place. Those wearing blue jumpsuits represented "administrative detainees": individuals with "credible fear cases" who had no criminal background. Those in orange had some criminal background but had committed nonviolent offenses. Individuals in red had committed violent felonies; some had completed sentences in US jails and were now awaiting deportation or release.

Haitians were administrative detainees wearing blue. All had arrived on two boats during the turmoil surrounding President Aristide's second election, reaching US shores on December 3, 2001, and October 29, 2002. In Building 8, a large room with sixty-eight bunk beds where many detainees slept, we were able to speak directly to seven Haitians. They spoke plaintively of feeling abandoned and wondered why their desperate pursuit of security and liberty was deemed a crime.

David Joseph's case epitomized the many conceptual, legal, and physical zones of indistinction employed to exclude Haitian asylum seekers. Although he was nineteen when we spoke, he had been detained with adults since his October 29, 2002, arrival and had turned eighteen while imprisoned. All Krome residents were presumed to be over the age of eighteen. Another agency, the US Department of Health and Human Services Office of Refugee Resettlement (ORR), managed detainees under age eighteen.

Only the biological body testified to the veracity of his age. In the absence of verifying documentation, dental X-rays and wrist measurements yielded either potential asylum and citizenship or exclusion and deportation (Physicians for Human Rights and the Bellevue/NYU Program for Survivors of Torture 2003: 130). These procedures resembled the late nineteenth- and early twentieth-century racial anthropometric practices (Kevles 1995)—that is, when scientists thought bodily measurements indicated a subject's purported intelligence, and physical, moral, and cognitive development. Contemporary medical experts challenged these biometric assumptions, arguing that there could be significant discrepancies between chronological age, dental age, and skeletal age. Furthermore, the standard to which present-day refugee measures were compared—the *Radiographic Atlas of Skeletal Development of the Hand and Wrist*, by William Walter Greulich and S. Idell Pyle—used upper-class White children from 1931 to 1942 as the norm. The method's relevance to current "multiethnic" populations was questioned (Physicians for Human Rights and the Bellevue/NYU Program for Survivors of Torture 2003: 130–31). Use of such technologies at Krome invalidated the voice, narrative, subjective experience, and human rights of the "minor" asylum seeker.

Measurement of suspect bodies was not the only discursive strategy restricting refugees' capacity to apply for asylum. Federal immigration policies toward Haitians as a legal class also inhibited their efforts to request asylum and await final judgment under more humane conditions. Although David was eventually granted release on bond pending an asylum hearing, he was denied discharge to a family in the United States because of changes in immigration policy toward Haitians. By the time of the October 29, 2002, boat, the US government had quietly instituted a "secret policy" against them:

> Following the December 3, 2001 arrival of 167 interdicted Haitians who were brought ashore to Florida, the Immigration and Naturalization Service (INS), which is now part of the Department of Homeland Security (DHS), adopted a secret policy directed solely at Haitians, which resulted in the prolonged detention of virtually all Haitian asylum seekers in South Florida, regardless of whether they arrived by boat or by plane, and despite the fact that all but two of the 167 had convinced U.S. Asylum Officers they had a "credible fear" of persecution upon return to Haiti. (Florida Immigrant Advocacy Center 2004: 10)

The federal government proclaimed that Haitians had to be detained for purposes of national security. Their parole could encourage a large, costly influx of "other aliens": "the release on bond of additional alien passengers from [the

October 29] vessel will cause a 'surge' in other aliens attempting to reach the United States by sea . . . there are insufficient resources to adequately screen the passengers of these vessels, which may contain aliens seeking to threaten the homeland security of the United States."[19] With the Board of Immigration Appeals upholding the immigration judges' decision to grant bonds, Asa Hutchinson, then undersecretary for Border and Transportation Security, asked former US Attorney General John Ashcroft to deny the release of all Haitians in this category.

Although of slight build, David appeared too thin, almost frail. He told us he had lost his appetite and he lamented having spent two Christmases in detention. He spoke passionately and with anguish: "Given the current situation, I came to the US to safeguard my life, not to be kept in jail. I got so sick I couldn't even eat. I don't hear from my family. I don't know how they're doing. Houses have been destroyed in Haiti [following the second ouster of Aristide] . . ." Overwhelmed by emotion, David stopped for a few moments, then spoke about the conditions under which they lived at Krome: "We aren't treated well. Haitians are humiliated here." All the detainees grieved their fate and shared disillusionment in hoping for US governmental assistance. They feared deportation to Haiti. Although Candace Jean, the Catholic Legal Services lawyer who interceded on David Joseph's behalf, was hopeful an appeal to the Board of Immigration Appeals might grant him asylum, on November 29, 2004, he was deported after spending more than two years in detention.[20]

David Joseph's case highlights how zones of indistinction are material spaces—like the detention camp or the land and sea borders between sovereign territories—as well as legal, symbolic, and conceptual spaces. In these purgatorial zones, humanitarian protection blurs into confinement, imprisonment, and punishment through a variety of discursive strategies—such as categorizing Haitians as "threats to national security" rather than as citizens possessing legal rights to seek asylum across borders, or as adults instead of unaccompanied minors. Once contained, a political and spatial order inculcates in detainees a sense of temporal indeterminacy while their future status, as incorporated or excluded, is determined.

BOYS TOWN

Boys Town, recently renamed the Unaccompanied Minors Program at Monsignor Walsh Children's Village, provoked moral and ethical questions about faith-based charity, national security, and the differential treatment of Haitians under US immigration policy. This case highlights how Catholic Charities' management of migrants on behalf of the state obscures any distinction between public and private realms, secular and religious administration, and pastoral, disciplinary, and repressive power. In so doing, Catholic institutions have become integral components of governmental apparatuses that police and confine the vulnerable while determining whether to incorporate them as future members.

Catholic Charities of the Archdiocese of Miami, Inc. links Boys Town to the controversial Operation Pedro Pan.[21] From 1960 until 1962, under President Fidel Castro's rule, Cuban parents who feared their children would be indoctrinated as Marxist-Leninists voluntarily sent fourteen thousand of them to be resettled with Catholic foster families in the United States. As director of the Catholic Welfare Bureau (now called the CCAM), Rev. Bryan O. Walsh placed these "children in temporary shelters in Miami," a fosterage practice that evolved into the Children's Refugee Program. When the capacity of local Catholic minor facilities was eclipsed, children were relocated to more than thirty other states through Catholic Charities' network of agencies.[22] Presumably, Boys Town was one of these facilities.

In 2004, Boys Town offered to unaccompanied minor children what staff members called residential "day treatment." Staff members called their facility a "soft detention" center caring for "minors," children ranging from infants to seventeen-year-olds. By the time of our March 10 visit, the fifty-six-bed center had already served 241 children. The majority spoke Spanish, Mandarin Chinese, and Haitian Creole. Staff fluent in the minors' languages offered educational and recreational programs (both on and offsite), psychological counseling, and food and clothing.

Our delegation met briefly with staff members, and was then led down a long driveway to another building containing a large recreation room. Inside, the children were assembled in rows before us. Seated in a semicircle in front of them, we could be attending an elementary school performance anywhere in United States. The children began a familiar song: "I am proud to be an American, where at least I know I'm free, and I won't forget the men who died who gave that right to me. And I gladly stand up next to you and defend her still today, 'cause there ain't no doubt I love this land … God bless the USA." Each child had a colorful map hanging from their neck representing a global nation. They waved handmade US flags and stood one by one to name their home country.

The musical show demonstrated each child was acquiring skills needed to navigate asylee status (if paroled into the United States), and potentially, permanent residence and citizenship. Secondly, their performance offered evidence of the normalcy, safety, and routines afforded to unaccompanied refugee minors while awaiting liberation. The song choice revealed the role soft detention facilities played in inculcating patriotic political dispositions in the children—a contemporary example of Catholic Charities' intercessory work to "reform" or rehabilitate children and prepare them for possible futures outside the purgatorial space. This was a positive outcome both for the children and for Catholic Charities, especially given continued questions about the roles of Catholic institutions in failing to protect children from clerical abuses. The children's earnest performance remains a bittersweet memory.

After the show our group divided to allow some to interview the Haitian children while others spoke with staff. There were ten Haitians, six boys and four girls ranging from five to seventeen years old. We were told there were difficulties placing Haitian children in the Haitian American community because of economic, legal, and other barriers. Children who could not be placed were routinely deported.

For some children Boys Town was not a benevolent pastoral space; it was a punitive one from which they hoped to flee. They shared heartrending stories of struggling to reach the United States and their fears one or both of their parents had died. They were frightened by the thought of returning to Haiti and felt isolated at Boys Town. Loneliness compounded psychological and physical complaints stemming from past traumas. The children also mentioned other minors who had run from the facility, preferring to navigate the shadowy world of illegality rather than await the award or denial of asylee status.

Boys Town raised questions regarding the roles of religious nonprofits as apparatuses of governmental security and as institutions attempting to inculcate moral, behavioral, and even political dispositions in those under their charge. As such, its "day treatment" resembled, but was not identical to, the 1960s work of Operation Pedro Pan or the early twentieth-century American Catholic charities refugee resettlement work. Each historical example demonstrated Catholics' capacity for civic responsibility and citizenship by means of rehabilitating, educating, and reforming wards of the state and other marginal populations. Even as faith-based organizations care for those served, by engaging in soft detention and refugee resettlement work, organizations like Catholic Charities have become components of a federal security apparatus that incorporates, while also policing, detaining, and expelling, so-called "unlawful migrants." In so doing, institutions like these operate between the poles of compassion and repression (Fassin 2005).

Since 1980, the organizations receiving the largest federal Office of Refugee Resettlement (ORR) subcontracts have been faith-based. In the fiscal year 2008, Church World Service, Episcopal Migration Ministries, Hebrew Immigration Aid Society, Lutheran Immigration and Refugee Service (LIRS), and the United States Conference of Catholic Bishops (USCCCB) were among the nine major ORR subcontractors. The USCCB—the public policy, evangelization, and social action agency of the Catholic bishops of the United States—describes itself as the largest resettlement agency in the world and has served as an ORR lead subcontractor.[23] When we visited, the USCCB and the LIRS were the only two agencies resettling unaccompanied refugee minors for the ORR. Under the USCCB auspices, Catholic Charities programs served the ORR's Unaccompanied Refugee Minors Program (URM).

The stated mission of the ORR Unaccompanied Refugee Minors Program is to help "minor refugees develop appropriate skills to enter adulthood and to achieve social self-sufficiency" while they await placement in foster families, unification with their own families in the United States, and regularization of their legal status.[24] As previously stated, if minors have not found placement prior to turning eighteen, they are transferred to an adult detention facility. If unable to obtain asylum, they are deported. Although Catholic Charities physically manages the program, children remain legally in the custody of the ORR during their stay.

The Catholic Church's history of resettling migrants on behalf of the United States government extends back to the colonial era (see Chapter 2). Until the early twentieth century, these efforts were organized at the local diocesan and parish levels and involved providing pastoral care, social services, and education. In 1920, American bishops established a national department of immigration under the National Catholic Welfare Conference. The conference had evolved from another national Catholic institution established in 1917—namely, the National Catholic War Council.[25] From concern for Catholic military chaplains and the need to formulate official Catholic positions on the war, "representatives from sixty-eight dioceses and twenty-seven Catholic societies met at The Catholic University of America and formed the National Catholic War Council, 'to study, coordinate, unify and put in operation all Catholic activities incidental to the war'" (Gribble 2008: 74). In 1919, the Council was made permanent with five departments, "Education, Legislation, Social Action, Lay Organizations, and Press and Publicity, each headed by a bishop" (Gribble 2008: 75), and in 1922, the Council was renamed the National Catholic Welfare Conference.

> Between 1920 and 1930, the Immigration Department, which had a presence at Ellis Island, had assisted more than 100,000 immigrants in their efforts to immigration. Following World War II and the passage of the Displaced Persons Admissions Act of 1948, the Church assisted in the resettlement of more than 100,000 European refugees. Catholic Relief Services (CRS) and the Catholic Committee for Refugees coordinated the provision of resettlement services.[26]

In 1965, the National Conference of Catholic Bishops and the United States Catholic Conference "assumed the work" of the National Catholic Welfare Conference under one joint institution, the USCCB (Oates 1999: 93). After its creation, the USCCB established the Migration and Refugee Services department to coordinate refugee resettlement activities, public policy, advocacy, and legal aid to immigrants.[27]

But the role of the USCCB as subcontractor for the federal Office of Refugee Resettlement is much more recent. On March 17, 1980, Congress enacted the Refugee Act of 1980 (P.L. 96–212) to establish "the number of refugees to be admitted to the United States" and created "the Office of Refugee Resettlement (ORR) within the Department of Health and Human Services to administer assistance programs designed to help refugees achieve economic self-sufficiency as quickly as possible" (ORR 1981: 1, 14). Responding primarily to the needs of hundreds of thousands of Indochinese refugees who were admitted to the United States following the Indochina Migration and Refugee Assistance Act of 1975, the new office coordinated efforts to resettle refugees accepted by the United States through grants made primarily to twelve voluntary agencies called informally by the term VOLAGs (ORR 1981; see also Ong 2003: 52–65). In fiscal year 1980, the USCCB and LIRS were two of the largest subcontractors resettling refugees, especially unaccompanied minors (ORR 1981: 14).

In part, the Church's support was motivated by its commitment to aid the poor, the sick, and the vulnerable, of which migrants are a particularly cherished population. In addition to theological imperatives to be charitable, policy statements also exhort Catholics to enact private acts of charity on migrants' behalf. In "Welcoming the Stranger among Us: Unity in Diversity,"[28] the USCCB describes Jesus as both migrant and refugee in order to inspire Catholics to welcome immigrant and refugee communities.[29] Catholics are also encouraged to advocate for immigrant human rights and laws that "preserve the unity of the immigrant family . . . [through] the extension of social services, citizenship classes, community organizing efforts that secure improved housing conditions, decent wages, better medical attention, and appropriate educational opportunities for immigrants and refugees."[30] As later chapters show, the Haitian Multi-Service Center sought to promote these activities as necessary for a dignified life. From examining this array of Catholic principled issues and charitable social services, the links among human life, health, social welfare, and the law are inextricable.

But the Boys Town example and the next case, Pwojè Lavi, also raises questions about the symbolism of children as objects of charity and humanitarianism. In humanitarian discourses, children have represented states of savagery and original sin, but also innocence, peace, hope, and truth (Liisa Malkki 2010). Children may also embody neutral, depoliticized ideals about the future for public and private actors in local settings, alongside more transcendent, universal values. At Boys Town, the song performance welcoming our delegation presented minor refugees as potential or "apprentice citizens" (Malkki 2010: 81), even while acknowledging ties to their home countries. Nevertheless, Boys Town was still a facility from which several Haitian children hoped to be liberated.

The next case, involving the 1992 release of Haitian minors from the Guantánamo camps, brings this story to Boston, and to another program Catholic organizations managed on behalf of the "caring state" (Daly 2009). Inaugurated by Cardinal Bernard Francis Law, this program shows how pastoral power can influence and critique state policies. Law's intervention evoked a centuries-old legal sanctuary tradition rendering a monastery or convent a space of protection and legal immunity from secular modes of detention and punishment. This narrative also queries the uses of charity to rebuild an institution's credibility in the face of scandal.

PWOJÈ LAVI (PROJECT LIFE)

Although portrayed initially as a safe location for asylum seekers, in the Guantánamo camps civil law has been (and continues to be) suspended,—producing the "state of exception" (Agamben 1998, 2005). In this purgatorial space, Haitian detainees existed at the level of "bare life" (Agamben 1998), lacking recognition of their civil and political rights. One Haitian parolee eventually resettled by the Haitian Multi-Service Center said of Guantánamo, "We felt that we were in jail the entire time. . . . We were under military surveillance. We had no freedom, even to go to the toilet" (Bennett 1992a).

Increasing numbers of Haitians fled by boat as repression of the prodemocracy sector escalated during the coup years. By January 1992, more than eight thousand Haitians were stranded in Guantánamo under conditions generating comparisons to Nazi Germany concentration camps. In keeping with the Reagan-era migration policy, the Bush administration argued that Haitians fled poverty rather than political persecution. Less than one quarter of these men, women, and minor detainees were permitted to apply for asylum. Haitians described how life was "marked by boredom, periodic violence and the near constant anxiety of having their fate in the hands of strangers" (Bennett 1992a). Another man who tested positive for HIV and was quarantined in a separate camp on the naval base said, "We lived in tents . . . men and women together. The women would put up sheets for privacy and to create their own space. When it rained, the water would come inside, and we ate rice and beans every day. There were wooden toilets set up without a flush. They were near where we ate and the smell was very bad" (Negri 1993).

In February 1992, many refugees were repatriated from Guantánamo. The Boston Haitian community called the Bush administration's refusal to grant the refugees an opportunity to enter the United States (while their asylum cases were pending) immoral and "evident proof of the insensitivity and selective application of the concept of human rights by the US administration" (Negri 1992). In the *Boston Globe*, Cardinal Law agreed, describing the repatriation as "legally justifiable" but "morally questionable" (Negri 1992). Despite efforts to mobilize moral judgment, there would be no change in US policy. By May 20, 1992, with 12,482 Haitians detained, Guantánamo had nearly reached its 12,500 capacity. Government officials suspended interdictions unless boaters faced imminent threat of death (Hansen 2011: 292). Two days later, in a direct letter to President Bush, Cardinal Law evoked publicly the collective moral failure permitting the Holocaust:

> The sad memory of Jews being refused entry before World War II should teach us that never again should we turn our back on a human being pleading for our help and hospitality. In the name of all that is decent, we cannot turn our backs on poor Haitians willing to take heroic measures in order to escape a hopeless situation which is made worse by a failure of resolve on the part of the international community. (Law 1992a)

Regardless of Law's effort to deploy pastoral power on the Haitians' behalf, on May 24, 1992, President Bush issued Executive Order 12807 authorizing the Coast Guard to return persons interdicted at sea without requiring "any procedures to determine whether a person is a refugee." In July 1992, as camp tensions escalated into demonstrations and rioting, the United States government launched a military operation using a warplane, bulldozer, and combat-clad soldiers brandishing weapons, to corral "the refugees into small holding pens while ransacking their shelters. . . . Haitians, male and female, their hands bound behind their backs [were] loaded into vans. Children and pregnant women were among those arrested" (Hansen 2011: 295).

Cardinal Law was eventually successful in obtaining the release of more than one hundred Haitian unaccompanied minors, including an infant, into the custody of the Archdiocese of Boston (Bennett 1992c). According to a staff person I interviewed from Boston's Catholic Charities, Law spoke directly with President Bush about the children. Bush agreed to their release, and Law obtained US Department of Justice and USCCB support to resettle them. The Charity sent staff members to Guantánamo to retrieve the children, and they all traveled by military plane to Boston.

The goal of Pwojè Lavi, Project Life,[31] was to help the Haitian minors acculturate and resettle, either with members of their own extended families or with foster families. The program operated between July 1992 and late spring 1994.[32] According to a former staff person, the children ranged from an infant to young adolescents. The children were first sheltered at the Espousal Center in Waltham, Massachusetts, a pastoral institution run by an order of priests, then removed a few short weeks later. I was told its staff lacked the language and cultural skills to work with Haitians and care for more than one hundred children. The Charity next asked the Sisters of the Good Shepherd to house the children.

Although the Good Shepherd sisters had not had much prior experience with housing unaccompanied refugee minor children, they had been involved in juvenile reform in Boston since the early twentieth century (see Chapter 2). The sisters had a contract with the Massachusetts Departments of Social Services (currently called the Massachusetts Department of Children and Families)—which deals with cases of abuse and neglect—and with the Department of Youth Services, which attempts to "protect the public and prevent crime by promoting positive change in the lives of youth committed to our custody."[33] A Good Shepherd administrator said in the mid-1980s that the sisters held a contract with the state to provide "residential treatment" to 120 girls who "failed to thrive" in foster homes. The girls had come before the juvenile court system because of mental health problems and social delinquency. Although some of the girls resided at the convent in a locked facility, others were not confined. The sisters provided to the Haitian children a fully accredited residential school, recreational activities, and access to religious services if requested. In 1992, Catholic priests and Protestant pastors were made available to meet the Haitian children's spiritual needs.

Pwojè Lavi had sixty staff members—including doctors, nurses, therapists, and lawyers—most of whom were Haitian and fluent in Creole. Personnel worked three shifts. Traditional Haitian cuisine was served. Each child had their own room. Much like Jean-Robert Paul's experience in Boston, however, a Haitian social worker directing this program noted some children acted out as a result of previously experienced traumas.[34]

Cardinal Law came regularly to share meals and celebrate the Catholic Mass with the children. According to a Haitian Multi-Service Center staff person who previously worked with Pwojè Lavi, Law wanted details of each child's welfare. The children liked him because he allowed them to play with his majestic black and red robes. To adult Haitians, the cardinal's willingness to allow Black children to touch him—children who had survived dire conditions in Haiti and imprisonment in the Guantánamo camp—was a moving demonstration of Law's care. By the program's end, some children had been reunified with parents and family members or placed with foster families. Others received asylee status and embarked on a path toward permanent residence and eventual citizenship. For years afterward the children stayed in touch with Pwojè Lavi caregivers who later worked at the Center.

• • •

Cardinal Law was able to circumvent US immigration policy restrictions and secure the release of Haitian children by shaming the United States publicly and through private pastoral appeals to President Bush. In so doing, Law helped procure a safe environment for these children. I am still struck by these stories of Law's pastoral care. The narratives pose stark contrasts to the cardinal's current image following the 2002 revelation of his approval of transfers of known predator priests in the archdiocese (beginning in 1984).

Because Cardinal Law's extraordinary advocacy for Haitians, especially children, occurred at nearly the same moment when victims of pedophile priests in the Archdiocese of Boston were publicizing their suffering, I am compelled to consider his public charity toward Haitians alongside the exposure of corporate Catholic scandal. On February 24, 1992, when the story of Haitian detainees was becoming prominent in the media, the *New York Times* announced the formation of a commission in the Archdiocese of Chicago to examine decades of accusations of clerical sexual abuse of minors. The Chicago priest and sociologist, Rev. Andrew M. Greeley, called the clergy pedophilia crisis the "S. & L. disaster of the Catholic Church," referring to the American savings and loan crisis from the mid to late 1980s. Then, on May 8, 1992, in the *Boston Globe,* nine men and women in southeastern Massachusetts alleged that Rev. James R. Porter had sexually molested them as children in the 1960s. With full knowledge of the misconduct allegations, the Church transferred Porter to two neighboring parishes where he allegedly assaulted other children before leaving the state in 1967. The nine adult accusers said they intended to sue the Church if it did not compensate them for damages and help them obtain justice.

The day after Cardinal Law's May 22, 1992, appeal to President Bush for clemency for Haitian detainees at Guantánamo, he was questioned about his church's response to the charges made against Porter in the 1960s. Law is reported to have responded as follows: the news media "has covered this story irresponsibly to paint all the clergy in a negative way" (Franklin 1992). At a mother's march against violence on the same day, Law publicly called down "God's power" against "the media, particularly the *Globe*," for their lack of coverage of the Church's benevolent work and disproportionate coverage of the emerging local scandal. The media described Law as "distressed by the absence of coverage of his own stand . . . criticizing the US decision to turn back Haitian refugees" (Franklin 1992).

The cardinal's reported displeasure at the lack of attention to his advocacy for Haitians suggests legitimate frustrations with the media's failure to use its power on Haitians' behalf. Perhaps Law was irritated about his exercise of pastoral power on their behalf not generating greater public outcry against unjust immigration policies or, possibly, personal forgiveness for his failures to safeguard other children. In this view, Law's intercession for the Haitian children in Guantánamo can be interpreted as a penitential act, one intended to balance his failures to protect James Porter's (and other predator priests') victims, especially as they came forward publicly to denounce the Church. Although I cannot definitively confirm this interpretation, Cardinal Law's intercession for Haitian minors reinforced the power of Catholic charitable institutions as agencies able to manage difficult cases. As the Charity administrator stated previously, other Catholic resettlement agencies considered Haitians "*a population that most people don't want to touch.*"

ASYLUM, SANCTUARY, AND LAW

For some Haitians, Boys Town, Pwojè Lavi, and even Boston's Haitian Multi-Service Center, offered "sanctuary" in the historical sense. In the Middle Ages, individuals were able to seek immunity from punishment at religious institutions like a monastery or abbey (Shoemaker 2011). Through confession and other penitential practices, the offender could be redeemed. Early Christian writers depicted churches as "spatial buffers against the spiritual contagion of theatres and pagan worship sites" (Shoemaker 2011: 17). The theologian Augustine of Hippo linked church sanctuary protections for fugitives to the intercessory powers of Catholic clerics in both secular and sacred realms of justice. In keeping with the obligation to offer charity, not only could Church officials petition courts for leniency on behalf of orphans and widows; the duty to provide charity could "require bishops to attempt to gain leniency or even clemency for malefactors tried before imperial magistrates" (Shoemaker 2011: 18). Furthermore, the practice of intercession "on behalf of the accused and condemned" had roots in the economy of salvation: "In Augustine's view, intercession aimed to turn the wrongdoer from his sin so that he might live free from it, while secular punishments only injured or killed the body without purging the soul" (Shoemaker 2011: 18–19). Over time, the church building itself was viewed as a sacred space able to offer asylum because of its sanctity. As a locus of spiritual activity, the physical building was inviolable or impenetrable by secular magistrates.

In contemporary times, religious actors have challenged secular law by using sacred spaces to offer sanctuary to undocumented migrants. In the 1980s, when US immigration policy was increasingly restrictive and political asylum claims were routinely denied not only to Haitian migrants but also to those from El Salvador and Guatemala, the church-based sanctuary movement (both Catholic and Protestant) shielded asylum seekers from "detection by law enforcement agencies who would have deported them back to an uncertain fate" (Van Ham 2009: 622).[35]

A final story tracing one of the Center's instructors from Haiti through Krome to Boston not only demonstrates the strategies and tactics Haitians employed to reach the United States but also how Haitian Catholics deployed pastoral power to critique, resist, and even limit state power.

CONTAINING THE STATE

Although desperation could propel Haitians onto paths resulting in their imprisonment, resistance was possible. Rénald St. Jacques, as I call him, spent nineteen months in Krome between 1988 and 1990, a time during which hundreds of Haitian men and women were detained beyond the facility's capacity. He was born in 1964 in Gonaïves, Haiti, into a large family whose older son was killed for political reasons. During the period of *ensekirite* that some have called "Duvalierism without Duvalier" (Trouillot 1990: 221–24), the escalating murders of young Haitians made him fear for his own life. The lack of job opportunities was an additional motivating factor. In 1988, Rénald fled for the United States without prior legal authorization.

In contrast to the thousands of Haitians who fled by boat, Rénald's family had some financial means. Given the restrictive American immigration policies, he knew there was little likelihood of migrating legally. Along with another friend, he purchased a false passport and visa, then flew to Miami. Both men presented their documents in the customs and immigration zone of indistinction (Agamben 1998). Although Rénald's identification papers went undetected, his companion's were discovered. Under questioning, this friend exposed St. Jacques's identification papers. Both men were sent to Krome:

> *ECJ:* If I can ask, what was Krome like when you were there?
>
> *RSJ:* When I [was] there, there [weren't] so many people in it. Like, maybe one hundred, [but later] up to seven hundred people. [It was] getting bad with [Mexicans] coming, Dominicans, Haitians . . . So, when it's too crowded, there's fighting. Fighting with officers, fighting with people. . . . Yeah, it [was] getting worse. They start[ed] deporting people. They sent people to take us. It was a bad experience.

Like the prisoners in Northern Ireland who used their bodies (and excreta) to protest the conditions in which they were imprisoned (Aretxaga 1993, 1995), the

Krome detainees announced in a letter to local leaders and the media that they would commence a hunger strike: "We [had] to do a hunger strike, to see if we can get out.... In [1988], we [had] a hunger strike for four days without food."[36] Although I do not know whether religious meanings of fasting informed the Krome hunger strike, I had learned in Haiti how religiously informed fasting was a common means to prepare for and focus prayers for deliverance from suffering and injustice.

The Miami Haitian community began protests outside Krome's walls on their compatriot's behalf. A *Miami Herald* story described the more than 180 Haitian detainees participating in the hunger strike as having left Haiti after the "Sept. 17 military coup brought Lt. Gen. Prosper Avril to power" (Lazo 1988). Avril had been leader of Jean-Claude Duvalier's presidential guard and was a member of the US-backed National Council of Government (CNG), "a military-controlled regime" that the US Department of State asserted "would lead Haiti on the road to democracy" (Trouillot 1990: 221–22). "Craving freedom more than food," the *Herald* reported, the detainees "turned down a special Thanksgiving buffet of Cornish hens, mashed potatoes and salad" and "would not eat . . . as a request that all Haitians be released from the center and given the same treatment received by Cuban refugees, who routinely get political asylum" (Lazo 1988).

The disparate treatment of Haitian migrants, in comparison to "unlawful entrants" from "communist" nations, had political roots in the Cold War. Like François and Jean-Claude Duvalier, Prosper Avril was not considered an enemy of the United States. In response, a well-known Catholic priest, Rev. Gerard Jean-Juste, who directed the Haitian Refugee Center (HRC) in Miami, deployed pastoral power in the tradition of Haitian liberation theology on the detainees' behalf. In addition to filing lawsuits against the federal government,[37] Jean-Juste framed the strike as a call to the public to consider these detainees' plight in the context of American ideals of liberty and justice: "I support the hunger strike. . . . This is a great day, Thanksgiving, and their call for freedom brings us to the roots of this country" (cited in Lazo 1988).

The hunger strike enabled more Haitian detainees to be paroled; however, as Rénald puts it, the public pressure and spotlight on Krome's conditions provoked the INS to expedite deportation proceedings:

> *RSJ:* After [the] strike . . . they [started releasing] people who have family here. But I didn't have family, so . . . they kept me. Nineteen months. . . .
>
> *ECJ:* How did you keep your spirits up?
>
> *RSJ:* Mostly it was very tense, [a] lot of tension, [and problems], because they [were] deporting people through [another] prison. When those guys came back, they [were] all lean, they didn't get food, they [came] with bone and skin. So, I was afraid.

With the overcrowding and strikes, some Haitian detainees were relocated to a Louisiana jail and another INS facility in Texas. After a lawsuit Rev. Jean-Juste's

HRC filed in protest of the transfers, the decision to relocate was overturned and the detainees were returned to Krome (Due 1989).

Eventually, with the support of two immigration lawyers—Cheryl Little, from the Florida Immigrant Advocacy Center, and another woman (whose name he could not recall)—Rénald was released on bond:

> So, I [called] Cheryl and I said, the way the tension is inside . . . you have to do something. Cause if you don't do anything, [they're] gonna send me to Louisiana because it's been getting so bad. So, they said, ok, we're gonna go back to the judge again to see if they can get a bond for me. So, they went . . . and they gave me a bond for five hundred dollars, so I got released.

After his release, Rénald met with the bishop of Miami and gave several interviews to the media to appeal publicly for clemency. Ultimately, his lawyers were not able to attain asylum status for him. They suggested he go to Canada, which accepted Haitian asylum seekers more readily than the United States did. Making another journey across national borders posed too great a risk, and he feared being apprehended once again.

In 1990, when many Haitians still grappled with the legacies of *ensekirite* and the climate of terror the Duvalier regime had established, Rénald chose life as an undocumented person in Boston. Social distrust was normal and even essential for day-to-day survival in Haiti. Pragmatic caution remained for many Haitians in the United States. Under such conditions, the Haitian Multi-Service Center became his home away from home. His Haitian host permitted Rénald to sleep on a couch at night; but he requested he leave the residence during the day. In the early 1980s, in the tradition of Haiti's liberation theology and the more recent sanctuary movements, St. Leo's pastor quietly allowed a small number of undocumented migrants to reside in the parish buildings until they could find other housing and, hopefully, regularize their legal status. The Haitian priest Leandre Jeannot mobilized pastoral power to support his flock and to bolster the professional expertise of civic leaders in the Haitian community to bring the Center into being.

. . .

Haitians with no other means have made their passage to residence in the United States through several purgatorial spaces. For some, the experience of internment merely preceded expulsion and the return to the conditions of insecurity that have plagued their country. My visit to Krome and Boys Town deepened my understanding of the stories of Pwojè Lavi and Krome that were later shared with me and that complicate a facile analysis of these very different purgatorial spaces. Although, on one level, all were spaces of containment resembling Goffman's total institutions, the extent to which each facility disciplined detainees varied according to perceptions of their worth. On a spectrum of "pastoral" power, Krome was closer to the repressive end; Boys Town and Pwojè Lavi were closer to the benevolent and compassionate end. In each space, detainees were inculcated into (or excluded from) a legal regime through normalizing routines and practices, whether those practices included a schedule of meals and exercise, or educational instruction and religious services. Unanswered questions remain regarding the governmental lease of for-profit corporate spaces like the Comfort Inn for women detainees and their children and the ongoing role of for-profit corporations like the GEO Group, Inc. in detainee management. How are the lives of asylum seekers in these hybrid spaces?

The intricate relationships between the state and religious and secular organizations partnering with, but subsidiary to, government, raise questions about the so-called separation of church and state. Against such spaces of containment, the Haitian Multi-Service Center (and St. Leo Parish) in Boston served as pastoral (and purgatorial) spaces offering shelter from many of these indeterminate migration conditions.

4

———

Memory Palace I

The Birth of the Center

*For a knowledge of intimacy, localization in the spaces of our intimacy is
more urgent than determination of dates.*
—GASTON BACHELARD

Toute vérité n'est pas bonne à dire. (Some things are better left unsaid.)
—FRANTZ PÉRALTE MONESTIME,
    FOUNDER AND FIRST HMSC EXECUTIVE DIRECTOR

The search for genealogical roots can be a labor of love and a puzzle to be solved,
especially for people of African descent. It is no less difficult to reconstruct our
institutional histories. As I began piecing together the Center's biography, available records were scant. My search eventually brought me to the Roman Catholic
Archdiocese of Boston (RCAB) Archives in Braintree, Massachusetts. After selling its Brighton location to Boston College for \$65 million, the Church moved to
a modern four-story, 140,000 square foot building in an industrial park owned
by longtime "archdiocesan benefactor," billionaire Thomas Flatley.[1] In February
2016, the exterior of the large reddish brown brick building reminded me of major
hospitals in Boston, as well as the new Yawkey Center (see Figure 10).

Like the Yawkey building, the RCAB headquarters had large windows, suites,
cubicles, and a feeling of sterility the ubiquitous fluorescent lighting projected
into its interior spaces. In contrast with many corporate offices and the other
Charity social service buildings I had previously visited, the display of religious
symbols in the Archdiocese of Boston Pastoral Center lobby was striking. Tables
near the entrance contained pamphlets in multiple languages advertising upcom-
ing spiritual retreats. Catholics Come Home® campaign materials invited lapsed
practitioners to return. Pictures of Pope Benedict XVI were on the walls. In contrast, Catholic Charities agency buildings did not overtly proselytize clients with

85

FIGURE 10. Roman Catholic Archdiocese of Boston (RCAB) Pastoral Center. Photo credit: Erica Caple James.

spiritual materials. Apart from personal items on Center staff member desks, religious iconography and images were absent during my work on-site between 2006 and 2007.

After checking with an awaiting attendant, I lingered near the informational materials until the archivist, Robert Johnson Lally, led me to a room containing many historical documents.[2] Walking down a corridor fragrant with incense, I glimpsed a Catholic Mass in progress through stained-glass windows in a large chapel anchoring the modern building in the faith. After entering the archives— a nondescript room with uniform shelving containing parish records, Catholic bishops' writings, archdiocesan directories, and other items—I was told all priests' personnel files were removed from public access when the clergy sex scandal erupted in the early 2000s. Apart from a letter initially assigning Father Leandre Jeannot as an auxiliary priest, documentation of his tenure at St. Leo's was not available. After its suppression in 1999, parishioners' private baptismal, communion, marriage, and other records were transferred to St. Matthew Parish.

At a small table I examined the small stack of papers Lally had compiled. The first, dated September 2, 1966, recorded Rev. Shawn G. Sheehan's "Profession of Faith" and "Oath against Modernism" made to the dean of the Archdiocese of Boston, Charles A. Finn, when Sheehan was appointed St. Leo Parish pastor. In 1907, Pope Pius X labeled "modernism" a heresy because of its historical approach to Jesus and the scriptures, its advocacy of secularism and church-state separation, and its foundation in rationalist philosophy. From 1910 until 1967 (when the Congregation for the Doctrine of the Faith rescinded the oath), "each diocese was to have a body of censors who were to watch over all literature in any way connected with the Church. The agencies were to observe strict secrecy in all their proceedings. . . . And, finally all priests and teachers were required to take an oath against Modernism."[3]

The next documents revealed routine collaborations between public and private, and religious and secular institutions—regardless of concerns each may have held about the others' moral, philosophical, or theological beliefs. An October 9, 1967, letter recorded Boston's inspection of St. Leo's clubhouse for use as a daycare agency. Another undated page itemized renovation specifications: a cover letter and leasing agreement that Cardinal Richard Cushing and Arthur J. Gartland, then president of the antipoverty agency Action for Boston Community Development, Inc., had signed to lease St. Leo's space for a Project Head Start childcare center.

The 1967 leasing agreement, addressed to the "Roman Catholic Archbishop Soul [*sic*]," revealed how the archdiocese and archbishop possess a secular body, the "Corporation Sole" (or "Corp Sole," as a Charity administrator would later call it), to conduct business with secular entities. In Boston the Corporation Sole is defined as "a legal entity created under Massachusetts civil law in 1897 to provide the Roman Catholic Archbishop of Boston with a means to operate within the public statutes of the Commonwealth of Massachusetts" (RCAB 2011: 12): "Corporation Sole statutes enable religious leaders—typically bishops or parsons—to be incorporated for the purpose of insuring the continuation of ownership of property dedicated to the benefit of a legitimate religious organization."[4] As a temporal leader, the archbishop (or cardinal) of Boston is technically the "owner" of these hybrid secular/sacred establishments, such as the parish buildings, schools, churches, and other properties. His relationship to them, however, is largely pastoral, taking the form of spiritual care for his "flock."[5] The ultimate ownership of Church properties became an issue after the 1999 St. Leo Parish suppression and a few years later, when Center stakeholders debated the future of the parish buildings and programs.

The RCAB archbishop also "serves as chairman of the board or president of numerous separately incorporated Catholic organizations that operate within the Archdiocese of Boston . . . [but] they are not under the control of the Corporation Sole" (RCAB 2011: 12). Although the archbishop does not "own" the institutions only affiliated with Corporation Sole, they are under his pastoral care. Corp Sole is responsible for, but does not directly manage, affiliated organizations, including the following: the Boston Catholic Television Center, Inc., a cemetery association, several Catholic high schools, and development foundations; health, retirement, and investment funds, trusts, and insurance groups; several seminary and missionary societies; mission-related institutions like the Society for the Propagation of the Faith in Boston; and finally, social service organizations, such as the Catholic Charitable Bureau of the Archdiocese of Boston, Inc. (the Charity).[6]

The collaborations revealed in the documents I reviewed among church, state, and private corporations (whether for profit or nonprofit) signaled two trends in social policy: federal funding for antipoverty initiatives was made available when the "caring state" (Daly 2009) strongly considered social welfare programs a right (as well as a responsibility). Secondly, third-party institutions fulfilled such needs when a neoliberal trend toward the privatization of social welfare arose (Wacquant 2009: 41–59). A page titled "itemization of non-federal share" outlined St. Leo's spatial contribution to ABCD's application to the Office of Economic Opportunity (OEO) Community Action Program for furniture and equipment. The OEO, the federal agency administering programs under President Lyndon Johnson's "War on Poverty," offered to pay heating and lighting costs for one year. The OEO also administered the Head Start program until 1969, when it was transferred to the Department of Health, Education, and Welfare (renamed the Department of Health and Human Services in 1979). Although genealogical links between this Head Start Program and the parish childcare and English as a Second Language (ESL) classes offered to Haitians remain unclear, the Church supported pastoral initiatives in partnership with and on behalf of government.

Given the limited written records, interviews with many Center stakeholders helped me reconstruct its history. Although their recollection of dates, events, and structural transformations was rarely exact, their stories provided rich testimonies of the dramas propelling the influx of Haitians to Greater Boston, and the roles the archdiocese, St. Leo's, the Charity, and the Center played in supporting them.

In contrast to the purgatorial sites in which Haitians had been detained since the 1970s, the Center was largely a space of security and remoralization rather than institutional violation and dehumanization (Frank and Frank 1991; James 2010; Kleinman 1988, 2006). The establishment of the Center at St. Leo's followed the paths of earlier groups of Catholic migrants to Boston and paralleled similar religious and secular institution-building initiatives among diaspora Haitians in Miami, New York, and other North American cities (Glick-Schiller and Fouron 2001; Laguerre 1984, 1998; Mooney 2009; Pierre-Louis 2006; Rey and Stepick 2009; Stepick 1998; Zéphir 2004). Haitians mobilized religious and other professional networks to amass the knowledge, expertise, and material and social capital to build the organization, while struggling with acculturation challenges themselves. By the 1970s, as the Greater Boston Haitian population increased, some archdiocesan resources were made available to support them and ensure they would remain incorporated in the Church. But Haitians offered as many material, symbolic, and spiritual resources to the archdiocese and its charitable institutions as they received. As the stories of its founders demonstrate, the Center has been a remarkable place from which to consider the relationships between migrants and public or private social welfare institutions, as well as how race, ethnicity, health, and legal status influence these social linkages.

THE MEMORY PALACE

In 1892 and 1893, the Impressionist artist Claude Monet painted over thirty portraits of Rouen Cathedral in France to capture its image at different times of day, and in different weather conditions and seasons. The series of façades suggests an edifice like a cathedral holds different meanings for those who enter and inhabit such spaces over time than for those who view them from a distance. Finished in a studio in 1894, Monet's memory colored the final images we view today.[7]

In *The Memory Palace of Matteo Ricci*, China historian Jonathan D. Spence (1988) describes how a Jesuit merchant missionary taught local Chinese scholars several mnemonic techniques to aid their preparations for governmental exams. Ricci hoped his knowledge gifts would encourage them to explore the faith that developed these memory arts. As elaborated by Society of Jesus founder Ignatius of Loyola, Society members were taught to apply all five senses to vivify scriptural passages under study, thereby creating an imaginal space (Csordas 1994; Nordstrom 1997). By constructing a mental structure of a real or fictive space, like a "temple compound, a cluster of government offices, a public hostel, or a merchants' meeting lodge" (Spence 1988: 1), one could store information in each room, depositing factual details like ornaments in precise order "around the walls, between the windows, on chairs, beds, tables" (Spence 1988: 7). When layered visually and spatially in the mental structure, details could be recalled precisely: "Once your places are all fixed in order, then you can walk through the door and make your start . . . and all the images are ready for whatever you seek to remember" (Spence 1988: 9).

The memory palace concept is evocative not only as a mnemonic technique but also for its understanding of the visceral, sensory nature of space and time, as well as the recollection and interpretation of the same. No two individuals will construct an imaginal space in the same way. The sensory details of the place from which one retrieves artifacts of experience are unique, regardless of whether a space is real or imagined.

As an ethnographic tool, the memory palace concept helped in painting the Center's portrait from the details of others' experience. Center memories were inextricably linked to those of St. Leo Parish. Each person recalled the parish architecture in a unique way, revealing the "social blueprints" mapped onto the Center—the ways persons of different statuses and social roles were connected to place. Remembrances of the institution also revealed each individual's "kinesthetic orientation" to the building and persons who occupied its spaces. These descriptions illustrated each speaker's "visceral ways of sensing" (Desjarlais 1997: 72) social space and encoded the aesthetic values and moral sentiments embedded in their experience. Center recollections vivified the narrator's feelings of safety and belonging, and/or vulnerability and exclusion. Each stakeholder's willingness to talk about its history was largely dependent on the emotions and sentiments institutional memories evoked.

Contested versions of the Center's origins are an indicator of stakeholder ambivalence. One account repeated by various Center staff and advisory board members identifies Father Leandre Jeannot and two social workers, Frantz Monestime and Evelyn Prophète, as its 1978 founders who, alongside other key Haitian and non-Haitian supporters, later formalized the program as the "Haitian Multi-Service Center."[8] Its founders, subsequent executive directors, staff persons, and community members intended the Center to become an independent Haitian-managed institution with no permanent oversight by either the Charity or Church, or by any other public or private agency. In this version, the Church provided space and administrative support, and the Center later joined the Charity; however, the exact date of the "merger" is disputed. Depending on to whom one speaks (or which texts one reads), the merger occurred in 1984, 1986, 1989, or even in the early 1990s.

The Charity's institutional website (as of this writing) presents the Center's origin story as follows: "Established by local Haitian community leaders, the Haitian Multi-Service Center (HMSC) began in 1978 with a single service, English as a Second Language for recent Haitian immigrants. In 1984, the HMSC became a community service center of Catholic Charities, Archdiocese of Boston."[9] Behind this simple statement are protracted and contentious struggles for control, as well as shifts in the structural relationships between the Church, Charity, and community-based charitable institutions in the Massachusetts Catholic Charities network. Perhaps these two versions are simply different sides of the same coin.

Disputes regarding the Center's origin, mission, and purpose reflect its stakeholders' struggles to determine how power—cultural, gendered, pastoral, and corporate—should be exercised and toward what ends. These disagreements also reflected Haitians' concerns about identity, justice, citizenship, and sovereignty. Their rights-based approaches to social incorporation sometimes conflicted with Catholic charitable authorities' requirement that the Center uphold the tenets and practices of the Catholic faith without exception.

These debates also concerned cultural intimacy. In his work on social poetics in the nation-state, Michael Herzfeld (1997: 14) contrasts the state's "official self-presentation" (its façade, a form of cultural nationalism) with stereotypes of cultural practices circulating outside the nation—images resonating uncomfortably as true "in the privacy of collective introspection." The disjuncture between public circulating representations and vernacular idioms and practices inside the nation-state produces cultural intimacy, "the recognition of those aspects of cultural identity that are considered a source of external embarrassment but which nevertheless provide insiders with their assurance of common sociality" (Herzfeld 1997: 3). Disputes about the Center's purpose reflected the broader Haitian community's aspirations to greater civic power but also ambivalence regarding their capacity to manage the Center independently, especially given ongoing troubling public and private affairs (whether interpersonal, institutional, or national).

Ever-present fiscal weakness and community need often surpassed the Center's institutional capacity. The HMSC frequently suffered budgetary deficits; and first the Church, then later the Charity, closed financial gaps with their own resources, personnel, and finances. Between 1986 and 1992, the Charity gradually assumed financial oversight. Some staff and advisory board members felt the merger would provide greater organizational and financial stability, but others fought to retain the Center's autonomy and connection to the Haitian community. It was difficult to sustain the flames of community voluntarism in the face of budgetary challenges.

INTIMATE MEMORY

Early stakeholders' sensory memories of the Center's physical, social, and environmental conditions were vivid. Apart from a prefabricated modular structure housing the daycare, St. Leo's old Victorian buildings—the 12 Bicknell Street Victorian "convent" where Haitian nuns resided (and eventually housed most of the social service programs), the Harvard Street rectory where Father Leandre Jeannot lived, and St. Leo Church on Esmond Street—were perpetually in disrepair (see Figure 11). Mice left telltale signs of nightly activities on staff members' desks. Water pipes leaked and the boiler often failed on many frigid winter days. In summer, the old Victorian buildings were hot and crowded.

Although St. Leo's offered shelter, education, and care, the surrounding urban landscape was sometimes hazardous. In 1994, a *Boston Globe* article noted the perilous surroundings:

> St. Leo's is located near a high-crime area, where drug dealers brazenly sell crack as they creep between Franklin Field and Franklin Hill housing developments. Prostitutes stroll along Blue Hill Avenue as if they are a legitimate part of the landscape. Left behind are the Christian values taught in the Bible . . . "In some respects, it is not that much different from the time when Jesus lived," said [Meyer J.] Chambers, director of the [Office for] Black Catholics [a part of the Boston Archdiocese]. "It's the struggle between good and evil." (Manly 1994)

The mixture of nostalgia and revulsion at these conditions invariably emerged in each interview. The physical spaces stakeholders endured created a feeling of cultural intimacy combining sentiments of embarrassment, aversion, and laughter, as well as feelings of pride, ownership, and solidarity. Although the desperation of its economically poor neighbors provoked perpetual break-ins, many described the Queen Anne Victorian with a wraparound front porch and third-floor gables as having a comforting "cozy feeling" (see Figure 12).

FIGURE 11. St. Leo Parish rectory, ca. 2004. Photo credit: Robert L. Powell.

During a 2007 interview, I asked a European American Charity administrator to describe the 12 Bicknell Street location. In speaking of the Center's "unchanging" quality—associated with domestic sociality and pleasures of traditional Haitian cuisine—their response evoked tradition and modernity, but also solidarity amid poverty:

FIGURE 12. Haitian Multi-Service Center, 12 Bicknell Street, ca. 2006. Photo Credit: Robert L. Powell.

> It was pretty much like it looks now, I mean, it never really changed. They have the big, the ESL classrooms, and the place was falling apart, full of people, you know an old computer lab, the childcare Center, um, it . . . you know it really never changed much. I mean I used to go there quite a bit, and it was always the same, but it was always full of clients. Full of clients. And you know the kitchen, and the cook, and the Haitian food . . . I used to love to go there so I could get a nice Haitian meal . . . there was always something breaking down, the water wasn't working, or the heat wasn't working, there was asbestos falling off the building [*laughing*] [and] lead paint! [*laughing*].

For this administrator, the Center was a "timeless" place, unvarying in routines and the ever-present needs and aspirations of numerous clients. But it was also a place in which one could encounter and consume authentic Haitian culture, improvise amid unexpected emergencies, learn, and feel at home. Although it might be tempting to interpret this administrator's recollections as a form of cultural stereotyping—as if the Center's "static" nature reflected the Other's timelessness (Fabian 1983)—I don't think the remarks were intended disparagingly.

At the advisory board meetings I attended, beginning in 2005, the feeling of camaraderie and shared purpose was enhanced by communally shared meals. Typically, these sensory feasts commenced with informal socializing over Haitian cuisine: fragrant plates of *diri kole*, white rice mixed with pinto beans spiced with garlic, onion, and cloves; and *legim*, a stew of dark leafy greens, cabbage, onion, and other vegetables. Carnivores savored *poule kreyòl*—chicken cleaned with sour orange halves, boiled, patted dry, then fried to a deep golden brown—accompanied by a spicy "creole" tomato sauce. We sometimes had stewed marinated beef (*vyann*) or another delicacy, *griyo*, crisp fatty pork cubes marinated in a spiced citrus rub prior to frying. As always, a platter of crisp fried green plantain chips was on hand. *Pikliz*, a piquant relish of cabbage, shredded carrot, vinegar, and habanero peppers added tart fire to these dishes. Through the conviviality and cuisine native Haitians remembered their homeland, diaspora-raised Haitians gained greater exposure to their cultural patrimony, and new and long-standing allies were able to share, recall, and learn afresh Haiti's cultural riches.

For "Susan Brown," a European American volunteer from the mid-1980s, memories of the physical plant and décor not only evoked the aesthetic riches of Haitian culture but also gender distinctions between the sexes:

> *SB:* I don't know if you saw the Haitian Center but . . . they are very artistic! . . . Well . . . the murals that they did . . . the murals would give all that sense of culture and beauty in detail.
>
> *ECJ:* Where were these murals?
>
> *SB:* On the first floor on the wall.
>
> *ECJ:* My big regret is that I don't have an image of what it looked like inside before the move.
>
> *SB:* . . . It . . . had a wood structure. I believe it was three floors. It had a porch . . . and a vestibule area. If you went straight ahead there would be . . . two at least large rooms with the daycare center. So, they were really large and had space for their activities.
>
> *ECJ:* So, the daycare was in the 12 Bicknell building, at first.
>
> *SB:* Yes, it was, and it had several places . . . a place to play, [for] eating, and . . . little classrooms . . . and so forth. So, when you go up the stairs that would be the place where we had our receptionist, a lovely Haitian woman who knew all. I felt like—I'm not trying to be biased in terms of gender—but there was a lot of maturity in middle-aged and even younger Haitian women, and a wiseness. . . . She was an older woman. I hope she's still . . .

As I participated in and observed programs between 2006 and 2007, I had similar impressions of the women staff members, especially the Sante Manman and health outreach staff. Susan continued:

> *SB:* Then we had ESL and [the] AIDS [program], and [an] administrative office—very small and almost movable. It was almost, again, emblematic of no administration. But the beauty was the direct service [and] the people, and the vibrancy of [their] coming for their services. But there was very little in the way of administrative space.

> *ECJ:* For the AIDS patients if they wanted confidentiality, was there a space
> for them?
>
> *SB:* Oh yeah, they had their own office—absolutely—and that was very
> honored, and the space for the counseling was private. . . . The doctor
> had his own space. . . . there was another floor where the ESL students
> were. . . . It was a big space, and it was a very well-developed program.
> I think that's all I remember about it.

In this volunteer's view, the direct care between staff members and clients, and especially the Haitian women employees' wisdom, rendered the space one of "feminine" pastoral power.

Not all stakeholders romanticized the Center. One European American staff member said of the 12 Bicknell building, "It was pretty much a shithole, physically. It was a terrible, terrible building . . . Anyone who says it was nice was lying. It was falling apart." For this individual, the visceral reminders of cultural differences between non-Haitians and Haitians were inescapable onslaughts to the senses: "We had a lobby. Some of the classroom people would just walk in and they would bring their food and you would always smell food, whether you liked it or not."

Undoubtedly, Center memories were communicated using such vivid language because for many it was a home away from home. In *The Poetics of Space*, the philosopher Gaston Bachelard (1969: 6) describes how intimate spaces evoke hope, security, melancholy, and nostalgia:

> We comfort ourselves by reliving memories of protection. Something closed must retain our memories, while leaving them their original value as images. Memories of the outside world will never have the same tonality as those of home and, by recalling these memories, we add to our store of dreams; we are never real historians, but always near poets, and our emotion is perhaps nothing but an expression of a poetry that was lost.

In recreating the Center through a palace of memories, I was reminded it literally was home for many stakeholders, and for others, a home away from a homeland left behind. The Haitian nuns resided in the convent, Father Leandre Jeannot in the rectory, and undocumented persons who were granted temporary sanctuary within its walls considered the space to be as much of a home as did St. Leo's parishioners, and later, the Center's clients, staff, and advisory board members.

WHITE FLIGHT

In a June 2007 conversation with "Harold Jackson," an African American St. Leo parishioner, I heard many stories about the demographic changes producing St. Leo's as a majority Black and Haitian parish. Boston African Americans once had their own parish in Lower Roxbury. After purchasing a former Protestant church for the Black community, Cardinal Cushing had dedicated St. Richard's in

1946. The Black parish was controversial, with some African Americans viewing it as a "form of racial segregation," while others thought it offered a sign of having achieved greater equality in the archdiocese: "Henry E. Quarles, Sr., a leading member of the local black Catholic community . . . argued that just like the Irish, French, and Italian Catholics before them, blacks wanted and needed their own parish" (Leonard 2009: 151–52). At the time of the *Brown v. Board of Education* ruling (1954) mandating desegregation of public schools, Cushing argued, "in light of the recent Supreme Court decision, I think we should do more . . . to incorporate the colored people in the parish in which they live" (Cushing 1956, cited in Leonard 2009: 153). St. Richard's closed in 1964 (Leonard 2009: 153).

Jackson described St. Leo's as predominantly White—Irish and Italian, specifically—until "we" (people of African descent) began moving in from Lower Roxbury, which had been predominantly Black. As the proportion of African Americans in the area increased, the neighborhood rapidly changed:

> *HJ:* At that time, I doubt very much . . . if there was two-dozen Haitian brothers and sisters there at the church. I doubt it. Ok, now, Father [Joseph] Gaudet. He took over, I think in 1967, or '68, . . . and then the church was damn near all Black then!
>
> *ECJ:* Wow . . . that was quick!
>
> *HJ:* Real quick! And um, there was a sprinkle of White folks still in the church. It was majority . . . Black Catholic, and then, all our Haitian brothers and sisters . . . and also Cape Verdean brothers and sisters.

St. Leo's having rapidly become a predominantly Black parish reflected (in part) the realities of racial segregation in Boston. Over the twentieth century Dorchester's demographic composition shifted radically as African Americans moved beyond Lower Roxbury to historically majority White areas of Dorchester. While some neighborhoods retained their Irish Catholic roots, the area surrounding St. Leo's was "unique in 1960: of the seventeen parish churches in Dorchester and upper Roxbury, only St. Leo's Church was surrounded on all sides by Jewish homes" (Gamm 1999: 91).

In the 1950s and 1960s, as the Jewish population fled to the suburbs and Blacks began to reside in the parish district near Franklin Park, Franklin Field, and Mount Bowdoin, the majority White St. Leo parishioners (residing mostly elsewhere) moved from the parish entirely. From a 1962 population of 5,810 parishioners, the population was 1,100 in 1970 (Gamm 1999: 91). By 1978, when St. Leo's housed the Haitian Multi-Service Center, both the church population and the surrounding neighborhood was overwhelmingly Black. The racial transformation occurred at a much earlier period than in Catholic neighborhoods north and south of St. Leo's (Gamm 1999: 91).

According to sociologist Regine O. Jackson (2007: 199), an influx of Haitians accounts for this demographic shift from White to Black.[10] Jackson's

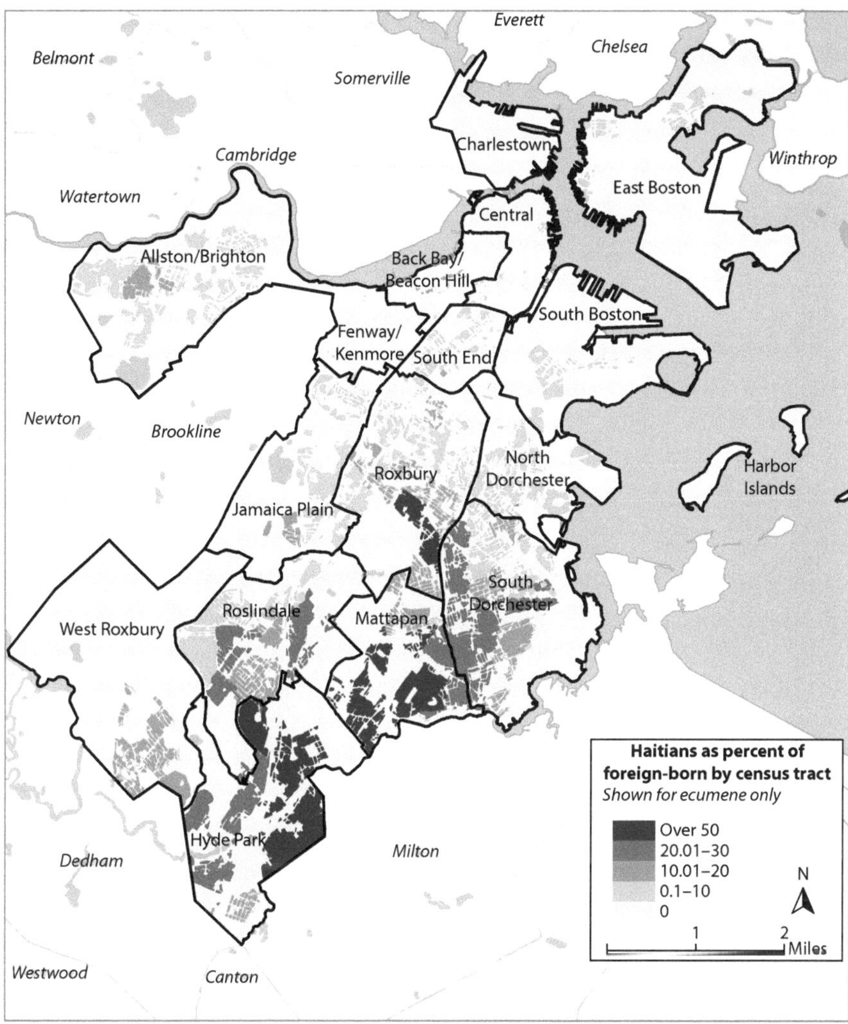

FIGURE 13. Haitian immigrants in Boston. Image credit: Boston Redevelopment Authority.

research on Boston Haitian immigrants indicates they migrated in four waves: "the *Pathfinders* (pre-1965); the *Core* (1965–1979); the *Boom* (1980–1991); and the *Newcomers* (1992–present)" (2007: 193). Haitian pathfinders comprised mostly middle-class professionals: "academics and teachers—participants in a program called the Congo Experiment who came to Boston when their contracts expired with the Congolese government; engineers seeking to take advantage of employment opportunities at General Electric and Polaroid; and physicians interning at Massachusetts General Hospital. Others were politicians in exile" (Jackson 2007: 196). After migrating, "pathfinders" selected where to settle in part to distinguish themselves ethnically from African Americans, against whom racial discrimination and segregation had been entrenched. They chose predominantly White residential areas in which multifamily housing units, "triple-deckers," were available as residences and investment properties later leased to new Haitians (Jackson 2007: 197).

Although each subsequent "wave" encompassed diverse sectors of the Haitian population, Catholicism became central to the Boston Haitian community because it provided "an important symbolic resource in the formation of an ethnic community" (Jackson 2007: 197). Since "Catholic churches coordinate residential behavior because they restrict membership to local residents" (Jackson 2007: 193), Haitian migrants chose housing and established local businesses in proximity to three Catholic churches (see Figure 13)—St. Angela's on Blue Hill Avenue, St. Matthew's on Stanton Street, and St. Leo's—the three parishes initially forming the territorial boundary for Haitian settlement.

St. Leo's became the unofficial "mother church" for the Haitian population (Jackson 2007: 198). In Haiti, parents typically sent their children to parochial schools, and the availability of Catholic education and "church sponsored recreational programs and activities for youth" (Jackson 2007: 200) made settling in Mattapan and Dorchester even more attractive. By the time the "newcomers" settled in Greater Boston, a 1996 *Boston Globe* article stated the growing Haitian population helped sustain Catholic institutions: "Haitian children are the salvation of parochial schools, from St. John's in Cambridge (89 percent Haitian) to St. Angela's in Mattapan (71 percent) to St. Catherine's in Somerville and Most Precious Blood in Hyde Park (both now about 50 percent Haitian)" (Radin 1996). In choosing parochial education Haitians may have given as much to Catholic institutions as they received.

But Haitian immigrants have not been equally successful financially. They also have obligations to sustain families across national borders. Analysis of 1990 census data suggested twenty percent of Massachusetts Haitians lived in poverty, and "71 percent were making under $15,000 a year. Even though many Haitians work multiple, menial jobs for minimum wages, almost all regularly send money to family and friends in Haiti, where unemployment is around 60 percent" (Radin 1996). Including himself among those providing for others in the United States and Haiti, Father Jeannot interpreted the exigencies of everyday Haitian life for outsiders:

> "The Haitian family here has to sustain not only itself but three or four families in Haiti," says Rev. Leandre Jeannot, pastor of St. Leo's Church in Dorchester, the unofficial mother church of Haitian Catholics in Massachusetts. "Everyone, even myself, compromises their living here to participate in that. Without the diaspora, Haiti would not survive." (Radin 1996)

In 1972, as the rapid demographic changes intensified, the archdiocese installed a Haitian priest, the future Monsignor Jeannot, at St. Leo's (see Figure 14).

FIGURE 14. Rev. Leandre Jeannot, as pictured in a Christmas card, 1981.

MONSIGNOR LEANDRE JEANNOT

Given Boston's racial history, the presence of a Black priest was significant. Father Jeannot was largely responsible for St. Leo's becoming the heart of Greater Boston's Haitian community (and the Center's base). Jeannot left Haiti in 1959 after having been persecuted politically there (under François Duvalier):

I was an elementary school teacher. . . . I was also a politician—a leader of the Mouvement Organisation du Pays. . . . Orders were given not to arrest me but to kill me. . . . I escaped by chance; I just happened not to be home when they came. It was not only Tonton Macoute [paramilitary forces loyal to Duvalier]. An officer from the army came, too. He declared to my family if they find me, they would shoot me." (Radin 1996: 18)

The Salesians of St. John Bosco hid Jeannot and he later escaped to the Dominican Republic (Radin 1996: 18). He joined the Salesian order and studied theology in Lyon, France, prior to his ordination in 1970 in Medellín, Colombia. In 1970, he came to the United States, first serving in the St. Theresa of Avila Parish in Brooklyn, New York, and then at the Lakes Parish in New Jersey in 1971 (Isidor 2001). Jeannot became pastor of St. Leo's in 1976, when Rev. Gaudet was "dispatched to a mission in Peru."

Recollections of Father Jeannot paint a striking picture of his personal charisma and pastoral leadership of the Haitian community. Pastoral power, to recall, is a power of care in which a "shepherd" attends to the physical and spiritual needs of each member of a collective flock through sacramental and charitable acts. According to Harold Jackson, a component of St. Leo's appeal was Jeannot's racial, ethnic, and national identity, as well as his position in the archdiocese:

> People flocked to our church because they had a Haitian priest in charge. OK? In charge. They came from Malden, they came from Somerville, they came from Brockton; they came from ALL of the cities surrounding Boston to our church. Our church was more or less the . . . main church for the . . . Haitian community. And you have to remember that Haitian folks are . . . about 90 percent Catholic. . . . He used to, now he was so busy—and God forbid, this may be part of the reason why his life was taken so soon, because he used to go do a Mass, do an English Mass in St. Leo's in Dorchester, then . . . a Haitian-Creole Mass on the same day, and then he'd go to Cambridge and do a Mass. Then he'd go to Brockton and do a Mass . . . and that was every Sunday. And that was every Sunday. It's amazing. He lived for his people.

In this account, Father Jeannot was a loving pastor who made personal sacrifices to ensure the safety, security, and salvation of his flock. Jackson continued:

> He would give them his last dollar if they needed it. . . . He would give him, he, the man would give away his whole—because he had a small paycheck from the archdiocese, and he would give it away most of the time. He would give his shirt, and he would give his everything, you know . . . because people needed things like that: clothing, food, and shelter. . . . He was just that, that loving towards his folks.

Until his death from cancer in 2001, Father Jeannot's pastoral work not only emphasized caring for others, but also political advocacy for Haitians. Like Father Jean-Juste in Miami, who advocated for more humane treatment of Haitian detainees (see Chapter 3), Jeannot protested publicly against Haiti's political crises. (Jeannot's religious order, the Salesians, were particularly prominent as supporters of his nation's pro-democracy movement).

FIGURE 15. Mass at St. Leo Roman Catholic Church. Photo credit: Robert L. Powell.

In 1992, at the height of unauthorized Haitian migration to the United States, Jeannot denounced publicly President George H. W. Bush's continuation of his predecessor President Reagan's deterrent policy to repatriate Haitian "boat people" without permitting them to apply for asylum: "It is not human, what they are doing. . . . The people in the boats, who have spent days hungry, they send them to hell. Instead of killing them, they make them kill themselves. How can they treat them this way? I am really sad. I couldn't even eat today. I will keep praying" (Weld 1992: 14). In 1987, after the self-immolation of Haitian immigrant Antoine Thurel on the steps of the Massachusetts State House, Jeannot described the suicide in political rather than theological terms. The death indexed the frustrations of Haitians who dreamed of returning to Haiti but could not: "We have all been hoping for democracy after so many years of dictatorship, but there is no peace, and there is much abuse. . . . The man who killed himself was like so many; after so many years away they wanted to go home and live quietly, but now they cannot" (Constable 1987).

In other accounts, a merciful Jeannot justified how Haitian Catholics' obligations to labor for near and distant family restricted their capacity to attend obligatory weekly Masses: "Most of the people who are willing to come have to work on Sundays . . . Some of them only have one Sunday off each month or they have to take care of their families, so it's hard for them to come" (Graham 1989). Although for other

Haitians, Sundays were reserved for celebrations of their collective religious faith (see Figure 15), on Friday evenings, Jeannot conducted charismatic services. Hundreds of Haitian men, women, and children assembled in a sacred celebration that countered the daily stressors of urban living and relieved some of their burdens.

The services made immanent a sense of life beyond the profane, a reminder of the spirit animating the corporate body of the Church:

> The beep-beep of car alarms switching on punctures the Friday twilight. But as night falls on the reminders of how mean these streets can be, a chorus of hallelujahs, sung in soft Caribbean accents to the tune of "Amazing Grace," floats through the air. Weather-beaten old St. Leo's is lighting up for the weekly Mass of the charismatics, people who practice a more emotive and demonstrative Catholicism than is the norm in traditional churches. Neatly dressed adults and carefully scrubbed children sway to beautiful music and the lilt of hundreds of voices raised in Haitian Creole.

As pastor, Jeannot mediated the connection between parishioners and the divine:

> Incense perfumes the air. Face grave, Father Jeannot moves slowly through the crowd, bearing before him a large ostensory, or monstrance—the ornate vessel that contains the host, central to the sacrament of Holy Communion. . . . The faithful surge forward to touch the gilded, sunburst-shaped container and to connect with this man who embodies both their faith and the events that set in motion the first wave of Haitians' flight from their homeland. (Radin 1996)

Parishioners connecting to Jeannot's sacramental and symbolic power shared healing and, literally, inspiration. I would later learn from Center program staff, particularly the women, how charismatic worship services were an integral component of their piety. A more "feminine" form of pastoral power rooted in Marianism, devotion to Mary the mother of Jesus, sustained the more public pastoral outreach through which they engaged individual clients and the community.

Although, Jeannot's personal charisma, pastoral care, and personal story contributed to his pastoral power, his depiction of Haitians to the media tended to reinforce negative stereotypes of Haitians' vulnerability and dependency:

> "Before I came, the Haitian people were timid and shy," he said. "It was sad. They felt isolated from the church. They were weak and easily exploited. Sure, I came here to perform services and give the sacraments. But I also came here to teach, to take care of the people, their feelings and their needs." The isolation was painful. In Haitian culture, Father Jeannot says, people depend on their priest to give them guidance on everything, from family matters to career counseling. "It's almost to the point of paternalism," he said. (Manly 1994)

At the time of his December 1994 statement, the upheaval of Haiti's coup years was only beginning to relent after the Multinational Force "restored" democracy on October 15, 1994. Regardless, rapid influxes of Haitian newcomers to Boston continued. (I return to Father Jeannot's pastoral care for Haitians in Chapter 5, when analyzing narratives challenging his benevolence.)

• • •

To step briefly outside this memory palace, it is important to note how depictions of the Haitian community as uniformly downtrodden, weak, blindly faithful, innocent, more authentically pious, and so on, have strategic uses. Ethical publicity—public representations of either individual or institutional accountability and responsibility toward those in need—can be useful when countering negative or scandal publicity (James 2010). These dynamics are no less present when considering public representations of pastoral care among religious actors, agencies, and institutions, as opposed to their actual practices.

Rather than seeing Haitians' reliance on Catholic leaders and institutions or their religiosity as apolitical—a sign of false consciousness, misrecognition of exploitation, or resignation to the injustices of temporal existence—I suggest the charisma and pastoral power flowing in private worship at St. Leo's provided the foundation for empowerment and civic action. As sociologist Margarita Mooney (2009: 78) writes of Catholic Charismatic prayer groups in the Miami Haitian community, such participation should not be viewed as a "retreat from social action, in particular, the kinds of social and political projects associated with liberation theology," nor should the flow of charisma be viewed as moving solely from pastor to parishioner as care, but rather, "praying . . . is a *way of giving to others*" (Mooney 2009: 77; emphasis in the original). Writing of members of Notre Dame d'Haïti Catholic Church in Miami, Mooney (2009: 77) affirms prayer not only fulfills a religious obligation; it is a form of labor enabling all participants to contribute regardless of material means:

> Members of Notre Dame attended church in part because they see worship as an obligation to God and also because prayer represents one potent way for them to give to others. Not everyone in the community can give material support to others . . . but they can all pray together. Even extremely needy Haitians said that through praying together, they transformed themselves into givers and not just recipients of aid [and infused] their social situation with a different meaning, a meaning that inspires them to become actors in their own drama rather than falling into despair or hopelessness.

A consideration of prayer as labor that enables the person praying to become an active agent, regardless of material circumstances, influenced parish efforts to support the community. This conception aligns with historical Catholic conceptions of charity as a reciprocal rather than one-sided exchange (see Chapter 2).

Over time, the pastoral programs at St. Leo's began transforming into a formal social service center. In response to social need, Jeannot was reported as inaugurating volunteer social service work out of his residence:

"My bell rings a lot," he said. "Sometimes a family will show up at my door. They have no money and they are hungry. Or someone will have their car break down and they need cab fare to get home." . . . Father Jeannot then opened his office and home, located in the Rectory, a few steps from the chapel, to the people. And they started coming in larger numbers, becoming a part of the church community, volunteering for groups to provide youth counseling and leadership training. (Manly 1994; the paragraphing is reversed.)

In a 2001 article in the *Boston Globe* memorializing Father Jeannot after his death, Pierre Imbert described him as someone who wove the diverse threads of the Haitian community into a single tapestry through the Center:

"He was a true father in every sense of the term," said Pierre Imbert, executive director of the Haitian Multi-Service Center in Dorchester, which Jeannot founded in 1978. "The sense of community didn't come until he came," added Imbert, wiping away tears. "Pe [pè—father in Haitian Creole] Jeannot was the glue that brought this community together." . . . Helping immigrants struggling for social and economic advancement, the Center is much more than a human service agency: It is the tightknit population's town square, the place they gather for news about Haiti or their community. And the one person who would never say no to any request for help was Jeannot. (Tench 2001)

One parishioner's 1994 media statement described St. Leo's as a place enabling her to live and feel part of a family: "St. Leo's is my life," says Carol Millien. "It's like a family. I love it so much. It's like I am in Haiti. I would like to move to Florida but I am staying here. I can't leave my family behind" (Manly 1994). The parish's success arose from enabling parishioners (and others) to tack between sacred and secular realms through the social services provided:

This is about the balance between the words of the Bible and the ways of the streets. St. Leo's has become more than a place of worship, where practicing Catholics can receive the sacraments, make confessions and study the Bible. St. Leo's also provides a myriad of social services to bridge the gap. (Manly 1994)

From the charism of pastoral power flowing among the pastor and parishioners, the Haitian Multi-Service Center emerged as a secular, professional, but "pastoral" institution—a bulwark against the external challenges of racism, crime, and legal insecurity—that promoted literacy, job training, health, citizenship, and "salvation" in temporal realms.

OPPORTUNITIES INDUSTRIALIZATION CENTER

While resident Haitian nuns began offering childcare, and volunteer parishioners taught ESL classes in St. Leo's' careworn Victorian buildings, a small group of Haitian professionals began meeting in another part of Boston each Sunday to draft a proposal for a Haitian social service center. The proposed program was modeled on the Opportunities Industrialization Center (OIC), a Philadelphia-based vocational training organization founded in 1964 by African American pastor Rev. Leon H. Sullivan.[11] Sullivan established hundreds of branches in the United States and developing countries.[12] In partnership with IBM, OIC provided a twelve-week, seven-hour-a-day course in a simulated office environment requiring a dress code. The federally funded Boston OIC branch gained recognition for "turn[ing] jobless, disadvantaged Boston residents into employees with salable skills in word processing, data entry, computer operations, and computer programming, at no cost to the students" (Kidder 1993). At the time, two Center founders, Evelyn Prophète and Frantz Monestime, worked at the OIC Boston branch.

The Center pioneers' proposal for a Haitians-serving-Haitians social service program was not the first, nor would it be the last. In the 1980s, other major Haitian organizations provided comprehensive services to Haitian refugees and immigrants. The earliest, the Cambridge Haitian-American Association (CHAMA), served the Haitian community from 1975 until September 1991 (when the IRS seized its assets for failure to pay back taxes). The League of Haitian Families, established in Boston's Back Bay in 1984, later moved to the South End until its closure as a result of bankruptcy in 1992. Both organizations suffered from common vulnerabilities facing grassroots nonprofits:

> Shoestring budgets, limited cash flow, burgeoning needs, and poor management all contributed to the demise of CHAMA and the league [*sic*]. Grants from private sources were always welcome, but they were rarely sufficient to meet operating costs. Government agencies such as the Department of Public Health and the Massachusetts Office of Refugees and Immigrants provided funding, as well, but only through a cost-reimbursement arrangement. The result: there was never enough money to keep up with the rent, the payroll, the telephone bill, the emergencies, and, most important . . . to pay closer attention to how money was being spent. (Ray 1992)

The League's former director remarked, "We come from a culture whereby if you had money and it was a choice between paying taxes and paying people, you pay the people. To us, that may be a good quality; to the IRS, it is not" (Ray 1992). This statement offers an important counternarrative to discourses of Haitian "corruption." The ethics of paying people illustrates a moral economy promoting "life as livelihoods" among Haitians who fought to establish sustainable advocacy institutions.

The third major Haitian organization assisting refugees, the Haitian Multi-Service Center, would not be immune from similar fiscal and material challenges. In 1992, a Center legal aid coordinator described additional obstacles Haitian social service organizations confronted to meet the needs of refugees: "There are so many emergencies that you can't keep up. . . . The refugees have medical issues and financial issues, and we have to respond to those. . . . We try, we really try, as much as possible to set them up in some comfort" (Ray 1992). At the time, the Center had an in-house refugee resettlement program. After the refugees' arrival in Boston, the program's staff members would screen them for literacy in English and place them in the Center's ESL classes or in an appropriate Haitian Creole class (for those who could not read or write their native language). Staff members also found refugees housing and employment opportunities and assisted them with the process of applying for political asylum. Staff even obtained clothing and furniture donations from factories to help the migrants with their transition. The Center also offered counseling, document translation services, training for nurses and home health aides, and maternal/child health education in the Sante Manman program (Ray 1992).

At a time when federal antipoverty programs were diminishing and anti-immigrant sentiments were growing, instituting a sustainable program would prove enormously difficult. Center founders' stories epitomize the trials of migration, social integration, and the tribulations of institution-building. In response to the Haitian community's growth in the United States, both Haitian cultural and Catholic modes of care informed the strategies and tactics employed to establish a formal institution, (re)producing a complex moral economy.

FOUNDER FRANTZ PÉRALTE MONESTIME

I was surprised by how much Frantz Monestime chose to share given his initial reluctance to speak (see Chapter 1). He was born on November 7, 1942, in Hinche, a small city in Haiti's Central Plateau, during an intense period of suppression of Haitian Vodou by the Catholic Church and Haitian state. With matrilineal connections to Charlemagne Péralte, the famous guerilla revolutionary who fought against the American occupation of Haiti (1915–34), he was a proud businessman who had accomplished much despite deadly obstacles.

Although my previous research should have prepared me, I wasn't expecting to receive his trauma narrative. The oldest of sixteen children (eleven boys and five girls), Monestime completed primary and secondary schooling in Hinche, then studied medicine in Port-au-Prince at the state university medical school until his studies were interrupted by political turmoil. Delivered in a factual manner, his words of rupture were jarring: "When Duvalier killed my father . . . we left Haiti to go into political asylum." Stunned by this disclosure, I waited for him to finish telling me he had completed a year of school in the United States and another year in Spain while in exile before returning to the United States permanently. Then I asked if he'd be willing to discuss the circumstances surrounding his father's death. He agreed, saying, "It is something everybody knows, and I have even spoken about it before on the radio."

Between 1957 and 1986, François and Jean-Claude Duvalier created a climate of fear through disappearances, random attacks on organizations and associations, and assaults against members of civil society previously deemed innocent and untouchable—women, the elderly, children, and clergy, and so on (Trouillot 1990). Among those targeted, however, were members of the Haitian army whom Papa Doc suspected of treason. Monestime's father was a prominent military officer who was executed at Fort Dimanche alongside four other family members serving in the military.[13] On that day, nineteen military officers were killed for reputedly plotting against the president.

After the three-day trial, Monestime told me, the execution took place on Thursday, June 8, 1967, at four o'clock in the afternoon, the same day the verdict was read. He learned about the execution from a local barber who heard the news on the radio before the stations were silenced. Monestime was told the news while on a night walk with his cousin, the Haitian vice consul to Canada. He had to mobilize his family quickly to avoid further reprisals. Later the same night the family hid to await an opportunity to seek asylum at the American Embassy. At twenty-four years old, Frantz became the de facto head of the family. He was now responsible for hiding and disguising them so they could make their escape. The journey to the embassy was an ordeal. The large group divided into two the next morning and pretended to be families dropping off their children at school. Monestime shared how frightened they were because Duvalier's *tonton makout* regularly surveyed the embassy. The family reached the compound and requested asylum. Duvalier ultimately permitted the women and children under the age of fifteen to leave the country, but he wanted to execute everyone over the age of sixteen. Although Frantz's mother and young siblings were able to leave in August, he and his brother were trapped at the embassy until January 1968. Diligent efforts made to solicit external support from the United Nations, the Organization of American States, the International Committee of the Red Cross, the Vatican, and President Lyndon B. Johnson ultimately yielded their freedom. Freedom did not come without scars. Frantz said for years he had nightmares about the flight to the embassy, his period of internment, and the escape from Haiti.

Although the details of the execution and flight were shocking and unanticipated, I was struck by his ability to speak publicly about the execution of his father in contrast with his stated reluctance or, perhaps, his refusal to speak about the founding of the Center and his role as executive director. What had made his tenure so challenging?

In May 1970, after settling in the United States, Monestime began working at the OIC of Greater Boston as an ESL teacher. With its mission of "Helping People Help Themselves,"[14] OIC trained Monestime to evaluate clients in reading, math, and other workplace skills using the Jewish Employment and Vocational Service (JEVS) Evaluation System.[15] He said OIC used a "theory of the whole person" and targeted programs to "the man who may be coming out of an institution" (i.e., a prison or drug rehabilitation facility) to enable him (or her) to become productive workers through literacy classes and other training. It was at OIC that Monestime first encountered Evelyn Prophète, the Center's cofounder.

EVELYN PROPHÈTE

I found Evelyn Jovian Prophète in January 2011 after a lengthy search ended at a Boston public school fewer than three miles from either St. Leo's or the new Yawkey Center. She was teaching Haitian children who had been evacuated after the 2010 earthquake to learn English and adjust to American culture. As some eight-year-olds had no prior schooling, her work involved basic literacy instruction. Prophète's service resembled the teaching and pastoral care she had previously offered at the Center and the formative expertise gained in vocational rehabilitation at OIC.

When the last student had left, we sat at one of the small round children's tables to discuss how she came to the United States and her role in launching the Center. She was born in 1958 in Léogâne, Haiti—the epicenter of the devastating 2010 earthquake—one of six children, four girls and two boys. Until the 1960s, her father worked for a large sugarcane manufacturing company with headquarters in Canada. He then decided to leave Haiti for Toronto but ultimately settled in Montreal. The rest of the family joined him when she was in high school.

Prophète did not have an easy time in Canada and returned to Haiti at a very young age to marry someone who was almost the same age as her father. It was an act of rebellion, she said, implying she had wanted to escape her family's control by marrying the older man. Marriage would not provide an easy escape—her husband was authoritarian and abusive. Her father managed to have the marriage dissolved (she did not explain how) and her parents raised her three children in Canada so she could go back to school. An aunt living in Boston told Prophète about a program in Roxbury, Massachusetts, providing English language instruction, job training, mentoring, and other services to the poor and newly arrived immigrants, while also paying students a small weekly stipend of $98 to $125 per week. As she described it, "OIC was the only place to learn English . . . look for a job . . . and learn a trade." The program accepted her from Montreal, and she came to the United States.

After meeting her at OIC, Monestime knew Prophète to be a "very smart young lady" who was "dedicated to what she was doing," but who also had a spirit of sacrifice. With his assistance (according to him), OIC hired her. Prophète described the generosity of Mrs. Anderson, an African American OIC administrator who decided to coach her for her employment interview with a manager. Prophète was successful and became a work sample evaluator who tested a person's psychomotor functioning, attention span, and capacity for various kinds of technical skills.

With two Haitian counselors—as well as a third, René George, who conducted intake interviews—Haitians began to flock to OIC. Of the 360 students recruited per month, a growing percentage was Haitian. Monestime said Father Jeannot would send Haitian clients to OIC periodically. According to another Center founder, the program grew to nearly 45 percent Haitian over time. Monestime rationalized how other social service organizations were 100 percent Spanish (it was ambiguous if he was distinguishing the predominant language or the ethnicity of the clientele), and, in addition to facing discrimination at other social service agencies, Haitians were "so hungry for knowledge." Attaining economic independence was also vital to promote family reunification for Haitians who had left loved ones in Haiti and needed to show sufficient income to the INS in order to sponsor them. There was another sociocultural component to their advocacy on

Haitians' behalf arising from gender ideals according to which men were expected to provide financially for their families. Monestime said, "He has to work, have a bank book, and go to immigration to show he can sponsor his wife and kids. We were helping them."

Monestime asserted this assistance was not solely around literacy; through OIC, they helped their compatriots with English language acquisition, and indirectly, immigration advocacy services. His colleagues also prepared Haitians without prior formal education and work skills to enter the "modern" labor force: "Some Haitians came who'd never seen a doctor, ever. . . . People from the countryside, boat people, who'd never seen a doctor or a light bulb." The staff inculcated new disciplines (Foucault 1979) and bodily praxes (Bourdieu 1977), enabling clients to "integrate" more fully into the workplace. Similar to their later assistance to refugees at the Center, Prophète said Monestime taught some OIC Haitian clients "hygiene"—that is, how to use a bathroom, wash dishes, and prepare themselves for laboring in American work settings. Monestime affirmed the Haitian staff made lists of Greater Boston companies' hiring needs, "what kind of work, products, [and] skills, [were] needed." Then the companies conducted trainings at OIC and offered future employment for clients.

In a 2007 interview, "Murielle Estimé," a Center health educator who assisted Haitian elders, told me she had attended OIC of Greater Boston. In 1979, she migrated to Boston as a "resident alien" sponsored by her husband, who had emigrated the previous year. She studied English, then completed training in microelectronics, working for seven years as a manufacturer at Teradyne (a corporation creating electronic systems to test semiconductors).[16] She next spent ten years in a similar capacity at Raytheon (an electronic defense systems company).[17] A few years later, Center volunteers provided similar, although less formal, vocational rehabilitation training and accompanied clients to their new places of employment to show them the routines needed to operate factory machinery.

By the early 1980s at OIC, the practice of favoritism for Haitian clients ultimately caused trouble for its Haitian personnel, and (perhaps) exacerbated the fiscal shortfalls OIC had already suffered as a result of cuts in federal funding. Both Monestime and Prophète described a visit President Ronald Reagan made to OIC of Greater Boston. Each linked the presidential visit to OIC's decline in the 1980s and, implicitly, to their own loss of employment. On January 26, 1983, Reagan visited three institutions in "enterprise zones" to highlight how partnerships between private firms and community-based NGOs combat urban poverty by preparing youth and disadvantaged persons to work in the high technology sector. OIC Boston staff members hoped the visit would yield additional funding for the national OIC organization and their local office. Cuts in federal funding for "manpower" programs (since Reagan had taken office in 1981) had forced the Boston OIC office to reduce staff from 110 to twenty-eight by the time of the 1983 presidential visit (Kidder 1983). Although one news article said Reagan's reaction to OIC appeared positive, someone present during the visit felt "the President was just 'setting up for the next election'" (Kidder 1983). When asked "whether the presidential visit had made any converts" of Reagan or his staff to the OIC anti-poverty model, an OIC administrator replied, "I don't think so" (Kidder 1983).

Both Monestime and Prophète asserted Reagan ultimately "shut down" the Boston OIC program because of his negative reaction to seeing the disproportionately minority (and Haitian) trainee population. Although I cannot verify the timing of OIC's eventual closure, and although neither Center founder admitted this directly, both Monestime and Prophète (as well as other Haitian OIC employees) were among those laid off around 1983.

Haitians perceived Reagan's administrative policy decisions to be anti-minority, anti-poor, anti-immigrant, and anti-Haitian, preventing them from accessing the OIC social service programs that once provided a path toward economic security and social integration. Indeed, Murielle Estimé attributed OIC's generosity to the benevolent policies under President Carter:

> *ECJ:* When you arrived here did you work right away?
>
> *ME:* No. I went to school. I went to school for almost a year . . . By this time, they had the school for immigrants. . . . You go to school and get your paycheck every Friday.
>
> *ECJ:* Really? . . . They pay you to go to school?
>
> *ME:* They pay you to go to school. You don't pay, and every Friday, each student gets his paycheck.
>
> *ECJ:* You're kidding!!
>
> *ME:* With Carter. . . . Jimmy Carter. This program ends with Ronald Reagan. That's when we lose the opportunities.

The macropolitical and economic shifts from the 1970s to the 1980s discouraged the expansion of the "charitable state" (Wacquant 2009) and likely played a role in OIC's eventual decline in Boston. Beyond the decline of the welfare state, the 1980s would pose tremendous difficulties for Haitians in terms of immigration policy (see Chapter 3), producing a sense of crisis in Greater Boston Haitians to which the Center's founders responded. Nonprofit institutions increasingly assumed the "burden" of providing social welfare to the poor and other disadvantaged populations and would extend assistance to help establish the Center—but not without a cost.

FOUNDING THE CENTER AT ST. LEO'S

From mid-1981 to 1982, as Haitian immigrants and refugees increased and institutional opportunities to help them establish new lives diminished, Monestime, Prophète, and other founders began planning to create their own Haitian social service center. Among the early founders were René George from OIC, André Charles (a young Haitian college student and OIC volunteer living in the same building as Prophète), Esther Lichtenstein (a woman the group met through Monestime's younger brother, Perard, a Catholic seminary student studying to become a priest), Monique Brun, who was a public school teacher, and a few others.[18] Perard Monestime had brought Lichtenstein to OIC to see the program and learn about Haitians' needs. She offered the group five thousand dollars to create a center "by Haitians, for Haitians." Each Sunday the group met in either Prophète's or Monestime's homes to draft a proposal, and the group eventually sought a space and additional financial support.

Although the group approached some Haitian Protestant churches for space, each requested rent, which would squander the limited funds in hand. The founders considered an abandoned building the City of Boston had sold for one dollar to another short-lived Haitian organization (Cecoama), but they felt the choice was too risky. The group approached St. Kevin's, where the St. Leo nuns had formerly resided, but space was unavailable. Ultimately, the Center found a permanent home at St. Leo Parish. As one founder reported, St. Leo's was a Haitian parish by the time the group began meeting, "and we had Father Jeannot. We were looking for a place with no money and went to see him."

According to Prophète, at the first meeting with Father Jeannot the group shared the troubles the Haitian OIC staff had had as well as the challenges of launching a social service program to serve "their own people." Although preferential access for Haitians could be considered "corrupt"—verifying external international and American depictions of Haitian institutions and professionals as lacking transparency and accountability—such tactics were "public secrets," likely arising from a moral economy rooted in critiques of structural injustices. They presented these events as evidence of bias in foreign and domestic policy against ethnic and racial minorities, and specifically, Haitians. In accepting how some founders' tactics at OIC curtailed Haitians' access to its social services, Jeannot's mercy reinforced a sense that St. Leo's was a space of cultural intimacy. At St. Leo's, where most founders once attended the Catholic Mass as parishioners, they found recognition and solidarity.

After the founders presented their Center proposal, Father Jeannot informed them it was timely because the nuns had a plan to open a formal daycare; furthermore, a parish council member and another woman parishioner had begun some informal English language programs. He suggested these efforts would be stronger if combined and offered space for a food pantry, clothing donations, classes, and other services. The group later met with the Haitian nuns. Acquiring archdiocesan approval was a last step before proceeding. Jeannot and Monestime met with Father Thomas Daily and other priests at the Chancery who agreed to provide administrative support, fundraising assistance, and a small stipend for volunteers.[19] Monestime became the first executive director.

The process of establishing the formal "Haitian Multi-Service Center" took a couple years. Each founder agreed that in 1984, the institution began to be presented as an autonomous program housed at St. Leo's under the umbrella of the Archdiocese of Boston. Despite its structural location, the founders affirmed the Center was a secular, rather than faith-based, institution. From the beginning, it operated primarily with volunteer support. Founders used their own vehicles and personal resources to solicit donations of food and clothing from area businesses. ABCD, Inc., the nonprofit housing its Head Start daycare program at St. Leo's in the 1960s, returned the gift of early support by providing chairs and desks for the Center's "school." The sisters cared for the children of students who came to the ESL classes. When it came to day-to-day financial matters, Monestime and another founder managed accounts. The archdiocese allowed the Center to use its 501(c)(3) nonprofit legal status for grant proposals. The first corporate funding (four to five thousand dollars) came from the Boston Gas Company. Other early monies came from state budget earmarks for refugee resettlement that the Massachusetts Office of Refugee Resettlement (MORI), established in 1985, received from the federal government.[20] Monestime and Prophète soon began retrieving Haitian parolees—who had been granted asylee status and were released into their custody—from the Krome Service Processing Center in Miami.

BRANDING THE CENTER

In March 1984, after the death of Cardinal Humberto Medeiros—who had struggled with "reorganizing the archdiocese, reinvigorating the Church, paying off the monstrous debt, and . . . the agonizing ordeal of the city's racial problems" (O'Connor 1998: 304)—Bernard Francis Law, then bishop of the Springfield-Cape Girardeau Diocese in Missouri, was installed as archbishop of the Archdiocese of Boston (Glendon 2002: xxvi). In response to mounting debts accumulated under his predecessors and demographic changes necessitating the restructuring of existing parishes (O'Connor 1998: 306–9), Archbishop Law began reorganizing the archdiocese.[21] According to a Charity administrator present during this period, Law initiated a formal assessment of Catholic social service programs at roughly the same time. The results suggested a shift from a regional model of service delivery—in operation since a previous restructuring in 1971—to a more centralized management structure with CCAB, the Charity, as the lead agency. The reorganization would not only standardize the quality of services offered across the agency but also reduce administrative redundancies. The meaning of "quality," however, would become a point of contestation: in addition to "quality control," a former Center executive director claimed the reorganization was intended to ensure all Catholics and Catholic institutions adhered to an "orthodox" interpretation of Church tenets and conformed to the corporate Catholic culture Law attempted to inculcate.

In a move provoking mixed feelings in the Haitian community, the Center became one of four formerly semi-autonomous programs administered directly by the Chancery to be acquired by the Charity (CCAB 1995: 19). According to some sources, the Charity was reluctant to manage the Center because it was not perceived to be "in the mold" of its other programs. But most of the early stakeholders with whom I have spoken (both Haitian and non-Haitian) felt the Charity "coveted" the public successes and social capital the Center had earned by the mid-1980s.

The Center's visibility increased in the Boston media, especially in 1986, when Haitian president Jean-Claude Duvalier was ousted. The burgeoning Haitian community congregated at the Center and St. Leo's as the political drama unfolded. During this period, a White employee lamented how Charity staff persons began to appear on-site for the first time to take photos of Haitian daycare children to be used for the Charity's promotional purposes: "The prominence of the Haitian Multi-Service Center was attracting attention from Catholic Charities. The archdiocese wanted it moved under the auspices of Catholic Charities, and they [Catholic Charities] were using a lot of the pictures from our day care center to raise money." On November 5, 1987, the Center was once again in the media, when Cardinal Law and Mayor Raymond Flynn (who had previously granted the Center $219,000 to fund the basic English language program) jointly issued press statements on-site in support of undocumented migrants. Both Cardinal Law and Mayor Flynn criticized federal immigration reform measures:

> Cardinal Bernard Law and Mayor Flynn, saying the federal amnesty program for aliens has been a failure, joined with the Massachusetts Immigrant and Refugee Advocacy Coalition yesterday in calling for an extension of the amnesty deadline next May. "The promise of the amnesty bill has not been fulfilled," Law said at a news conference in the Haitian Multi-Service Center in Dorchester. Fear, he added, is keeping thousands from applying to the Immigration and Naturalization Service for legal status.[22]

Many of the Center's clients were among the populations fearful of pursuing amnesty through the program. Nonetheless, the HMSC provided a visual backdrop against which Cardinal Law and Mayor Flynn addressed these political barriers to migrant incorporation.

What was particularly interesting, however, were the underlying racial politics embedded in the debate. Further analysis reveals additional symbolic roles the Center and its clients played not only in the archdiocese but also in city politics. Two weeks before the press conference, on October 23, 1987, Mayor Flynn testified before the Senate Judiciary Committee's Subcommittee on Immigration and Refugee Affairs, telling the committee members, "It is wrong that literally tens of thousands of young people from Ireland and other nations must today live shadow-like existences in our nation's largest cities such as Boston, New York and Chicago—cities that their family members from previous generations helped to build" (Blake 1987). According to estimates made at the time, there were roughly equal numbers of "illegal" Irish and Haitian immigrants in Boston (Blake 1987). On October 1, the city had opened the "Immigrant Rights Unit" aimed primarily at aiding undocumented Irish immigrants because of the city's Irish heritage (although persons of other national backgrounds would be eligible). In response, David Johnson, one of only two European Americans who served as the HMSC Executive Director (ca. 1987–90), overlapping with Dr. Helene Hayes (ca. 1986–88), was publicly critical of the new program in a statement to the *New York Times*:

> "To target the Irish has to do with race and is not helpful across the board," said David E. Johnson, director of the Hatian [*sic*] Multiservice Center. "We have strong cultural and ancestral ties to Ireland but we also have strong business and foreign policy ties to Haiti and Central America."[23]

Given Johnson's critique of Boston's program, it seems reasonable to assume the church and state officials also held the November press conference at the Center to demonstrate their respective accountability to undocumented persons of other racial, ethnic, and national backgrounds in Boston. Haitians (and the Center) became a visual representation of the care and advocacy these church and municipal leaders extended to undocumented migrants of color.

By the late 1980s, when it became clear the Charity would definitively acquire the Center, leaders in the Haitian community began meeting to discuss whether the merger could be stopped. The group received an appointment with a former Charity president, Dr. Joseph Doolin, to talk about the proposed merger.[24] Over the next fourteen years, until his resignation a few months after the 2003 Dorchester community service center sign unveiling ceremony, Doolin would play a pivotal and controversial role in the Center's future. In July 1989, Doolin succeeded Rev. Richard J. Craig to become the first layperson to serve as president of the Charity. He came to the position not only with extensive experience in human services but also as an archdiocesan insider. The South Boston native had earned a doctorate in sociology and social work from Boston University and a master's degree in public administration from the University of Massachusetts at Boston. For many years he had been a development officer for Federated Dorchester Neighborhood Houses, an organization founded when three settlement houses combined to offer education, health, human, and social services to area children, youth, and adults.[25] After leaving this position, he served ten years as an executive director of the Kit Clark House, a program that "provided health and social services for more than a third of Boston's elderly," including transportation, a mobile feeding program, and housing (Franklin 1989). Doolin next became the director of the Archdiocesan Office on Aging.

One Haitian Center stakeholder present at the meeting with Doolin described the occasion in terms that recalled Michael Herzfeld's (1992) discussions of bureaucratic indifference. In his view, the "delegation" was neither accorded respect nor recognition. The feeling of humiliation this individual conveyed highlighted the limited civic power Haitians possessed, despite the many successes they and the Center had previously achieved:

Delegate: The people in the community were not too happy about [the proposed merger] and started to have big meetings [with] many people and many community leaders. . . . It was not quite totally clear that they [the Charity] were taking over at the beginning or quite right away. Because at the point there when [the community] finally realized that and people started to talk about . . . it in a way, trying to attract other people's attention and to start people talking about that. . . . I think it was a little after 1987 [*sic*]. . . . We had a delegation of people and went to meet with Doolin [*laughs ruefully and with chagrin*]. DOOLIN!! He was like, "Hunh, what are you talking about?" . . . He gave an impression that I was making up stories, and I was fabricating something, OK, because he "knows nothing about this."

ECJ: Did you believe him?

Delegate: I was shocked . . . that this gentleman didn't know anything about the existence of the Center. In other words, . . . it was like I was making a false claim! . . . I decided I didn't need to talk to him anymore and I walked away. I decided to stop giving money to the Center, too. Because whenever there [were events] for fundraising, I always gave something. . . . But these people . . .

Since Doolin only joined the Charity in 1989, it is possible he may not yet have been aware of the turmoil the impending transfer of the Center from the Chancery had caused in the Haitian community. Haitians perceived they were being cut off from the locus of pastoral power to which they previously had access by being in direct contact with archdiocesan administrators. In nearly all my interviews with Haitians, individual archdiocesan clergy were remembered fondly, especially Cardinal Law.

But there were other reasons for the community unrest over this transfer. One Center founder said in early conversations with Chancery clergy there had been an understanding the Center would ultimately become independent. This person likened the eventual transfer to the Charity as a betrayal of trust, and a deep violation of the blind faith this person had in the Church:

Founder: To the community, to us it was like dealing with God. It was like . . . believing in you, like, blind . . . you know that. If I am in the hand of God, what do I have to be afraid of? And then when I turn around and find out I was in the hands of . . . [*long pause*]. You know!?! Then, ah, you become a different [person]. You become a different [person].

ECJ: In what ways do you become different?

Founder: [*Long pause*]
The way I used to see them, I can no longer in my whole life see them like that again. . . . They are different people now, probably. It's like, these people . . . are bringing God to me. They are the one's putting *l'Eucharistie* [the Eucharist] on my tongue. They are the ones putting the host on my tongue. And I told you that, we trust[ed] them like God.

A European American volunteer described how in the mid-1980s there was tremendous ambivalence between the Haitian and non-Haitian Center staff members seemingly rooted in racial and ethnic differences. Some staff members also felt they were not treated as "equals"—either as persons or as an organization—to other programs in the Charity network, which included having their own board of trustees, rather than having (at the time) a relatively weak advisory board:

> My memory of this was that the board of directors, the board of trustees for Catholic Charities, was *the* board, so that they were the umbrella group, and that all we could have was an advisory board. And I think we began to have the advisory board . . . but . . . it just felt as though there was a power struggle a little bit with the desire for Catholic Charities to have [the Center], 'cause it was an attractive program right in the inner city—but then at the same time . . . I think that the staff, some of them . . . would have wanted their own board of directors. There was an ambivalent relationship. Dependent, hostile-dependent . . . and I didn't touch that one.

This same individual felt that the archdiocese, through the Charity, kept the Center in a position of tutelage or dependency, rather than support it to become independent. Possessing the Center and its clients was "useful":

> You know I did not know much about the other agencies and Haitian programs [outside the Charity network], but I believe the HMSC was the most stable and in the growth mode. And it was almost as though they were kept somewhat dependent on the archdiocese. And then when the archdiocese wanted to do a fundraising pamphlet or something, [it seemed as if they said,] "It would be very nice to have all of these beautiful little Haitian children in the picture." . . . The Haitian staff that I worked with were very bright and they kind of got it that we only saw this . . . person with the camera once in two years or something. So, there was some of it, but I also think that it's the powerlessness of the Haitians that I perceived operating, and there would be a sensitivity to any suggestion that they couldn't run their own show.

After the acquisition, some Haitians felt that they as an ethnic immigrant group and the Center had lost independence (and social status). Others felt the move engendered greater stability and financial support. These tensions solidified in the institutional relationships among the Church, Charity, and Center over the next decade, and would erupt into disputes in the media around issues of sex, sexuality, and Catholic social teachings.

5

Corporate Secrets

I have this saying after working with some of the small villages where the women get trafficked, . . . like how they say, "power corrupts," [pausing, and speaking with deep sadness], *powerlessness corrupts, too!*

—SISTER "MARGARET CHAPMAN," HAITIAN MULTI-SERVICE CENTER VOLUNTEER (CA. 1985–87)

Voice has the function of alerting a firm or organization to its failings, but it must then give management, old or new, some time to respond to the pressures that have been brought to bear on it.

—ALBERT O. HIRSCHMAN

In many of their founders' stories, Haitians and Center stakeholders who supported them banded together against external societal forces (or institutional authorities) blocking their incorporation as equals in either church or state. Their memory palace depicted the Center as a predominantly benevolent pastoral space. But their memory palace also holds shadows. In almost every interview with the Center's pioneers, I received dramatic stories of rupture, disappointment, loss, and even scandal, all of which challenged its public image as a sanctuary.

One interview raised questions I wasn't sure I wanted to pursue. At the conclusion of a long conversation with a 1980s volunteer, I was handed a stack of documents that had been saved for nearly thirty years. There were fragments of grant proposals, a paper written on Haitian understandings of illness and the body, and a draft of a curious letter from the "Committee Against Injustice in the Haitian Community" (hereafter, CAIHC), the text of which addressed an unnamed "Dear Bishop." I quickly read the letter and asked what prompted the CAIHC to write it. Its contents and the other written fragments accompanying it complicate the portrait of the Center I have painted thus far, especially regarding its relationship to St. Leo Parish and the archdiocese. I shared the letter in subsequent conversations with other Center stakeholders who were active in the early 1980s, and I asked what may have provoked its drafting.

The text is reproduced below, exactly as written and in its entirety (but with names of parishioners removed). It reveals how the St. Leo Haitian community struggled to determine who could legitimately exercise pastoral power at the parish. Overcoming difficulties with the English language, the letter's authors appealed to Catholic authorities outside the parish not only to intercede in these interpersonal disputes but also to advocate on behalf of the rights of vulnerable Haitians living under conditions of legal insecurity. The letter also shows its authors perceived themselves as members of the universal Church possessing rights to raise their voices in protest to archdiocesan authorities.

Committee Against
Injustice in the
Haitian Community

May 5, 1983

As Haitian and as Parishioners of St. Leo's Church located in Dorchester we are writing to you, not only to voice our opinion but also to make you aware of the real situation at the Parish. For we do believe that there are always two sides of a story. And the best decision can be made upon hearing both sides.

We are aware that you have been recently visited by Father Jeannot the Parish Priest, and we understand that he had voiced his objection against the sisters presence in the parish, on the basis that they are not doing anything, and they are psychological sick. It is a shame that Father Jeannot did not tell the real reason, and we are sure Reverend, that you know the history of St. Leo's ever since Father Jeannot set in. But we would like to share some facts with you.

1. There is no such thing as the Parish Council as Father Jeannot would want you to believe. There is of course a Triumvirate made up of ________, ________, and ________.
2. The same Triumvirate not only controls Father Jeannot, but influences his decision. Sad but true.
3. This Triumvirate has no voice in the community as claimed, therefore cannot speak for the community.
4. This triumvirate has failed to have the community raise against the sisters. They threatened the sisters over the phone as the last recourse.
5. This triumvirate has made false accusations against the sisters by saying that they are not doing anything.
6. Whatever the activities that the sisters try to undertake, this triumvirate is always after destroying them.
7. Finally, this triumvirate really thinks that it controls the church.

Unless the power of this triumvirate is curbed Dear Bishop, we would predict that in the next two years, one will see the Parish wither away. It will happen, if the sisters get deported under the pressure of the triumvirate. The Parish is not made up of this triumvirate, but of many of us. It is now a cry in the community in regard to this triumvirate's action to have the sisters deported.

As concerned Parishioners, we take the liberty to voice our opinion against such injustice. We can assure you, Dear Bishop, that there are many voices like us in the community. And we join together in this endeavor to see that the sisters stay and continue their work that is so needed in the Parish as well as the community.

The power struggle seems to be between the triumvirate and the sisters. All it comes down to is that the triumvirate feel threatened by the presence of the sisters in the Parish. It is a sad situation. For a moment we thought Father Jeannot would not have succombed to the power of those three.

But alas, we were more or less hoping that he could develop a better channel of communication with the sisters. It seems to me that bond is broken.

In closing Dear we would like to say that before making any decision please consult with the other party. You will be surprised. But we guarantee that there are a lot of us who are working to see that St. Leo's Parish become a better Parish, our aim is rather to end the power struggle that is going on now. For with such atmosphere, a lot of parishioner decide to stay home instead of being parts of it.

If necessary we can provide you with a petition signed by members of the community just to prove to you that it is not the community that does not want the sisters, rather a miniature group as the triumvirate struggling for its own power in the parish.

Please receive our salutations and best wishes.
Thank you.
Sincerely yours

. . .

The Center and St. Leo Parish did not provide sanctuary to all. For some of its more vulnerable Haitian members, these institutions were spaces of insecurity, exploitation, and, possibly, abuse. Each institution could resemble not a refuge but a purgatorial space—a disciplinary, normalizing, but also oppressive place of temporary waiting—especially for undocumented migrants, until external actors determined their fates.

But what if these organizations produced exclusion rather than incorporation and inclusion? How are social theorists who analyze the social lives of organizations to understand the relationships between the benevolent public face or brand of value-based entities, organizational decisions perceived as having negative effects, and private or secret practices belying the legitimacy and authenticity of their stated mission? Are these actions—the compassionate and caring, the disciplinary or conversely, the negligent, and the repressive or abusive—related and even intertwined dimensions of pastoral power? As previously described, pastoral power occurs along a continuum from benevolent to malevolent acts. Its force can be generated through spiritual and corporal works of care or "mercy," but also correction or discipline, and public advocacy in civic realms.

Another kind of pastoral power is produced in exploitative or even abusive situations. Although the Center and St. Leo's community engendered cultural intimacy, the negative dimensions of pastoral power also irrupted intermittently. Malevolent pastoral power comprises acts and social processes intended to fracture rather than heal, shame rather than support, and exclude rather than incorporate. Corporate secrets held about an organization in realms of cultural intimacy tend to reinforce, reify, and give "definition and authority to [the organization's] shadowy power" (Herzfeld 1997: 10). Such secrets can also reinforce the power of those persons involved. These conditions created an "atmosphere" that reportedly deterred parishioners from participating in the sacramental life of the Church. By raising their voices in writing, however, the plaintiffs perceived they would be heard, and the Church would respond.

The letter, and the alleged facts underlaying its production, demonstrated unseen aspects of the charitable practices of everyday life. In many respects, the letter was a sign of escalating underlying tensions. It also shows how rumor, jealousy, and accusations of malfeasance could develop into threats and, as will be discussed later, even attempted violence. Although not identical in form or context, these social processes reminded me of the negative dimensions of "bureaucraft" (James 2010)—the way rumor, gossip, accusations, and scapegoating among Haitians and international aid workers developed into symbolic and actual violence in Haiti. Sharing such knowledge drew me more deeply into realms of cultural intimacy among the Center's stakeholders, producing new ethical dilemmas of whether to remain silent or reveal what I had learned.

Father Jeannot, one of the letter's subjects, cannot contest these next allegations, having passed away in 2001. A stakeholder told me many letters were sent to the Archdiocese of Boston about what had happened—but seemingly to no effect. In conversations with other stakeholders with whom I was particularly close, a few suggested letting sleeping dogs lie. Although his words were not necessarily directed at the events described here, as Frantz Monestime has said, some things may be better left unsaid. Others have suggested it is my obligation to analyze these stories and their reputed events in as scholarly a manner as possible. For those who drafted the letter, saved it for nearly three decades, and then gave it to an "outsider," what was at stake is another's sense of injury and justice denied, not merely retribution or my own unease.

Stories about the letter revealed additional obstacles pioneers faced founding the Center in a faith-based governance structure—one subject to pastoral power and lacking transparent accountability mechanisms with which lay complainants could resolve pastoral disputes. These narratives also highlighted the tensions for stakeholders who held knowledge of practices occurring in "private" realms of cultural intimacy—secrets shared among Haitians in the parish, at the Center, and possibly, with clerics in the Church—and modes of representation or display intended for those "outside," such as Center funders or administrators. Depending on the context and to whom one spoke, the boundaries of inside and outside—whether of the parish, the Center, the "Haitian community," or other "imagined communities" (Anderson 2006)—shifted.

Given the realities of everyday charitable life at St. Leo's, the other documents accompanying the letter suggested advocating on the Center's behalf with "outsiders" required framing Haitians' needs effectively to solicit material, financial, and in-kind support. Embarrassing, shameful, and perhaps "sinful" practices became productive objects for intervention, creating opportunities for staff members and other Haitian professionals to develop and display their expertise in social welfare provision and promotion of public health. At the same time, Center staff recognized, accepted, but also attempted to transform harmful cultural practices and behaviors that reproduced negative psychosocial legacies of Haiti's troubled past.

• • •

"Louis Léon" was one of the Center's pioneers. He migrated to the United States with his family in the early 1970s, and he completed undergraduate and graduate degrees in business administration at a time when the Haitian community was being stigmatized unjustly as a vector of HIV/AIDS (Farmer 1992; Sabatier 1988). In the early 1980s, he aided the Center with administrative work and grant writing. While I sought clarity on the relationship between the Center and the parish, and the roles each played for Haitians, a Center founder referred me to him.

I was also curious to speak with him because I had received the CAIHC letter prior to the meeting and was still attempting to interpret it. Why were the Haitian sisters considered a threat to the "triumvirate" and to Father Jeannot's administration of the parish? Why were they being threatened with deportation? I knew the sisters cared for Haitians' children during their evening ESL classes, and eventually, during the day to allow parents to work. Harold Jackson described them as "civilians," perhaps because their professional (and legal) status at St. Leo's was uncertain. As the letter indicates, not only was parish governance in dispute, but also who could claim and receive sanctuary onsite.

Léon and I met at his office; he served as a higher education administrator. We made small talk as I looked at photos he had mounted on the walls. One framed news article depicted Jeannot receiving what Léon said was the Center's first corporate donation, a check from the Eastern Associated Foundation (affiliated with the Boston Gas Company). As the caption described, the gift's intent was "to help convert the parish's convent into a community center," which provided "child-care facilities, family life education and other services to Haitian immigrants, who now number about 10,000."

In response to my query about the relationship between the Center, St. Leo's, the Church, and its Chancery, Léon carefully distinguished each entity and hinted at management problems arising from the Center's link to Catholic institutions.

> *LL:* St. Leo Parish's was like a Haitian parish, and we had Father Jeannot. We were looking for a place for the Center, and we didn't have any money. So, we went to see Father Jeannot and the rectory was basically empty. There were many rooms there. Then we contacted ABCD [Action for Boston Community Development, Inc.] and they gave us some chairs and old desks . . . and that was the beginning of it. . . .
>
> *ECJ:* I've heard people mention a woman named _______.
>
> *LL:* [*laughing cheerfully*] She was very active in the Church.
>
> *ECJ:* Did she have any kind of program [at St. Leo's]? The reason why I am asking is that Catholic Charities still lists a date of 1978 for the start of the Center on its website.
>
> *LL:* That's where the confusion came. . . . St. Leo's Parish existed. . . . It was like a place for Haitians to come and gather, but it wasn't a Center. The Haitian Multi-Service Center basically started after, and we need to distinguish between the two. . . .
>
> *ECJ:* Did you all incorporate?
>
> *LL:* [After the Center began operating at St. Leo's,] I ended up sending a proposal to the archdiocese and they liked the idea and wanted to meet with us. And it was very difficult for us to raise funds so that's why we came under the archdiocese to make it easier for us.

Léon told me part of the reason the archdiocese was interested in supporting the fledgling Center was the attractiveness (both pastorally and financially) of a predominantly minority institution offering social services to Haitian immigrants and refugees (and other poor minority populations): "Haitian refugees were high profile. We got money to do refugee resettlement of Haitians from Florida." His views echoed those of other volunteers who worked with the agency at the same time.

According to a Charity administrator who worked at the Massachusetts Office for Refugees and Immigrants (MORI) in the 1990s, the Center's early funding for refugee resettlement likely came from the DHHS Office of Refugee Resettlement's contract with the USCCB (see Chapter 3). Federal dollars were "passed through" to MORI, which oversaw how the Center implemented the contract as the local archdiocesan agency. Some funding helped relocate Haitians paroled from the Krome Service Processing Center while regularizing their legal status. At the end of 1982, Prophète and Monestime flew to Miami to receive these released Krome detainees, and Center staff members housed them in an apartment rented for them.

The institutional partnerships between government agencies and private faith-based organizations to provide migrants and refugees (among others) social welfare had implicit roots in an economy of salvation. To recall, the term "economy" incorporates a notion of managing a household or community's resources, supervision of bodies and regimens of living, and in the theological sense, the divine governance of creation.[1] For most Center pioneers, the Center's purpose was ethnic and even nationalist, rather than solely charitable. Given the structural impediments to achieving a sustainable nonprofit, especially in the 1980s, Léon suggested the relationship between the Center and Church was mutually beneficial and enabled the founders to raise funds despite the climate of racial and ethnic discrimination against Haitians in Greater Boston and the United States. He told me Center staff members wrote draft grant proposals, the archdiocese would "make corrections and sign off," and then send the proposals out under its own name and nonprofit legal status.

> *ECJ:* So how did that work?
>
> *LL:* Whatever proposal we did they signed the proposal. . . . Most of the decision-making was basically with us. In terms of payroll later on, [they handled it].
>
> *ECJ:* Were they kind of a grant manager?
>
> *LL:* You could say that.
>
> *ECJ:* You didn't incorporate as a nonprofit?
>
> *LL:* No.
>
> *ECJ:* Who was able to sign checks?
>
> *LL:* Day-to-day things required two signatures, Monestime and I.
>
> *ECJ:* Did you have your own bank account?
>
> *LL:* Yes, an account was set up through the Archdiocese of Boston. . . . We did have a checkbook.

When the grants were disbursed, Léon said, "Whatever money would come [in] was sent to [the archdiocese]," which would reimburse the Center for costs incurred in running programs. Oversight of day-to-day administration of the Center was left in its founders' hands: "Most of the things were left for us to do."

The arrangement resembled the model I had observed in Haiti in the 1990s of America's Development Foundation (ADF), a secular 501(c)(3) "private voluntary organization," serving as the "procurement structure" through which federal dollars flowed from USAID in Washington, DC to USAID/Haiti, and through ADF to the Human Rights Fund. In the example of the Center, however, founding staff members were not initially paid and programming was rather ad hoc. "Did you get paid?" I asked. Léon responded, "Actually I didn't for over a year. Well, I was young . . . I didn't even know what to do with my money. Every day I rode my bicycle from Cambridge to the Center—I was young and had energy—and the next day I did the same thing. Finally, the archdiocese decided to give me a stipend, probably like two hundred dollars [a month], I don't even remember."

Monestime, Prophète, and other founders had used personal resources to solicit donations and supplies, until a later point when the archdiocese provided limited stipends to staff members, including, it seems, the nuns for their childcare. In a context of a high demand for services, especially because of the large influx of Haitian migrants to Boston in the 1980s, conflicts over flows of donated goods, programming routines, and labor stipends eventually precipitated an administrative crisis. Léon attributed many challenges to fellow Haitians' social and cultural practices.

> *ECJ:* How did people find out about the Center?
>
> *LL:* Well, St. Leo's Parish was right there. The word got out that there's a Center there and we started out by offering ESL. But the demand for ESL was unbelievable. But the problem was that volunteering was not part of the Haitian [custom] at the time. . . . So many volunteer teachers would disappear without telling you anything . . . sometimes I had to take over. It was hard at the beginning; then later on things started working fine.
>
> *ECJ:* When you say Haitians don't have a history of volunteering . . .
>
> *LL:* The idea of "What's in it for me?" is always there.

Scholars of Haiti have described several types of mutual assistance organizations, especially in rural Haiti. These include, among others, the *sosyete*—large, hierarchical civil society organizations carrying out collective labor (i.e., transporting loads, construction), adjudicating disputes, and offering support in times of sickness (Smith 2001: 104–13)—and *konbit*, agricultural work parties (Smith 2001: 83–92), as well as rotating credit schemes like *sòl* or *sang*, in which members contribute money to a communal pot the total of which each receives in turn (James 2010). Scholars of diaspora Haitians have also described the role of "hometown associations" in organizing humanitarian aid for natal communities while also aiding Haitian immigrants to "affirm their culture and language" when in the minority (Pierre-Louis 2006: 7). Léon suggests the model of individual volunteerism and philanthropy, perhaps without an expected return gift, was not customary, or part of the "habitus" (Bourdieu 1977) of Haitians with whom he worked. In some respects, this statement accorded with those of others I interviewed and with Haitian social service providers' 2005 qualitative assessment of the strengths and weaknesses of the Greater Boston Haitian community (see Chapter 6).

Léon next described how an absence of "discipline" on the part of Center volunteers and parish clerical staff made it difficult to fulfill donor expectations of accountability and transparency. He began to reveal ambivalence about working out of the parish. Some challenges ultimately related to Father Jeannot's pastoral practices.

> *LL:* For most Haitians it was like that. It was tough. Even the discipline of things was hard for them.
>
> *ECJ:* Say more about what that means "the discipline of things."
>
> *LL:* I'm a very disciplined person . . . And my word is my word. For most Haitians it's not the same way, and after a while that really got to me. Working even with Father Jeannot was like . . . tough.

ECJ: Really? How come? . . .

LL: As I said, discipline was not there . . . because Father Jeannot was like an undisciplined person. With us [at the Center] it didn't go well. For instance, we had a grant for food and shelter . . . and food from Boston Food Banks [was] transported to a Rectory room. Every Sunday Father Jeannot would open the door and let people go in . . .

ECJ: And just take things?

LL: And I don't work that way, I had to document everything . . . It was like a challenge for me, and I couldn't deal with it. I had to record everything that I do . . . so when I [came] on Mondays and [saw] things all over the place, I said, "Geez!" And during the week [when I was there] everyone had to fill out a form . . . so that I could do a report for Boston Food Bank of how many people . . . we [served].

ECJ: But people wouldn't fill it out?

LL: Not with Father Jeannot when they go on Sunday.

One can analyze the tensions Léon describes as conflicts between modes of pastoral power, both religious and secular. In contrast to the divine judgment of charitable acts in the economy of salvation, the Center was subject to the largesse and judgment of private and public actors in largely temporal realms.

GIFTS, KINSHIP, AND PATRONAGE CULTURES

Although classifying and demarcating the boundaries between gifts as secular or sacred, and public or private, is difficult (if the distinction has every truly existed), the giving of material gifts after sharing the spiritual communion of the weekly Eucharistic Mass might have been seen as another kind of reward for parishioners, one for loyalty to Jeannot in this world. Father Jeannot might have felt obligated to respond to his flock's need for food and other basic items by giving out the resources at the parish's disposal without regard for the required administrative auditing—the paperwork tracking the distribution of corporate and foundation donations—the more secular mode of pastoralism required.

As the "sovereign" at the parish, perhaps Jeannot felt that it was his right to make such life and death decisions to aid parishioners (Foucault 1979). It is also possible Jeannot's pastoral obligations as priest intertwined with cultural expectations for him to be a *patwòn* (patron in Haitian Creole) of a *lakou* (family compound, courtyard). The cultural tradition of the *gwo nèg* (big man) in Haiti, a patron of clients bound by ties of loyalty and reciprocal obligations of care and exchange (James 2010: 243–46), may have informed how Jeannot responded to his parishioners' requests for assistance and how he related to them as an authority figure. As one example, St. Leo parishioner Harold Jackson told me he regularly helped to order the parish financial records and sometimes tidied Jeannot's living quarters. The priest had not been accustomed to maintaining the domestic sphere and had admitted to Jackson he had "never gotten his hands dirty a day in his life" until well into adulthood. Given Haiti's extremes of poverty and wealth, it is possible Jeannot had grown up with servants even without being a member of the elite class. Furthermore, sex and gender norms in Haiti typically required women to manage the domestic economy, alongside performing other duties (Lowenthal 1987; Maternowska 2006).

GENDER, CLASS, AND DISCIPLINING THE HOUSEHOLD ECONOMY

Gender and class dynamics and ideas of obligation and reciprocity also influenced the conflicts unfolding at the parish. I next raised the question of the CAIHC letter and told Léon a Center founder gave it to me. I asked if he knew what it was about, and said I found it fascinating and, in some ways, an historian's dream. Léon looked over the letter, chuckling as he tried recalling the details, but then grew serious: "There were sisters, three of them, coming from Haiti. Some will come, go back to Haiti and come again. . . . When we got to St. Leo's they were there. We felt a little bit . . . sorry for the sisters because they were not treated well." In other interviews I was told a dispute developed between Father Jeannot and the nuns over the stipends they eventually received from the archdiocese for their childcare. One interviewee said Jeannot withheld the sisters' payment for use at St. Leo's; however, the sisters wanted to send the money to their own religious order in Haiti.

As previously discussed, there have been conflicts in Catholic institutions regarding power and authority between men and women religious, and the sexual division of charitable labor. Interviewees emphasized how the dispute between the sisters and Jeannot had more complicated roots. "Margaret Chapman," a European American religious sister who volunteered at the Center in the mid-1980s, provided additional context. We met at her Massachusetts convent, a large, pastoral campus set apart from mundane life, but not an isolated cloister.

Sister Margaret learned about the Center when a Charity priest asked her to assist with administrative work. The Center's staff was overwhelmed with running the flourishing program, overseeing the building renovation, completing program documentation, and meeting new Haitian arrivals' needs. Although the Church continued to pay staff salaries, Center staff could not always complete the monthly invoices recording their service provision to receive reimbursement for program costs in a timely manner. (Similar challenges remained during my time onsite between 2006 and 2007.) The archdiocese reimbursed cost outlays after receipts and paperwork had been submitted; without documentation charitable funds did not flow.

Staff members served as mediators and brokers between clients and federal, state, and municipal agencies. As Sister Margaret explained, by 1986, services included ESL; a well-run daycare that would soon gain national recognition for excellence; mental health, medical, and legal services; and family counseling for clients to learn new parenting skills. The family counseling work exemplifies how Center staff members attempted to transform the culturally intimate practices in their clients' homes to accommodate the norms of American society. Sister Margaret described how newly arrived Haitians frequently faced legal problems falling under section 51A of the state's public welfare laws. This statute requires "mandated reporters" to notify the Massachusetts Department of Children and Families of suspected abuse or neglect of children. Some Haitian families were confronted by state actors under this statute because of the corporal punishment of their children—a disciplinary practice customary among many families in Haiti (and in the United States) that may nonetheless be categorized as child abuse:

> We did . . . go out to legal cases, court cases, about the 51As in particular, but it was also like a learning . . . a socialization process for them [Haitians] as to what's allowed in this country, and so forth. They were not . . . we didn't really deal with "real" out-and-out abuse. It was charges made by others because they were seeing something . . . but it really wasn't that they were totally abusive toward their children. It was what [others] saw and what was done to [Haitians] in terms of something that they brought from Haiti, and it was really hard to break that.

The processes of inculcating new practices within the family or workplace recall Foucault's discussion of the disciplinary roles social institutions (like the family, religion, schools, the military, clinics, and others) may play in the lives of those subjected to their power. Both individual bodily regimens and interpersonal social practices were targets of reform. In this respect, the Center operated as a corrective or domesticating apparatus, in a pastoral rather than punitive mode.

At the same time that Center staff members advocated on behalf of Haitians with powerful external authorities, they gained expertise in preparing clients to acculturate, succeed in the workplace, and integrate better with the non-Haitian majority. Over its first five years, the Center's expanding programs and successful fulfillment of contracts with governmental agencies in Massachusetts (i.e., the Department of Social Services and others), indicated to its Haitian staff an independent future was a possibility. Sister Margaret told me a "movement to become a 501(c)(3) was in their minds." But what Haitians anticipated would be a transition toward institutional independence and sovereignty was thwarted when the Center merged with the Charity.

During these early years, in spheres of cultural intimacy and private realms of social interaction, staff members confronted obstacles to institutional autonomy when long-standing negative sociocultural practices posed barriers to the Center's success. I also asked Sister Margaret to review the CAIHC letter for additional background. She placed the conflict in terms of the structural inequalities in economically "developing" societies provoking some men and women to enter religious life. Although she only implicitly questioned the authenticity of Haitian men's and women's religious' piety, she highlighted how acceptance of vocations in situations of dire poverty may produce variances between "local" gender, kinship, and cultural norms, and the Church's "universal" religious ideals.

In joining a religious order, men and women faced double binds of how to uphold the sacred and technical "disciplines" and "rule" of their religious family versus the temporal obligations to his or her gender, culture, and "natural" family:

> *Sister Margaret:* I do have something to say on this. Wow. . . . What I [have] to say about the Haitian community and the informal grapevine and all . . . was that it really could be quite insidious.
>
> *ECJ:* It's quite a letter.
>
> *SM:* Oh my! . . . Power struggles all the time. I have this saying after working with some of the small villages where the women get trafficked, . . . like how they say, "power corrupts," [pausing, and speaking with deep sadness], *powerlessness corrupts, too!* . . . I'll be praying for you. This is a prayer [and] fasting time and you'll need a discerning heart. I'll say what I know about the sisters . . .
>
> *ECJ:* Do you know where they were from?
>
> *SM:* I know that they were Haitians and they were working in the daycare . . . and a dispute arose regarding the payment they would get from Catholic Charities.[2] . . . I think they would probably get a stipend, as sisters [they] would get less than a full salary. . . . That's always understood in terms of our [vows of] poverty—that it goes to the [religious] community. It's not that you don't get everything that you need in terms of clothing and food . . . but it's really that you're not . . . keeping a bank account and things like this. Well, what happened is . . . what I was hearing was that the sisters or one or two of the sisters were sending to their natural family in Haiti their paychecks. And this was a dispute between the community and the sisters.

If the sisters had chosen to send to their own families the material resources the parish leaders viewed as belonging either to the corporate Church or to Father Jeannot, one tension is between the individuality of the nuns and seeming lack of respect for a more communal orientation. A second tension is between feminine and masculine forms of power, in that pastors typically are considered sovereigns in the territory of the parish. But, as the letter indicates, observers of these dynamics depicted Father Jeannot as being vulnerable and subject to the influence of the parish council members. The nuns' reputed thwarting of priestly authority reflected ambivalence about his failure to exercise power. But there was more to the story:

> Secondly, that they were not necessarily, ummm . . . documented. But I never asked. And then thirdly, I think the reason they were sending the money home was the complete destitution of their family. And also, it may be true to say that they wanted to be here in the United States, and they wanted to find a way to have money and help their family and have a future, but it would not necessarily translate into a religious

life vocation. I understood that over time there was one who just left, you know . . . and then another, I don't know whether it was a mailman or who, but . . . [she had] some relationship along the way. So that their primary . . . ties were to family, and that's always true. But when you enter religious community, also there [are] commitments there.

Just like other entrants who have come to the United States under legal means (tourist visas, student visas, etc.), a couple of the sisters may have elected to overstay the terms of their "temporary religious worker visa" and remain at St. Leo's as undocumented laborers until they could regularize their status. Again, I am uncertain, but this explanation offers one interpretation for the sisters' vulnerability to threats of deportation referred to in the CAIHC letter. But, if the sisters' legal status was not in question, such threats of expulsion may still represent a dispute regarding benevolent aid resembling the conflicts I previously observed among Human Rights Fund beneficiaries (James 2010).

The sisters' status was also uncertain under canon law. Another dimension of the social drama concerned gender, power, and the maintenance of discipline in the parish and Center. In the religious sense, the sisters apparently prioritized their freedom to exercise spiritual practices, regardless of Jeannot's wishes as parish priest. In the secular sense, the sisters may have been among those individuals whose initial inconsistent labor practices impeded the maintenance of reliable childcare (and other) services:

> The other feature was that it was hard for Frantz and the director to have any control over the three sisters.[3] When they decided . . . they would go on vacation or retreat . . . they would just go. I didn't know of any connection with Father Jeannot. But like Frantz, Jeannot was a one-on-one kind of gentle guy. He wasn't overbearing. I just don't understand all that—implied in [the letter]. But I wouldn't know whether Jeannot was trying to pull them in the sense of, "when you're at the Center you have to let the director know if you're not going to be there." So, in a way they were elusive.

Sister Margaret next suggested Haiti's structural inequalities and desperate living conditions likely pushed the nuns toward a religious vocation:

> This happens in terms of religious life sometimes with Third World groups. And it's really out of desperation . . . but they see [the religious life] as a means of education and three square meals, and bed and board, but it wouldn't translate into a life commitment. And the family would then—the needs of the family would be primary.

The meaning of family, as social or as natural, and conflicts over what obligations are owed to support the family as defined, seemed at the heart of this dispute. But there were other issues at another level of gender and kinship.

In addition to the nun's uncertain legal statuses—as well as the questions of gender, labor, and authenticity of religious vocations in Haiti (and other resource poor settings)—other complicating factors arose from sexual politics. Louis Léon said hesitatingly, "And also, Father Jeannot was like a . . . probably people already told you [he] was like a ladies' man. That was well known in the parish. And people would be on the big [advisory] board saying he was sleeping with the . . . It was a mess." At this point he did not clarify with whom Father Jeannot was reputedly engaged in sexual relations—whether with one of the nuns or someone else—but later in the interview he suggested not only was the priest involved with one of the sisters; he also carried on a long-term sexual relationship with a member of the parish council. Léon clarified his remarks about Jeannot "lacking discipline" were directed toward this interpersonal practice. But the exact details of the story were still a matter of hearsay.

> *ECJ:* Was he?
>
> *LL:* He even admitted it. He wasn't cryptic about it . . . .
>
> *ECJ:* Do you think they [the sisters] were taken advantage of?
>
> *LL:* Ahhh. From what I understand, from what I heard, one of them was. And that was one of the things too because she was like, taking [comments] from the sisters and would report to Father Jeannot what they were saying. . . . She was like a detective . . . finding out what was going on [in the community] and reporting it to Father Jeannot.

If these rumors were true, a Haitian priest engaging in a sexual relationship with a parishioner was not necessarily unusual. Indeed, in June 2010, because of "allegations of sexual misconduct" stemming from a long-term sexual relationship with an adult parishioner (or more than one), the Archdiocese of Boston revoked the "faculties to perform public ministry" of a Haitian priest from the Archdiocese of Cap Haïtien, Rev. Gabriel Michel.[4] Gabriel had served as parochial vicar at the predominantly Haitian St. Angela's Church in Mattapan. For a brief period, he was an HMSC Advisory Board member. Several Haitians whom I interviewed spoke of widespread sexual dalliances of priests, including priests of other nationalities, in Haiti.

Léon related the dispute between the sisters and the "triumvirate" to the reported sexual practices of some Catholic priests in Haiti: "It's still going on in Haiti. Actually, a priest was just arrested in Léogâne for going around with a young girl, and she's pregnant. It just makes me sick sometimes." There were rumors mentioned in other interviews that Father Jeannot had reportedly fathered a child with one of the parish women. But, in Léon's characterization, the nun was actively in pursuit of the liaison and strategized to find ways to strengthen her influence with Father Jeannot by accumulating and sharing others' secrets.

I next asked to what extent Father Jeannot's reputed failure to uphold a priest's vows of celibacy was known either to the parish or to the archdiocese:

> *LL:* Back then even people complained about that, but the Church didn't do anything. That's the problem. It wouldn't have gotten [so much worse] had they addressed the issue.[5]

> *ECJ:* Did [the Church] know?
>
> *LL:* Oh yeah. Letters were sent to the archdiocese regarding Father Jeannot's [behavior]. The thing is they think they're [pause] untouchable. People will complain and the archdiocese will not do anything, and they continue. They continue. A lot of people wrote . . . they should have [done] something.

Recent revelations of sexual relationships between Catholic priests and adult parishioners around the world suggest the practice is widespread.[6] There are also reports alleging priests have abused nuns sexually, including in Italy, Ireland, and the United States, but increasingly in African countries in which the AIDS epidemic is particularly virulent.[7] In such cases, nuns were assumed to be free from the virus and were coerced into having sexual relationships with priests.

Although the global clergy sex scandal has emphasized the travesty of pedophilia, sexual improprieties in religious organizations (and more broadly, in private institutional settings) arise from abuses of power, especially pastoral power, rather than theological views of celibacy or sex (Scheper-Hughes 1998; Scheper-Hughes and Devine 2003). Indeed, the violation of the vows of celibacy is a "public secret"— "that which is generally known, but cannot be articulated" (Taussig 1999: 5)—whether between consenting men and women religious (and lay adults), between priests and religious or lay individuals who were somehow coerced, as well as between nuns (whether consensual or not), and, at the most egregious, as acts of pedophilia between men and women religious and minors (Chibnall, Wolf, and Duckro 1998).

The hidden side of sex among a minority of Catholic clerics speaks to more troubling dimensions of power, sovereignty, and impunity manifesting across a variety of social institutions. As Taussig (1999: 7) states, "wherever there is power, there is secrecy, except it is not only secrecy that lies at the core of power, but public secrecy. . . . To put it bluntly, there is no such thing as a secret." Léon went on to describe that Father Jeannot's relationships were not only well known, but that some parishioners also protested his reputed behavior publicly and felt he should not have been celebrating Mass:

People walked with big signs outside the church protesting Father Jeannot. Every Sunday. . . . As I said every Sunday there were people outside protesting. It was just like a matter of fact. . . . When you are in a certain position you don't take advantage of people below you. You don't do that and that's what happened.

Other Center stakeholders affirmed Father Jeannot's relationships with parish women were a public secret. If true, culturally intimate knowledge that could cause scandal if revealed outside the community—where representations of Haitians have frequently been negative—may have compelled some parishioners to keep the alleged secrets of St. Leo's pastor. After Vatican II, Haitian Catholic leaders' pastoral power was directed more toward transforming entrenched political and economic injustices than issues of personal moral behavior (see Farmer and Walton 2000). The personal practices of Jeannot—one of few priests, if not the only priest, of African and Haitian descent in Boston at the time—may have been a carnal matter of little concern to most parishioners. If the archdiocese was aware, on the one hand, perhaps the matter was privately confessed and forgiven. On the other hand, the alleged intimate relationships occurring at St. Leo's may have been ignored.

The issue of cultural differences suggests another interpretation regarding norms of sex, gender, and kinship in Haiti. Stories of Father Jeannot's confessing or, perhaps, boasting about his relationships may be an indicator of tensions between ideals of sex and gender and public expressions of masculinity and femininity in Haitian society. To recall, Frantz Monestime wanted to launch the Center in part to help Haitian men gain an ability to sponsor their families for immigration. Haitian women tended to find work more easily in the United States, especially in domestic work, nursing, elder care, and hospice settings.[8] Shifts in gender roles were also becoming prevalent in Haiti in the mid-twentieth century (James 2010; Maternowska 2006: 64). Haitian men tended to experience more challenges finding employment during the resettlement process in the United States. Other Haitian male staff interviewees perceived Haitian men to have greater difficulties than women in finding steady employment and in achieving gender ideals in the United States.

The experience of Sister Margaret's international religious order informed her comments on the roles of gender, culture, and sex in Catholicism and at St. Leo's. When I asked her about the CAIHC letter and the comment about Father Jeannot lacking discipline, she was unable to confirm the rumors but deepened my understanding of the cultural stakes of the dispute:

> *SM:* But I do know that culturally, you know I'm not sure in terms of the valuing of celibacy . . . and I think I'm going to [give the example of] Africa, where we have [missions] in Kenya, Ethiopia, and South Africa, and you know, the sisters were talking about how hard it is really for the priests, because the culture does not value . . . celibacy, and they feel that a young man is a man when he has a child. Once he's a father, then he is an adult. . . .
>
> *ECJ:* What some people have said is . . . there are many priests in Haiti who have . . . partners—
>
> *SM:* —yes, on the side, and I've heard it said in different places in the world that they don't want to become bishops, because then they would have to turn in the little woman . . . 'cause then there'd be . . . more visibility . . . so that they don't want to be bishops. I think our church has a problem with imposing such a thing . . . on a man.

Cultural ideals of gender in Haiti link heterosexual relationships with women as essential to public masculinity, especially among the poor: "It is common and generally accepted for men to have several partners at one time and to have children with several women" (Maternowska 2006: 50). The man is expected to "perform his role as provider, planting gardens and tending livestock for all of the women and . . . the women are expected to remain sexually faithful to the man" (Maternowska 2006: 50, citing Schwartz 2000: 260). Attaining a social and gendered role as parent is also critical to identity: "Eschewing these roles is unheard of, since childlessness, according to [anthropologist] Lowenthal (1987: 309), 'is a virtually untenable status, ultimately undermining efforts to live a proper and meaningful life.' . . . In all unions, producing children marks a critical entry into adulthood" (Maternowska 2006: 52).

Anthropologist James Lorand Matory's analysis of controversies regarding the "public secret" of homosexuality among male Candomblé priests in Brazil suggests, "while people might appear to be conforming to the norms of one imagined community, their visible actions, as well as their private symbolism and narratives, might simultaneously embody alternative imaginations of self and community" (2004: 157). Norms and expectations of sex, gender, and kinship in Haiti are interwoven and in tension with the theologies of embodiment in Catholic orthodoxy and actual off-stage practices.

But, to return for a moment to this ongoing consideration of pastoral power, Foucault (2007: 172) states: "Just as on one side the pastor's merit and salvation are due to the weaknesses of his sheep, so too the pastor's fault and weaknesses contribute to the edification of his sheep and are part of the movement, the process, of guiding them towards salvation." Perhaps the public secret of Father Jeannot's interpersonal parish relationships were humanizing and elicited some parishioners' understanding. Such loyalty, however, was not solely as Catholics but as diaspora Haitians: "diasporas, like nation-states, propagate secrets and defend their own intimate zones. Diasporas often share the *materia prima* of secrets with other, overlapping communities, including regions, nations, civilizations, and transnational social movements. Moreover, these communities regularly contest and reinterpret each other's secrets" (Matory 2004: 184; emphasis in the original).

Overlapping imagined communities intersected at the Center regarding the public secret of sex. Controversies about carnality produced embarrassment and frustration for some, in part because Haitians were already stigmatized in the United States (and elsewhere) for their so-called aberrant sexual practices in relation to the growing prevalence of HIV/AIDS. Secondly, if men and women religious and parish council members were conforming to cultural norms of gender and sex in Haiti, the reputed or disputed relationships among them in zones of cultural intimacy were to be defended against those outside the community. As Matory (2004: 171) argues, "the African diaspora is constituted by secrets and can be reconstituted through reselections and reinterpretations of secrets that need to be defended."

The controversy was also a matter of public secrets about sex among Catholics, and growing debates about celibacy, not only among the religious but also among the laity. Some Haitians felt the Archdiocese of Boston's seeming failure to act to censure Jeannot—when "letters were sent" to notify the hierarchy that its cleric was reportedly celebrating the Catholic Mass in violation of his vows—signified the Church's relative disregard for Haitian Catholics' authentic religious piety. By failing to act, some felt the RCAB communicated Haitians' lack of worthiness of a celebrant who upheld the norms and practices "on display" as components of the Catholic brand. These issues would come to a head from the late 1980s to mid-1990s, when the Center came more fully under Charity management.

Regardless of these interpretations, the ambiguities and tensions in the personal and working relationships among the sisters, the members of the parish council, and Father Jeannot, contributed to the threats made against the sisters, and the exodus of some of the sisters and two founders from the Center. Although an exact time frame is uncertain, my assumption is these events occurred between 1983 and 1984. Léon asserted that what ultimately drove him from the Center in 1984 was the treatment of the sisters and the administrative challenges of working at the parish. One of the Center's founders continued volunteering for slightly longer, but also left because of the treatment of the sisters (and the stipend was inadequate compensation for the challenges of supporting the fledgling institution):

> *ECJ:* Did you leave because it joined Catholic Charities?
>
> *Founder:* I left before Catholic Charities . . . One of the reasons I left is because of the injustice to the sisters. . . . I know so many things that happened to the sisters . . . in order to kick the sisters out. So many things.
>
> *ECJ:* Like what?
>
> *Founder:* They went to a point that they destroyed the convent. Only one sister, only one sister survived [with her faith intact]. Sister ______. The other ones, you know they left the convent.
>
> *ECJ:* Who destroyed it?
>
> *Founder:* Ahhh . . . [*laughter*] . . . Oyy! [the founder revealed the identity of the person, but it was ambiguous whether I was to keep the name a secret.] This is one of the reasons that I really quit . . . because I know the injustice. . . . So, the [sisters] left the convent . . . and went and married. . . . You know [one] union [marriage] did not even survive [and] . . . she regretted it. She regretted marrying and leaving the convent. She's the one who talked to me about everything.

The alleged destruction of the sisters' residence was not the only threatening act. During the interview with Frantz Monestime, I showed him the CAIHC letter and asked whether he knew to what it referred. He shared a story about an horrific act—the culmination of tensions at the parish—reminiscent of malevolent bureaucraft processes (James 2012):

> *FM:* The sisters were under the archdiocese. There was conflict between some people in power at the parish and the sisters. They came in and were in their own convent and shouldn't [have been] seen as a threat. They worked in the daycare. One night I was there [working late]. . . .

> The wall [was] cracked in the daycare and we [repaired] everything ourselves and . . . And while I was there . . . I heard a [gurgling noise]. . . . Someone was trying to set fire in the building there where the daycare was! In the building where the sisters were living!
>
> *ECJ:* Was that the 12 Bicknell building? [the Victorian house]
>
> *FM:* Yes. Probably at eight or nine o'clock p.m. Madame, I was shocked to see this! Ok?!. . . I worked so hard to build this . . . and for someone deliberately to go in and to do something like this! [Frantz's voice bellowed with exasperation.]
>
> *ECJ:* So, you think the act was directed to harm the whole Center [or] to harm you personally?
>
> *FM:* If there is no building, there is no Center. At the same time, also, nobody was there but me . . .
>
> *ECJ:* When did this happen?
>
> *FM:* I don't remember . . . I shook my head, and I said, "No, this is not possible." Because I did not expect to fall so low. Ok? And I did not realize that there was somebody who hates like *this* [voice rising at the end in incredulity]?
>
> *ECJ:* Why do you think that someone would do that?
>
> *FM:* [gesturing at the CAIHC letter] Well, you saw. After that I shook my head and I walked away. I stopped and did not think about it, and I did not get [involved]. Because I wanted to focus on the Center and really go in and keep it out of whatever kind of conflict there could be . . . but there was some really bad conflict. But . . . I am the wrong person to ask about this because I [would] not get [involved]. . . . and Father Jeannot, he was a nice guy. Nice guy. And he was also too soft. And aahh, too nice. Because sometimes when you are too nice, they take you for stupid, too! But there [were] . . . some problems. There are things that . . . I will not say.

The story of the attempted arson was confirmed in an earlier interview I had conducted with Harold Jackson. He mentioned the incident almost in passing, with a chuckle, as a sign of the trials and tribulations of aiding his "brothers and sisters" at St. Leo's, in the context of infrastructural problems at the parish:

> *HJ:* Ok . . . I was the Building Chairperson for the building. And we put in that building, I'll bet you, from 1980, till we moved out, . . . at least a quarter of a million dollars or more. Patching!
>
> *ECJ:* wow. Wow!—
>
> *HJ:* —[*laughing*] patching up the [place]. They set a fire to it one year!
>
> *ECJ:* Oh my gosh!
>
> *HJ:* The pipes froze, four or five times, even while Mr. Pierre [Imbert] was there. Ok? The pipes froze, and you know that when they thaw out, they break, and oh boy, what . . . damage. Uh, and theft! Oh! They used to break in every week . . .

> *ECJ:* Really? That's what people say! They say, everywhere . . . every week!
> *HJ:* *Every* week! They do. Break in! Take the televisions, the computers, and the archdiocese, of course on account of charity, of course, always tried to help us replenish some of that stuff . . . and so forth, but, uh, the building was in, the building, could be ah . . . the building's a fabulous building. It's just, it's old, and we didn't have the right resources or . . . enough money . . . to put into the building to make it real nice.

. . .

St. Leo Parish and the Center were places of sanctuary and cultural intimacy, but they were also more complicated than their public faces indicated. One could call them purgatorial spaces, especially for those whose legal statuses were ambivalent and who were expected to submit to the pastoral authority of the priest and parish council. But the lines of power were ambiguous and contested.

The recurrence of the trope of discipline in these stories recalls earlier discussions of purgatorial spaces as sites of transformation in which individuals make the passage from one status to another through various kinds of labor. Léon used the term "discipline" to describe both the maintenance of order through administrative practices and the observance of rules of chastity and obedience expected of men and women religious. Another sense was invoked in Sister Margaret's discussion of the challenges some Haitian parents had adopting American sensibilities regarding corporal punishment—external actors felt they disciplined children's bodies too much. These examples also demonstrate the extent to which St. Leo's and the Center were sites of struggle over bodily practices and care, the carnal and the corporeal, and intimacy and secrecy.

There were also multiple resistances to practices deemed unjust, exploitative, or immoral. The nuns appear to have decided at will to abstain from expected duties to provide childcare. Add to these resistances the visible or scriptural forms of protest in which stakeholders crafted texts to appeal to the ethical norms of outsiders: the CAIHC letter, the petition in support of the nuns the letter mentioned, and the public protests using picket signs outside the church during Mass. But modes of resistance also occurred in the shadows. Uncertainties and ambiguities about how power flowed provoked rumor, gossip, accusations, and even threats (by phone). The combination of the more visible, textual modes of protest and the secret and culturally intimate modes of conflict contributed to a social process resembling bureaucraft. Indeed, these dynamics culminated in the attempted arson—an act intended not only to destroy property but possibly to murder.

I have not yet considered another interpretation of this story. Perhaps this dispute was about love and jealousy. One interlocutor worked with the woman with whom Father Jeannot was alleged to have had an enduring conjugal relationship. Each day, the interlocutor said, the priest dropped the woman off at her place of employment and picked her up when she had finished for the day. Such routines of domesticity and care suggest a deeply profound and tragic situation of double binds. If this latter interpretation is also true, it must have been tremendously difficult to have chosen a vocation that expects self-sacrifice, obedience, charity, and chastity, and then to have found love, but under circumstances forcing it into the shadows. As Sister Margaret suggests, the religious vocation is a challenging one. The weight of cultural conceptions of gender, sex, and kinship may make the path that much more difficult for religious aspirants. By most accounts, Father Jeannot was a loving and caring person who was, if anything, "too nice."

. . .

In 1999, St. Leo Parish was suppressed (closed). The remaining RCAB archival materials indicated how structural weaknesses in the "St. Leo Church" foundation required external support: *"This floor should be braced from the basement below until such time of the rebuilding of the foundation"* was the June 23, 1998, statement Phil Barrett, a building inspector, made to a Mr. Reilly, following his June 18, 1998, examination of the beloved house of worship. In this extended memory palace, I could not help but interpret these words symbolically. External authorities may have felt the moral and spiritual foundations of the parish also needed to be rebuilt.

At the Presbyteral Council Meeting on March 12, 1999, a committee of bishops met with Cardinal Law to discuss liturgical matters and the suppression of several churches (Our Lady of the Assumption Parish, St. John the Baptist Parish, St. Aidan's Parish, and St. Theresa of the Child Jesus Parish). The agenda included St. Leo Parish and a proposed "Alteration of the Territory of St. Matthew Parish" to incorporate St. Leo's still vibrant community after the suppression. The bishops agreed to the "Relegation to Profane Use of St. Leo Church, Dorchester" in order for the Charity to receive much-needed "space for its Multi-Service Center."[9]

On April 14, 1999, using regal terminology, Cardinal Law signed a "Decree" taking effect at "12:01 A.M. June 1, 1999." In order "to allow for a more efficient and effective use of Church resources in the Dorchester Section of the City of Boston," Law decreed:

> that Saint Leo Parish, Boston, be suppressed,
>
> that the territory pertaining to Saint Leo Parish be territory of Saint Matthew Parish, Boston,
>
> that the canonical registers of Saint Leo Parish be kept at Saint Matthew Parish, Boston,
>
> that the goods and obligations of Saint Leo Parish belong to the Archdiocese of Boston,
>
> that the rectory and adjacent property of Saint Leo Parish become the canonical property of Saint Matthew Parish.

FIGURE 16. Cardinal Bernard Francis Law, Monsignor Jeannot, and clerics at the final Mass celebrated at St. Leo's. Photo credit: Robert L. Powell.

The term "suppression" is a curious one. It is tempting to think of it in psychological terms as an inhibition or repression of emotions, drives, or bodily desires, in medical terms as the control of illness symptoms, or in sociopolitical terms as the restraint of unruly behavior, rebellion, and resistance. But the language above contains no hints of these conditions. Rather, suppression appears to refer to a bureaucratic act made on behalf of Corporation Sole to regulate Church resources in the Catholic economy of compassion.

In a moving ceremony, Haitian parishioners celebrated St. Leo's last Mass, with Monsignor Jeannot, Cardinal Law, and other archdiocesan officials (see Figure 16). Center advisory board member Mr. Robert Powell, whose beautiful pictures capture the poignancy of the church's closure, photographed the procession accompanying the St. Leo statue to its new home as they said goodbye to their parish home (see Figure 17).

Three years later—after Father Jeannot's 2001 death and Cardinal Law's fall from grace—Law transferred ownership of St. Leo's to the Charity. The decision

FIGURE 17. Procession of St. Leo's parishioners after final Mass, May 23, 1999. Photo credit: Robert L. Powell.

was the culmination of years of struggle (and triumph), during which the Center emerged from its turbulent birth to seek autonomy and sovereignty over its territory, goods, and obligations, only to meet with resistance from the Charity (and some Haitians) to let the Center go. But between 1984 and 2002, the Center would expand and gain public recognition for the quality of its services, becoming the voice of the Haitian community in Boston.

6

Corporate Schisms

Life and Death between Church, State, and Law

> *We started as a grassroots organization [and] now we've become a church-based organization. . . . Now we have a church making decisions for the community.*
>
> —DR. RÉNALD RAPHAËL, FORMER DIRECTOR OF THE
> HMSC SANTE MANMAN AND AIDS PROGRAMS (CA. 1988–96)

In June 2005, I attended my first HMSC Advisory Board meeting at its annual retreat, an event at which the board, Charity, and Center staff members, and a few clients strategized about the Center's future. In addition to participating in the retreat's group activities, new members received a separate orientation to the history between the Center and Charity. A document titled "Summary of Facility Related Conflict with Catholic Charities" described ongoing disputes regarding the ownership and management of the original 12 Bicknell Street property at St. Leo Parish. It was not clear whether the roots of the tensions involved miscommunications, disagreements over how best to serve the Haitian community, cultural differences, racial and ethnic clashes, some combination of these, or other factors. Its then executive director, Pierre Imbert, was on a much-deserved sabbatical in South Africa after having received a fellowship.[1] Imbert had been at the Center for thirteen years, and he was executive director for eleven. He joined after working with the Pwojè Lavi program (see Chapter 3). At its closure in 1994, the Charity invited Imbert to serve as the Center's business manager. In 1996, at the height of a struggle over the Center's mission, the Charity appointed Imbert interim director, then executive director. Although I never experienced the Center under Imbert's direction—what many consider its golden age—I looked forward to serving the board he had shepherded. But just after the 2005 retreat he resigned to accept then Governor Mitt Romney's appointment as director of the Massachusetts Office of Refugees and Immigrants (MORI). MORI administered the state's federally funded refugee resettlement programs.

140

I was later able to hear stories of the Center's early history and interactions with the Charity directly from Pierre Imbert. In November 2005, before the move to the new Yawkey building, he returned to the advisory board to help strategize how best to work with the Charity. Imbert told us the institutional relationship resembled those in some homes or families, a "love-hate" relationship. His description recalled a volunteer's characterization of the organizational connections between the two entities as "hostile dependency." Both the kinship and psychological metaphors used to describe these organizational entanglements influenced my conception of "corporate Catholicism."

This and subsequent chapters expand the Center memory palace with reflections on its work from key stakeholders as well as members of Greater Boston's Haitian community. In many respects, moral conceptions of corporality or corporeality—material or embodied experience often captured discursively in texts—and carnality, "the unintegrated, errant aspect of materiality" refracted especially through sexuality (Povinelli 2011: 108), clashed in the episodes recounted. Attending to both registers, the corporeal—the discursive understandings of and interventions directed toward the corporate body at a population level—and the carnal, the more intimate and fleshly dimensions of interpersonal exchanges, are important components of this ongoing analysis of corporate Catholic charity.

. . .

Imbert's version of the Center's origin and early history underscored the emotional ambivalence embedded in these institutional linkages. Before the Center formally entered the Charity network (from the late 1980s until the early 1990s), Cardinal Law reportedly instructed then Charity president, Dr. Joseph Doolin, to adopt the program. Doolin agreed reluctantly because, as Imbert put it, "No one had ever said 'no' to His Eminence." This deference remained until Law's resignation in 2002 for his role in the clergy sexual abuse scandal.

Imbert said the Center had begun in a single room in 1978. Although the archdiocese processed payroll by phone with no real sense of the budget, "the organization was growing, and it needed to become the center that the Haitian community longed for." He celebrated the organization becoming one of the most comprehensive social service sites in Massachusetts, and even in the northeastern United States, for its "ethnic focus" and "service to the current and emerging needs of the Haitian community."

Imbert also invoked the renewed covenant between the Church, Charity, Center, and the City: "The new task at hand was how to serve more than [the Haitian] community." With a broad smile, he continued, "You're just too good for one community." When immigrants from Liberia, Congo, Trinidad, and other nations came asking how to replicate the Center's successes, he laughed, "I had to apologize for the appearance [of the buildings]." He reminded us we knew how it looked when we each joined, but we believed in the cause. This dedicated belief, or allyship, in contemporary parlance, mobilized a racially, ethnically, and economically diverse group to join Haitians' labor, talent, resources, and time to further its mission.

But Imbert also confessed to joining the Center reluctantly because he didn't want to work in his own community: "Haitians have a history of self-destructive behavior." In the early 1990s, at his very first meeting, the vexed relationship between the Center and the Charity was discussed. Remembering the variant on this same struggle articulated at my board orientation, I wondered if protracted disagreements with the Charity had become a marker of the Center's brand. On another reflective occasion, a long-standing advisory board member said of Haitians, "We have a revolutionary tradition, not a democratic one." Implicit in these statements is a recognition of traumatic histories of exploitation by external actors against which Haitians liberated themselves, but also inegalitarian and authoritarian forms of governance bolstered by elusive external and internal elites in the postcolonial and democratic eras.

When formally adopted into the Catholic Charities network, Imbert continued, the Charity discovered a large operation but little budget management. In the mid-1980s, the first of two European Americans managed the Center. Dr. Helene Hayes became director when "Haitian community leaders were no longer in support of the project." An advisory board member working at the John Hancock financial services company brought funding for program support. Then, for a few years, David Johnson was executive director. Of his own journey to employment at the Center, Imbert said that when he was introduced as business manager in 1994, the Center had been losing momentum because of challenges working with the Charity.

As I continued formal research on the Center's history and traced the connections between the Center, Charity, Church, and external stakeholders, I received many other descriptions resembling Pierre Imbert's kinship metaphor. Throughout these episodes, the assemblage of affiliated organizations and actors resembled members of a corporate family, one in which sentiments of love and hate had created antagonism, separation, and even what could be considered "divorce," but also an intense bond. What other roles had the Center played in the lives of Boston Haitians?

THE METRO BOSTON REACH 2010 COALITION

At the June 2005 advisory board retreat, I was appointed liaison to a network of Haitian advocacy organizations working to reduce racial and ethnic health disparities in Greater Boston—the Metro Boston Racial and Ethnic Approaches to Community Health 2010 Coalition (hereafter, Reach 2010 Coalition or the Coalition). Two Coalition facilitators, Nesly Metayer, a sociologist who once served as an AIDS program manager at the Massachusetts Department of Public Health, and Judy Freiwirth, an expert in nonprofit management, both facilitated the retreat and presented the outreach effort. Both facilitators noted cultural factors the community needed to overcome, not only to reduce HIV disparities but also to demonstrate how organizational collaboration *could* work to resolve social problems. The cultural factors reported were mistrust, a lack of commitment, "deceptive practices" (never explicitly defined), and then two seemingly contradictory factors—a desire for association, but also a rejection of association with others.

As I participated in the Coalition during subsequent months, I learned a tremendous amount not only about the agencies involved but also about how Greater Boston Haitians perceived the legacies of Haiti's *ensekirite* in their diaspora lives. Although these conditions were not ubiquitous, the Coalition's assessment had identified several common areas warranting programmatic interventions: relationships between the sexes; intergenerational conflicts; class, political, and cultural conflicts; and ongoing public health crises.

I attended my first Coalition meeting on June 28, 2005, at the headquarters of the Center for Community Health, Education, and Research (CCHER). Since the late 1980s, the prominent Haitian community-based organization had worked to reduce the prevalence of HIV/AIDS in Greater Boston. CCHER led the Coalition with a grant from the Centers for Disease Control and Prevention (CDC) to implement health disparities programs for new immigrants, and underprivileged and underserved populations. Staff from other Haitian medical, social service, and grassroots advocacy organizations participated. Many of their representatives had previously worked with—or had received social assistance, training, and other support from—the Center. In sum, these institutions served a large cross section of the Haitian population in eastern Massachusetts.[2]

CCHER was one of twenty-two "Action Communities" the CDC had selected nationwide to implement REACH 2010 programs. In 1999, the CDC instituted the national REACH 2010 program as the "cornerstone of . . . efforts to eliminate racial and ethnic disparities in health . . . that occur by race, ethnicity, education, income, or geographic location." The program was designed to implement the CDC's strategic objectives by "addressing health disparities in critical life stages (infants, children, adolescents, adults, and older adults)." The CDC solicited proposals offering "innovative approaches . . . in communities, health care settings, schools, worksites, and after-school programs." Six areas were intervention priorities: breast and cervical cancer screening and management, cardiovascular disease, diabetes mellitus, immunizations, HIV/AIDS, and infant mortality.[3]

The CCHER offices were in a large Victorian house located within a mile of the new Yawkey building. Their physical proximity was not the only factor linking them. Dr. Eustache Jean-Louis, CCHER's executive director, formerly managed the Center's Haitian Community AIDS Outreach Project (established around 1987). Another prominent Coalition organization possessed kinship ties to the Center. The Haitian-American Public Health Initiatives (HAPHI), founded in 1989 by a group of health care professionals, also targeted Boston Haitian's health issues. Between 1989 and 1996, Jean-Marc Jean-Baptiste, the HAPHI executive director, served as the HMSC executive director.[4] Another HAPHI staff member, Dr. Rénald Raphaël—whose lament opens this chapter—founded the Center's Sante Manman Se Sante Pitit (Healthy Mother Healthy Child) program (in 1988 or 1989).[5] During their tenure at the Center, both individuals expressed publicly their frustration with Catholic institutions. Their attempts to meet the Haitian community's needs without violating Catholic doctrines ultimately led to a dramatic crisis.

INSTITUTIONAL DRAMAS

The 1980s were exceptionally difficult for Haitians not only because of the emergence of HIV, but also because of stereotypes of Haitians as "disease carriers" (Farmer and Kim 1991: 214). There was also stigma inside the diaspora community. One former Center staff person described the time as frightening: "Everyone was scared, and no one knew how to deal with the disease. . . . Being diagnosed was seen as a death sentence. Family members expelled people from their homes who were identified as suffering from the disease [at a time] when the community was still finding itself economically, socially, and politically." This same individual said the HIV/AIDS program started at the HMSC during this crisis: "It was a support program for people diagnosed with HIV and with AIDS and included case management, peer social work, and financial assistance, including housing."

David Johnson, the Center's executive director in the late 1980s, described the epidemic's impact on the Haitian community as another blow to its collective self-esteem. Johnson, a native of Dover, Massachusetts, was a former seminarian whose wife's career prospects led them to Boston. In Boston he became, by all accounts, a thoughtful and important advocate for Haitians. According to another staff person who worked with him regularly, Johnson "had a real reverence for human beings." Haitians were not the first African diaspora community he assisted. While at Boston College, a Jesuit instructor from Jamaica urged Johnson to serve others, so he taught English and religion at a Jesuit school in Jamaica for a couple of years. He also worked with inner-city youth in Kingston and volunteered in a prison. He considered studying to enter the priesthood and attended seminary before eventually choosing to marry.

I asked how he compared the two different Caribbean populations and was struck by his using the Christological language of "woundedness" to characterize Haitians—in the sense they had suffered external blows unjustly. But he also thought internal social conditions harmed the community, particularly, a tendency toward maintaining social class and status distinctions. Johnson described an occasion when the Center furnace had (once again) ceased to operate and he attempted to fix it himself. Haitians present objected to the director getting his hands dirty. Johnson compared this attitude to the concerns for titles and stature common in some European societies in the nineteenth century, in which social rank was determined by relationship to a sovereign (Foucault 1979).

Other internal factors posed obstacles to reducing the increasingly severe impact of the AIDS crisis. At that point, with little knowledge about how the virus spread and blame against Haitians as a vector, Johnson said rumors circulated that Haitians should not go to the hospital because they might be killed. Or conversely, some questioned how an invisible little germ could kill a man. Dr. Jean-Louis (director of the AIDS Outreach Program) and he attended one or two funerals each week for Haitians who had perished from the disease.

A view of the strategies Haitian professionals employed to combat disease in their community came from an individual whom I call Dr. Bernard Brutus, a Haitian public health administrator who served as the Center's executive director from late 2005 to 2008. Brutus was also involved with launch of the Center's AIDS Outreach Program. He told me the project was initially housed at the Center because it needed a fiscal agent to receive grants.

The controversy leading to the fracturing of this program concerned obstacles staff members faced operating between church and state. When Cardinal Law was installed in Boston (in 1984), he ordered the reorganization of Catholic institutions and emphasized strict observance of Catholic doctrine. One theologian at the University of Notre Dame called Law "one of the most conservative, right-of-center bishops in the US hierarchy" (Golden 1990). Law railed against politicians for their stances in favor of abortion rights, and during a 1986 commencement speech he reprimanded Boston College, accusing it of losing its Catholic identity.[6] A media commentator observed, "Instead of taking a more visible role against racism or AIDS, Law has crusaded against individuals and institutions that he has regarded as heterodox" (Golden 1990). When Mayor Flynn inaugurated a clean needle exchange program in Boston (to help prevent the spread of infections among intravenous drug users who shared needles), Law denounced his colleague's plan (Golden 1990). Although the cardinal launched a "comprehensive AIDS education program" in the archdiocese in 1988 (Davis 2003) and founded a hospice center for people dying of the disease in 1992, he would write the following in an introduction to a pamphlet called *AIDS and Adolescents*:

> Ultimately the only adequate response to the prevention of AIDS and the elimination of sexually transmitted diseases lies in the behavior of human beings, men and women like you and me, who have to reflect on how they act and take responsibility for their actions. Whatever be a person's thoughts about certain devices [condoms or contraceptives] the real problem at issue is human behavior. (Law 1992b: 7)

According to Catholic tenets, the way to resolve this public health crisis was to promote abstinence. The 1968 papal encyclical on the regulation of birth, Pope Paul VI's *Humanae Vitae*, proclaims use of contraceptive technologies a violation of natural law because it would inhibit the procreative purpose of sexual activity (sec. 11).[7] This perspective would fundamentally clash with the state's public health approach to prevention. It would also conflict with the framework Center staff members used to prevent HIV/AIDS.

When the Center AIDS program began, it received public funding from the Massachusetts Department of Public Health (DPH) through the AIDS Action Committee. Among other sources, Johnson said, the AIDS Action Committee provided one grant for housing people with AIDS.[8] Beginning in 1989, the DPH commissioner, David Mulligan, a former Catholic priest who married after leaving the priesthood, launched many of the state's AIDS programs.[9] In addition to promoting a public education campaign and working to establish a needle exchange program, Mulligan actively worked with the gay community to combat the disease. He proposed condoms be distributed in private establishments catering to homosexuals and exhorted gay partners to disclose their sexual histories and to use condoms. The Center also disseminated education and prevention strategies among clients to fight the primarily heterosexual transmission among Haitians and to combat mother-to-child virus transmission.

As a former employee from this era recounted, the DPH began to "regulate the AIDS prevention movement," by requiring grantees to implement more comprehensive programs. The department insisted condoms be distributed in programs it funded. The Center's AIDS program was soon caught between what the church and state each demanded. This double bind precipitated an institutional crisis when the Center was increasingly coming under Charity management. As the charitable arm of the archdiocese, the Charity insisted there could be no talk about contraception in its programs, much less distribution of condoms onsite; programs should promote abstinence.

At roughly the same time these controversies were unfolding at the Center, the Charity's restrictive policies reached media attention regarding another program:

> In a dispute over AIDS prevention, Catholic Charities of Massachusetts has banned condoms from a homeless shelter it operates with public funds and will dismiss the shelter's director. In addition, plans for an AIDS education program at St. Patrick's Shelter for Homeless Women in Somerville that has discussed condom use will be halted, according to shelter workers. Joseph Doolin, the Charities' archdiocesan director, yesterday said AIDS education will continue, but "abstinence must be the approach." (Neuffer 1991)

The Charity later fired the Somerville shelter director because she supplied condoms to unhoused women, "a measure she elected to take under a general state directive to provide an AIDS education program" (Canellos 1991). The ensuing controversy raised legal issues regarding the separation of church and state, not to mention the ethics of firing employees caught between these powers. How could a publicly funded organization fail to observe what the state had determined to be the best course of intervention?

At issue were conflicts between two constitutional principles. On the one hand was the freedom of religion, here for corporate "persons" (see James 2019). This freedom protected the Charity's right to observe Catholic moral tenets on sexuality and contraception. On the other hand was freedom *from* religion, in this case "protection against state-sponsored religious indoctrination," which religiously motivated restrictions on condom availability could be said to impose on clients of faith-based organizations (Canellos 1991). One legal scholar argued religious freedom was problematic because it privileged the rights of institutions offering a service over consumers. Furthermore, the approach assumes these institutions operate in a free market and clients are also able to exercise choice freely in seeking services. Instead, as legal scholar Renee Landers argued, "the government's first concern . . . should be the rights of the clients, who have little freedom to begin with [and for whom] there's not much choice . . . and . . . at that point the restrictions become a problem" (Canellos 1991).

When questioned about the firing in an interview, Joseph Doolin stated the employee "was fired for violating Roman Catholic principles in AIDS education. He said the charity would fulfill its mandate to teach the homeless about AIDS by advising abstinence from sex" (Canellos 1991). Then governor Bill Weld affirmed the state required an AIDS education program, but it did not mandate condom distribution onsite. Therefore, as a "corporate person" with rights, the Charity could not be compelled to violate its freedom of religion. This example shows the degree to which the Church and affiliated Catholic institutions had accumulated greater civic power and corporate rights than the vulnerable populations (and employees) who were dependent on their services—forms of social support the city and state could not, or would not, provide directly.

These controversial issues about religious freedom, the promotion of life, and the prevention of death provoked the Center's AIDS Outreach Program staff to meet with the DPH Refugee and Immigrant Advisory Committee (on which Brutus served) about how best to resolve the conflict between church and state. A group comprising some Haitian physicians, Nesly Metayer, the former program manager for the DPH HIV/AIDS program (and REACH 2010 Coalition facilitator), Brutus, and other Haitians, discussed with Mulligan and his staff members the challenges of working in a Catholic institution. The group then asked whether the AIDS program could be removed from the Center to enable the program to offer comprehensive HIV/AIDS work, including condom distribution. According to one meeting participant, Mulligan was "not going to go against the Church." The solution, this individual said, was to "divide the baby in two." This phrase refers to the biblical story in 1 Kings 3:16–28. Two women claim to be a child's mother and King Solomon, to whom they appealed, orders the child split in two. To save the child the true mother relinquishes her claim and Solomon returns the baby to her. In the AIDS Outreach Program case, rather than determining a true "mother," the state split the funding. Dr. Jean-Louis took half the budget and started a comprehensive AIDS program that developed into CCHER. The Center used its half for prevention education classes, outreach to new immigrants, case management, and counseling support. The program continued operating at the Center until a second crisis erupted in the mid-1990s.

. . .

In the early 1990s, the Charity assigned to Greater Boston Catholic Charities the task of managing the Center's finances.[10] Although the archdiocese had previously overseen the payroll, I was not able to ascertain whether Jean-Marc Jean-Baptiste had fiscal oversight of the HMSC following David Johnson's departure (ca. 1990). When Pierre Imbert was identified as a promising candidate for an administrative role, Ellen Parker—former head of the Charity regional office (and subsequently Executive Director of the Massachusetts antihunger organization, Project Bread)—invited him to serve as Center business manager.[11] I was told that Greater Boston Catholic Charities and two private philanthropies—the Boston Foundation,[12] a community development organization, and the Hyams Foundation, a family foundation seeking "to increase economic and social justice and power within low-income communities in Boston and Chelsea, Massachusetts"—jointly funded Imbert's position to "build capacity" and promote the necessary "institutional leadership," eventually enabling the Center to have greater independence.[13]

But the Haitian community was concerned the Center had lost institutional autonomy, especially as waves of their compatriots sought asylum during the coup years from 1991 to 1994. As executive director, Jean Marc Jean-Baptiste had become a prominent public voice, especially when the Center began resettling adult Haitians paroled from the Guantánamo camps. As discussed previously, the United States Conference of Catholic Bishops (USCCB) held a large contract with the ORR. The Charity was the local VOLAG (voluntary agency) implementing the USCCB contract in Massachusetts.[14] In press statements, Jean-Baptiste advocated for more funding to help refugees until they could find jobs (Bennett 1992a). He lamented the negative depictions in the media compelling Haitians to live in the shadows: "There are many Haitians here, but they are not that visible, because of color, because we are poor. And because of bad publicity of things associated with us, like AIDS, we tend to stay away from the majority culture, which is sad" (Bennett 1992b). Jean-Baptiste would also speak out against discriminatory US immigration and foreign policies toward Haiti, and especially the "porous" international embargo that harmed the poor more than its target, the coup regime (Mallia 1994). Jean-Baptiste also advocated for relief after Hurricane Gordon devastated Haiti in November 1994.

But in 1996, another crisis fractured not only a single Center program but the entire staff. The conflict involved intractable controversies between two distinct frameworks on how best to define and promote life. For the archdiocese and the Charity—its policy enforcer at the programmatic level—the focus on life seemed to involve aligning Haitians' moral and bodily practices with Catholic teachings. For Center staff members, promoting life meant aiding their clients to live with dignity—through housing, education, and job training to assist individuals and families to become incorporated—perhaps, as future American citizens. These distinctions recall earlier discussions of the different modes of pastoral power employed through organized charity in Haiti versus in the United States. In this context, Center staff members felt increasingly restricted by both Catholic doctrines on sexuality and, as I was told, the reporting requirements of the federal grants. It became difficult both to provide and document acts of care, a point of conflict I would later observe firsthand at the Yawkey Center.

One Charity administrator told me Jean Marc Jean-Baptiste was conflicted about working with an agency prohibiting condom distribution, instruction about conventional contraceptive methods, and needle exchange programs—components of secular medical and public health best practices. The Charity was eventually tasked with enforcing Catholic discipline. On April 10, 1996, Jean Marc Jean-Baptiste called an unscheduled staff meeting to announce he had resigned. After the meeting, I was told, Charity staff members escorted him to his desk and packed up his personal items; within two hours he had left the building.[15] A few days later, Carol Chandler, his deputy, also quit. Dr. Raphaël was fired. Over the next two months, five other administrators also quit.

As a news article reported, years of disputes between the Center and its "corporate parent, Catholic Charities, over birth control and AIDS-prevention practices at odds with Catholic teaching" precipitated the crisis (Nealon 1996). The previous fall, the Charity ordered Center staff members to refrain from holding English classes in a building where condoms were distributed in a health clinic. In this theo-spatial logic, proximity to such services meant promoting, condoning, or materially supporting them. By policing its charitable borders using a logic of quarantine, both clients and staff members were kept within prescribed moral boundaries protecting the corporate Church from a contagious source of moral temptation to sin. Then, in April 1996, Dr. Raphaël, who directed both the AIDS and Sante Manman programs, was told the only authorized contraceptive method was natural family planning, "a method that involves pinpointing a women's fertile time by carefully monitoring bodily changes" (Nealon 1996). Reportedly, on May 29, "all staff members in the AIDS program were asked to sign a letter agreeing not to mention condoms in discussions with clients" (Nealon 1996). In attempting to regulate Center practices by policing consciousness, volition, speech, bodily interiority, and external space, the Church exercised pastoral biopower.

The Center's human development and public health approach to promoting life and equitable access to care was compassionate. Haitian staff recognized cultural determinants in promoting health and social empowerment. Their clients' near 80 percent nonliteracy, lack of English fluency, and unemployment made preventing sexually transmitted infection by procuring prophylactics themselves extremely difficult. Some staff responded pragmatically (and mercifully) through alternative spatial practices by ignoring when private actors "just happened" to visit the 12 Bicknell Street Victorian building to distribute condoms to clients waiting for services. Very rarely staff might step off private Church property onto public land to give condoms to clients themselves—a practice of compassion as private persons.

The 1996 crisis was not confined to health-related staff. In solidarity with their colleagues, long-standing Adult Education Program staff members also quit. Center staff members appealed to public and private donors to adjudicate the ongoing dispute, as had occurred with the division of the AIDS program:

> On April 22, 17 staff members wrote to funding agencies warning that Catholic Charities "has assumed a proprietary role over our work in the Haitian community." The Boston Adult Literacy Fund, which gives the center $10,000 annually, is considering withholding a scheduled payment in July. "For us there's the purely subjective concern over what happens to the study center and the whole adult literacy program when such pivotal personnel leave," said Joanne Appleton Arnaud of the literacy fund. (Nealon 1996)

The Massachusetts Department of Education, which gave the Center a two hundred thousand dollar, five-year contract, announced its own investigation. Interestingly, the Boston Adult Literacy Fund commentator compared the crisis to a structural problem involving mergers between values-based institutions and "secular" ones: "Arnaud likens the situation to Cardinal Bernard Law's recent refusal to sanction a merger between Carney Hospital, a Catholic institution, and Quincy Hospital because the Quincy facility performs abortions and provides birth control" (Nealon 1996). In speaking of the Center schism, Joseph Doolin put the controversy in straightforward terms: "If there are people who chose to leave because they can no longer live with our policies then we have to scramble around and get other good people" (Nealon 1996). The Charity, as "corporate parent," named Pierre Imbert interim director and then executive director the same year.

THE METRO BOSTON REACH 2010 COMMUNITY ASSESSMENT

When I began working with the Coalition in 2005, I had no knowledge of these past institutional struggles. Despite this history of organizational friction, the Center's AIDS program staff members had already been working with the Coalition for years. The Center was a CCHER grantee for the REACH 2010 program. At this point, the Center's AIDS program staff did not know their program would end in fall 2006. All clients and case files would be transferred to CCHER (see Chapter 9).

The Coalition was conducting a Haitian community assessment using a qualitative survey instrument administered to five focus groups in Brockton (1),

Cambridge (1), and Dorchester (3).[16] The discussions were held in Haitian Creole and English (according to the preference of the participants). The questions elicited responses from and dialogue about each participant's experience in their respective communities and reflections on the internal and external perceptions of the Haitian community. The participants were also asked about the community's strengths and weaknesses, obstacles to advancement at the individual and group levels, and possible interventions to resolve the problems the groups identified. (I helped code and interpret data from the focus group transcripts.)

The collaborative research process was innovative. It was designed as a capacity-building exercise to improve the participating organizations' technical skills. The research process was intended to build interpersonal and interorganizational trust, and promote greater trust between the organizations and the communities each served. Although unplanned, the focus groups were almost therapeutic—an example of pastoral power in a benevolent secular sense. After the groups were completed, the facilitators led the entire Coalition in an exercise to code one transcript together; then smaller groups analyzed the dialogue from individual focus groups to identify recurring themes. Recurrent themes were then aggregated to form more general conclusions about Greater Boston Haitians.

In October 2005, Nesly Metayer, the same public health expert who facilitated the HMSC Advisory Board retreat, presented the conclusions publicly to a small but engaged audience in Dorchester's Codman Square Great Hall. Metayer discussed the Haitian community's concerns about lacking social, political, and economic power, and sociocultural challenges in realms of cultural intimacy. After describing the Coalition's history, the focus groups' composition, the research methods, and data analysis procedures, he showed how the focus groups had independently identified common themes regarding the community's struggles: mistrust, disunity, disorganization, and resentment toward institutions.

One problem expressed across the groups involved crises in the family. An insufficient level of education and professional experience prevented many Haitians from obtaining skilled employment. Skilled labor positions would permit them to be at home with their families to a greater degree:

> *Pwoblèm ki vi-n rive, paran Ayisyen yo, a fòs ke yo pa gen nivo entèlektyèl ase elve pou li fè yon sèl dyòb, sa vi-n pouse li fè 2 dyòb e li pa gen tan pou timoun nan e timoun nan se deyò ka-p ba-l edikasyon.*[17]

The problem is that Haitian parents, because they don't have a sufficiently high educational [literally, intellectual] level to do a single job, that pushes them to do two jobs, and they don't have time for the children, and it's [forces] outside [the home] that give children an education.

The inability to find a single job to meet family expenses meant parents were not at home as much as needed to instill the desired cultural and moral values in their children. External forces had more influence in the family. Focus group participants linked an insufficient level of education to a person's challenges being incorporated into majority populations. A lack of skills inhibited their capacity to aid newly arrived Haitians (and themselves) to access social support programs. Inadequate education also prevented Haitians from exercising their rights as laborers.

Respondents discussed youth identity crises related to the stigma attached to Haitians among non-Haitian populations, in the media, and in "external" communities:

> *Anpil ti jèn . . . yo pa vle idantifye yo "as Haitian." Menm kreyòl la yo pa vle pale pou pa konnen ke yo se Ayisyen. Paske yo asosye tout bagay negatif a Ayiti. Fò-n kòmanse montre yo, fè istwa avèk yo pou yo ka konnen kisa ki Ayiti-a. Media pa ede non plis, paske lè yo ap bay yon bagay sou Ayiti se tout kote ki pa bon yo montre w, moun kap pouse bouwèt, moun kap pote chaj sou tèt, se sa yap montre de Ayti.*

> Many youth . . . do not want to identify themselves as Haitian. They even don't want to speak Creole in order not to be revealed as Haitian. Because they associate everything negative with Haiti. We must show them and share stories with them for them to know what Haiti [truly] is. The media doesn't help at all, because when they show something on Haiti they show every [thing] that isn't good, people pushing wheelbarrows, people carrying loads on their heads, that's what they show of Haiti.

These debates about identity, the "presentation of self in everyday life" (Goffman 1959), and the role of the media in representing Haiti and Haitians negatively, are elements of cultural intimacy (Herzfeld 1997). In critiquing the stereotypical, traditional representation of economically disadvantaged urban and rural Haitian men (who typically push wheelbarrows) and women (who most often carry large loads on their heads), these respondents are fighting to control narratives of themselves and to brand themselves as a modern, professional people of diverse class backgrounds. But they were also responding to the legacies of stigma against Haitians historically and more recently.

LANGUAGE, ETHNICITY, AND STIGMA AGAINST HAITIANS IN BOSTON

In 1992, Ehrl Lafontant, former member of the Cambridge Haitian-American Association (CHAMA) board (see Chapter 4), described how Boston's reception of Haitians changed after successive waves of immigration: "Before the 1980s, Haitians were received here with open arms, and we were viewed as hard-working, respectful, and all those good attributes. The community was still not very large, and during those years you probably had the more professional Haitians living in Boston" (Ray 1992). Sociologist Michel Laguerre, who was in Boston at the time, commented: "Historically speaking, the people who came earlier were a little more educated, and they felt that they had a special status" (Ray 1992).[18] In the mid-1980s, however, the stigmatization of Haitians as HIV/AIDS carriers, Vodou practitioners, and destitute, exacerbated the growing intolerance against all Haitians in the United States. Laguerre noted how Haitians "realized that just getting an education would not be enough. That experience has forced Haitians to better understand the black American situation" (Ray 1992).

For the 2005 Metro Boston REACH 2010 focus groups, negative external representations also reflected class conflicts inside the Haitian community that were reproduced, but also transformed, in the diaspora:

> *Nou te gen you seri de kesyon klas an Ayiti, men isit nou tout nan menm bòl, ki fè pou nou bliye sa, pou nou kòmanse òganize, pou nou konnen an tan isit nou tout se menm. Gen nan nou ki konn li, gen nan nou ki doktè, gen nan nou ki avoka, men nou tout ap sibi menm pwoblèm yo.*

> We've had a bunch of class questions in Haiti, but here we're all in the same bowl, which requires us to forget [class] in order to begin to organize [together], to recognize that here we're all the same. There are those among us who can read, some are doctors, some are lawyers, but we all suffer the same problem [referring to the pain of discrimination by non-Haitians].

Challenges with internal class discrimination were also linked to a lack of community leaders who could help its members surmount a tendency toward individualism, mistrust, and a lack of unity. By doing so, Haitians could mobilize their strengths to meet the community's needs:

> *Feblès (kominote a) se yon mank de leadership ke li genyen; . . . feblès li se lè nou rantre la . . . nou viv nan yon sans kòm si pa gen anyen otou de nou menm. . . . Nou bezwen yon vizyon kominotè . . . pou n kapab pran pwòp kilti ayisyèn an epi devlope strateji, pou ka pèmèt Ayisyen eseye reponn ak bezwen yo.*

> The weakness of the community is its lack of leadership; . . . its weakness is that when we enter here . . . we live in a sense as if there is nothing [or no one] around us. . . . We need a community vision . . . for us to be able to take authentic Haitian culture and then develop strategies to permit Haitians to try to respond to [our] needs.

The groups emphasized a need to reclaim and mobilize aspects of Haiti's culture and history as a means toward empowerment and social solidarity.

The focus groups highlighted several community strengths: its hard work ethic, high educational aspirations, cultural pride and traditions, and strong family values [there were no Creole quotations provided to illustrate these assets]. In sum, the groups suggested several interventions to improve the community's status:

- Change the negative views of the Haitian community.
- Strengthen leadership in the community.
- Build trust within the community.
- Establish a climate of respect for one another.

- Educate the community to search for and use available resources and services.
- Break existing social barriers in the community.
- Integrate within other communities while maintaining our Haitian identity.
- Revitalize the Haitian family.
- Be more responsive to the needs of our Haitian youth.

The groups perceived these interventions, although somewhat oriented toward individual practices, as solutions to augmenting Haitians' collective well-being. Furthermore, these social intercessions were perceived as necessary steps to reducing disparities of health status and access to treatment.

MOBILIZING THE COMMUNITY

To begin implementing the community assessment recommendations, on November 18 and 19, 2005, the Coalition sponsored a workshop at UMass Boston called "The Future of the Haitian Community: Moving Toward—Trust, Unity and Collective Action!" More than 120 community members representing the professional sector, senior citizens groups, artists, promoters, and entertainers attended. Churches, political activists, and community organizers also participated, as did technicians and business leaders. A variety of nonprofits, community-based and faith-based organizations, and clients of the social service organizations participated, as well as teachers and members of the media. These individuals dialogued using a modified "Future Search" process—a community planning method originally designed for nonprofits—in which participants tell stories of significant past events, analyze the current state of the organization or group, and envision the future in a collaborative manner.[19]

The evening of November 18, participants identified critical events for both Haitians in Haiti and the diaspora from the 1960s to 2005. Among these were the rise to power of dictator François "Papa Doc" Duvalier (1957–71), the American civil rights movement, the 1968 global student revolutions, the 1971 accession of Jean-Claude Duvalier after the death of his father, the 1973 oil crisis, and President Jimmy Carter's promotion of human rights internationally. Pivotal events in Greater Boston included the early 1970s desegregation of public schools. Racial tensions escalated into violence and Haitians were among the targets of hate crimes. From the 1980s, participants noted the negative impact of President Ronald Reagan's policies against Haitians—particularly immigration interdiction policies. The groups also emphasized the appearance of HIV/AIDS in their communities and the 1986 ouster of Jean-Claude Duvalier. Another significant moment in Boston was the 1987 immolation of Haitian cab driver, Antoine Thurel. Thurel set himself on fire on the steps of the Massachusetts State House "as a sacrifice for the liberation of Haiti." At the time, Haiti was in the throes of the postdictatorship period (called "Duvalierism without Duvalier"), a time of reciprocal violence between anti- and prodemocratic forces disproportionately harming impoverished social justice activists.

For the 1990s, the groups identified the December 16, 1990, presidential election of former priest Jean-Bertrand Aristide and the September 30, 1991, military coup ousting him less than eight months after his February 1991 inauguration. With great solemnity, participants spoke of the reign of terror the coup regime and the FRAPH organization inflicted on the prodemocracy sector. They also expressed appreciation for the MICIVIH intervention, the United Nations and Organization of American States International Civilian Mission of Human Rights Observers.[20] MICIVIH's members had documented human rights abuses during the coup years and had aided persecuted Haitians alongside military and other humanitarian actors when the US and UN Multinational Force intervened to restore democracy in fall 1994 (see James 2010). Lastly, the assemblage focused on the present by reviewing the Coalition needs assessment findings on issues currently facing the Haitian community.

The next day participants reviewed the Coalition needs assessment in small groups. The facilitators asked the groups to devise possible short- and long-term goals to implement the recommendations. Several groups hoped Boston's Codman Square or Mattapan Square be renamed "Haitian Square" or "Haitian Town" to create a "*blòk solid*," a visible, recognized Haitian social and political space in the city. Some groups suggested the creation of a Haitian credit union or bank to improve the community's economic prospects. Another group hoped the Boston Haitian community might receive a fifty million dollar grant to support community-organizing efforts in Haiti. Other groups proposed the community pursue greater political connections to the Haitian communities of New York and Miami. All these efforts involved increasing the community's visibility in civic space, achieving political recognition, and accumulating greater wealth.

Most striking to me was a proposition common to almost all the groups: Haitians in Greater Boston needed a community center—a cultural center with an identified leader who could spearhead such initiatives and provide a social space for youth to hang out, learn about their culture, and improve their language skills in Haitian Creole. Others thought a center could offer educational opportunities and job skills training. As each group highlighted a similar aspiration, I wondered why the existing Haitian Multi-Service Center or the new Yawkey Center could not fill these roles? Or, for that matter, why couldn't any of the other Coalition organizations?

Perhaps a new Haitian organization was desired because the relationships among many of the Coalition institutions resembled too closely models of family and kinship. Perhaps their respective mandates were too narrow to meet Haitians' multifaceted needs. Embedded in the historical intraorganizational linkages were strong sentiments, friction, and frustration, but also deep commitments to continuing the struggle to aid their constituents. Some of these tensions were structural and arose from the challenges of operating between church and state, and voluntary and private sector donors. The double binds that were created had influenced several past crises. At the heart of such institutional dramas, however, were conflicting frameworks regarding how to define and best promote life.

. . .

The Charity was not immune to these moral and organizational tensions. In operating between the Church and public and private donors, the agency faced another set of intractable controversies. On May 17, 2004, same sex marriage was legalized in Massachusetts. Then, in October 2005, the *Boston Globe* published a story revealing how the Charity had facilitated thirteen adoptions to same-sex couples in the previous eighteen years, despite Catholic pronouncements that "allowing homosexuals to adopt children is 'gravely immoral.'" The children had been difficult to place—some suffered from physical or emotional difficulties, others were older—and the Charity had quietly fulfilled its contract with the state because doing so was in the best interests of the child (Wen 2005).

When questioned about the contradictions between the Church's stance on the practice of homosexuality and the Charity's adoption work, Rev. Bryan J. Hehir, the then president of the Charity, "described Catholic Charities' decision to permit these adoptions as a legal accommodation in the name of a greater social good. He said that if they did not comply with the state's nondiscrimination clause, they would not be able to do the state work that enables them to place hundreds of foster children in stable homes" (Wen 2005). The Charity had had a long-standing contract with the Massachusetts Department of Social Services and could not discriminate against any eligible couples. According to law, the Charity could not exclude same-sex couples from adopting; doing so would violate the terms of its contract. On the other hand, the Charity could not engage in acts violating Catholic tenets. When the authenticity of the Church's brand was questioned publicly amid the ongoing clerical abuse crisis, theological compliance was particularly important. Any additional evidence of institutional hypocrisy or violations of its rules called into question the Archdiocese of Boston's stated commitment to transparency and the corporate Church's efforts to regain legitimacy.

In December 2005, the Charity Board of Trustees voted unanimously to continue fulfilling same-sex adoptions as an essential component of its Christian mission. On February 28, 2006, the four Massachusetts diocesan bishops requested from Governor Mitt Romney an exemption from the obligation to facilitate adoptions to gay couples. The bishops' statement emphasized the Church's one hundred years of providing adoption services to Massachusetts (an articulation of the Catholic charitable brand), then requested the state respect its "Constitutional guarantee of religious freedom" and desire to continue serving "without violating the tenets of our faith."

In response to the bishops' assertion of religious freedom and request to exclude gay couples who desired to adopt, seven Charity trustees resigned: "We 'cannot participate in an effort to pursue legal permission to discriminate against Massachusetts citizens who want to play their part in building strong families,' the seven members said in a statement" (Wen 2006a). Some Charity donors stated they would withhold customary donations. According to one trustee who resigned, Peter Meade, executive vice president of Blue Cross Blue Shield of Massachusetts and former chairman of the CCAB Board of Trustees, "he has already heard from some current contributors to Catholic Charities who say they will pull their donations because of the bishops' plan. Last year, the agency raised $7 million, roughly 20 percent of its income, from individual donors, foundations, and corporations" (Wen 2006a). Meade also argued the request for a legal exemption was uncharitable and sent "an unfair message to the 13 gay couples who have already adopted through Catholic Charities. 'Does this new policy suddenly render the love and care they have given their children worthless? Of course not,' he said" (Wen 2006a). The same day the resignations occurred:

> Hehir and O'Malley met with Romney in his State House office to make their case for an exemption, but Romney said he lacked the authority to do so. Hehir and O'Malley left the State House feeling that nothing could be done soon for their cause. The bishops had considered launching a court challenge, but Hehir said he and O'Malley realized it would cost "too much time and energy"—without any certainty of victory. "It became clear our options were narrow," Hehir said. (Wen 2006b)

On March 10, 2006, after archdiocesan instruction, the Charity announced it would discontinue adoption services altogether, a core work of mercy since the organization's founding in 1903.

. . .

As I watched these events from 2005 to 2006, the Center was preparing to move to the new Yawkey building. The 12 Bicknell Street era was coming to an end. I had many questions about the Center's role in the Haitian community and its link to the Charity network. I did not know if the Center could fulfill the Haitian community's need for a cultural center, or if it ever had previously. Nor was I certain whether the social and cultural barriers that Haitians themselves had identified as obstacles to their successful incorporation in Massachusetts had influenced the Center's history. Despite the episodic turmoil both internal and external events would provoke as challenges, the Center had nonetheless endured and served for nearly thirty years. The Haitian community had also struggled to overcome historical and cultural barriers to social trust, collective action, and health, and had been strong supporters. However, the social assessment and "future search" workshop process showed the Greater Boston Haitian community still longed, as Pierre Imbert called it, for a space of their own.

7

Memory Palace II

Everyday Life and Death at the Center

Despite the brutal reality of racial apartheid, of domination, one's homeplace was the one site where one could freely confront the issue of humanization, where one could resist.
—bell hooks

The memory palace expanded throughout this chapter complicates a notion of "everyday life" as habitual or static (Das 2010). In January 2006, the Haitian Multi-Service Center commenced operations in the Yawkey building, coproducing charity among clients, advisory board members, and community stakeholders. The stakeholder assemblage, a corporate body, embraced "strangers" and "the vulnerable" from cradle to grave. Center "keepers of the flame" (Hopgood 2006), its long-standing staff members, emplaced anew their advocacy and care practices in the new structure while adjusting to a new executive director, a public health administrator whom I call Dr. Bernard Brutus. Although a majority Haitian program, African Americans, international migrants, and some European Americans also received food, housing, and charitable aid.

Center care, education, and advocacy practices were "spatialized"—rooted physically in bureaucratic spaces, but grounded sensorially in places offering shared cultural orientations, memories, natal languages, and aspirations. Amidst everyday emergencies, managerial requirements for the Center to become a predictable, procedural space, rather than a cultural and even spiritual "homeplace" (hooks 1991), underlay new administrative crises and interpersonal disputes.

In her seminal volume, *Spatializing Culture: The Ethnography of Space and Place*, Setha Low (2017) traces how scholars analyze the meanings of 'space' and 'place,' with an emphasis on anthropologists' definitions. In early ethnographic works, *space* connoted the material foundations of culture, such as the physical architecture of built environments, the design of human settlements, and topographical components of social structures. *Place* suggested a locale to which sensory, affective, and embodied memories were attached, providing an intimate locus of identity, kinship, and community. Commonly, space is "the more encompassing construct, while place retains its relevance and meaning but only as a subset of space. Place is defined as lived space made up of spatial practices and is phenomenologically experienced, such as the culturally meaningful space of home" (Low 2017: 12).

Contemporary population mobility—whether international migration, forced displacement, rural to urban shifts, gentrification, or economically driven homelessness, and so on—untethers the fixity of place, space, and especially "home." Center staff members often defined home as their natal province or village, a neighborhood in their birth city, or the schools and religious institutions attended. For others, home signified ease in culturally and linguistically familiar surroundings rather than a geographic location. The Center was homelike, a site of remembrance and cultural anchoring, with safe places for improvisation, creativity, learning, and imagining.

To recall, at St. Leo's the Center was also a literal home for its resident clerical staff and a temporary sanctuary for clients in a city less kind to persons of color or the poor. Although interpersonal strife previously diminished the refuge provided (see Chapter 5), the parish Center nonetheless embodied Black feminist theorist bell hooks's (1991: 384) concept of "homeplace":

> Historically, African-American people believed that the construction of a homeplace, however fragile and tenuous (the slave hut, the wooden shack), had a radical political dimension. . . . This task of making a homeplace was not simply a matter of black women providing service; it was about the construction of a safe place where black people could affirm one another and by so doing heal many of the wounds inflicted by racist domination.

While both St. Leo's women and men enabled the Center to become a homeplace, the care Haitian women staff gave their clients and each other—through domestic education, the aesthetic environment, and advocacy practices—deepened this sense of home. Being welcomed at the Center conveyed to stakeholders a sense of validation, dignity, and social and political recognition, regardless of legal and economic status, or race. In the Yawkey building, however, pressures on staff to consistently achieve best practice benchmarks curbed improvisational care practices.

CARE AND EDUCATION ROUTINES

In the new building, the Center's identities as Haitian or Catholic, and secular or religious, remained contested, as did its capacity to offer a homeplace. In June 2006, a striking lobby wall facing the reception desk displayed images of prominent Haitian revolutionary figures. Although welcoming, the visual acknowledgment of Haitian culture and history was not easily conveyed to clients (see Figure 18). After the "merger," a receptionist who spoke Haitian Creole was not

FIGURE 18. Yawkey Center lobby, June 2006. Photo credit: Erica Caple James.

consistently available. Rather than interpreting this as an administrative decision to reduce redundancies, many staff perceived this change as a Charity strategy to diminish the Center's care and advocacy for Haitians.

Programmatic mergers provoked disputes over whose charitable labor, culture, and history should be commemorated onsite. The cumbersomely named Yawkey Konbit-Kreyòl Center for Early Education and Care represented one compromise. The Church and Charity sought to acknowledge the Yawkey Foundation, whose five million dollars enabled completion of the new ten million dollar building. Like prior struggles to place "Haitian Multi-Service Center" on the new building's exterior, the HMSC Advisory Board insisted the daycare name acknowledge Haitian voluntarism, teamwork (*konbit kreyòl*), language, culture, and families. Renaming the program solely after philanthropists who had not directly contributed to the daycare was considered an erasure of history.

These concerns about naming and increasing the visibility of ethnic minority contributions to civic life would later be reflected in other conflicts over the Yawkey name in Greater Boston. In an era when the racist, sexist, and otherwise reprehensible behaviors of prominent contemporary and historical figures has led to the removal of their names, effigies, and likenesses from both public and private spaces, the 2018 decision by Boston Red Sox principal owner John Henry to rename the famed "Yawkey Way" in Fenway Park to "Jersey Street" provoked tremendous public debate. Thomas A. Yawkey, who owned the Boston Red Sox baseball team from 1933 until his death in 1976, and the Red Sox organization "front office," the last major team to integrate African Americans, were both alleged to have practiced systematic racial discrimination in the team's early decades. A National Public Radio media story highlighted the ambivalence of Yawkey allies and grant recipients about the naming controversy.

> "It's a very slippery slope and ultimately a very divisive slope," says Rev. Ray Hammond, pastor at the historically black Bethel AME Church in Boston, and a Yawkey Foundations trustee. The street name Yawkey Way is nothing like the Confederate memorials that deserve to be dumped, he says. Yawkey's 'sins' don't compare, he says, and must be considered in the context of the era, his personal growth, and his generosity. And he says, one must allow for his redemption. (Smith 2018)

At issue was whether the individuals' negative acts should define their legacy and compel recension of their public recognition or whether individuals who have expressed remorse, been "redeemed," and have practiced penitential corporate philanthropy, should still be honored publicly.

But debates over commemorating the legacy of controversial figures like Thomas Yawkey reveal the underlying economy of merits and faults and roles of charity and philanthropy in this salvific economy. Yawkey family foundation grant and gift beneficiaries, including the Charity, quickly defended the Yawkey family and name and advocated for its retention, but to no avail. Among those supporters, Cardinal Seán Patrick O'Malley, successor to the infamous Cardinal Law, and Debbie Rambo, then President and CEO of Catholic Charities of the Archdiocese of Boston [the Charity], were signatories to a March 15, 2018, letter advocating for the retention of the Yawkey name:

> The Yawkey Foundations have donated hundreds of millions to charities, many of which support the underserved. . . . As direct beneficiaries of the Yawkey legacy, we are proud to include his name on the buildings, facilities and programs made possible by generous grants from the Yawkey Foundations. We believe it is not overstating things to say that removing his name from Fenway Park will forever taint his legacy, both as the historic owner of the Red Sox and throughout the city of Boston. It will force people to take sides over how to treat the Yawkey name and, we fear, create conflict rather than consensus over what we all need to do to make sure Boston is welcoming to people of color. (Yawkey Foundation 2018; Labbe 2018)

Although I have not seen this argument extended to the legacy of individuals like Cardinal Law, or other clerics who violated their ethical charge, the underlying moral assumptions conceive charitable giving as redemptive for the donor, provider, or practitioner. Secondly, charitable and philanthropic practices somehow purify and cleanse the negative legacies of individual and institutional actors. Third, institutional grant recipients portray themselves to be "beneficiaries" of aid, even as they serve as providers or donors themselves. Additionally, charity and philanthropy are means of improving racial injustice by "welcoming people of color."

But in 2005, when the Center Advisory Board and staff struggled to have the Haitian origins and contributions to the daycare at the Center recognized, these implicit assumptions about philanthropy and disputes about naming remained private and internal to the corporate Catholic community. The unwieldingly named Yawkey Konbit-Kreyòl Center for Early Education and Care was the compromise choice symbolizing many of these ethical dilemmas.

In everyday practice I knew the daycare services reflected none of these (bio) political debates. With no infant childcare spots available at my university, I was grateful my daughter Ayanna was offered an unsubsidized place in the Center's new infant program. Only later did I learn firsthand how Haitian women's personal sacrifices established the program.

. . .

In a rural community about an hour outside Port-au-Prince, I waited with anticipation for Center daycare founder "Sister Yvonne" to dismiss parochial school students for the 2017 summer. After several years of searching I had finally found her. I was excited and a bit nervous. She was the sister whose vocation remained after the tumultuous period of the Center's establishment in St. Leo Parish (see Chapter 5). Wearing a royal blue habit over a crisp white collared blouse, she encouraged the youth to help their parents and to remain chaste during the break. Although demanding compliance, the tiny woman radiated warmth, pride, and love.

Sister Yvonne represented a less visible category of immigrants, religious laborers. In the late 1970s, as Greater Boston's Haitian population expanded, Cardinal Medeiros invited her religious order to serve. Medeiros had met Mother Monique, the religious community's superior, when she was receiving medical care in Boston. Mother Monique asked the cardinal for sacred relics for their chapel in Haiti. After her return home (in 1977 or 1978) the cardinal wrote, requesting some nuns to help meet diaspora Haitians' corporal and spiritual needs in Boston. In 1981, Sister Yvonne emigrated with the third group of religious sisters.

Although Sister Yvonne said she felt she had been called to religious life since childhood, after meeting with a priest to discuss her vocation, an opportunity came serendipitously. Her older sister happened to be teaching a religious sister at a school in Port-au-Prince and learned their order needed a good teacher. She wrote the almost nineteen-year-old Yvonne to come to the capital. "Upon arriving, Mother Monique didn't give me much credit because I was thin and looked very young. . . . And then she talked to me. Not in the context of becoming a Mother. She just chatted with me. . . . After, when I was twenty-two, I entered the community, and now I am sixty-four. So, I have been in the community for 42 years." In her spiritual biography, an intense personal commitment to serve, care for, and educate those perceived as less fortunate later allowed her to launch a daycare program while enduring migration challenges and parish crises.

At St. Leo's, Sister Yvonne was the first to offer childcare: "We lived upstairs, and the children were downstairs. . . . The daycare was the first activity. . . . Afterwards, Monestime brought in the 'Haitian Outreach,' giving classes for adults, adults' school." Demand for English instruction was high, Yvonne continued: "In fact, when there wasn't enough room, they used to give English classes at night [in the room] where the kids were." She also confirmed the Center received archdiocesan support directly: "the Cardinal . . . used to pay us a small salary so that we could have some money." Sister Yvonne returned to Haiti around 1983, when tensions in St. Leo Parish produced factions for and against the religious sisters.

As the daycare formalized and included trained lay staff persons, it earned renown providing bilingual education and care. The National Academy for the Education of Young Children (NAEYC) later accredited the program. According to "Mirlande St. Jean," the daycare was one of the only accredited Haitian-run programs in the United States. Mirlande first volunteered from 1987 to 1989, then became a paid preschool teacher, and eventually, manager. With funding from the Massachusetts Department of Social Services (now the Massachusetts Department of Children and Families) and other sources, the Yawkey Konbit-Kreyòl Center offered classes in English. French- and Creole-speaking instructors helped establish for students "a foundation for the future and connection with the home country."

Although the state and NAEYC accrediting agency required the inclusion of children's home language in the curriculum, I soon learned the programs were no longer rooted predominantly in Haitian culture and language. Their goal was achieving facility with American English and culture. The identity of the daycare as a Haitian place, or ethnically and linguistically indistinct space, remained contested.

INITIAL RESPONSE

Clients facing everyday emergencies often accessed the Center through Initial Response, which combined the Center's and Greater Boston Catholic Charities' emergency aid programs. In a May 2007 interview, a Center administrator estimated twenty individuals requested admittance daily. Most encountered "Dr. Oscar Fils-Aimé," a Haitian physician studying to earn his US medical license while working with Initial Response and the HIV/AIDS program.

Dr. Oscar became accustomed to managing medical emergencies during his training in Haiti's capital. A native of northern Haiti, he earned his medical degree in 1994 at the Faculté de Médecine et de Pharmacie—Université d'État d'Haïti (UEH) [Faculty of Medicine and Pharmacy, State University of Haiti] in Port-au-Prince. He was interning prior to President Aristide's restoration to power and said during the three years of unlawful military rule (1991–94), soldiers frequently entered the hospital to terrorize patients and clinical staff. These antidemocratic forces even shot their targets in the hospital emergency room. The ongoing *ensekirite* (insecurity)—political and criminal violence that ebbed and flowed unpredictably—contributed to his family's decision to migrate to the United

States. An older sister moved first, then sponsored their mother. In 2000, their mother sponsored remaining family members (one sibling remained in Haiti). For six months, Oscar, his wife, and daughter lived with his in-laws in Boston until they could afford their own housing. In the meantime, he struggled to obtain English fluency, master the public transportation system, conserve savings while seeking employment, and acquire the certifications to practice medicine in the United States. Dr. Oscar became an American citizen in 2005, but not all of his extended family were lawful residents. He also lamented the requirement to give up his Haitian citizenship after naturalizing; dual citizenship between Haiti and the United States was not legally possible.

Dr. Oscar contrasted how obstacles to integrating into American society affected migrants of different class and gender backgrounds: "It's an issue of expectation. Those with lower socioeconomic status have lower expectations. Those of higher socioeconomic status and education in Haiti have higher expectations. . . . When they can't meet them, they have a [psychological] breakdown." In his analysis, Haitian professionals, especially men, who could not work at the level they had previously or who, because of linguistic difficulties, might never attain the socioeconomic status held in Haiti, had greater adjustment difficulties: "Usually society expects more from men. If we consider this, maybe men have more challenges."

Initial Response enabled Dr. Oscar to mitigate the emergencies Haitians (and others) confronted daily and to employ the health expertise he had earned in Haiti. Oscar began working at the Center part time (in 2002) to help implement its REACH 2010 subcontract with CCHER (see Chapter 6). He would subsequently conduct public health outreach in the Center's redesigned health promotion program (see Chapter 9).

Although Initial Response provided much needed aid, its Haitian-centered justice orientation was diminished in the Yawkey building. At St. Leo Parish, Dr. Oscar said, the Center's emergency relief services offered immigrant and refugee legal assistance. He regretted how the Center "has changed . . . and is moving away from what it has been or should have been in terms of a Center for Haitians where people can come for services or to get connected." Before the Yawkey merger, immigration support "was a centerpiece" of the Center's work. He emphasized how people came for all kinds of reasons—for the telephone number of the Haitian Consulate, for help with finding housing, or to ask how to donate money to Haiti after hurricanes. "After the new director's arrival they decided to take [immigration services] out." He told me, despondently, how those services had been centralized in the Charity headquarters in downtown Boston. An immigrant in search of legal assistance might have first contact with Charity staff members only in English.

Center staff linked limitations placed on the language of first contact to the shift away from the "Haitians-Helping-Haitians" mission. In May 2007, a former Adult Education Program staff member scorned the change:

> So, . . . we're talking about thousands of people . . . So, if that program changes from
> Immigration Services . . . it's very important that people have access to these services,
> and this money and whatever, but what is the Haitian Center then? I mean, this in-
> stitution is very important to the Haitian community because of the services that it
> provides, and they have to do with the immigration services.

I was not able to confirm whether the Charity's decision to centralize refugee and immigrant services was part of agency-wide restructuring—perhaps in response to increasing financial constraints—or signaled less willingness to sustain the Center's independent legal and political role as an immigrant rights advocate. Regardless, the restructuring reinforced staff suspicions about deliberate efforts to shift the Center from a homeplace to a bureaucratic workspace.

The merged Initial Response emergency aid program exemplified charitable biopolitics with its focus on mitigating everyday crises at the individual and family level. Dr. Oscar said the program offered "wrap-around" services with two main amenities for eligible clients: (1) a food pantry provided standard bags of donated food items monthly; and (2) financial assistance for rent and utility payments was available. To attain eligibility, prospective clients completed an intake form requesting biographical and demographic information—such as race, ethnicity, marital status, disability status, and the source of referral—and household composition data: the name, sex, social security number, date of birth, and age of all members. All sources of monthly income were required, ranging from employment payments, disability payments, pensions, social security, and any other forms of social welfare or unemployment compensation, to alimony and child support. Monthly household expenses were to be enumerated for all members, then the "cause of need." Personal and familial, but also external crises were categorized: problems with budgeting, childcare, and child support; death, domestic violence, "desertion, divorce, and separation"; and illness/disability and substance abuse. Other categories included disaster, eviction, and relocation, robbery, and refugee and undocumented alien status. Conditions like unemployment, underemployment and "income below cost of basic needs," "security deposit/other housing issues," "rent too high," and "public agency delay" could also render eligibility. Applicants had to provide government issued identification, social security cards, and proof of address for food pantry assistance, plus a landlord's letter to authenticate need of rental assistance. After legitimating need, the program provided limited financial assistance using funding from multiple sources.

I was surprised to learn Initial Response received partial funding from the Federal Emergency Management Agency (FEMA). I had assumed FEMA provided humanitarian assistance only in the aftermath of "natural" disasters or large-scale environmental cataclysms that received formal recognition from political leaders. However, after the September 11, 2001, terrorist attacks, FEMA and twenty-two other federal agencies would be linked in 2003 to compose the Department of Homeland Security. FEMA's mission expanded to include responses to so-called natural and man-made disasters affecting homeland security.[1] The agency would also provide grants to social service agencies across the United States through the Emergency Food and Shelter (EFS) Program. Catholic Charities USA, the national federation of United States Catholic Charities agencies, was an EFS member. FEMA grants were intended "to supplement food, shelter, rent, mortgage and utility assistance programs for people with non-disaster related emergencies" in order to "help prevent homelessness, and feed and shelter the nation's hungry and homeless."[2] Dr. Oscar said FEMA funds were restricted to US citizens and permanent residents or aid recipients with legal status like asylees; however, undocumented clients could be aided through other resources. At the time, the United Way provided almost one hundred thousand dollars per year to the rental and utility assistance program through the Charity. Similarly, the Gillette Fund offered Initial Response financial support.

Initial Response also aided persons who were "food insecure." Food insecurity describes "the limited or uncertain availability of nutritionally adequate, safe foods or the inability to acquire personally acceptable foods in socially acceptable ways" (Weiser et al. 2010: 2, citing Normén et al. 2005). Sister Yvonne described how the food assistance program had been one of the Center's earliest services:

> The Salvation Army used to provide foods . . . rice, canned food, beans, corn . . . And [for] the kids also. . . . We used to have a camp program for the kids. When we had camp, we were given a lot of food. Kids didn't have to bring any food. They came without anything and went back home with their belly full. In fact, our refrigerator had plenty of leftover[s], which we gave to families in need.

At St. Leo's, donated food came from individuals, institutions like the Salvation Army, and local grocery chains with surplus goods. As the Center's services formalized, it received governmental and nongovernmental grant funding, Project Bread food donations, and Greater Boston Food Bank food distributions.

Through its institutional location in the Catholic Charities network, Initial Response received indirect federal support from TEFAP, the United States Department of Agriculture's "The Emergency Food Assistance Program." In 2006, TEFAP provided donated nutritional support to "state distributing agencies" in the form of commodity food items for "low-income Americans, including elderly people, by providing them with emergency food and nutrition assistance at no cost."[3] In 1981, the Temporary Emergency Food Assistance Program was launched to "distribute surplus commodities to households." Under the 1990 farm bill the program's name was changed to the Emergency Food Assistance Program. TEFAP was "designed to help reduce Federal food inventories and storage costs while assisting the needy."[4] To mitigate the economic effects of the Great Depression on low-income families in the United States, in the 1930s the federal government provided food to families and aid to farmers with unsaleable products by buying "surplus commodities" and donating them as food aid, especially to school lunch programs.[5] Both humanitarian relief and corporate subsidies were joined through this program via the distribution (and, at times, purchase) of surplus commodities from agricultural producers. At the time of my research, TEFAP mandated each state's allocation of the United States Department of Agriculture (USDA) nutritional resources derived from the number of unemployed persons and people with incomes below the established poverty level in the state. State food aid allocations were then distributed to food banks that in turn dispensed food items to local organizations like community action agencies, soup kitchens, and food pantries. These programs provided food directly to eligible individuals and families (USDA 2006). In Massachusetts, the Greater Boston Food Bank was the primary agency designated to manage food distributions from TEFAP.

In addition to receiving governmental emergency food resources from FEMA, the food pantry received both funding and food donations from several national, regional, state, and local nongovernmental institutions: the Greater Boston Food Bank, one of the largest hunger-relief agencies in the United States; regional grocery food chains like Stop N' Shop; Project Bread, a statewide antihunger advocacy agency that provides public education, networking, and funds to a variety of food initiatives; and local private supermarkets. As described by Ellen Parker, a former Charity manager who also worked with Project Bread, the Greater Boston Food Bank was part of a national network of agencies taking surplus foods from grocery stores for redistribution. These stores received a tax deduction for the donated food: "It was valuable to the grocery stores because they didn't have to pay to get rid of the food, and there's a big tax benefit for them. . . . It's kind of a good deal for Big Ag[riculture]. They get to take the entire market value off on their taxes. It's been a big thing for them." She next outlined the relationship between corporate food production, charitable food pantries, food security, and culture:

> The Greater Boston Food Bank is one of the larger ones [food distributors] for a lot of reasons not having to do with need, but they take surplus food. Originally, they only took surplus food and gave it out, so it was really kind of mixed. It was like Coke and sugar cookies. But now, because they have a lot of money, they purchase food through the same kind of purchasing agents that big supermarkets purchase through. So, because they're really led by supermarket official executives, it has the whole culture of a supermarket. . . . They don't worry about, "Does the person eat the food when they take the food out of the food bank?" For years, they never worried about what kind of food they gave away. So, there's a lot of problems with ethnic food. They've changed somewhat.

Next Parker suggested the growth in Greater Boston Food Bank's capacity to distribute food responded not to a national rise in chronic hunger, but rather to the charitable partnerships between the commercial and nonprofit sector. She distinguished the Food Bank's approach from Project Bread's:

Well, Project Bread . . . at least when I was there . . . had an advocacy role. It used to raise about $3 million a year and give it away. And we had a lobbyist. . . . We were really advocating for change in the quality of school lunches because, for example, in Boston, there's like 59,000 kids that get [one third] of their calories from school lunches. . . . So, the quality of the lunch is super, super important.

A current Project Bread staff member said the Haitian Multi-Service Center's 2003 grant application recorded 350 families served annually by its food pantry. That year Project Bread gave a grant for nine thousand dollars. Eventually, the Center—and later, the Yawkey building food pantry—depended greatly on the Greater Boston Food Bank, but had limited capacity to provide food meeting clients' needs. Parker continued:

I mean, the Food Bank had a very straight, clear job which was to collect and distribute food. The Haitians used to get screwed by the Food Bank because . . . the most cost-effective way for the Food Bank to distribute food would be to distribute to really large food pantries like the Red Cross food pantry, which could give out tons and tons of food to lots of people, because volume and number of people are two major measurements for them, reporting measurements. [But] the Haitian Multi-Service Center never had any place to keep inventory. So, the food had to be given out, and they didn't—other food pantries had these very fancy refrigerators and stuff like that. [The] Haitian Multi-Service Center never had that.

In January 2009, three years after moving into the new Yawkey building, a local news article highlighted the struggles Dorchester food pantries, including the Yawkey pantry, faced in supplying demands (Harding 2009). Beth Chambers, the Yawkey Center food pantry manager, noted: "Our numbers have tripled since Catholic Charities moved from Bird Street [the Greater Boston Catholic Charities former Uphams Corner location] here to the new Yawkey Center in January of 2006 . . . And there's no sign on [the] door or publicity that we even have a food pantry. It's all word of mouth." In December 2008 over seven hundred families were served. The high demand forced the Yawkey pantry to limit visits to once every other month (Harding 2009).

Although the demand for emergency food services can be considered an indicator of local, national, and even global financial crises, the intervention of religious nonprofit organizations to mitigate the urban public's acute and chronic hunger has been normalized. Should the state guarantee the public's food security directly with vouchers or financial aid, rather than through purchases and subsidies to agricultural producers and distribution through corporatized charitable food agencies?

. . .

In her *Sweet Charity: Emergency Food and the End of Entitlement*, Janet Poppendieck (1998: 12) argues the growth in soup kitchens and food pantries in the early

1980s represented a retreat from support for a federal food stamp program. From a voucher program enabling the bearer to purchase desired food items reliably, the recension of New Deal entitlements forced reliance on "haphazard local provision" of charitable food assistance. Such programs "were a retreat from rights to gifts. Poor people might be, and often are, very well treated in charitable emergency food programs, but they have no rights, at least no legally enforceable rights, to the benefits that such programs provide" (Poppendiek 1998: 12). Such a shift is a characteristic of neoliberal charity.

The privatization and "charitization" of food support are not limited to the United States. The reduction in government social welfare and outsourcing of state care to private voluntary institutions is a global phenomenon (James 2019). Paul Cloke, Jon May, and Andrew Williams (2017: 704) describe the rise of food banks in the United Kingdom as a form of "voluntary service provision in the context of austerity." Referencing North American social analyses, the authors assert "food banks are themselves symptomatic of insecure and corporatized food networks [that] depoliticized issues of poverty by institutionalizing food poverty as deserving of charitable emergency aid rather than collectivist welfare entitlements." While acknowledging its interpretive importance—linking increasing nonprofit social care to entitlement reduction—the authors criticize how this framework fails to interpret "food banks as spaces of care that potentially serve to articulate a newly emerging and not yet fully formed ethical and political response to welfare '*in the meantime*'" (Cooke, May, and Williams 2017: 704; emphasis in the original).

Although food banks may offer spaces of care and an alternative ethical model of redressing economic inequality and food insecurity, should government guarantee public safety and security and the means of subsistence? Do humans possess inherent rights to basic needs or is access to the means of subsistence solely an earned privilege? Should public or private actors provide individuals and families the means to fulfill these needs "in the meantime"?

At the (Yawkey) Center, similar tensions recurred between viewing access to food as a human right and an entitlement secured by the state or an earned privilege bestowed through private charity, human services, and voluntary care. These politics of hunger, basic needs, and emergency relief truly reflected a biopolitics of charity. Regardless of its theoretical importance, from 2006 to 2007, the food pantry distributed supplies long before the month's end. Because the Yawkey Center food pantry was accessible to the public from the main floor atrium, I would sometimes see clients waiting patiently to receive their monthly allotment. I was also aware of Center case managers' food package deliveries to eligible clients. The commodity products available for fiscal year 2006 were canned and dried fruits, canned vegetables, fruit juice, dried egg mix, meat/poultry/fish, nonfat dry milk, pasta, peanut butter, rice/grits/cereal, and soups. Although atypical of foods Haitians (or clients of other ethnic backgrounds) would consume, there was little variety in a food program reliant on donated surplus items rather than the options voucher programs offered aid recipients to purchase customary food items.

Why perform "corporal works of mercy" or, simply, charity, with only minimal capacity to meet clients' needs? In describing her personal acts of compassionate care in retirement, Ellen Parker addressed a perceived conflict between charity as neoliberal care that normalizes structural inequalities and charity as a means toward food security and justice:

> So, the one thing that I do is every week . . . I make ten pounds of collard greens and I hand it out [at] this homeless dinner in a park. There's about seven of us, and I'm part of this team. And we give it out. I'd always have been down on these homeless meals programs and [this] charitable stuff, yet I know kind of in the moment that I'm giving up collard greens [and] that these people are actually really hungry, and they don't have any place else to go. . . . I mean, because working for justice wouldn't feed them on Thursday night. So, it's an interesting thing.

I am struck by the implicit charitable economy articulated here between personal sacrifice, mortification,[6] or penitential practices in giving up an item to others without expectation of a return, and its contrast with more bureaucratic sites of meal distribution. The outdoor setting, a recreational space, has become a place in which a meal is provided intimately to those without a homeplace. Alongside her team, Ellen's offering of something material, collard greens—presumably to those for whom this is an accustomed food—and giving time, labor, and resources to meet unhoused persons' needs, could be a step on a path toward justice, an intangible good. In her view, perhaps echoing Cloke, May, and Williams's notion of "in the meantime," direct charity provided face-to-face helps to sustain everyday life while advocating for empowerment and equity in the long term. Haitians, she said, were experts in this kind of improvisation: "The other thing I feel like about the Haitians . . . maybe because I knew them better as a group, but I feel like their self-reliance is just really—they just seem, as a group, really able to cope with huge amounts of things and also be self-reliant or community-reliant." For Parker this capacity to be "self-reliant or community-reliant" in the face of routine personal and social ruptures is admirable.

I've wondered whether food provision, like gift giving, conferred as much or more benefit to the donor as to the recipient. In 2006, I worked alongside staff members to assemble bags of staple foods for distribution with free turkeys to clients for Thanksgiving. It was a collective activity fulfilling a work of mercy— to feed the poor—and it enabled us to extend care and compassion tangibly. Although many of us questioned how clients would receive less than culturally ideal items, we had no discussion of charity's capacity to address structural issues of economic inequality and injustice. Undoubtedly, charitable food aid is a pastoral activity aligned with the Catholic principle of subsidiarity, an ethic seeking to limit the role of government in solving problems of insecurity for citizens and eligible residents. The food pantry provided needed sustenance, gave volunteers opportunities to aid others directly, and offered clients temporary relief—all likely better than receiving no nutritional support. But food pantries could neither provide food nor engender food security sustainably.

THE ELDER PROGRAM

The elevator ascended slowly to the third floor of the building. Impatient (and fit) stakeholders mounted the stairs, an easier task for adult learners seeking the second-floor classrooms and computer lab, or who met with the employment counselors. Rising by mechanical lift or by foot was a difficult choice for those in the Elder Program, which had been misguidedly designed for the third floor. But the large room where elders met and received lunch several times weekly was welcoming; it was a place of advocacy and education, and a homeplace empowering elders to strive for citizenship.

The program responded to Haitian elders' isolation and urban immobility. One near full-time staff member, another part-time member, and volunteers served the program. The Center's shared driver and van transported some clients; others came by public or private means. The program met from Mondays through Thursdays from nine o'clock in the morning to three o'clock in the afternoon and offered social activities, field trips, and guest speakers who presented topics related to the elders' needs. Staff members gave practical trainings, English as a Second Language (ESL) instruction, and citizenship classes. The program served elders over the age of fifty-five, most with limited literacy in either Haitian Creole or English and lacking fluency with spoken English. Such limitations often correlated with lower economic status.

Most of the twenty-six clients were permanent residents between the ages of fifty-five and nearly ninety (for the oldest Haitians dates of birth could be uncertain). Prior to becoming Center clients, most had been unaware of the benefits to which they were entitled as lawful US residents. With program assistance, elders made the passage from immigrant to citizen, and from social isolation to social incorporation. But apart from the elders' participation in external religious activities, the Center frequently became the focus and locus of their independent social lives.

A 2007 interview with a twenty-five-year-old social work intern illuminated the obstacles Haitian elders faced in Greater Boston. In 1993, "Cassandra Isidor," born in 1981, emigrated from Port-at-Prince, Haiti, through family sponsorship. After graduating high school, she majored in criminal justice in college and aspired to become an immigration lawyer. A documentary about twenty-first-century aging convinced her to pursue a master's degree in social work, eventually fulfilling the second year of a required internship with the Center's Haitian elders. Although most of the elders were physically healthy, some suffered high blood pressure, back and knee pain, and dental problems. Cassandra hoped to offer psychotherapy but told me these clients first required accompaniment to the Massachusetts Department of Transitional Assistance, and help with healthcare provider appointments—everyday basic needs and care crises. Expressing a sense of humor tinged with resignation, Cassandra said, "You have to meet clients where they are. They need housing, food, cash—both to live here and to send money to Haiti."

There was limited opportunity to reduce elders' trauma from past sociopolitical ruptures in Haiti or their newer vulnerabilities in Greater Boston. Cassandra described these seniors as struggling with depression and posttraumatic stress but asserted: "They don't really comprehend it. They relive moments—watching a son murdered by *zenglendos* [bandits or gangs in Haiti circa 1991 (see James 2010)]—and another lost six children back-to-back, year after year." Grief and shock from familial losses and the psychosocial legacies of living with *ensekirite* were not the only sources of depression and PTSD. In addition to the threats formerly posed by *tonton makout, zenglendo,* or criminal gangs, many had lived in fear of unseen or supernatural entities, such as *lougawou.* In summer 2006, I volunteered alongside Haitian high school students to help the elders prepare for their citizenship exam. To encourage communication we designed a folklore project that enabled the elders to share their experiences with us. I once asked the elders to explain *lougawou* to us, thinking the youth might be as inexpert as I. Admittedly, I had encountered stories about them in Haiti and I was curious whether these entities' baneful power retained potency in the United States. *Lougawou* are individuals possessing supernatural powers. They shapeshift, leaving their homes in spiritual form by night to extract the life force from the vulnerable, such as children or the elderly. Other similarly feared occult actors are the *chanpwèl* secret societies, groups using malevolent magic to govern physical space and mobilize power. In response to my query, each elder explained their spiritual combat with such entities in Haiti. Some acted out cleansing the roof of a household of negative spiritual influences using brooms and various protective prayers. The program manager, whom I call Melissa Plancher, remarked that this folklore session was one of their most animated.

Conversations with a small group of advanced English learners (portions of which were filmed for the short documentary, *Doing Anthropology*)[7] revealed how even for "younger" clients (below the age of fifty-five), the threat posed by occult actors exists in Boston. One woman's uncanny story produced anxious laughter in fellow students:

> *Student:* In our country we say "Chanpwèl." There are "Chanpwèl" here. There are people who fly, there are people who do everything, but what they do in our country, they do here as well. Here is what I experienced. I was going to pick my husband up for work. . . . In Roslindale . . . I was going by Hyde Park. Ok, as I went through Hyde Park, I went by a cemetery. It was midnight, close to a quarter past midnight, I went to get my husband. As I was speeding up, I thought I saw someone on the

> road, and I slowed down. . . . As I slowed down, I looked behind me and
> realized that these people were behind me. The same people who were in
> front of me, were now behind me. And my husband told me, "Speed up."
> I sped up. And the people stood in the middle of the street, and I took off
> really fast. My rear-view mirror broke off and [I] no longer saw anyone.

ECJ: Wow.

Student: I did not see anyone. My husband told me to go back so we can pick
up the mirror because the car was new. I said no, I would not go back.
[But eventually] I went back, I found the mirror on the [ground], I bent
over and picked it up. When I got farther . . . when I got to the little
hill in Hyde Park to come off on Blue Hill [Avenue], I found all [the]
people I had seen earlier. Ok? I was at a red light, I was waiting. When
the light turned green, I took off. As I sped up, the people were running
after me. . . .

The reality of unseen forces, pervading both the Catholic faith and Haitian
Vodou, was a component of everyday experience for many stakeholders.
Cassandra told me one elder admitted to being cursed supernaturally and afflicted
with reproductive problems as part of a love triangle. The potency of interpersonal
ill will, expressed socially through sorcery or other baneful means, exacerbated the
material insecurities of life in Haiti *and* in Greater Boston.

The menace posed by actors possessing secret or invisible powers accompanied
a general apprehension regarding trusting others socially. Cassandra's clients were
reluctant to divulge any personal information for fear of negative repercussions,
like adverse impacts to sponsoring family hoping to migrate to the United States.
Like the Human Rights Fund Rehabilitation Program beneficiaries in Haiti,
Center elders often preferred to see non-Haitian clinicians. Cassandra said they
worried another Haitian might disclose their problems socially. To assuage their
fears, she (and other staff) offered informational sessions on American patient
privacy laws (HIPAA), the patient's bill of rights, advanced directives and medical
proxy agreements, and issues like domestic violence.

Despite Cassandra's efforts to advocate for and build trust with clients, apprehension remained a component of everyday life outside the program. Her role
as translator and culture broker sometimes posed conflicts when accompanying
elders to medical appointments. She desired to promote clients' well-being and
coordinate their treatment, but they were often hesitant to accept her advocacy.
Once, when visiting a hospitalized client, the medical staff members had removed
a breathing tube indelicately and Cassandra's client was bleeding. Cassandra
wanted to complain, but the client was afraid to protest the injury, perhaps in fear
of retribution or from feelings of powerlessness.

The reluctance to complain to external authority figures about mistreatment
extended to the households in which elders resided. Most lived with their adult
children or, if living independently, had regular contact with them. Elders' children
and in-laws often expected them to contribute to childcare, cooking, and cleaning.

Although most clients enjoyed babysitting, Cassandra said they sometimes felt exploited because of their lack of education. The elders saw themselves as dependent on their children and vulnerable to mistreatment by their children's spouses. Greater linguistic and cultural fluency would likely engender greater independence and social mobility in the United States.

Haitian elders' domestic lives could be isolating, exploitative, and even abusive. One elder program client had a daughter who had married a European American man. The woman and her son-in-law did not get along and eventually he asked her to move out. In another example, an elder woman's daughter-in-law was mistreating her. One day, the elder was sick and vomiting repeatedly into a bucket. She eventually collapsed and her head fell into the bucket. Instead of providing care, the daughter-in-law left her and later forced the woman out of the home. However, such cases of domestic precarity (and abuse) were not routine.

Cassandra described a more frequent form of elder vulnerability arising from "social neglect," such as when a client's family would not maintain contact if the elder resided outside their home. A woman client who had had a stroke struggled to rent a bedroom for four hundred dollars a month without a regular income or any familial support. She was forced to rely only on her faith to find future financial aid. In another slightly different example of isolation, the oldest program client, a woman in her late eighties or early nineties, was caregiver to an adult son who had been disabled by a stroke. She also babysat regularly for her great-grandchildren. Cassandra and I likened the exploitation of elders for unremunerated domestic labor to the plight of young *restavèk* in Haiti. *Restavèk* worked for extended family members in exchange for housing, food, and even education, but sometimes under conditions resembling enslavement.

In describing her motivations to serve, Cassandra lamented elders' lack of opportunity to access education and employment in Haiti. She felt compelled to honor and respect her clients despite their vulnerability, and in some cases, their powerlessness. But she mentioned the challenges of doing so given the Center executive director's views on how best to empower clients. Director Brutus, she said with chagrin, regarded showing clients compassion unprofessional. "How can they learn if you don't show them first and then teach them?" Many other Center plaintiffs wondered if the Charity had ordered the director to inhibit staff caring.

Despite perceived pressures to limit merciful client interactions, there were many moments of celebration among this elder group and their advocates. One of my first opportunities to meet Center clients arose when I was helping elders learn the history and composition of the American government for their naturalization exam. For many elders, this civics education instruction was their first class. The English materials made learning more difficult for the Haitian Creole-only speakers, but they persevered to memorize responses to complex questions with enthusiasm. While filming *Doing Anthropology* in late spring 2007, the class celebrated an intrepid elder who passed her citizenship exam. An instructor asked her to recount her experience:

> *Instructor:* How did the interview with the immigration go for you?
>
> *Elder:* The interview was not easy for me because they took a lot of leeway to ask me questions. But, with my intelligence . . . I succeeded. . . . I was the victor. . . . I answered all the questions they asked me. They asked me questions from the book. They asked me about when I moved to the US. I came in to be a babysitter. . . . They saw that I used to pay the income tax. They know as much about me as I know myself. . . . They spoke to me about my children who had made me come to the US. I answered everything. All the questions in the book. I think they asked me even up to seven questions—I answered them. And then they said, "Madam, you pass."

A March 2011 interview with a new Center health program manager, "Dr. Raymond Fleur"—a Haitian physician who had served the most ostracized persons in Haiti (individuals with leprosy, Hansen's disease)—placed in context elder students' citizenship successes:

> *Dr. F:* I'm happy to see that they have a place where they, after a few years, they can read, they can read Creole, their own language. They discover that there are words, and words can be written. That you can use a pen to express your ideas. . . . To have a place to express their opinion, no matter what it is. Two, two years ago we had fourteen pass their citizenship.
>
> *ECJ:* That's amazing!
>
> *Dr. F:* Fourteen of them passed . . . the citizenship [exam] after a couple of years or so of learning all the questions and so forth. . . . So, I feel that there are perhaps some sad things, but there are still some great successes and good stories, good stories to celebrate when I talk about the elders.

"TRAUMA IS LIKE THIS HAND": RUPTURES IN ROUTINES

Wednesday, February 21, 2007, was a beautiful, sunny day. At nearly 45 degrees Fahrenheit, it was much warmer than expected. After finishing work, I collected ten-month-old Ayanna and dressed her in her bulky winter coat. We said goodbye to her teachers, then signed out at reception. It was about 3:25 p.m. I carried her behind the building to our car, secured her in her car seat, then drove through the parking lot onto Columbia Road. A narrow grassy median strip separated double lanes on either side of the well-trafficked boulevard. There was little traffic, however, only a bus I passed picking up passengers in front of the Yawkey building.

A police car parked in the front of the middle school—two blocks north and on the opposite side of the boulevard—abruptly sped forward with lights flashing. The car crossed the divider separating Columbia Road and entered northbound traffic going south in my lane. I panicked. The bus was on my right. I could not move aside. The Black officer motioned vigorously for me to move out of his way. I was stuck. At the first opening I changed lanes. I continued gingerly, wondering what sparked such commotion. Several more police cars, an ambulance, and other law enforcement vehicles came south (on the proper side) toward the direction we had just left. The wailing sirens, flashing lights, and numerous security personnel suggested something serious had happened. Thankfully, the remaining commute was uneventful.

At eleven o'clock p.m., a chilling story was on the news. The anchor announced a homicide occurred at 3:30 p.m., just north of the Center on the boulevard's opposite side. Unknown assailants had shot a young male pedestrian multiple times. Another person was injured. The murder likely occurred while I secured my daughter in our car, but from behind the Center I heard no gunfire. I didn't remember seeing crowds or anyone hurt on the street—I was focused on entering traffic and circumventing the bus. Learning about the killing prompted my husband and me to debate my return the next day; with good health, Ayanna would gain another brother in roughly six months.

As I reflected on staff members' commitment to their clients, I knew witnessing how violent episodes affected them individually and as pastoral care providers was critical. The next morning, after settling my daughter in her class, I spoke with teachers, other parents, and program staff about what had happened. After work, one teacher had walked southwest on Columbia Road to catch the number 19 bus on Washington Street, and had then seen the flashing blue lights of a single squad car, followed by at least twenty different police vehicles. The police immediately roped off the area with yellow tape and began questioning pedestrians. The officers chased a man running on a side street, but he was only jogging, not fleeing, as it had been a warm day. Parents and teachers commented that one could never predict when something cataclysmic might befall us.

Yawkey Center directors called a debriefing meeting for later the same day to permit discussion of the shooting and implications for building security. Before attending, I went outside. From archival research on violent crimes in Dorchester, Mattapan, and Roxbury—the communities the Center most served—I knew fear of reprisals often inhibited individuals from sharing what they might know about such incidents. The culture of silence prevented many residents from joining public commemorations of tragedies or disclosing local knowledge of criminal activity, unless an act affected them or their family members directly. I felt ambivalent about wanting to view the site and the growing memorial. Was I guilty of the professional voyeurism criticized in the social sciences and media studies (Kleinman and Kleinman 1997)? Even if so, wasn't it important to document how neighborhood residents marked, memorialized, and remembered not only the dead, but also the violence in their community?

Along Columbia Road, I passed dilapidated apartment buildings and strewn debris, then crossed the wide boulevard to arrive at the murder and memorial sites. Remnants of grayish powder clumps of which had turned a dark reddish brown remained next to the curb. Seven-day votive candles in multiple colors were lit around the base of a street sign. A photo of the deceased, a teddy bear, and other items were mounted on it. I entered the convenience store and asked the owner if I could take some photos—he said that he didn't care. Outside I nodded to those holding an informal wake, then introduced myself to a minister consoling pedestrians and mourners on the sidewalk. After exchanging greetings, I explained my research to Minister Michael A. Person, and he allowed me to witness his counseling passersby.

Minister Person, a well-known victim-witness advocate and child trauma counselor, often aided survivors after violent crimes. The area was located between several "hotspots"—zones the municipality designated as having higher concentrations of crime and violence. He spoke with a man in his twenties and another woman in her thirties about the history of violence in the neighborhood. After their departure, a young man whom I call Ronald approached. The minister told Ronald and me he had been a drug dealer in his youth. Only after praying for God's help could he change course. He told us he ultimately attended cooking schools in Europe and worked as a chef in the United States. He now actively encouraged children and adolescents to avoid violence.

Person stated a major problem the community faced was the media's primarily negative depictions of Dorchester neighborhoods. Historically, international political critics also portrayed Haiti negatively (Lawless 1992). Whether for Haiti or contemporary Dorchester, ongoing positive work was rarely highlighted beyond the local print or visual media. Person next lamented how the absence of jobs and opportunities contributed to youth social disorder. Without such opportunities, he said, young adults more easily resorted to violence and crime to solve problems.

Ronald's affirmation described how opportunity scarcity affected him personally. He was completing a bachelor's degree in audio/media technologies after having earned an associate's degree. He told us about the recent funeral of a friend who was murdered in Boston, and his own efforts to persuade others to finish their education rather than become involved in gangs and crime. But Ronald felt it was useless to try to eradicate violence from the streets, "It feels like it will always be this way."

Minister Person encouraged Ronald to keep up the struggle and continue pursuing his education despite how hard trauma is to fight. While showing an outstretched hand in front of his own face, Person said: "Trauma is like this hand. You can move it to the left or right and try to shift it behind you, but it is always there. It's like a part of your body once it's there . . ." The minister then shared that his son was murdered in 2001 and his sister had been murdered in a liquor store. Altogether, assailants had killed eight members of his family. Person lamented the 294 murders in Boston in recent years. He had gone to each site to console the grieving.

Minister Person's description of trauma, as a part of one's body, a presence that cannot be expunged or exorcized, resembled the descriptions I'd heard in Haiti from survivors of many kinds of violence. His posttrauma ministry showed how the labor to care for others, or what Catholics call the corporal and spiritual works of mercy, arises not only from desires to fulfill religious duties. Sometimes charity arises from a hope to prevent others from suffering the losses one has experienced.

. . .

I did not anticipate learning how traumatic experiences were everyday personal challenges for Center staff. The third-floor seminar room, a space I associated with advisory board meetings, hosted an intense discussion of the shooting and its implications for building security. The Center and Greater Boston Catholic Charities directors and staff members packed the space. I was surprised to see in attendance an archdiocesan leader who worked with the Charity whom I call Father Peter Thompson. In the ensuing conversation, spatial and geographical issues were critical: because the shooting occurred just a half block away, the perpetrators could have run toward the Yawkey building. There were concerns about the unpredictability of local gang and youth violence. The new health prevention program director, "Roberta Johnson," a lifelong Boston resident (see Chapter 9), asked whether there was a relationship with the police or participation in a community policing program, especially because staff members made client home visits. Center director Brutus mentioned he had a meeting scheduled with the new Boston police commissioner related to routine matters, but it was a month away. The archdiocesan leader was lobbying the state legislature to advocate for initiatives against youth and urban violence. He told us that the Boston TenPoint Coalition, a network of Christian clergy and lay leaders organizing the community around issues facing Black and Latino youth, was working diligently to acquire funding to address youth violence.

Although the Center and Charity leadership shared their ongoing civic efforts to address urban insecurity, staff members were concerned about their everyday work vulnerability. One person spoke on behalf of a receptionist who staffed the front desk daily after five o'clock p.m.: "Maria [a pseudonym] has the worst job. She doesn't know who is coming." In soft tones, Maria responded that her son "Alejandro" actually witnessed the shooting and saw four people running from the crime scene. He overheard them say, "He's dead. Let's run." She told us she'd asked him, "Did you have your hoodie on?" "Yes." With some assurance his clothing may have concealed him, another staff member said that routine police brutality nevertheless posed a risk to everyday safety. The police might have assumed Alejandro was involved in the crime rather than simply being a bystander. The risk of being harmed by gang or police violence, whether inadvertently or intentionally, was not solely an external reality; staff members still faced potential risks inside the Center building. The adult education classes met as late as 8:30 p.m. and the advisory board also had regular evening meetings. The custodian, "Alcide Isaac" (whom we will meet in Chapter 8), sometimes worked after nine o'clock p.m.

The porosity of the building raised questions about staff, volunteer, and client failures to sign in and out at the reception desk. In their rush to drop off and pick up their children, the daycare parents were particularly guilty of this procedural lapse. It was vital to regulate who was onsite at all moments. Sometimes intoxicated neighborhood residents (and even clients) entered the building. How could current and prospective clients be distinguished from suspect members of the general public? Should there be a guard at the entrance? (This option was chosen to provide greater security.) Father Thompson interjected, "The question is how to keep the Center secure, but user-friendly, and not like Bank of America." He continued reassuringly, "You folks influence thousands of people's lives. We've got to keep you safe. We can't control everything, but we've got to keep you safe enough to do what you do." Although the unpredictability of everyday violence remained, this pastoral concern from the Charity leader was heartening and demonstrated the benevolent side of charity governance extending from the headquarters to the programmatic periphery.

The shooting evoked memories and stories of near misses, threats, and the hazards of delivering human services at clients' homes. A Sante Manman staff member recalled another shooting during her visit to a client in Roxbury four years before. After the police cordoned off the site, she and her covisitor were initially unable to leave the apartment building parking lot. Only by showing the Catholic Charities identification card as evidence of being visitors were they eventually able to leave.

The debriefing debate escalated around the emergencies clients could face if services were interrupted for safety reasons, whether at the Yawkey Center or at a residence. An Initial Response staff member said a client had called, desperate for a food delivery. She had a disabled husband and three children at home. Because the client lived in an area known for crime and gang violence, the staff member was reluctant to visit alone. A Sante Manman staff member next exclaimed, "We are safe when we are here [in the Center], but not when we go out." In response to statements about the risk calculus staff members performed each time they visited homes in insecure neighborhoods, Father Thompson responded solemnly, "Take no chances. If there is any doubt, don't try it."

STRUCTURAL DEFICITS

Although the Yawkey building did not belong solely to either of its two main organizations, Center stakeholder recollections evoked a sense of ownership, hope, safety, and security. However, another crack in the foundations of the Center as homeplace had begun since the merger. Unfortunately, unanticipated financial constraints negatively impacted its programs and personnel. To the best of my knowledge, the archdiocese had previously absorbed the rental and maintenance costs at St. Leo Parish. In the new building, both the Center and Greater Boston Catholic Charities—and ultimately, the Charity—were financially responsible for the facility's expenses. According to a former Charity employee, in the late 1980s, the Charity received overhead on grants awarded to it on the Center's behalf. With consternation, this individual said it was unfair the Charity "charged" the Center a higher overhead rate than other Charity programs. Furthermore, in the Center's "golden years"—described as a period of majority Haitian management, in which only four European Americans had either volunteer or paid roles—this extra overhead likely contributed to Haitians' perceptions that the Charity unfairly "taxed" the work Haitians conceived, designed, and implemented themselves:

> *FCE:* Well, part of it is that the Haitians were very appealing. The Haitian Multi-Service Center was very appealing to the private donors and to the Department of Public Health. There was a project there . . . the health of the mother is health of the baby [Sante Manman]. And they got a lot of money from [the Department of] Public Health to do that. They were very effective at doing it, very effective at outreach around prenatal care for Haitian women. They used Haitian outreach workers and it was really good. But Catholic Charities, because they were sort of the central [agency]—It's hard to know what all the truth is, but one of the truths was that Catholic Charities had a much, much higher—what do you call it? Like a management fee . . . to keep the organization running.
>
> *ECJ:* Like overhead?
>
> *FCE:* Yeah, they applied a much higher—they had established a pretty high overhead fee. The Haitians—this is probably true of a lot of smaller groups, but they didn't have high salaries. They didn't spend like that. . . . The Haitian Multi-Service Center also suffered somewhat from its association with Catholic Charities because a lot of people didn't want to give to Catholic Charities but wanted to give to the Haitian Multi-Service Center.

This statement confirmed a complaint echoing through many stakeholder interviews that the Charity was profiting from their labor.

In the late 1990s, former Charity program staff had made similar charges against Charity headquarters of disparate administrative and fiscal treatment of ethnic-specific programs in the Charity network. In a complaint against Catholic Charities lodged with the Massachusetts Commission Against Discrimination, "a leading youth advocate and former director of El Centro Cardenal has accused her superiors of ordering her to falsify state records after an internal audit of the center turned up discrepancies" (Latour 1999). Three days after filing the complaint, El Centro's director, Ruth Rubalcava, was fired. Furthermore, other El Centro staff asserted, the Charity ordered their center "and the city's other minority-run center, the Haitian Multi-Service Center, to comply with stricter reporting requirements"

(Latour 1999). In response, "Joseph Doolin, president of Catholic Charities, said the allegations of a racial double standard were 'frivolous . . . they're utterly baseless'" (Latour 1999).

As the next chapter affirms, reporting requirements and fiscal solvency are inextricably linked to governance over the corporate Catholic network. But for the Haitian Center in the new Yawkey building, the cumulative overhead the Charity charged increased because of unanticipated new operating costs. In July 2007, Father Thompson returned to the HMSC Advisory Board to explain the Center's dire fiscal status and how economic scarcity affected the Charity. Director Brutus said the budget for fiscal year 2008 would show a deficit of $414,000, mostly driven by new building costs. Because the Center operated primarily from program grants, raising the additional six to eight hundred thousand dollars needed could take three to four years. The advisory board chair, a Charity trustee, said the depreciation cost charged to the Center would be two hundred thousand dollars—yet another unanticipated infrastructure expense.

The Center's budget shortfalls were not the only challenge; the Charity itself faced financial difficulties. Father Thompson said the United Way (of Massachusetts) had changed its funding priorities. Rather than support umbrella organizations like the Charity, the United Way intended to fund independent programs targeting four "problem areas": child development, teen services (to reduce gang violence), emergency relief services (like those of Initial Response) and affordable housing for low- and moderate-income families. In partial response to such shifts, the Charity planned to develop a program specific marketing campaign. Then Father Thompson reiterated the conditions under which the Charity was awarded the Columbia Road site: a building exclusively focused on the Haitian Multi-Service Center's ethnic interests did not accord with the City's expectations of the land's uses. One of the reasons the daycare programs had merged in the Yawkey building was the requirement of outreach beyond core constituents. Still, Thompson continued, the merged daycare Center enrollments had not increased to anticipated levels, which contributed to budget shortfalls. As a result, less-regularly used building sections would be offered for lease to community organizations to supplement the income needed for unanticipated costs. In later years, parts of the Yawkey building would be rented to other organizations for long term use. Such financial shortfalls likely underlay the conflicts I witnessed between 2006 and 2007 and that I will discuss in the next chapters.

8

Inscribing and Incorporating Life

The "scriptural" is that which separates itself from the magical world of voices and tradition. . . . Thus one can read above the portals of modernity such inscriptions as "Here, to work is to write," or "Here only what is written is understood."

—MICHEL DE CERTEAU

"We operate in a structure, a reimbursement structure, where if it's not written down, it didn't happen. . . . If it's not in writing, it didn't happen."

—"SALLY BRASCO," CHARITY ADMINISTRATOR

Throughout its social life, Center programs attempted to improve the corporal well-being of clients by reducing health disparities among Haitians (and others). Interventions included material support, access to care, educational opportunities, and public health outreach, all offered while also incorporating clients as residents of Greater Boston. These human service practices helped to improve "health literacy." Coined in 1974, the concept of "health literacy" was acknowledged internationally as critical to health promotion in 1997 (Fernández-Gutiérrez et al. 2018: 55). In its Health Promotion Glossary, the World Health Organization (1998: 10) defines health literacy as "the cognitive and social skills which determine the motivation and ability of individuals to gain access to, understand, and use information in ways which promote and maintain good health." The WHO distinguishes health literacy from the mere ability to read; individuals must possess nuanced skills enabling them to apply health information to their own and their community's lives (WHO 1998: 10). Establishing charitable social service programs to improve health literacy among refugee and immigrant populations recalls decades of work Catholic institutions have performed in North America to incorporate Others through bodily care, public health, and civic interventions (see Chapter 2).

Although the Center's adult education and health programs provided clients robust "wraparound" services to improve their health, livelihoods, and health literacy, this chapter analyzes another dimension of corporate Catholicism enacted through charity—namely, how funder requirements to record human service encounters frequently produced individual and institutional dilemmas. From 2006 to 2007, the Charity managed more than 140 projects across multiple institutional sites.[1] A critical condition of social assistance was recording each project's activities, especially the successes and failures of care. A March 2011 interview with "Sally Brasco," a Charity executive with decades of Center involvement, illustrated the challenges of implementing what she named "the human service and social justice orientation of Catholic Charities." We discussed the agency history and structure and the impact of crises like the 2010 Haitian earthquake on charitable giving within the archdiocese. I later asked about former Charity staff claims that the ethnic and minority programs were burdened with more administrative duties than others. In response, Brasco said, "There are things that we have to do as a social service agency when we're dealing with contracts that require . . . a lot of writing and documentation. And I don't think everybody comes to this work wanting to document. It's a hard thing to do."

Brasco acknowledged the political, economic, and ontological insecurities (existential precarities) impoverished immigrants and refugees suffer while adapting to another culture. Social service providers needed to capture these complexities using specific forms of writing. Brasco continued:

> If English isn't your first language and we're asking you to document in English, that's a challenge. So, it just makes the work a little bit harder. . . . I understand, culturally there's some really good reasons not to document things. I understand the . . . cultural mistrust of people and authority, the cultural mistrust of government . . . and so I think . . . there are times . . . it's challenging for people for whom . . . this is not their first world . . . to understand.

Staff members' ability to record caring transactions—and extract descriptions of clients' aspirations, everyday behaviors, mental health statuses, and efforts to sustain their lives—necessitated trust. Working with populations mistrustful of authorities, such as actors fomenting *ensekirite* in Haiti or those causing (and responding to) violence and crime in Greater Boston, also required tremendous time, patience, and sensitivity. Trust-building labor could be simultaneously pastoral, political, and risky, especially for undocumented clients. Nevertheless, in exchange for aid, the gift of services obliged clients to accept formal programmatic inscription, administrative visibility, and ongoing monitoring. Yet, in 1999, the Charity was accused of requiring its minority-run programs both to pay additional overhead on funding received and to complete additional documentation of services "not required of white-run agencies" (Latour 1999). To what degree are fiscal and textual taxes levied more heavily against independently run, ethnic-specific human services? What is the cost to compassionate care?

Although I can neither confirm nor deny any explicitly racialist rationale for disparate administrative practices across the Charity network, I will discuss in this chapter how the documentary obligations of social service work could constrain institutional freedom. With hearty laughter, Brasco described how human service organizations like the Charity must transcribe charitable practices into written texts to receive institutional payment: "We operate in a structure, a reimbursement structure, where if it's not written down, it didn't happen. So, you know you have that really stark reality. If it's not in writing, it didn't happen."

Both the Center and Charity operate in what I have described elsewhere as the "grant economy" (James 2010; 179–80), an economy pivoting between gift and commodity economies. Grantees receive public and private funding, as well as subcontracts, to render services on behalf of the state and other private entities. Social service providers in grant economies are increasingly subjected to an audit culture. Knowledge about clients' lives is elicited, transformed, accumulated, and shared with donors—a form of commodification increasingly common in grant funded programs. There are differences between faith-based and secular social service agencies that merit distinction. Although many FBO laborers are concerned for their clients' souls in the theological sense, grant-funded compassion economies also compel such "pastors of the soma" (Rose 2007: 29) to recount their client's physical, mental, legal, economic, and other statuses—components of the secular soul—to external monitoring entities (see Chapter 2). While the documentary procedures analyzed here resemble the benevolent bureaucraft practices and processes I observed previously in postconflict Haiti, the textual production in Greater Boston conforms more closely to a *scriptural economy* in a relatively secure, rather than fragile, nation-state.

THE SCRIPTURAL ECONOMY

To recall, the historical concept of economy in the West composes control of resources in a household or community, management of bodily regimens, and theologically, the divine order governing creation and drawing humanity toward salvation. Jesuit scholar Michel de Certeau describes the "scriptural economy" as an "apparatus of modern discipline" (1984: 131). In this economy, textual writing—inscription—is an act of production permitting scribes to order and control a space, such as a blank page, to make legible and provide meaning to (and sometimes for) the vernacular voices and bodies of Others (Certeau 1984: 134–40). Scriptural practices are markers of modernity and progress in Western societies. An expanding technocratic class with mastery over language and tied to economic production produces the scriptural economy (139). Certeau affirms: "For the past three centuries learning to write has been the very definition of entering into a capitalist and conquering society. Such is its fundamental initiatory *practice*" (1984: 135–36; emphasis in original).

In my usage, "scriptural economies" incorporate embodied subjects into a regime of life and mode of living through writing and other textual practices. A goal is securing the health of the individual, community, institutions, and states monitoring such practices, a form of secular salvation. In many respects, contemporary population health work initiates an organization's educators, caregivers, and clients into secular scriptural economies. But theological exhortations sometimes motivate scriptural laborers to resist the textual obligations of secular auditors.

As our interview continued, Sally Brasco acknowledged how institutional reporting obligations instilled particular disciplines in service providers, but not without challenges:

> Compared to . . . a caregiver who says, "How could I possibly capture everything that I've done. *And* you might be asking me to capture things that I don't want to talk about in writing," so, we . . . constantly train [regarding] what's necessary to be part of a good note, what's not necessary to include, because there's a skill and a craft to that. And I think it's a training issue. That said, there are some biases that you can't get past.

By "biases" I am not sure whether she meant cultural inhibitions against revealing personal information, or staff desires to aid but not document others, as required of historical scientific charity and contemporary case management best practices (see Chapters 2 and 9). Staff reluctance to reveal social and cultural intimacies elicited through obligatory confessional practices might inhibit the transcription of clients' biographies. Regardless of the meaning of "biases," penning clients' private lives rendered these individuals visible and legible to donors, and potentially to civic authorities.

Health literacy educators, counselors, and case managers ultimately deploy a kind of pastoral biopower in their charitable labor. Pastoral biopower combines the affective power of care with the regulatory cultures of biopolitics on the state's behalf to propose "disciplines of the body and the regulations of the population" around issues of "propagation, births and mortality, the level of health, life expectancy and longevity" (Foucault 1990: 139). Furthermore, the scriptural obligations imposed on health literacy work also govern individual and collective lives to produce legible (secular) souls—whether counselor, instructor, case manager, or client—who collectively labor to reduce health disparities posing risks to populations, institutions, and state security. The programs also benefitted from an internal reservoir of available participants attending Adult Ed and other programs. The Center's health literacy programs' success rested as much on the faith and souls of its staff members as on the scriptural practices they enacted with students and clients to provide evidence of compassionate care in their respective management systems.

In this chapter, two cases—the Center's adult education and maternal and child health programs—illustrate how the textual communications among federal, state, and municipal funders, Catholic Charities and the Center, and Center programs and their respective clients compose a contemporary scriptural economy. This economy was simultaneously pastoral, textual, biopolitical, monetary, and normalizing. The obligations of scriptural economies affected how Charity intermediaries—the Center's program managers—circumscribed the exchanges between staff members and their students or clients. Both Center programs demanded specialized documentation at every level of interaction with the Center's clients. In each case, staff members grappled with desires to offer education, social support, and compassionate care in a manner conflicting with the reporting requirements of funders and the Charity. Each case also demonstrates how increasingly bureaucratic practices with real economic repercussions disciplined student/client/customers, educator/providers, and the social service institutions themselves. Each also highlights the affective, moral, and ethical stakes of serving marginal populations at the intersections of the Center, Charity, Church, City, and State. Nonetheless, improvisation and resistance to the bureaucratic routines of service provision occurred regularly.

THE SCRIPTURAL ECONOMY
AND ADULT EDUCATION

Alongside the daycare, the Adult Education Program was the Center's oldest and received state and municipal funding from the Massachusetts Department of Elementary and Secondary Education (henceforth, the DOE) and the Mayor's Office of New Bostonians. Adult Ed, as it was called, served individuals of mixed legal statuses. The program offered preliteracy classes (in both Haitian Creole and English), three levels of English as a Second Language (ESL), math, computer literacy, Adult Diploma, citizenship classes, and educational counseling (see Figure 19). In 2006, the Charity website stated the Center's education programs were designed to "provide Haitian and other adults with essential skills that will lead to life-long learning . . . literacy, and economic self-sufficiency." This description reminded me of Certeau's statement, "learning to write has been the very definition of entering into a capitalist and conquering society."

When I began volunteering as an English tutor, the program was transitioning under a new manager whom I call Catherine Hansen. From her I learned the Charity had hired her directly and she was instituting "a culture change" with a revised curriculum, "new activities and teaching techniques," and a student-centered, rather than a teacher-centered program. This culture change complied with a scriptural economy obligating educators to record clients' personal data for DOE consumption. At the time, the DOE required grantees to use a database to which it had direct access to monitor class sizes, enrollments, attendance figures, students' personal information, and their future goals—the System for Managing Accountability and Results Through Technology (SMARTT).[2]

Hansen told me the Center's teachers did not always know what the students' goals were. This reputed lack of awareness of students' aspirations was not solely

FIGURE 19. Adult Education bulletin boards. Photo credit: Erica Caple James.

a question whether instructors adequately pastored or mentored clients, but whether they successfully elicited student data textually. Such digital inscriptions influenced how well the DOE evaluated its grantees using the "2006–2010 Performance Standards for Community Adult Learning Centers."[3] "We get credit for them," Hansen said of the accounting practices documenting achieved results. A precise calculus determined one program performance measure, "Setting and Meeting Student Goals": "Total number of goals set divided by the number of students enrolled in the program" and "Total number of goals met divided by the number of students enrolled in the program." These figures were compared to a benchmark in which "programs set, on average, at least two goals per student per year," and "meet, on average, at least one goal per student per year." Another assessment was to "document goals met according to the Countable Outcomes Definitions and Required Documentation Chart of the Student Goal Sheet." When all performance measures were tabulated for each student—attendance, average attended hours, pre- and post-test percentages, learner gains, student goals, and educational functioning level completion—the average for all students was determined and converted into the program's "performance points." The programs' performance points for the previous four years of a typical five-year grant were averaged and called "cut points." Each institutional contractor needed between eighteen and twenty-five cut points to become eligible for refunding.

What textual practices were required of clients and educators to meet these criteria? To continue with "Setting and Meeting Student Goals," the Adult Ed counselors—typically multilingual speakers of English, Haitian Creole, French, and Spanish—met privately with students to set and record their educational goals on a digital "Student Goal Sheet" containing several predetermined categories. The first, "Countable Outcomes Requiring Valid and Reliable Data/Documentation," ranged from "enter employment" and "obtain GED" to "apply for U.S. Citizenship" and "receive certificate of citizenship at oath ceremony." The evidence could range from data matches—using the student's social security number or, in cases of students without social security numbers, a self-report—to copies of application receipt notices or certificates of citizenship.

The accounting practices generated among counselors, instructors, and clients were means of tracking adult lives over time. A set of goals categorized under "Countable Outcomes Requiring Student Self-Reporting and Teacher Verification" obliged instructors to monitor clients' everyday livelihoods and behaviors. Student goals were categorized as economic (i.e., "be removed from public assistance"), educational (i.e., "increase computer literacy"), health ("quit smoking", "learn about HIV/AIDS"), parenting ("join an organization at your child's school"), societal ("enter military"), employment ("create a resume"), financial literacy ("develop a personal and/or family budget"), and others "not for performance accountability measures." The counselor entered each goal, the dates set and met, then progress toward student's goals were assessed and updated each quarter—at least in theory. This goal-setting exercise attempted to translate the personal desires, experience, activities, and knowledge of Center clients into technical data to be surveyed, tabulated, and converted into percentages and points benefitting the overall program—a modern economy of merits and satisfactions (see Chapter 2). The students undoubtedly achieved many goals through regular class attendance, attaining greater proficiency in their natal language or in English, and successes in the American labor environment.

The Adult Ed instructors and program manager inevitably faced double binds working in this scriptural economy. One point of frustration between Hansen and the teachers concerned daily records of student attendance and class size. Certain "rate-based" courses were to have a "fixed schedule, meet minimum requirements for intensity and duration, [and] have a fixed number of student seats or slots . . . the eligible cost of which [was] determined by an established rate per student instructional hour." Calculations for optimal numbers of students per class correlated with rates the DOE paid per student slot. Several Center teachers did not always record attendance figures accurately or in a timely manner. But to ensure agency payment, totals had to be entered into the SMARTT database. For some teachers, failure to enter this information was resistance; for others, the bureaucratic annoyance was not fully understood.

Instructors shared their exasperation with program manager Hansen's enforcement of DOE expectations. Several Haitian teachers felt some Haitian clients—especially the elders—attended classes for social support rather than to achieve literacy in Haitian Creole or proficiency in spoken and written English. One conflict between instructors and Hansen regarded two nonliterate Haitian elders who periodically attended the "Pre-Literacy ESOL" class without formal enrollment.

If discovered during a spontaneous DOE site visit, the two additional students could jeopardize the program's overall performance rating. To the chagrin of teachers, the two elders were ultimately barred from the class.

The scriptural practices the DOE compelled were intended to craft instructors who complied with circumscribed student-centered practices and clients who could become disciplined workers in a capitalist environment. The reported threat of impromptu DOE performance audits, both onsite and by database surveillance, provoked supervisory staff fears the program could be found noncompliant. This secular audit culture compelled difficult choices—whether to discourage teachers' spontaneity and flexibility to conform to donor rules or to bend the rules to extend compassion to clients. Those programs possessing disciplined scribes produced sufficient countable outcomes and could be rewarded with renewed funding.

Some staff members feared this form of outcome-based adult education could become another source of risk, particularly for undocumented students. Through the SMARTT database computer program, the DOE was able to access much of the performance standards data, including information on the student goal sheet. In order to receive services, students signed a release acknowledging the DOE monitored its institutional grantees to determine their success in helping students achieve their educational goals and future employment. Students were informed their records might be matched against the Massachusetts Department of Revenue's wage records, and their name, social security number, address, educational goals, GED test scores, and employment history could be checked. Although personal information remained confidential, one staff member feared the state would inevitably use this information to monitor students directly and to ascertain which clients might have undocumented legal status. If undocumented students' legal status became legible and visible to third parties with program data access, the educational classes would no longer provide sanctuary from the legal insecurities of everyday life. For some students, attendance in Center classes might pose a risk of being apprehended and eventually deported by public authorities.[4]

SCRIPTURAL ECONOMIES AND SANTE MANMAN

In contrast to the Adult Education instructional and goal setting work in the classroom, Sante Manman's program included extensive monitoring of pregnant clients through educational programming both on- and off-site. Case managers regularly completed detailed reports on services while incorporating clients into a geographical network of care in Greater Boston. Services ranged from instruction and health examinations to travels to various medical appointments and support groups. This form of mobile "accompaniment" (Farmer 2013; Watkins 2015) reduced barriers clients confronted in accessing care, whether linguistic, cultural, educational, or legal. Undocumented pregnant clients were eligible. In a September 2006 meeting with Sante Manman staff members, the Center executive director reported that roughly 50 percent of the program's eighty-five clients had legal status.

Sante Manman staff members humanized the city while also working to incorporate their clients into a biomedical system from which they might have been excluded without such assistance. The program's mission paralleled the Charity's contemporary concern for healthy families and historical work to retain Catholic immigrant infants, children, and families within the corporate body of the Church. Although the program did not overtly fulfill an explicit religious charism, its maternal and child health focus interpolated charitable biopolitics within an emergent scriptural economy that primarily documented the lives of secular souls.

Much like Adult Ed, Sante Manman's life work was situated at the nexus of another set of networked public agencies, institutions whose interventions were mediated through clients' bodies. The constellation of maternal and child health interveners engaged in forms of what has been called "reproductive governance": "the mechanisms through which different historical configurations of actors—such as state institutions, churches, donor agencies, and non-governmental organisations (NGOs)—use legislative controls, economic inducements, moral injunctions, direct coercion, and ethical incitements to produce, monitor and control reproductive behaviours and practices" (Morgan and Roberts 2012: 243). Sante Manman's maternal and child health interventions posed similar ethical dilemmas for staff members to those in Adult Education.

TRACKING BLACK LIVES IN INFANT "DEATH ZONES"

"It's like a way of life to let black babies die," charged Allen Ball, director of the Harvard Street Neighborhood Health Center on Blue Hill Avenue in Dorchester. "This is the medical mecca. They shouldn't let the infant mortality be as high as Third World countries." (Kong 1990)

"It's like a way of life to let black babies die." I am sitting with Director Ball's reported statement for a moment. Letting others die as a form of life, a way of being in the world, suggests some lives are not worthy and their loss is normal or natural, especially when invisible. The second part of the statement—that in the "medical mecca" infant mortality should not reach the level of "Third World countries," also disturbs me. Apparently, the preponderance of deaths in some nations is also normal or natural, if still invisible. The proximity of Black infant deaths to centers of Boston's medical expertise creates more moral outrage, as if the disparities are more uncivilized, barbaric, or unthinkable precisely because of their nearness. But I cannot parse here why infant deaths are so high in the so-called Third World and what relationship those deaths may have to the medical achievements in so-called developed worlds.

In 1990, as reported in the *Boston Globe* newspaper, Boston's 1988 infant mortality statistics demonstrated the racial gap was widening between the deaths of White and racial and ethnic Other infants:

> Among whites in 1988, there were 7.9 deaths per 1,000 live births; among blacks, the rate was 24.4 deaths per 1,000. By comparison, Costa Rica recorded an infant death rate of 13.4 per 1,000 last year. The Globe's review of death certificates for 1989 shows that 70 of the 108 infants who died in Boston were black, while only 18 were white. Twelve babies were Hispanic; 8 were listed as "other." In the first half of this year, 32 of the 61 babies who died in Boston were black; 14 were white. The deaths were concentrated in Roxbury, Mattapan and Dorchester. (Kong 1990)

In comparing Boston's infant mortality rates to those of so-called Third World countries, the news report implicitly mobilized alarm, and perhaps shame, to suggest these health disparities were comparable to those reputedly resulting from nation-state underdevelopment.

Disaggregating infant deaths by race and ethnicity obliquely directed fault or responsibility for infant deaths primarily at the behaviors of impoverished individuals and populations of African descent. The causes were not solely reduced to individual behaviors and adverse health, but also included socioeconomic factors. Nevertheless, the disparities in infant mortality rates in Roxbury, Mattapan, and Dorchester—coupled with crime, violence, and entrenched poverty—caused state officials to label these neighborhoods "death zones."

> "Death zones" is the term state public health officials use for the Boston neighborhoods with high infant mortality rates. A review of crime, health and economic statistics for one zone, a 10-square-block area in Mattapan where 17 babies died in the last three years, offers a window on the problem: More than 30 percent of the families live in poverty. (Kong 1990)

The public health officials' assessment spatialized deaths within an ungovernable racial geography of poverty lacking adequate pathways to care. The ontological insecurity in such zones undoubtably produced stressors that disproportionately affected the bodies of Black pregnant women and their babies.

However, conditions like poor housing, interpersonal violence, crime, and other infrastructural harms rendered infant mortality as just one indicator of what has been termed "syndemic suffering." The concept of syndemic suffering describes "a set of intertwined and mutually enhancing epidemics involving disease interactions at the biological level that develop and are sustained in a community/population *because of harmful social conditions and injurious social connections*" (Singer and Clair 2015: 429; emphasis in original).

In addition to disease comorbidities (co-occurrences), social scientists Merrill Singer and Scott Clair (2015: 429) argue harmful social situations are also direct determinants of health. Health statuses like "malnutrition, substance abuse, and stress," when combined with "health-threatening social conditions (e.g., noxious living, working, or environmental conditions, or oppressive social relationships)," produce a "dangerous synergism" that "contribute[s] thereby to syndemical enhancement of disease" (Singer and Clair 2015: 429). Media reports of high infant mortality rates in Greater Boston from the late 1980s and early 1990s suggest a syndemical context for poor maternal and child health:

> In 1987 and 1988, 51 babies were born weighing less than 5 1/2 pounds, including 11 who weighed less than 3 1/2 pounds; 42 mothers got inadequate prenatal care and three got none; 25 girls age 17 and younger gave birth. At least 70 children were poisoned by lead between 1979 and 1985. Last year, there were two murders, six rapes, 74 robberies, 129 aggravated assaults, 151 simple assaults, 47 calls for family trouble and 179 auto thefts reported to police. (Kong 1990)

High infant death rates were just one symptom of a heightened level of physical and environmental risk for the majority Black residents of these areas. Although infant mortality does not necessarily occur solely because of disease, its high rates reflected a public health crisis for marginalized racial and ethnic populations living in an industrial nation possessing immense biomedical resources. Because these high rates occurred within mere miles of "29 neighborhood health centers and 26 hospitals—16 of them teaching centers," one frustrated area clinician suggested:

> "Why don't we just shoot these pregnant women?" asked Dr. Yvonne Gomez-Carrion, director of obstetrics at Roxbury Comprehensive Community Health Center. "We tell them, 'Say no to drugs,' but there is no treatment for them. We say, 'Get yourself together and get off welfare,' but there are no jobs for educated blacks, let alone untrained welfare mothers. Shooting them starts to sound like a reasonable option." (Kong 1990)

Dr. Gomez-Carrion emphasizes systemic inequalities here, the lack of healthcare to mitigate the so-called personal moral failure of drug addiction. By stating even Black persons of higher socioeconomic statuses faced obstacles to attaining livelihoods in an economy lacking jobs, however, the physician calls attention to the challenges of structural racism and economies of scarcity. Proposing murder as a solution, even in exasperation, demonstrates the deep weariness and impotence caregivers felt to remedy the socioeconomic disparities negatively affecting both vulnerable and higher status Black communities in Greater Boston.

Geographer Ruth Wilson Gilmore (2007: 247) defines racism as "the state-sanctioned and/or extralegal production and exploitation of group-differentiated vulnerability to premature death." High infant mortality rates among populations of African descent epitomize "group-differentiated vulnerability to premature death." Despite the racial and socioeconomic determinants of poor maternal and child health, some clinicians still identified the etiology of infant mortality primarily in pregnant women's biology and individual moral and behavioral failures. Another clinician supervising three community health workers who advocated for pregnant women in the Mission Hill area of Roxbury (near Harvard Medical School) thought there might be a medical reason for the high mortality rates, such as "an unusual strain of chlamydia." She later said, however, "It's not about some unusual strain of chlamydia. It's about unmet basic human needs" (Kong 1990).

At issue here is the degree to which infant mortality is a problem of sexually transmitted infections and, by extension, individual moral fault, structural inequalities like the lack of education or employment, racial and gender discrimination, and the effects of entrenched poverty, or some combination of these. Infrastructural problems like inadequate housing, environmental toxicity, and lack of transportation complicate these factors. For racial and ethnic immigrants, like the predominantly Haitian clients in Sante Manman, cultural and linguistic barriers, domestic violence, and legal insecurity intensified these complex material, social, and economic conditions. Although regular reporting of client statuses was a component of their duties to improve health literacy, it was difficult for Center staff members to capture textually how their clients lived with syndemic suffering.

The state of emergency that infant mortality rates posed to Greater Boston and, as will be discussed below, to the nation as a whole, provides context for Sante Manman's work tracking Black lives while seeking to improve client's health literacy. The program served hundreds of women and their families from 1989 to 2014 through tangible and intangible exchanges of care, information, and a model of case management now called "accompaniment" (Farmer 2013; Watkins 2015). Over its history, the program became a component of a scriptural economy incorporating pregnant women and their infants into a public health apparatus, one aspiring to mitigate the emergency of high infant mortality rates (deaths occurring from birth to age one) in the United States. In a 2002 television interview for a Catholic EWTN segment, former executive director Pierre Imbert described Sante Manman as an essential community-based program serving the most vulnerable:

> The Haitian Multi-Service Center is the only site in the Haitian community for pregnant women in the fight to decrease infant mortality and help women deliver healthy babies, fight against low birth rate, and to help families deliver babies of a weight that can guarantee survival. The focus is on the whole family and on the mother at a critical stage of pregnancy. We also assist the mother after the baby is born with breast-feeding. The . . . program helps fight domestic abuse through education and educates older mothers [regarding] breast cancer.[5]

Sante Manman was designed to fight disparities in infant mortality rates between so-called racial and ethnic populations, on the one hand, and White populations, on the other. Infant deaths were especially high among the native-born Black populations; they were extremely high among immigrants who self-identified as Black. The use of martial language to commence the campaign against Haitian infant mortality and maternal illness, and to promote health, positive relationships, and good parenting was highly significant.

In 1989, when Sante Manman began offering services in the 12 Bicknell Street building, social conditions were no better for the Blue Hill section of Dorchester: "Signs of economic abandonment are everywhere, except for a plethora of billboards advertising cigarettes and alcohol on Blue Hill Avenue. One billboard towers over Morton Street with a picture of a baby and these words: 'If only they came with instructions'" (Kong 1990). As many Center staff members previously attested, the Franklin Field area off Blue Hill Avenue was similarly plagued with crime and multiple forms of violence. Given the routine suffering and "violences of everyday life" (Kleinman 1997) in these neighborhoods, what interventions could address the structural challenges communities faced in so-called death zones? Given the syndemical roots of such social suffering, should government donors, hospitals, and public health agencies propose "community-targeted" interventions or should "community-derived and controlled" interventions informed by local sociocultural specificities be developed (Plough and Olafson 1994: 223)? What role did scriptural economies play in the maternal and child health practices in everyday life?

The high infant mortality rates publicized in 1990 sparked tremendous community outrage in areas where prenatal care was least available. In response, the Boston Department of Health and Hospitals (the predecessor to the Boston Public Health Commission) organized the "Walk for Healthy Babies." Alongside care providers and politicians, hundreds of mothers pushed babies in strollers from Roxbury's Grove Hall (two blocks west from the Yawkey Center) down Blue Hill Avenue to a rally at Franklin Field (two blocks from the original Center at 12 Bicknell Avenue in Dorchester) (Ribadeneira 1990). These health advocacy efforts produced several public health and community-based interventions—Sante Manman, for example—to reduce disparities in infant deaths in the city.

In 1991, one umbrella intervention emerged to target the infant mortality crisis in Greater Boston, the Boston Healthy Start Initiative (BHSI). At the time, BHSI was a consortium composed of the Boston Department of Public Health, community advocates, and local health institutions. BHSI was one of fifteen national Healthy Start projects aimed at implementing a standard community-based approach to reducing maternal and child health disparities. The Maternal and Child Health Bureau in the Department of Health and Human Services' Health Resources and Services Administration (HRSA) funded Healthy Start. In 1994, the Haitian Multi-Service Center's Sante Manman program became one of fourteen subcontractors for BHSI, Healthy Start's urban grantee in Massachusetts (Howell et al. 1997: xiii).

Despite this city-wide, community-based program to improve maternal and infant health outcomes, reported 1996–2000 statistics in BHSI project neighborhoods showed "obstacles to gaining access to care and disparities in underlying health status and socio/economic well being continue to exert influence on perinatal outcomes . . . particularly for Black women." The analysis stated, "race and ethnicity continue to be predictors of poor perinatal outcomes in these neighborhoods." The same assessment identified additional problems related to lower health insurance coverage among "minorities and low-income individuals" plus troubling demographic statistics: "30% homeless or doubled up in housing, 25% who abuse alcohol during pregnancy, and 40% with repeat severe social risks." The majority of those whose infants died "experienced fragmentation and discontinuity in health care and that of their infants, including lack of follow-up and linkages across time . . . and across systems of care (medical and social)." In addition to domestic abuse preceding repeat unwanted pregnancy, the same report stated that 38 percent of cases displayed patient-provider challenges: "Interviews with women of color, in particular, emphasized how race, class and cultural differences between patients and providers often lead to miscommunications that leave women feeling disrespected."[6]

To reduce this broad array of factors maintaining disparities, BHSI sought to increase the number of women receiving prenatal care and case management from the first trimester through the postpartum period and to increase the percentage of infants tracked by case managers through age two. The program had extensive community training and organizing activities, including the "Father-Friendly Initiative." Another goal was to decrease the percentage of participants experiencing maternal depression, which could result from personal or family history, marital challenges, and unwanted pregnancy. [7]

Like other grant-funded projects previously analyzed, the BHSI model displayed a form of "results-oriented management" defining specific objectives and outcomes to be audited periodically (see James 2010, Chapter 4). For example, the BHSI Project Period Objective 3 sought to ensure "100% of BHSI participants during the inter-conception period will receive family planning counseling and services . . . in a culturally and linguistically sensitive manner to women and their partners at their postpartum visit." Case managers were to guarantee provision of family planning education and attendance at "scheduled family planning service visits" (Boston Healthy Start Initiative 2005: 37).

As a nonclinical subcontractor housed in a faith-based institution whose rules prohibited promoting or providing access to contraception or abortion (see Chapter 5), I was curious to understand Sante Manman's approach, especially since facilitating access to family planning was a mandated component of the Healthy Start/BHSI model of care. Once again, I draw on the memory palace method to consider the role of scriptural technologies in incorporating and tracking client lives. Given Sante Manman's dependence on cyclical grant funding to secure programmatic life, what modes of being, care, and self-auditing were employed in Sante Manman's maternal and child health literacy practices? When the precarities of pregnancy in so-called death zones surpassed BHSI scripts, how did staff

FIGURE 20. Sante Manman infant clients. Photo credit: Erica Caple James.

members cope? What kind of affect and improvisation did everyday emergencies produce and were such acts captured in writing? Could such documentary practices accurately capture the determinants of improved Black lives?

. . .

It is August 2006. I have just begun working with the Sante Manman Se Sante Pitit Program on the Yawkey Center third floor. The bright suite of rooms offers safety, knowledge, advocacy, care, and material assistance to clients. In a large closet to the right of the main reception area, freshly laundered secondhand baby clothes are stored as gifts for prospective parents. Another small room to the left contains a chaise lounge for clients to wait and rest, as well as a table and chairs. This space doubles as a classroom. At the far end of the room are large glass windows. Sunshine illuminates the interior. Plants native to Haiti flourish in pots along the windowsills, almost to spite the coldness of the fluorescent lighting and Boston's winters. On the left wall adjoining the windows, photos of many Haitian infants and children born to clients since the late 1980s form a multihued halo around a central indigo poster (see Figure 20).

Under the poster's bold cursive title, *Philosophy of Birth*, a wreath of pastel flowers surrounds a creed:

Birth is normal, natural and healthy.

The experience of birth profoundly affects women and their families.

Women's inner wisdom guides them through birth.

Women's confidence and ability to give birth is either enhanced or diminished by the care provider and place of birth.

Women have the right to give birth free from routine medical interventions.

Birth can safely take place in homes, birth centers and hospitals.

Childbirth education empowers women to make informed choices in health care, to assume responsibility for their health and to trust their inner wisdom.[8]

These walls are iconic. Their images enshrine Black maternity, nativity, infants, and families as worthy. They testify to the program's success in aiding Haitian and other women of African descent to deliver their babies successfully.

Throughout the Sante Manman suite, additional emblems of life promote biomedical conceptions of pregnancy and birth. A poster of a White baby warns about sudden infant death syndrome (SIDS). In the classroom, an abstract poster of a cobalt blue mother nursing a baby carries the message, *Lét manman se richès bebe* (Mother's milk is baby's riches). Anatomical models of the cervix in various states of health display graphically "Why Pap Tests Can Save Your Life." Each educational item promotes reproductive health literacy and healthy family life. Each also attests to the unseen presence of external authorities to which the program was accountable.

. . .

Imparting public health information to primarily immigrant clients was part of the processes of promoting health literacy and incorporating clients into the public health apparatus. One of Sante Manman's early successes was its outreach to and education of the Haitian community on women's health. A 1997 Sante Manman Se Sante Pitit (SMSSP) "Breast Cancer Prevention Program Report" describes the program's efforts to educate Haitian women on the anatomy and physiology of the breast and to increase their knowledge about breast cancer. Like other program components requiring documentation of activities and interactions with clients, Sante Manman's public health objectives were similarly outlined as goals to be achieved:

- Educate Haitian women on the anatomy and physiology of the breast
- Educate them on the importance of the breast and its functions
- Increase their knowledge about breast cancer
- Educate women on breast self-examination and clinical breast examination and encourage them to get into the habit
- Increase their knowledge on mammography and its benefits
- Inform them on methods of treatment of breast cancer

Such trainings epitomized how poor, ethnic, immigrant clients were encouraged to adopt new biomedical sensibilities and senses of embodiment as they sought fuller civic incorporation. As the report outlines, objectives were achieved through "a carefully planned radio campaign that [included] live radio shows with guest speakers, public service announcements on [the Center's] weekly radio show, and a series of breast cancer prevention workshops [and] video shows conducted both at the Haitian Multi-Service Center and other community venues." Center program grant documents estimate its radio programs reached nearly forty-five thousand Haitians. Staff members also conducted workshops at the Episcopal Church of the Holy Spirit and St. Angela Parish in Mattapan.

The breast cancer report also outlines how Sante Manman staff presented the breast cancer training to women students of the Adult Education Program, an in-house community outreach effort occurring with each new health prevention initiative undertaken at the Center. The public response to these programs was animated. After one radio show hosted by Dr. Nissage Cadet, a breast surgery specialist, the Center received twenty-five calls from "listeners anxious to have specific questions answered. The community asked questions about signs and symptoms of breast cancer and sought to calm their fears of mammography. Callers, often women with legitimate fear, were invited to attend subsequent workshops." In response to the education campaign, clients with undiagnosed breast issues were referred to medical centers. Haitian senior citizens who were already scheduled to have a mammogram were encouraged to keep their appointment and not fear the diagnostic technology.

Although Haitian women responded well to the breast cancer prevention program, continued outreach and education in the Haitian community was needed to eradicate "false beliefs and taboos" that "constitute barriers to many women taking effective measures to detect early and prevent breast cancer" (SMSSP 1997). The breast cancer program report concludes with an example of a workshop attendee named "Alice." At fifty-five years old, she had never previously conducted a breast self-examination or had a mammogram. During the workshop she found a lump in her breast and became very upset. Alice feared to seek treatment, stating, "I don't have anyone in my family who has a lump in her breast or cancer." The Sante Manman staff members referred her to Boston Medical Center and the Mattapan Community Health Center for a follow-up. Through mammography the lump in her breast was confirmed and removed. The report notes her appreciation of the program and that "even her husband called to say thanks for the program that prevented his wife's condition to become worse."

Informational materials that could be retained away from the Center supplemented Sante Manman staff members' direct instruction of clients. Once given to clients, however, the booklets, pamphlets, and brochures were not simply public health promotional resources one might find at a supermarket, library, or other mundane public space. From tangible reminders in English and Haitian Creole of how to improve one's health and health literacy, they became gifts of knowledge. These corporeal items offered opportunities for staff members to share their expertise and their facility not only with the English language but also with biomedicine. In sum, the materials Sante Manman staff members gave clients became secular icons of care, knowledge, and advocacy that resembled the emblems of faith its staff members displayed in their personal spaces.

FAITH AND FAMILY PLANNING

Sante Manman staff were observant Catholics dedicated to advocating for vulnerable pregnant women, especially Haitians, while following Catholic prohibitions against promoting contraception or abortion. In addition to family photos, their workspaces contained small, framed images of the Madonna and Child. Other cubicles displayed small pictures of Catholic saints or framed inspirational prayers. Some staff members wore small pendants of the Virgin Mary or a crucifix on thin gold chains.

Just below the large windows, two Haitian case managers, "Marguerite Roy," a veteran who began working when the program started in 1989, and "Roseline Dorvil," a social worker who joined the program in the early 2000s, had large adjoining work cubicles. The program director, "Pascale Verenette," a Haitian nurse practitioner with more than twenty years of healthcare experience, had a private office to the right of the suite entrance in which she examined clients. She began working with Sante Manman in 1994, when it joined BHSI. Anatomical drawings of the human body lined the walls of her workspace, and other medical images designated her area as a clinical space of care and healing. A bathroom scale used to weigh clients lay on the floor near her chair. A stethoscope and blood pressure cuff were other biomedical technologies used regularly to monitor client health.

I met Nurse Pascale in summer 2005 at an HMSC Advisory Board meeting. She did not wear nursing attire, but carried herself with an air of authority that made a uniform unnecessary. Her presentations were efficient, and she was serious about her work with clients and her obligation to report the Center's status to the board. Briefly, in 2005, she became interim Center director when Executive Director Imbert went on sabbatical and did not return.[9] I did not know she would become a good friend, one whose resignation in 2008, after fourteen years of service, was a source of sadness and grief for many stakeholders. Nurse Pascale was one of more than fifteen staff members who left the Haitian Center between 2006 and 2008. The departure of employees would parallel a similar exodus of core advisory board members during this same period (see Chapter 9).

At one of its weekly meetings, Sante Manman staff members shared how they viewed their program, its history, and challenges of operating between BHSI and the Charity. In early years, the program offered support including case manager home visits, parenting education classes, translation assistance, referrals to other medical facilities, transportation to clinician appointments, and other services. The program sought to improve children's health, prevent developmental delays, and reduce child abuse and neglect. Recognizing how the lack of mobility posed barriers to clients' ability to keep both prenatal and pediatric appointments (Giffin,

Curry, and Sullivan 1999: 43), in 1994 Nurse Pascale added transportation support explicitly in Sante Manman's proposal for inclusion in BHSI.

Offering maternal and child health services with primary financing from a publicly funded consortium posed challenges. In spring 2007, Sante Manman had to begin finalizing work for the close of the fiscal year at the end of June. There were eighty-five clients being seen by the two case managers and the goal was to enroll a few more by May 2007. Nurse Pascale explained, when their child reached age two clients neared the end of their enrollment. The staff needed to replace departing clients to maintain a stable cohort through spring 2009, the grant's scheduled end. As in Adult Ed, preserving a client base was a delicate process. The three staff women continued discussing the pros and cons of program registrations.

In previous cycles, there were problems if too many women were enrolled without sufficient funds to cover expenses at the end of a grant. At a minimum, the program needed to sustain a caseload of sixty women; the maximum was ninety. Staff strove to enroll pregnant women in the first trimester in order to see Nurse Pascale and have baseline vital statistics measured for comparison throughout the pregnancy, such as their weight and blood pressure.

I then asked about contraception and whether they could speak about it with clients given the program's location in the Charity network. In terms of family planning, rather than facilitate such services directly, the staff members referred clients either to their primary care providers or to other health centers offering counseling and access to available contraceptive methods. At no point did the Sante Manman staff members facilitate access to abortion, and as discussed below, these women sought a wide variety of external resources to enable a woman to carry out a pregnancy, improve her mental health, and aid her family.

Without articulating either personal or programmatic prohibitions against providing reproductive knowledge to clients, the staff discussed with some trepidation the risks of imparting contraceptive knowledge directly to clients. One case manager said in Massachusetts the morning-after pill was available to women aged nineteen and older. Prospective users needed to show identification to buy this contraceptive. If a woman was eighteen or younger, she required a prescription; while not exactly an over-the-counter drug, the medication was still accessible with parental support. In strong terms the staff stated concerns about the side effects of birth control pills and reported how an underage girl had died after taking it. Marguerite, the most senior case manager, speculated about the potential harms if individuals who were nineteen years old or older purchased the morning-after pill and distributed it to others. Who would be responsible if the side effects of these medications harmed the client or someone else? Pascale exclaimed, even as a nurse she would not deal with contraception.

I was struck by the sense of risk emerging in this discussion. The fear was not about being found noncompliant with BHSI's mandate. Neither was the risk of sharing contraceptive information and training about violating Catholic proscriptions against its use. Rather, concerns about liability for harm befalling a woman because of side-effects or the unlawful distribution of medication was a sense of risk I'd not previously heard debated at length in contested reproductive discourses. I wondered if the potential for harm to befall someone in relation to staff members' work inculcated a more widespread sensibility of fear among Center staff.

Despite outsourcing the family planning component of the subcontract, Sante Manman staff reported achieving stronger outcomes than the other thirteen hospital and community health centers in the BHSI network. Once when attending a meeting at the Massachusetts Department of Public Health, Nurse Pascale said someone criticized Sante Manman's nonclinical approach because it didn't provide birth control education. Such education and care should be a responsibility of health centers, she argued, especially because the Center could not offer injectable contraceptives like Depo-Provera or other modes of birth control, nor could they provide tubal ligations or IUDs. But in terms of birth outcomes, Sante Manman was most successful because clients' infants were typically 6 lbs. or more at birth, theirs was the best community outreach, and caseloads met benchmarks more than the clinical health centers with case management. Furthermore, at their audits, Sante Manman was able to have all client children immunized when the health centers did not. Hospital and health center clients might not attend postpartum check-ups even when located in the same facility as their prenatal care. In having a line item for transportation, the Center was more easily able to help clients keep appointments and, as a result, their tracking of client benchmarks was better than clinical facilities.

In comparison with historical reproductive governance strategies that abandoned, repressed, and even sterilized Black women in the United States (see Bridges 2011; Briggs 2017; and Roberts 1997), the Sante Manman program was pro-life or pronatal, improved birth outcomes, and promoted the health literacy, social welfare, and livelihoods of Black women clients and their families. What other factors made Sante Manman's efforts effective, even at points when the program faced termination?

Although staff members and program managers deemed the program efficacious, there was no guarantee Sante Manman could operate in perpetuity, regardless of its positive outcomes. In 2002, as the clergy sexual abuse scandal exploded, backlash against the Church and affiliated Catholic agencies reduced private donations to the Charity. The state, from which the Charity received more than half its revenue, was also in crisis. The remainder of the Charity budget was composed of "private contributions, United Way grants, and client copayments," but with "less than 2 percent of the agency's money" coming from the archdiocese. According to the *Boston Globe*, in 2001, the Charity "ran a deficit for the first time since the early 1990s, spending $720,000 more than it took in" (Abel 2002). By 2002, spending exceeded revenues by more than one million dollars. The Charity announced in

March 2002 its intent to "cut their $40 million budget by 15% and lay off up to 200 of their 1,400 employees" (Abel 2002).

Although Sante Manman's scope of work closely aligned with the Charity's historical mission to serve families, in 2002 it was reported as one of several programs for immigrants, racial and ethnic minorities, and mothers and children, slated for termination in the Catholic charitable network.[10] Although the *Boston Globe* article does not state what other fiscal management issues might have affected the Charity's budget, it continued, "Despite its distance from the church, agency officials say the current scandal has led many contributors to withhold checks. The agency canceled its annual garden Party at the cardinal's residence in Brighton; last year, that event raised $1.4 million" (Abel 2002), the majority of which would fund the Charity.

The Yawkey Foundation contributed five hundred thousand dollars in emergency funding to the Charity, which in turn gave Sante Manman one hundred thousand dollars to maintain the program until July 2002. In the scandal's wake, Sante Manman's contributions and the meritorious labor of the other programs at risk of termination—"El Centro del Cardenal, a youth education program for Latinos in the South End, the Edwina Martin House, a substance abuse treatment program for girls in Brockton, and Roxbury's Nazareth Residence for Mothers and Children [which provides] housing, medical care, and other services for poor families affected by AIDS" (Abel 2002)—yielded media attention for this major saving gift to the Charity. This gift came just a year before the Yawkey Foundation pledged five million dollars for the new building. At a time of corporate scandal it is likely Sante Manman's successes became emblematic of the Center's, and by extension the Charity's, care for the City's children.

PASTORAL BIOPOLITICS
AND SCRIPTURAL ECONOMIES

Throughout the years of client care, BHSI affiliated providers were to offer "health education related to self-care and infant care; nutrition, breastfeeding information and . . . other health education [about] HIV, STI's [sexually transmitted infections], substance abuse, family planning, reproductive health, [and] parenting support" (Boston Healthy Start Initiative 2005: 7). Sante Manman's client base was primarily composed of "refugees or immigrants with low literacy skills, limited or no English speaking ability, no health insurance, and no or low paying jobs.". Clients often suffered from "family isolation and survival stress" (Sante Manman Se Sante Pitit 1997). The program maintained extensive health records for both mother and child. Although I did not have access to study such records, staff members once showed me tall stacks of lovingly handwritten notebooks containing client information from the program's earliest years. (I later helped to enter intake forms into the computer, without analyzing the data in any detail.)

As part of the intake process and during pre- and postnatal services, Sante Manman staff members administered to clients two psychological assessments, the Women's Health Questionnaire (WHQ) and the Beck Depression Inventory-II (BDI-II). The WHQ, a survey instrument designed by the BHSI consortium, contained "63 questions about the health and social well being of the participant woman." It was administered three times, "at intake, end of 1st year, and 2nd year after delivery" (Boston Healthy Start Initiative 2005: 68). The BDI-II was similarly administered three times during a client's participation (Boston Healthy Start Initiative 2005: 52). BHSI mandated case managers make nine home visits during a client's participation in the program, including in the first days after giving birth. Case managers monitored child immunizations and, for those in secular community health centers, client utilization of family planning (Boston Healthy Start Initiative 2005: 52). The program also solicited feedback through "client satisfaction surveys . . . at the end of pregnancy, 1st year, and 2nd year after delivery," that BHSI staff analyzed to discern programmatic results from year to year (Boston Healthy Start Initiative 2005: 68).

Similar to the Adult Ed program's SMARTT database and the access provided to the Massachusetts DOE, BHSI clients' health data were accessible to the BHSI main office, and by extension, to the federal Healthy Start funders in HRSA. Although each national Healthy Start site used different management information systems, they were required to submit a "minimum data set" (MDS) to HRSA incorporating 241 variables on twelve maternal categories: "characteristics of client, key dates of services and providers, pregnancy history, medical risk factors, behavioral risk factors, prenatal care, psychosocial services, scope and content of case management/facilitating services, individual development services, psychosocial and supportive services; other family members, delivery, [and] postpartum care" (Howell et al. 1997: 77). Each program was obliged to report 159 additional variables for infant clients: "demographic characteristics; characteristics at birth; health status at first pediatric visit and at age one; use of medical services; use of psychosocial support services, facilitating services, and individual development services; and mortality data" (Howell et al. 1997: 78).

According to HRSA's 1997 Healthy Start outcome report, none of the fourteen national sites succeeded in submitting complete data. Reasons for inconsistency included lack of access to collect data correctly, lack of incentives for clinicians to "comply with burdensome data collection requirements," particularly when program funding was only a small part of their revenues, and inconsistent entry of variables into local program site's own data management systems (Howell et al. 1997: 78).

Records of the clients' health status and all components of service delivery— calls, visits, and even missed appointments—were to be recorded and shared by formal report with the BHSI consortium. Each local program site received computers containing software providing BHSI direct access to client data. Clinical data—such as client medical records, intake forms, prenatal progress records, labor and delivery records, and the six weeks postpartum record—were extracted from each of the fourteen program sites. Trained "medical record abstractors" collected infant health and pediatric visit records. Program staff members submitted monthly aggregate data reports to BHSI to "capture, besides the usual demographics, important non-clinical aspects of the BHSI component" such as depression rates and other "interconception aspects" (Boston Healthy Start Initiative 2005: 68). BHSI was also able to monitor uploaded program data through site visits and by using the MS ACCESS Database software (Boston Healthy Start Initiative 2005: 68). Nonetheless, Sante Manman staff members sometimes struggled with both the hardware and software the BHSI system required. "Something's wrong with the computer," was a regular refrain among case managers who needed to input their client's intake and mental health information. Indeed, computer crashes were frequent and contributed to the backlog of information requiring entry.

Besides the lengthy WHQ and BDI-II inventories, there were intangible aspects of the "direct relationships between case managers and families" not easily captured by these scriptural inventories (HSNRC 1997: 19).[11] The Sante Manman staff members facilitated far more than "care coordination," "women's access to and use of the perinatal health care and social services they need," "client empowerment," and improved "client and provider satisfaction" (HSNRC 1997: 19). Although its case managers hoped to recruit clients in the first trimester of pregnancy, doing so required trust and willingness for the client to be documented biomedically for nearly three years. In addition to educating clients and transporting them to and from their many health providers, other care practices included taking groceries to clients (those enrolled in Initial Response), lengthy discussions with partners and family members about maternal and child health, instruction about parenting and domestic relationships, and supportively counseling the pregnant woman.

Another component of care likely unique to the Center was gift giving. BHSI initially purchased cribs for clients, but discontinued the practice. Sante Manman staff members continually obtained donated items like baby clothing, equipment, and other paraphernalia and attempted to ensure clients' children and family members received gifts at Christmas. Other items were given at the Mother's Day celebrations (see Figure 21).

In many respects, such practices brought clients into a quasi-kinship relationship with Sante Manman staff members and the Center. In addition to the mentoring and accompaniment received, treating clients and their families as kin encouraged program participants to access services in a health network comprising St. Elizabeth's Hospital, Boston Medical Center, Mattapan Community Health Center, Bowdoin Street Community Health Center, and Carney Hospital. BHSI consortium members met monthly with willing clients to offer additional support (a program component to which I did not have access). The 2003 Sante Manman "Program Abstract" attributes program successes to the relationships between

FIGURE 21. Sante Manman Mother's Day gifts. Photo credit: Erica Caple James.

caring staff members and clients "built on longevity and trust." These clients in turn referred family members, friends, and other associates to enroll during their own pregnancies. Such associations were able to "empower clients to maintain healthy lifestyles after they have left the program" (Sante Manman Se Sante Pitit 2003: 2).

CENTER MARIANISM

A favorite time of day was when the Sante Manman staff joined with health promotion and elder psychosocial support program women staff members for a mid-day meal. Most brought food from home, and we sat in the small second floor room overlooking the rear yard. Each of the primarily Haitian women had their own culinary specialty. Nurse Pascale typically brought flavorful and filling rice and beans, and sometimes *legim*, meat slowly simmered with vegetables and spices to liquefy into a fragrant stew. I wondered how they found time to prepare meals, care for client families, complete their professional work, and support extended family in the United States, Haiti, and elsewhere. A stroke suffered years before had disabled one woman's husband; another's adult son suffered mental health challenges and lived at home. Another woman managed adult-onset diabetes and was a single parent breadwinner in household that included her dependent mother. How did they care for loved ones at home, navigate the complexities of Center work, and aid clients to live securely in the United States?

At one lunch in March 2007, I asked, "How do you all do it?" I knew there was no magic formula, but the workplace ambiance of peaceful detachment and conviviality dispelled the vexations of everyday life. I knew their journeys from Haiti and the process of starting anew in the United States had never been easy. Struggles with the English language remained to varying degrees, especially when staff had to transcribe interactions with clients into reports of program activities. (After all, "if it's not written down, it didn't happen.")

In answer, one woman spoke of rising before dawn to cook supper for her immediate family before leaving for work. Another lived with extended family in a triple decker compound that provided some benefits of a familial safety net. She also labored as a nursing home caregiver while attending night school for an advanced professional degree. Their personal and professional achievements became benchmarks to which clients could aspire, but these successes required tremendous effort.

Center staff women deepened the Haitian American roots sown in Greater Boston through paths furrowed by courage and perseverance. As much as the obligations of transnational kinship and family could permit, their concern was to empower clients and care for their communities (and themselves). Indeed, as case manager Marguerite told me, "Even when I go on home visits, I am helping my people and doing something spiritually for God." Each went far beyond the scriptural requirements of professional charity to help clients achieve their own goals.

I admired the Sante Manman team (and other Center staff members) and was honored to experience the place of kinship and maternal care they had created. As I recollect and now write, I know I could have asked them to analyze further the gender dynamics in their own lives. I could have questioned whether they considered their work a form of reproductive governance replicating the asymmetries of power between the sexes in the United States, Haiti, and globally. I also could have challenged more aggressively Church doctrines on life, gender, sexuality, contraception, and marriage, as well as the hypocrisy of the abhorrent clergy sexual abuse scandal. But interjecting such questions into these intimate exchanges might have prevented my learning other lessons—about ethics, care, mercy, and how to persevere, despite the many obstacles at work and in everyday life.

For most of the Center's women staff, active involvement in their respective churches, especially prayer services, sustained private piety. I marveled at their faithful certainty; matriculation in divinity school and extensive training in anthropology had done much to deconstruct my own. Several of the women encouraged me to learn to pray the rosary as another path to explore religious faith. In the rosary, a scripturally based meditation, repetition of the Hail Mary prayer frames contemplation of significant episodes in the lives of the Madonna and Child. Encouragement to explore this devotion suggested prayer and connection to the Virgin Mary underlay their own faith and life practices.

At a lunch in late March 2007, several women shared their experience attending a conference for Catholic women in Boston, especially how the keynote speaker's story demonstrated the power of the rosary.[12] Marguerite spoke at length about Immaculée Ilibagiza, a survivor of the 1994 Rwandan genocide. Immaculée was hidden with seven other women in the tiny bathroom of a Hutu man who was sympathetic toward the persecuted Tutsis. While concealed, the women repeated the rosary as many as forty times a day. They were not detected during repeated Hutu death patrols of the area. Although every member of Ilibagiza's family was slaughtered, she shared with the convocation, "I didn't know how to move on, but I said to God, 'God, I have just met You in the bathroom. I know You can act.'"[13]

I've since pondered whether the story was so compelling to the staff because Ilibagiza, like many struggling Haitian women, left a nation scarred by cycles of political violence and persecution. Perhaps the story reaffirmed the efficacy of piety. Although the Center women's devotional practices occurred amid different difficult circumstances, the women were no less fervent or sincere. In the context of shared meals, these caretakers taught me much about what could sustain and promote life. In their own way, these women staff members deepened the quiet reservoir of pastoral power at the Center's heart to be shared with the clients and each other.

MOTHERCRAFT

With professional maternal expertise, the Sante Manman team conveyed care and appreciation for their colleagues' and clients' dignity through "mothercraft." Historically, mothercraft referenced an early twentieth-century mode of public health instruction of women and girls. Rooted in positive eugenics—the promotion of desired population propagation—mothercraft aimed at creating hygienic families and improving public sanitation. Negative eugenic ideals sought to curb the reproductivity of populations deemed morally or physically degenerate, feebleminded, or socially disordered (Klaus 1993: 14).

As population health was correlated with national health and productivity, the maternal and infant health movement became an international one. Women's bodies and social roles became the nodes at which so-called public and private spheres converged. In early twentieth-century France, radical republicans "focused their attention on women's wage labor as the most important cause of infant mortality and an important factor in the decline of the birthrate and the disordered state of working-class morality and family life" (Klaus 1993: 14). In early twentieth-century Britain, "Child-rearing was becoming a national duty not just a moral one . . . To be good mothers they now needed instruction, organized through the various agencies of voluntary societies and local government, in the skills of what came to be known as mothercraft, as they were being defined by the medical profession" (Davin 1978: 13).

Immigrant women's literacy, behavior, and bodily health similarly became targets of early twentieth-century American interventions to mitigate perceived declining patriotism and lowered national standing resulting from diminished public health. Programs intervened to preserve the primacy of elite Whites:

"Race suicide," a concept widely accepted among Progressive reformers of all varieties, reflected a concern with the changing composition of the American population, as upper- and middle-class whites bore fewer and fewer children while more prolific immigrants from southern and eastern Europe filled the factories and slums.... Urban public health officials in the United States traced the causes of infant mortality partly to poverty and defective public hygiene, but they placed the primary blame on the ignorance of immigrant mothers." (Klaus 1993: 16).

In 1920, Nurse May Bliss Dickinson, chair of the Mothercraft Committee of the Massachusetts Federation of Women's Clubs in Boston, presented "the Mothercraft Movement" before the American Public Health Association as an emerging solution to this crisis:

> Mothercraft, now introduced into twenty-five states and several foreign countries, is a very recent development in public health education. It seeks to utilize the maternal instinct of young girls and build on it a knowledge of simple hygiene and sanitation. The child carries this instruction to the home and the standard of home health is raised.[14]

The mothercraft system's instruction of girls "leads them naturally into the subject of baby hygiene and the right care of the baby in the home" (1920: 201). The Massachusetts mothercraft movement envisioned supporting government agencies such as state and local departments of education, departments of hygiene, and Red Cross efforts to solve "urban and rural problems" (1920: 202).

Mothercraft practices expanded throughout Europe and its colonies to improve infant and maternal mortality, and to mitigate the impact of population losses on national and colonial productivity. British "maternal imperialists" (Allman 1994: 25, citing Ramusack 1992) implemented public health policies among colonized Asante women in Ghana designating infant mortality as a "failure of motherhood." Colonial efforts to control the reproductive labor of Asante women were inextricably linked to control over their productivity in the colonial economy (Allman 1994: 28). Similarly, early twentieth-century Belgian "doctors, Catholic missionaries, and state agents lamented the low birthrate as well as the high infant death rate in the colony" (Hunt 1999: 241). The declared demographic emergency conveyed modern anxieties about population loss, infertility, and low birthrates among Europeans in the metropole and among Congolese laborers and their families in the colony (Hunt 1999: 243). Although Belgian copper mining industrialists in the Congo executed "a pioneering maternal and infant health care program," Catholic nuns were among the missionaries who intervened to transpose "ideas emanating from social Catholic pronatalist movements in Belgium" to the colony on behalf of the state. Historian Nancy Rose Hunt asserts: "understanding this Belgian colonial exceptionalism requires noticing how integral maternal metaphors and procreative logic were to the convergence of interests among capital, church, and state on Congo's Copperbelt" (Hunt 1999: 244). In all these examples, conceptions of race were inextricably linked to ideas of sex and gender, health and hygiene, education, and the productivity of the nation-state.

These early twentieth-century relationships among capital, church, and state, and maternity, migration, and (re)productivity, reemerged in late twentieth- and early twenty-first-century infant mortality interventions in North America. Although conducted in very different political and economic contexts, there are similarities between the medical missionary work in the colonial era and the hybrid governmental and nongovernmental tracking of life in the Healthy Start and BHSI programs. A particular similarity recalling Lynn Morgan and Elisabeth Roberts's definition of reproductive governance is the public deployment of secular and faith-based community organizations to educate women and transform their bodily practices and hygiene in their private homes. This kind of instruction recalls both the historical senses of mothercraft and what Katharine McCabe (2016) calls "neoliberal mothercraft."

In contemporary neoliberal governance regimes, the state outsources the fulfillment of social welfare, healthcare, education, safety, and other public entitlements and infrastructure needs to private corporations and agencies. Under such conditions, privatized markets or economies converge with new sociocultural norms, as well as expert knowledge and technologies, to transform citizens into self-governing, risk-bearing consumers: "Experts derive their power from teaching citizens normalizing scripts for how to contend with social insecurity and manage risks which are in part accentuated by neoliberal divestment in public resources" (McCabe 2016: 178). Neoliberal "intensive mothering" projects impose "gendered expectation that mothers manage risks and adopt moralized maternal identities through their consumption behaviors" (McCabe 2016: 178). Scriptural and documentary practices provide the evidence of services delivered, maternal mentalities educated, immunized children, and other outcomes of strategic objectives designed to affect public health on the state's behalf.

Contemporary comparisons of infant mortality rates in the United States to other developed countries above also recall historical concerns with national health, eugenics, race, and immigration. At this writing, the national Healthy Start program states:

> Though infant mortality has declined in the United States over time, the U.S. has been slower to improve our consistently higher average rate of infant deaths than other industrialized countries. According to one source, in 2019 the U.S. ranked 34th out of 44 countries, with countries such as China, India and Turkey the only ones with worse IMRs. Russia's IMR was better than the United States at 5.1 deaths per 1,000 live births.[15]

Embedded in such comparisons are concerns with national health and development, the reputed degenerate effects of marginal populations on public and national health, and questions of the obligations states or governments have to care for, protect, and improve the lives of others. The statistics also point toward the modest success of programs like Healthy Start and drive a larger question: why are women's health, fertility, morality, and nativity the focus of demographic interventions rather than the structural, racial, political, and socioeconomic conditions that strongly give rise to population vulnerability?

. . .

In their own words, the care staff members provide to clients is maternal, engendering biopolitical charity with ideals of motherhood, protection, discipline, and gentle correction—producing a feminine or maternal form of pastoral power. But the efficacy of such work also lies in case managers' patience, expertise with Greater Boston's health resources, and perseverance to remove barriers to client success. Roseline Dorvil, a Sante Manman social worker, emphasizes staff commitment to help clients solve social problems as integral to programmatic success:

> *ECJ:* Why is this program effective or why is it successful?
>
> *RD:* The program is very successful. Because, when a client comes to the program, we do a lot with the client. We start doing prenatal education and . . . we make the client comfortable to talk about herself, and by talking about herself the client shares things with us regarding her own house and . . . family. By this we can see what needs the client really has and we help, we try to help her on those, too.

Through the establishment of rapport and sustained contact, staff empower clients inside and outside their families and homes, even when living under precarious circumstances. Roseline continued:

> For instance, there are some clients [who] don't have a house. . . . If they have three children, a husband, and herself, they probably have, maybe, two rooms. And that client always tells you, "I'm looking for housing." And what we did in the program, we referred the client to the Boston Housing Authority. We give them the address. . . . If they can't go by themselves, we go with them. If we cannot go with them, we tell them to bring the application we help them to fill out the application.

Housing instability, a major determinant of health, is a condition of living with overcrowding, having difficulties affording rent and household expenses, or paying most of one's income on housing. Another feature of housing instability is living in contexts exposing residents to health and safety risks.[16] Roseline claims that eviction from a residence and homelessness pose extreme threats to clients' health and access to healthcare. That kind of everyday emergency in the context of syndemic suffering requires exceptional interventions from case managers. Roseline explained:

> Some clients . . . are pregnant, but they are living with somebody else, and the baby is going to be born [but the client has] no house [of her own]. We explain [to] the

client how we have a shelter that has . . . [worked] with us [for] a long time . . . and that shelter only receives prenatals. If she wants to go, we call for them, set up an interview. If they have space, they [accept] the client for us. . . . The shelter helps the clients to apply for AFDC;[17] now the client can have an income by herself. And, [in] the same way the client can also apply for housing . . . because when you are in the shelter it's better for you to find a house [as soon as possible]. So, we did all of those things. You know, we worked with the client every day, anytime they want us, you know, any concern they want to share, any issue . . . And like a mother. We can say like a mother, right Marguerite?

Contemporary, pastoral power "works through the relation between the affects and ethics of the guider . . . and the affects and ethics of the guided." Such affective exchanges or economies are "translated into a range of microtechnologies for the management of communication and information" (Rose 2007:74). In their deployment of mothercraft, case managers addressed social, cultural, and linguistic barriers to care, while developing familial relations with clients—"like a mother." There developed an affective exchange between staff member and client conveyed through a variety of communicative actions engendering pastoral power.

As confirmation of the affective kinship produced between case managers and clients, Marguerite lamented in an interview how case managers were prohibited from touching clients for several years, even to provide supportive comfort.[18] Although she was unable to console clients using touch, she continued, she might, sometimes on a home visit—after administrative check-ins were completed and only if the client was in extreme distress—read Christian scripture passages to lift their spirits. This statement, made on a single occasion, was one of the only times I heard faith described as gift or remedy one could offer clients. The only semi-public indicators of piety were the discreet personal items at a few staff members' personal workspaces. Perhaps entering a client's homeplace relaxed any customary restrictions against sharing the faith in Catholic charities agencies.

Other intangible dimensions of the pastoral, caring relationship not easily recorded in a case note were present on the few occasions I accompanied staff on home visits. As mentioned previously, case managers were scheduled to make nine home visits to clients, and clients came to appointments at the Center in between home visits. One sunny morning in July 2007, Nurse Pascale invited me to accompany her to see a young Haitian mother who had just delivered a son. Because my research terms limited observation of individual meetings between Center staff and clients and any access to individual case files, I quickly agreed to go. I could not resist an opportunity to visit a client's home. We drove through sections of Boston with high concentrations of Haitian businesses and residents to reach the client, whom I call Guerline Isidor. On our arrival at a small reddish brick apartment building, a friend met us at the door and led us to the room where Guerline was resting. Rather than using formal assessments, Nurse Pascale checked Guerline's health and mental health through pleasant conversation and admired her son, whom I call Mathieu. During this tender exchange, I was, I am embarrassed to admit, transfixed by two components of the domestic scene: throughout the discussion a cigarette brightened to a glowing ember with each of Guerline's deep inhalations. Secondly, although I did not know his weight, baby Mathieu was tiny, barely six pounds. I wondered if Guerline had smoked throughout the pregnancy or if her smoking was rare. If routine, could smoking have had any relationship to Mathieu's lower weight? After Pascale shared more warm words of encouragement, an embrace, and gratitude for Guerline's willingness to have me visit, we left for the Center.

I was curious how the visit would be documented and whether Pascale would record Guerline's smoking in the obligatory case notes. While en route I asked her about the young mother's cigarette use. She said many Haitians have one cigarette in the morning and that it was not such a big deal. She chided me (gently) and stressed a more critical issue. Guerline had been in an abusive relationship. She was starting over alone with support from the Center. I was justly admonished, but still wondered about Pascale's report. If she disclosed cigarette use, or commented on the reputed cultural difference in their consumption in Haiti, would this information alarm BHSI's central administrators? Conversely, would Pascale document the kind and motherly way she congratulated and reassured Guerline whenever she transcribed the encounter? After all, "if it's not written down, it didn't happen."

In an interview, senior case manager Marguerite expressed exasperation with the burdens of inscription: "The services offered to clients are less than the paperwork." In late July 2007, Marguerite brought me to visit two clients. Although she had confirmed the appointment with the first client just before we left the Center, when we arrived, the young woman had left the home. Perhaps her absence was a form of resistance to case management. In hindsight I worried the client regretted agreeing to have an unknown visitor enter her homeplace. Marguerite was nonplussed and said sometimes clients missed appointments. We left to visit "Beatrice Sanon," a pregnant Haitian woman in her late thirties who had two children living in Haiti. Marguerite had already completed the WHQ, the BDI-II, and other intake forms by phone. What remained was a face-to-face meeting for Beatrice to sign the documents, one of which allowed the Sante Manman staff to request personal information from her health care providers should they be unable to reach her. Marguerite told me clients were sometimes difficult to trace. They moved frequently and sometimes left the city or state in search of work or other means of living.

Beatrice resided with her boyfriend and was expected to deliver her baby in early August, just a few weeks before me. Her sparsely furnished, air-conditioned basement apartment in a modest building on the border of Mattapan and Hyde Park was comfortable. Once seated, Marguerite spoke with Beatrice mostly in English. From her slight accent I would not even have guessed the client was Haitian until the conversation shifted to Creole. Beatrice had been faring well but lamented not having family nearby close to her delivery. She was frustrated her partner couldn't take leave from work to stay with his child. Moreover, her sister was having her first child in New York in August. As their mother lived closer to her sister, she was going to remain at home rather than travel to Boston for Beatrice's birth. Marguerite reminded her it was her sister's first child and that she also needed support. Marguerite's own daughter was also expecting her first child. Although compassionate toward Beatrice, she shared her enthusiasm about her first grandchild as another perspective on Beatrice's mother's decision.

The conversation was familial and pleasant, then unexpectedly shifted to differences between giving birth in Haiti versus the United States. Beatrice said she had decided never to give birth in the United States after witnessing how hard it was for American women, especially single mothers of limited means, to manage parenting. She mentioned seeing a woman with a newborn at a laundromat trying to do laundry alone. The woman appeared exhausted. Beatrice vowed never to have another child. "Yet," Marguerite said, "here you are."

I asked how things were different in Haiti. I remembered working at the Chanm Fanm clinic in Martissant the day a young woman in active labor came, asking to give birth inside. She was turned away. The physicians were not mandated to do deliveries and could not admit the young woman. Perhaps the staff also feared accepting the risk to provide care when the outcome was unauthorized and uncertain. She ended up having the child in the street.

Marguerite, the oldest child of ten, told us the story of her mother giving birth in a Haitian hospital. In the days following her release the doctor visited their home to check how her mother was feeling. Nurses came to give her sponge baths and her mother remained upstairs with the newborn to rest and recover. She recalled that the family prepared special meals to help fortify her mom—oatmeal in the morning, and bread and hot chocolate before she went to sleep. It was a time of pampering for a month following delivery. Marguerite and Beatrice were nostalgic for the care and loving attention shared postpartum in Haiti, likely under situations of relative security, as opposed to the individual and sometimes solitary experience of giving birth in the United States.

When back at the Center I asked Dr. Oscar, the Initial Response physician, about traditional birthing practices for mothers in Haiti. Within twenty-four to forty-eight hours after a birth, he said, mothers are given a hot steam bath, then massaged with *lwil maskriti* (Palma Christi oil or Haitian black castor oil). While our discussion of traditional Haitian birth practices continued, we unexpectedly learned more from a staff member with whom I had had only passing, but pleasant, interactions. By chance, Alcide Isaac, the Yawkey Center custodian, joined us and greatly enlivened the conversation. In Haiti, before her death, Alcide's mother was a *fanm chay* (*fanm saj*, midwife). He had served as her assistant and gathered firewood and herbs for an herbal bath for the delivering mother. Dr. Oscar added that women in Haiti often know in advance when they are going to deliver. They might go to the market earlier in the day or run errands, and then would call the *fanm saj* toward evening.

Alcide shared there are *tizàn* (teas, infusions) given to help *chofe* (heat up, accelerate) labor if it is not progressing properly and other remedies to lessen contraction pains. After the birth, the steam bath is given. Water is heated in a bucket, then a variety of herbs and leaves from mango, papaya, and sapodilla trees (among others) are added. When ready, the new mother stands over the bucket. As steam envelops her body, she is washed with the water. The bathing helps the *move san* (bad blood) to *desann* (descend) and *sòti kò-a* (leave the body), "*espesyèlman san ki gen tan 'clot' deja*" (especially blood that has already clotted). After the bath, the new mother is massaged, especially in her abdomen, to stimulate her womb and encourage the blood to leave the body (*san vide kò-a*). Without receiving the massage, he said, the woman could suffer from *matris tonbe* (collapsed/prolapsed womb/uterus). When walking she could stumble and her womb could fall or be misplaced, affecting her future fertility.[19] Normally there are three baths given, three nights in a row, in the evening before sleep. If the woman has someone with her, she may not leave the house for two to three months.

In subsequent days I asked the Sante Manman staff members about these traditional modes of labor and postnatal care. Caseworker Marguerite said some Boston hospitals had permitted Haitian women to receive the postnatal massage. Although prenatal care was much better in the United States, she affirmed postnatal care was better in Haiti. But whether postnatal care could consistently be as healing and restorative as described remained a question, particularly given Haiti's cycles of *ensekirite*.

. . .

The stories in this chapter show how life, health, education, and everyday care practices become objects of textual production, of translation and transcription, to demonstrate an intervention's efficacy and to enable institutions to demonstrate accountability to grantors. Attempts to convert life achievements into attainable objectives tend to individualize and naturalize many everyday life challenges. Goal-setting exercises, confessional practices, and formalized inventories of subjective states are affective performances and productions between staff members and clients. Such practices provide means of encouraging reflection, evaluation, and opportunities to seek expert assistance. In Sante Manman in particular, such steps facilitate the incorporation of women clients into the American biomedical system of birth, pediatric care, and organizational surveillance on behalf of municipal, state, and federal agencies. In both Adult Ed and Sante Manman, health literacy practices incorporate clients into scriptural economies that may stop short of enabling full citizenship; nevertheless, they facilitate paths toward civic inclusion. Some aspects of everyday charitable lives that may exceed scriptural templates of programmatic successes and failures involve culture—expressed through different ethics, moral senses, and caring practices—and structural inequities like racism, the roots of which appear unchallenged.

9

Bureaucratic Disenchantments
and Wounds of Charity

Disenchant, *v.*
To set free from enchantment, magic spell, or illusion.

—*OXFORD ENGLISH DICTIONARY*

Though we laud charity as a Christian virtue we know that it wounds.

—MARY DOUGLAS

*The Word of God inflicts a wound, but it does not produce a sore. There is a
wound of righteous love, there are wounds of charity, as she has said, "I am
wounded with love" (Cant. 2:5).*

—AMBROSE, BISHOP OF MILAN, COMMENTARY ON THE SONG
 OF SOLOMON 2:5

One of the conundrums of charity, especially faith-based charity, is that it can
wound. In concluding this ethnographic history's postmortem assessment, I further untangle the knotted strands of care and antagonism among the Center, Charity, and Church as the Center was made into something different in the Yawkey
building. As in previous chapters, I am deliberate about distinguishing the sensory
and affective components of "space" and "place." To improve human services and
produce an efficient, disciplined "workspace," Center managers compelled procedural changes, thereby altering the practices and mood in the "homeplace" (hooks
1990). Alterations in everyday charity transformed the Center's daily environment from conviviality, collaboration, and care—engendering a mood of collective joy or "communitas" (Turner 2012)—to hesitation and inhibition, producing
individual insularity, defensiveness, and even flight.

In the years since I witnessed these events, I have asked whether any organization can maintain its identity and mission when changes in operational routines are
experienced as imposed, negative, and hostile. Are sentiments of solidarity, respect,
loyalty, and dignity necessary among stakeholders for organizational survival,

215

especially in mission-driven work? I suggest efforts to routinize and bureaucratize Center services reduced its capacity to offer the Haitian community an intimate place of empowerment, solidarity, care, and justice. Between 2006 and 2009, the threads tying the Center, the Charity, and the Church together continued to fray and even snapped. The vignettes recounted show how corporal and spiritual works of mercy can be benevolent but potentially corrective, disciplinary, and even punitive and harmful to those subjected to their power—but not without resistance.

Seemingly arbitrary administrative changes confused, debased, and even sickened some Center laborers, resulting in some staff members abdicating responsibility, others' banishment, or even their flight from the worksite, as if from something spoiled. Increasingly bureaucratic interdictions against assistance and a lack of workspace transparency produced friction between managers and several Center educators and caregivers—especially the most outspoken Haitian staff. The correction and standardization of charitable practices deepened staff members' fears any noncompliance could produce retribution. Although arising as much from structural factors as from the personalities and behaviors of those involved, such tensions contributed to deteriorating morale and cut ties binding many stakeholders (including donors) to the Center.

Some Center staff members felt the Charity was deliberately attempting to dismantle long-standing programs serving Haitians through inflexible program manager directives. Those experiencing the Center as increasingly disciplinary and less Haitian-focused shared with colleagues their feelings of anger, disbelief, frustration, and betrayal. Staff who were wounded from attacks on their care work sought other employment. Aggrieved charitable laborers who depended on the Center and Charity for their livelihood felt dread on entering the building. In private, several shared how such experiences were embodied—producing negative emotions and distressing physical symptoms. I was not immune from the emotional and physical distress such events caused.

Advisory board members who learned about the punitive practices and diminishing morale also became disenchanted—especially by the disruption of communications among the board, the Center, and the Charity. Long-standing board volunteers transferred their loyalty and affective support to other Haitian nonprofit organizations, abandoning decades of dedicated work on the Center's behalf. Other stakeholders withdrew monetary support and withheld participation in the Center's "liturgical" calendar—activities such as the annual Mother's Day celebration, Adult Education Program graduation, health fair, fund-raising gala, and cultural commemorations—which deepened a sense of organizational insecurity. An environment intended to be a place of refuge for clients, providers, and the community was perceived as indifferent.

In the ensuing years it has been difficult to discern whether these events mark typical challenges of institutional reorganization and reform, the underside of Catholic charity, or the emergence of more negative styles of nonprofit governance that I observed previously and characterized as "malevolent bureaucraft" (James

2010). Perhaps all these dynamics were present. In the attempt to characterize how the cumulative discord disconnected the institution's long-standing partisans from the goal of establishing an independent institution "by Haitians, for Haitians," I am reminded that charity can move from compassion to repression, as Didier Fassin (2005) has described the shift from aiding to incarcerating and expelling undocumented migrants in France in the early 2000s. Similarly, Catherine Besteman (2019), drawing on Jacques Derrida (2000), shows how charity can encompass both hospitality and hostility, producing "hostipitality." Her ethnographic work in the United States is a particular touchstone as she documents the agonistic charitable relationships between Catholic Charities, native Maine residents, and Somali Bantu refugees in Lewiston, Maine. In Besteman's example, race and racism, ideals of citizenship and belonging, and disputes about whether refugees were unentitled recipients of charity or deserving beneficiaries of welfare—a distinction based on legal status and rights to receive public assistance—negatively charged civic debates about African newcomers to a predominantly white town. These ethnographic examples portray similar paradoxical tensions of care, control, inclusion, and abandonment seeming to underlie some of these events at the Haitian Multi-Service Center.

In contrast to ethnographic works describing the institutional extension of charity to, or the withholding of it from, refugees and migrant clients, the uncharitable practices I now present were directed toward the human service providers and charitable volunteers who advocated for their (compatriot) refugee and migrant clients. The shift from a hospitable homeplace to a bureaucratically routine but hostile workspace had predictable effects—such as the production of activities fulfilling projected programmatic outcomes but largely perceived to have failed in terms of stakeholder participation. I interpret four specific episodes: a September 2006 general staff meeting, the hiring of a new health program manager, the 2007 health fair, and finally, the Center's thirtieth anniversary fundraising celebration (held belatedly in 2009)—a celebration that lost more funding than it earned. Interwoven among these episodes were confrontations among the Center management and stakeholders regarding ethical gift giving. These interludes showed the Charity did not, and perhaps could not, always monitor how program sites implemented human services. The intra-organizational contests over care, charity, and advocacy were enmeshed with issues of race, class, gender, and even ethnonationalism. These protracted dynamics eroded a sense that the Church, Charity, Center, and even the City could be aligned to aid Haitians.

SETTING THE SCENE

By late summer 2006, I was still having difficulty communicating with several of the twenty-five plus full- and part-time staff members beyond engaging in simple pleasantries. Requesting formal interviews proved especially challenging, as the staff members were busy with program labor both on- and off-site. I would later learn all was not well under the surface of everyday routines. For some staff members, my connection to the institution's programmatic changes was unknown, and perhaps even suspect. Most challenging was earning the trust of providers in the HMSC AIDS Client Services Program (hereafter, the HIV/AIDS program), which was scheduled to close later that fall. Since the late 1980s, the HIV/AIDS program had offered peer support, counseling, and accompaniment (Farmer 2013; Watkins 2015; see also Chapter 8) to HIV+ clients and those living with AIDS (including some children). As is now well known, the virus first emerged in Haiti in the early 1980s when the disease was brought to the nation by international travelers (Farmer 1994). Initially, the path of infection was unjustly attributed to Haitians, who, alongside hemophiliacs, heroin users, and homosexuals, were viewed as members of the ill-reputed "4-H" club—populations considered vectors of the pandemic. For Haitians who emigrated to the United States at this time, association with the disease meant additional discrimination, professional prejudice, and a long struggle against misinformation about HIV/AIDS from majority populations.

The HIV/AIDS program manager, whom I call Dr. Maurice Calixte, later described to me the struggles of his clients against stigma *within* the Haitian immigrant and refugee population. Many Haitians still feared the disease could be contracted via passing physical contact. Others worried that any interpersonal exchanges with infected persons could transmit infection and were potentially deadly. Infected clients feared social ostracism from their compatriots and especially their families. A 2003 Center grant proposal identified other ethnic and cultural circumstances thwarting HIV/AIDS prevention:

> Haitian pride, denial, gender biases and voodoo [*sic*] beliefs inhibit recognition of high-risk behaviors and the willingness to test for HIV/AIDS. Even when diagnosed, they are not likely to seek treatment until they become very ill. Frequently, family members with HIV/AIDS care for others who have AIDS and may be neglecting their own care. These care givers are traditionally women, and are at high risk for early morbidity. Elders have the least access to HIV/AIDS information in their own language. They face more intense cultural barriers as well as age-related barriers to appropriate care.

But Dr. Calixte strongly emphasized how reducing transmission rates required addressing the socioeconomic conditions in which many impoverished Haitians lived. Some clients shared housing with many others who both worked and slept in shifts. The exchange of sexual favors sometimes occurred, was often expected, and even coerced among precariously housed residents. Domestic violence remained a large factor inhibiting Haitian women's ability to protect themselves from sexually transmitted infections (Jean-Charles 2002).

Given these conditions, the Center's program had been well positioned to provide the Haitian communities in Greater Boston, Somerville, and Cambridge trusted resources and public health education to reduce racial, cultural, and ethnic health disparities. The Boston Public Health Commission AIDS Services and the Massachusetts Department of Public Health AIDS Bureau granted most of the program's funding. These two public health divisions received federal funding from the United States Department of Health and Human Services HRSA (Health Resources & Services Administration) Ryan White HIV/AIDS Program (RWHAP) Part A. As currently described, RWHAP Part A offers "medical and support services to Eligible Metropolitan Areas (EMAs) and Transitional Grant Areas (TGAs). EMAs and TGAs are cities/counties that are the most severely affected by the HIV epidemic."[1] Similar to federal grant programs previously described, state and municipal public health office grantees administer funding to clinical and nonclinical subcontractors like the Center, as well as to other service providers in Greater Boston and eastern Massachusetts.

The Center's HIV/AIDS program aimed to improve the health and mental health of those directly affected by the disease at the local or community level. The Center's 1996 HIV/AIDS program draft grant proposal stated case managers accompanied approximately seventy-five Haitian clients (thirty-four infected with HIV and forty-one diagnosed with AIDS)—of whom 39 percent were male and 52 percent female, with children composing 9 percent. At the time services included:

> Case management including the functions of intake, on-going assessment of client needs; on-going service planning; coordination of and referral to services needed; monitoring and follow-up; and discharge and planning based on the HIV/AIDS Case Management Standards of Care that are divided into the following sections: personnel; client's rights; intake; assessment/reassessment; service planning; coordination and referral; discharge and planning; agency policy, procedures, and supervision. (HMSC 1996–97)

Through its peer support program and two peer leaders, Center clients had access to all services on-site and found social acceptance among others living with HIV. By 2003, the client base had grown to 110 individuals. Public health and educational outreach, especially to new immigrants, were offered to clients and outside communities via the Center's subcontract with the REACH 2010 initiative (see Chapter 6). The program's successful operation was indicated by an award a case worker received on December 1, 2002, from the Collaborative of Providers Serving the Haitian [Community] for "commitment to the health of the community members" (HMSC 2003).

The Center's program also received public recognition for community health services at critical transitions in the archdiocese's institutional history. When budget shortfalls led the Church to close the archdiocesan Office of AIDS Ministry—a unit established by Cardinal Bernard F. Law in 1988—the Center was lauded in the *Boston Globe* as the entity assuming the Church's ministry.[2] That the Center's own program would close in late fall 2006—ostensibly because of a failure to submit a grant proposal—was a devastating blow to staff members, clients, and their communities. In both the archdiocesan and Center closure cases, budgetary issues were critical. I suspect, but cannot confirm, that Church ambivalence regarding observance of medical best practices in reproductive healthcare and education—including instruction on use of contraceptive measures to assist in preventing the spread of sexually transmitted diseases—also underlay a willingness to allow these programs to close. Regardless of the motive, the closures seemed to indicate to many stakeholders that the Charity and Church were less committed to supporting vulnerable lives in Greater Boston, especially the lives of clients of Haitian (and African) descent.

The HIV/AIDS program staff members had dedicated their professional lives to advocating and caring for Haitians in Haiti and the diaspora. Dr. Calixte, a soft-spoken Haitian physician in his fifties, had directed a major hospital in Haiti in the 1990s and led the HIV/AIDS program since 2000. Dr. Oscar Fils-Aimé, the Haitian physician who worked in the Center's Initial Response program, also served as a liaison from the HIV/AIDS program to the REACH 2010 Initiative. In addition to providing interviews about health topics on local Haitian radio stations, he gave public lectures on a variety of health conditions. Two Haitian women case managers, "Bernadette Hilaire," who had worked at the Center for nearly fourteen years, and "Danielle Elie," who had started with the program in the late 1980s, accompanied their clients in a similar manner to the Sante Manman Se Sante Pitit case managers. Bernadette and Danielle (we used first names) supported their compatriots in everyday life by reminding clients, over discreet phone calls, to take antiviral medications, supplying household items and groceries, helping newcomers who did not speak English to navigate the city of Boston, counseling clients on disclosing their status to their families, and, more generally, by providing translation assistance, social recognition, and care without judgment. Although the program performed a critical community service by offering a place for clients to meet in security and without stigma, it remained somewhat cloistered inside the Center.

By early fall 2006, I had become aware the HIV/AIDS program was in trouble and scheduled to be closed permanently. The program was then serving forty-seven clients—forty-five Haitians, one African American, and one an African national. The majority lived in Dorchester. As an institution operating in multiple economies (gift, grant, compassion, scriptural, market, etc.), the Center's reliance on public grant monies constrained the form and content of the care provided. Challenges relating to documenting overall program activities and individual acts of care also contributed to its impending closure. Like the scriptural requirements in the Sante Manman program (see Chapter 8), each encounter between staff and clients had to be recorded in a case file, regardless of whether such care took the form of groceries delivered personally or conversations by telephone. Although I never had direct access to program records, my understanding was they were not religiously maintained. The Center executive director told me in early September that the Department of Public Health had recently cited the Center (in July 2006) after an assessment found fault with the HIV/AIDS program's filing system. By September, a report explaining what measures the team had taken to redress any oversights was overdue; it had not yet been submitted to the Charity for review and submission. I would later learn from case managers that there was resistance to recording caring interactions, as if their inscription somehow reduced or minimized the expressions of solidarity and quality of accompaniment between staff members and clients. Like other Center programs, an inability to produce complete records of human service delivery created problems because of requirements to demonstrate to funders clients' improved (health) literacy and (bio)psychosocial statuses, and staff member compliance with best practices in HIV/AIDS case management.

The issue of documentation remained a sensitive one stemming not only from staff resistance to bureaucratic forms of client surveillance but also, with respect to HIV/AIDS, from concerns regarding patient privacy. But reluctance or inability to produce documentation negatively impacted the HIV/AIDS program's continuation. When Pierre Imbert, the Center's longest serving executive director, was on sabbatical in 2005, a critical grant had not been submitted to the state to renew the HIV/AIDS program. To mitigate this lapse, Imbert asked Mayor Menino's office to request a special grant of $160,000 from the state to extend program support. Imbert also approached private donors, one of whom gave ten thousand dollars. But in anticipation of potential fiscal shortfalls, the Center also asked CCHER (the Center for Community Health Education and Research, see Chapter 6) to provide direct services to any clients whose services might be discontinued because of a potential funding gap.

Despite the uncertainty around the HIV/AIDS program's future, spirits remained high regarding the expectation that the Center would continue to be a hopeful place and expand its client base as promised to the City. Through attendance at the HMSC Advisory Board meetings in late April 2005, I knew overall prospects were still good for sustaining and expanding programs. The finance committee reported a grant for Adult Ed had been successfully funded—increasing the overall budget by seventy thousand dollars for the next grant cycle—and the fiscal year 2005 budget would have no deficit. (As we later learned, the maintenance and depreciation costs of the new building were not included in the existing program budgets, thus a $414,000 shortfall existed upon occupation of the new site.) Ultimately, the failure to complete the needed client paperwork and grant submission proved devastating for the HIV/AIDS program.

In seeking to understand further the events that took place between the missed grant submission, Imbert's 2005 resignation, and the discontinuation of the HIV/AIDS program a year later, I learned more about the structural and financial relationships among the Charity, Center, and their respective funders. A 1996–97 draft report outlining the Center's health-related activities greatly aided my understanding. The excerpt clarifying such connections was included in a request for funding from the Boston Public Health Commission. In the draft, the direct applicant on behalf of the Center's AIDS-related programming was the "Catholic Charitable Bureau of the Archdiocese of Boston, Inc., d/b/a Haitian Multi-Service Center." This "d/b/a" is significant and shows how at least from the mid-1990s the Charity acted as the legal and administrative entity in which the Center was subsumed. In doing business as the Haitian Multi-Service Center, the Charity provided nonprofit status to the Center and could present itself as a "Haitians-serving-Haitians" institution. If this draft report accurately represents these organizational relationships, the Center was neither structurally nor legally independent. Administratively, the Charity was the lead agency in this kind of grant application for state funding. On the other hand, the document offers another model of networked governance (Laguerre 2011) epitomizing the intricate connections among Catholic corporations globally.

That these nested institutional linkages could generate both benefits and restrictions for the Center and Charity influenced each organizational site and its respective administrative routines, and not always for the better. From a March 2011 interview with "Sally Brasco," a high-level Charity administrator who served as the Center's interim executive director when Pierre Imbert resigned, I learned Dr. Calixte was not solely at fault for the failure to submit the HIV/AIDS program grant. When it came time to tender the application, Brasco said she and other Charity liaison staff members did not recognize the grant proposal as a *renewal* rather than a new submission; thus the Charity headquarters failed to pursue the funding from the Department of Public Health. Although the ultimate responsibility for the failed grant renewal might rest with the Charity, the nested corporate structure and disruption in leadership and communication during a personnel transition undoubtedly contributed to this state of affairs. However, the lack of transparency about these processes exacerbated the fragile trust between Center stakeholders and the Charity. Their underlying suspicion of Charity indifference—and even hostility to this racial and ethnic minority human service center—was confirmed by the failure to resubmit the grant proposal. It was well known that the Charity intended to streamline services offered in the Yawkey building and to broaden (or reduce) the Haitian-centered focus of onsite programming. More broadly, many Catholic institutions remained ambivalent about issues related to corporeality, sexuality, contraceptive prevention, and HIV/AIDS care work.

Although these communication and funding challenges framed the scene at a disturbing staff meeting, they were not solely responsible for the outburst that occurred. By fall 2006, Executive Director Bernard Brutus increasingly displayed bitterness and anger at having inherited a financial deficit (among a litany of other perceived problems). He shared such complaints with me in informal chats as I sought to understand the Center's history. Brutus had assumed Center leadership in December 2005 and had been an enthusiastic and collegial stakeholder for many years. In spring 2006, Brutus hired the same facilitators who had worked with the REACH 2010 initiative (and the 2005 advisory board retreat) to aid staff members in drafting the Center's five-year strategic plan using the "Future Search" planning method (see Chapter 6). I had known Dr. Brutus from my role as advisory board liaison to the REACH 2010 coalition, at which he represented another ethnic health organization. In our early one-on-one conversations in the Yawkey building in summer 2006, he lamented the level of staff professionalism and record-keeping practices, his lack of access to past program documentation (although the Charity possessed prior Center grant proposal submissions), and what he characterized as lax employee discipline. Perhaps his apparent ease in communicating these challenges to me was related to my advisory board member role and represented an effort to justify any problems I might perceive or witness. However this may be, this early informality in communication suggested to some Center staff I fully supported him in his role and attitudes. Undoubtedly, the pressures for Brutus to succeed were high on multiple fronts. But from 2006 to 2007, his private expressions of frustration erupted increasingly in more public settings. "Things are changing!" was a phrase he pronounced frequently with menace; however, the level and depth of change to which he referred never became fully clear until it was too late.

RUPTURES IN ROUTINE STAFF MEETINGS

At first the September 2006 meeting seemed routine. Alongside the executive director, roughly twenty-five staff members were present in the large, cheerful classroom where we met on the second floor of the Yawkey Center. In turn, managers of the Adult Education Program, the Elder Program, Sante Manman, and the HIV/AIDS program gave status reports. Their presentations offered a comfortingly familiar recounting of tasks completed and outcomes achieved, which ordinarily would elicit constructive feedback and discussion of future steps. An outburst changed my perception of these meetings. Dr. Calixte had nearly finished describing successes in fulfilling the REACH 2010 HIV/AIDS prevention subcontract for CCHER when Director Brutus interrupted him. In front the entire assembly, and with a dry, disdainful tone laced with scorn, the director belittled the quality of Dr. Calixte's presentation. Brutus next reminded him of the past administrative error that (initially) resulted in the loss of much needed programmatic funding: "But yet *you* failed to submit the grant that would have renewed the Center's own AIDS program and now the program will close." The director had spoken publicly an unmerciful partial truth by casting the full blame on Dr. Calixte.

The impending program closure could be likened not only to the severing of one of the Center's own limbs but also the loss of a bulwark against the spread of HIV/AIDS among Haitians in Greater Boston. However, if the closure was the result of failures in communication and oversight between the Charity and

Center, why did the director choose to publicly reprimand Dr. Calixte? Was this a form of fraternal correction in the sense of the "spiritual works of mercy"—described as an admonishment of an individual intended to reform or to prevent further fault—or a formal public rebuke by an authority because "the offender has already in advance relinquished whatever right he possessed to have his good name safeguarded?"[3] Was Brutus ambivalent about closing the program when the need remained in the Haitian community? Were there other unknown pressures or stressors provoking this punitive, shaming behavior?

Despite the potential loss of grant funding, all was not lost. The Center still operated as subcontractor for REACH 2010. Through Pierre Imbert and (then-) state representative Marie St. Fleur's advocacy, other funding had been procured. At the time of the distressing staff meeting, the state commitment of new funding from another budget line item was already known. But the funding required that the Center revise and expand its public health work, perhaps at a cost to clients living with HIV/AIDS. In alignment with the Massachusetts Department of Public Health's general concerns about racial and ethnic disparities, the Center health programs' new focus would be addiction and cancer prevention. To address these public health target areas, Brutus decided to reorganize all Center programs categorized as "health promotion and prevention" into a single division under a new director. In effect, this decision removed the administrative authority of existing health program managers and represented a fundamental structural shift. As will be discussed later, the process of hiring the new health program director revealed widening cleavages between some program managers and their staff. Unanswered was whether the state mandated the Center focus on addiction and cancer because they posed greater risks to public health or if the Church and Charity's prohibitions against promoting contraceptive protections reduced the Center's capacity to promote STD prevention successfully. Regardless, the Charity and Center remained viable recipients of public health grant funding.

Director Brutus's open reprimand and exclusive blaming of Dr. Calixte produced a stunned silence. The reminder of a lapse already known by everyone assembled reopened old wounds and was a form of moral shaming. Dr. Calixte later told me he had never been so professionally humiliated before this incident. The public institutional disrespect would continue when, at the closure of the HIV/AIDS program, its staff members were told they all had to reapply for any new positions in the restructured Health Promotion and Prevention Program. Nobody was rehired. The Center later transferred the entire HIV/AIDS program to CCHER. CCHER's programmatic inheritance was especially ironic. CCHER was founded in the 1990s because of the irresolvable divide among Center and Charity staff members regarding how best to provide health care and education to Haitians about STDs, especially HIV/AIDS. As one of several incidents of public controversy in the 1990s over organized healthcare for Haitians, staff who could not accept the double bind—between complying with Catholic teachings barring use of contraceptive methods and medical best practices advocating use of barrier contraceptive methods to help prevent the spread of infection—left the Center to form other Haitian health organizations (see Chapter 6).

Immediately after the September 2006 staff meeting, I asked several attendees privately if this kind of public reprimand had happened previously. I was told it had not by some, but others remained silent. It's possible my question sparked concerns about whether I could be trusted with a response, or—as an HMSC Advisory Board member—whose "side" I was on, that of managers or program educators and caregivers. Nonetheless, several in attendance expressed their shock privately. My outreach to staff about this event may have been the key opening doors to interview several reticent Center staff members about their lives and history of charitable work—but other events preceded such new openness.

WITHHOLDING GIFTS

The public disparagement of Dr. Calixte was not the only incident provoking a palpable sense of disruption and unease; nor was it the only example I witnessed on-site. I would learn from other staff members a similar style of public correction and reprimanding of teachers occurred regularly in the Adult Education Program meetings. A new program manager chastised teachers for failing to add voicemail greetings to their phone extensions or for receiving any non-client visitors on-site—another transformation of the Center from homeplace to a more bureaucratically oriented workspace. Adult Education staff members who had held positions for many years, such as the native language literacy instructor—who instructed nonliterate speakers to read and write in Haitian Creole—were fired, ostensibly for failure to pass English language proficiency exams. Over a short period, instructors who taught at a satellite site in Mattapan were also terminated; these included Rénald St. Jacques, whose story of immigration, imprisonment, and undocumented life preceded his finding refuge at the Center, then naturalization and hire as an English instructor (see Chapter 3). Another instructor, a charismatic voice in both the Haitian and diaspora media, also left. His departure was a significant blow, as he hosted Center public health programs and advertised its services on the radio. Rénald claimed the teachers whose positions were rescinded for technical reasons of language proficiency had been the most outspoken critics of the new management regime. In his view, these firings were ultimately intended to inhibit employee independence and capacity to resist, and to bring the program further into conformity with Charity goals and Catholic teachings.

A few months before the public castigation of Dr. Calixte, the Charity had hired a new education program manager, Catherine Hansen. In contrast to previous (and subsequent) managerial job searches, Center staff members reportedly were not involved in this hiring process. Although there may not have been a connection to the Charity's decision to hire a new manager without staff input, earlier in 2006, and for only three months, there had been yet another Adult Education Program director whom I call Nora Wagner. Several of the Center's women staff encouraged me to reach out to her. The conversation we eventually had was troubling. At the close of her three-month probation period, Ms. Wagner was terminated. She later filed a harassment complaint against Director Brutus and Catholic Charities with the Massachusetts Commission Against Discrimination.

Although Ms. Wagner could be characterized as a disgruntled employee, her words aligned with much of what was reported to me about the increasing managerial aggression toward some staff members and growing lack of administrative transparency regarding the Center's future identity and mission. Nora (as I was invited to call her) had worked in international development in Haiti and served for many years as an education specialist with the Peace Corps in North Africa. In our interview she contrasted her approach to human development with the Center executive director's using examples from her previous work: "In development . . . you could be in a hurry and get things done, in which case you do it yourself, . . . or, you decide that you want to create something meaningful, lasting, and appropriate—in which case you're going to take a lot of time and have a lot of dead ends, but in the end, the people you work with develop ownership of what you do." She went on to say she thought the new executive director was frustrated with what he perceived as the staff members' inadequacies, whether in tasking them with producing a strategic plan or in trusting them to work professionally.

Nora gave additional examples of frustrating Center practices that evoked her prior challenges teaching English in Algeria:

> Another thing is . . . I learned the expression, "Who has the keys?" Everything was locked up. If you wanted books as a teacher, you had to go get the key to the book room. The supply closet was locked. The telephone, if you want to call outside of the immediate Boston area, you had to go through [the executive director's] secretary. I understand some people had to use the phone at one point, but there's a way to do it, you give everybody a phone call, whatever. But it was all very withholding, which reminded me so much of Algeria.

Nora's complaints about the withholding of material resources and disciplining of staff were not the first I had heard about Charity-managed projects (see Latour 1999). But the norm of cultivating solidarity amid scarcity seemed to have changed dramatically from St. Leo's to the Yawkey Center.

Although the new rules may have been an attempt at professionalization and guarding scarce resources, their effect was to create an environment of correction rather than care. Nora continued:

> This is supposed to be a place of refuge. I was really, really, uncomfortable. It went against my values that I had developed, the work I had done before, which [was] what drew me to the Haitian Center in the first place. Because it was more than ESL [English

as a Second Language], it was a continuation of development work. I mean, I'm sure I have my negatives too, but [the director] wouldn't talk to me. He was hostile.

Nora's description of Brutus's demeanor as hostile raises a question about the extent to which hospitality and hostility can intertwine in both individual and institutional encounters, whether in charitable or development work. But I also had unanswered questions about gender, and whether the director potentially objected to or discriminated against Nora as a (non-Haitian) woman, one with outspoken perceptions of how educational labor should progress at the Center. Perhaps the Charity objected to a manager who sided with long-standing Center staff members against the new director. An adult education counselor whom I interviewed suggested the dispute derived from temperament and sentimentality on Nora's part, which this individual considered excessive. But this same counselor would resign within the year from their own emotional distress and physical exhaustion, saying, "my health is not worth staying in this job."

Nora Wagner named the director as the impetus for withholding practices. Center stakeholders suspected the Charity had authorized staff chastisement to create a more compliant and tractable workspace, rather than a less formal but effective homeplace—one that could enable employees to continue developing professionally. At one of our late fall 2007 meetings, an advisory board member reported a disturbing encounter that increased board suspicions the Charity ultimately planned to dismantle the Haitian Center. The member reportedly informed Tiziana Dearing, the Charity's new president and first woman and lay Catholic to lead it, about the troubles under the Center's new management. She reputedly responded the Center "was being brought into the twenty-first century." The implication that the Center was backward or unprofessional was conveyed in the tone the board member used to convey Dearing's reputed words. The statement held undercurrents of paternalism, colonialism, and even racism, as if the Charity's mission was to convert souls through modernization, correction, and discipline, and its managers acted as the overseers of this transformation. Managerial claims of worker noncompliance and incompetence could facilitate a goal of removing a Haitian-centered focus completely. I leave aside these issues temporarily to contextualize the links between public reprimands, workspace shaming, and the paradoxes of aid, especially when an institution is dependent on the grant economy.

MOBBING

Anthropologist Noelle Molé has analyzed phenomena of toxic workplace behavior in Italy—such as the bullying of subordinates in one-on-one or group settings— and refers to some of these behaviors as "mobbing." Molé (2008: 189) defines mobbing as "psychological or emotional harassment entailing the marginalization of a single worker by another individual or group of either same-level colleagues or superiors." A phenomenon described in the social science literature since the 1990s, mobbing arose from efforts by the Italian state to shift the labor economy to one "more flexible and casualized" (Molé 2008: 189). Longer-term guaranteed work contracts protecting employee security were giving way to short-term non-traditional employment characteristic of a neoliberal economy (Molé 2008: 189). Routine mobbing behavior or professional bullying also included "events such as unexpected changes to schedules, the seeming invisibility of figures in charge, and the psychological weariness from constant changes in staff" (Molé 2008: 190). Additionally, mobbing comprises behaviors like "attacks directed at the target's communication networks, social relations, image, professional level and tasks, and well-being and health" (Molé 2013: 24). Molé's examination of worker harassment cases demonstrates how less direct negative mobbing practices can also produce experiences of "isolation, idleness, or boredom," resulting from "social exclusion to accusation[s] of a lack of productivity, abruptly reassigned work responsibilities, job transfers, and being assigned to an isolated or shabby office space" (Molé 2013: 25). Mobbing practices "make the workplace hellish to compel workers to quit" (Molé 2013: 26).

As workers increasingly linked the stress of this negative kind of professional climate to deteriorating bodily health, mobbing was formally "medicalized" in Italy (Molé 2008)—identified as an illness meriting treatment and, in rare cases, compensation. Molé's careful analysis of Italy's mobbing employment cases helps characterize the "affective toil" (Molé 2013: 37) working under precarious and hostile labor conditions can impose. I propose such negative and harmful behavior can also arise when nonprofit actors and agencies like the Charity and Center operate in insecure grant and gift economies characterized by impermanent sources of funding, and flexible, nonsalaried, and volunteer labor.

ILLIBERAL GIFTS

Governmental outsourcing of social welfare to the nonprofit sector benefits, but also produces stressors for, those institutions operating in and reliant on publicly funded grant economies (James 2010). In addition to the institutional insecurities accompanying dependence on grants and monetary gifts, in the realm of faith-based administration, nonprofit corporations like the Church and, by extension, the Charity, rely on the benevolence faith can generate in terms of "in-kind" support (Clemens 2019)—such as donations of goods, professional services, volunteer labor, administrative support, material space for programs, subsidized rent, and so on. Thus, at several levels, these networked institutions are in a structural position of worthy gift recipients or grantees. Faith-based organizations are also presumed to desire and promote benevolent practices throughout their networks, thereby generating complex moral economies encompassing multiple forms of caring exchanges between and among individuals and institutions. I suggest that bullying, and additional examples of mobbing behavior that will be described below, are more likely to emerge under situations of fiscal precarity, producing visceral, penetrating wounds from which their targets cannot recover. Such toxic behaviors were interpreted as bureaucratic malevolence because stakeholders expected the Center's work environment to sustain and regenerate the care extended directly to clients, donors, and volunteers.

. . .

To the disconsolation of several staff members, the discontinuation of an annual Christmas activity—the collection of Christmas gift donations—affected their ability to support clients. When considered alongside additional alterations, the cessation of gift giving can be characterized as a form of mobbing. Various employees, but especially those in Sante Manman, typically solicited Christmas gifts for their clients. Formerly an organized practice, by 2006 the Christmas gift activity was ad hoc; although occurring outside the mandates of a particular program, gift solicitation and distribution were still routine among staff.

In a late August meeting, Nurse Pascale Verenette informed the Sante Manman staff about the gift practice suspension in her summary of the regular program managers' gathering with the executive director. The managers' meeting outlined expected activities for the remainder of the calendar year, such as the October staff performance evaluations, the Center's annual fundraising gala (November 2006), and various Christmas activities. She said the director voiced concern—presumably the Charity's—over the potential duplication of donors and services between the Center and the Greater Boston Catholic Charities programs in the Yawkey building. Center managers were told to instruct staff not to solicit Christmas gifts for clients. It was not clear if the gift practice was being centralized, suspended temporarily, or discontinued permanently, but by all indications the cessation was irrevocable. Also unclear was whether the ban on gift solicitation included the gifts routinely given to expectant and new mothers in the Sante Manman program (see Chapter 8).

Sante Manman staff members recounted how donated Christmas gifts were placed in a large room at St. Leo's. Parents were given fake money to go "shopping" for gifts for their children. The staff interpreted the suspension of this festive activity as a loss for clients and their families. In hindsight the discontinuation can be interpreted as an attack "directed at [staff members'] communication networks, social relations, image, professional level and tasks and well-being and health" (Molé 2013: 24). Nurse Pascale repeated woefully Director Brutus's exhortation during the meeting, "Things are changing!" These words had become a mantra foreboding unknown new routines.

The origins of the programmatic gifting practice show why its termination was painful and much lamented, appearing to staff as another form of punitive employer behavior. I learned more about the tradition from a 2011 interview with

Sister Veronica, as I call her, a religious sister who formerly worked extensively with the Center. In addition to taking vows of chastity, poverty, and obedience, sisters in her order took vows of service. Then at seventy-eight years old, she remained a sharp-witted woman after a long and distinguished career as a scholar, educator, and university administrator. She had supported Vietnamese refugees at an American military installation in the 1970s. As she neared retirement, she hoped to continue working with impoverished immigrants. With fluency in French plus experience teaching Haitian university students, Sister Veronica asked her provincial (the regional head of her order) if she could next serve Haitians in the United States. She was deployed to St. Matthew Church in Dorchester in summer 1996 and began learning Haitian Creole at the UMass Boston summer language institute in the summers of 1997 and 1998. In 1998, after a serendipitous meeting with then executive director Pierre Imbert, Imbert invited her to establish a volunteer program at the Center. The program later became an internship site affiliated with the PULSE Program at Boston College (BC).[4]

The PULSE program, which still exists at this writing, seeks to "educate . . . students about social injustice by putting them into direct contact with marginalized populations and social change organizations and by encouraging discussion on classic and contemporary works of philosophy and theology."[5] The opportunity for student volunteers to be "in direct contact with marginalized populations and social change organizations," and to reflect on such immersive service-learning experiences, enacts what the Jesuit moral theologian James Keenan (2008: 9) defines as *mercy*—that is, "the willingness to enter into the chaos of another." Although greater power and resources tend to reside in those who are merciful toward others, Keenan's formulation, drawing on the work of Judith Butler (2004, 2012) and other theorists of social precarity (Han 2018), reveals additional dimensions of charitable exchanges of care in voluntarism. Keenan asserts that the willingness to enter the chaos of others' lives requires the donor, caregiver, or Good Samaritan to become vulnerable themselves: "Here too is the invitation to surrender one's dominance or privilege, to enter into solidarity with the other, not through a condescension but rather through an accompanying meekness that allows oneself to be trained precisely by the precarious one" (Keenan 2020: 141). The student volunteers' service-learning "experiment" generated social intimacy and multiple forms of gift exchange with the Center's predominantly Haitian clientele. The focus on encouraging direct contact with the marginalized also reminds me of the remark a Charity staff member made about the Charity's work to "reach out to a population that most people don't want to touch" (see Introduction). Such outreach was a core tenet of corporate Catholicism, reflected here in pedagogy.

Sister Veronica told stories showing how the "corporal works of mercy" could transform all parties to a charitable encounter, especially when enacted between receptive donors and recipients of care: "And it was so touching, the bond they developed with the Haitian elders . . . the most charming people on the planet. . . .

Then they worked with the ESL classes. They worked in daycare with the children. Some of them worked in Initial Response at the food pantry." Because the service-learning opportunity also offered university credit, students with interest in human services came from other Boston-area universities, such as Lesley College (now Lesley University), Northeastern University, and Bentley College (now Bentley University).

Sister Veronica's comment lauding university volunteers implied most were non-Haitian; their immersion experience occurred across racial, cultural, linguistic, class, and other lines:

> It was wonderful for the Center because they had [others to help out]. It actually turned out that because . . . there was academic credit involved, they always showed up. The only thing, which isn't always the case with volunteers, . . . they got very, very close to the people. And interestingly enough, . . . [in] the second or third year, we began getting Haitian Americans.

"The people" referenced here, Haitians, reveals some of the subtext aligning poverty, race, and ethnicity in this Catholic nun's understanding of charitable voluntarism. That non-Haitian volunteers got "very close to the people" suggests the immersive program helped bridge gaps not ordinarily surpassed through organized voluntarism at their universities—language, geography, class, race, and even touch. Perhaps such charitable labor and vulnerable social exchanges enhanced the worthiness of both care givers and recipients in the economy of merits and faults.

Sister Veronica's story about her encounters with Pierre Imbert shows the elision of ideas about who constitutes "the least of these" and why one who was not obligated to serve would choose to "enter the chaos of others":

> [The building at 12 Bicknell] was falling apart. I mean, I was glad it never fell down around our heads or burned down around our heads. It's a miracle. But what happened, one day, they emptied out a food pantry and moved it over to another place. And that was going to be the office for [a staff member] and me. And we're there moving furniture, finding anything we could find, putting it in, and Pierre Imbert looks at me and said, "Sister, why did you leave [your] university to come here?" And I said, "Pierre, I'm a [name of her religious order]. And I wanted to be closer to the truly poor. That's why I did it."

In contrast, Sister Veronica described the motives of Haitian university volunteers who came to the impoverished Center as something personal or private, and related to identity, in addition to receipt of academic credit for charitable labor:

> I asked them—because I had to do one-on-one supervising—I asked them, and . . . before we accepted them, I [would say], "Why do you want to come here? The place is falling apart. It's not easy access." And the Haitian American students said, "I want to know something about where my roots are." And it was wonderful for them, too.

A desire to learn about one's roots suggests the Haitian American students viewed the Center as a repository of cultural expertise and a (home)place able to teach them about their national or ancestral heritage. Although offering aid from a position of greater social, economic, and even racial privilege, the Haitian volunteer students received training and multiple forms of social capital from client experts.

Another one of Sister Veronica's stories shows how the Center gift program facilitated benevolent moral and ethical exchanges among volunteers, clients, and staff who served them. Student volunteers helped her request gifts from commercial vendors and nonprofit programs like Toys for Tots. Even armed forces officials gave gifts for Center children who had written to Santa with requests. The students also instructed Sister Veronica ethically, encouraging her to allow the Elder Program clients to select gifts they could give to others: "And one of the students said to me, 'Sister, have you thought of giving the elders something that they can give to a child?' I said, 'No.' So . . . all the [donated gifts] came in. We put [them] out on benches in the church. And they came over to pick out stuff for [their] grandchildren. And I said to the student, 'You're a genius.' He said, 'I know.'" As discussed previously, a Sante Manman staff member shared that the clients were later able to "purchase" gifts with play money as the program developed. Despite being a simulation of commercial Christmas shopping, the provision of play money to "buy" a chosen object encouraged these clients to participate symbolically in the American commodity economy. Perhaps the activity endowed them with hope for future independence and economic self-sufficiency in the United States.

Building others' capacity to give was a form of empowerment and a critical but undocumented mode of charitable work at the Center. Stories like the following helped me understand why the discontinuation of the Christmas gift program and additional limitations placed on staff members' personal service to clients were so emotionally devastating:

> *Sister Veronica:* But we had the AIDS program at the time. And at that point, one Christmas, [a woman client] was in the hospital, [a] woman who had AIDS. . . . And we got the presents and sent them over to the hospital. And children who were teenagers came. And she said . . .
>
> *ECJ:* Her [own] children?
>
> *SV:* Her children. She said this was the first time in her life that she had ever been able to give her children what they'd asked at Christmas.

A critical dimension of charity, enabling others to give—especially those like this AIDS patient whose health and other vulnerabilities made it impossible to partake in cultural gift-giving practices—was an intangible form of care amidst everyday emergencies.

The tradition of gifting strengthened clients' capacity to perform "spiritual works of mercy" themselves, by instructing those offering services or donations.

Sister Veronica told a story of an Elder Program client who wanted to thank a social work intern by giving her a gift he had brought from Haiti. The intern did not want to accept it—thinking it would be unethical or a violation of the terms of her professional position—and she asked Sister Veronica to intervene. The intern's client told them both: "To receive is also to give, because it is a gift of self." In deeply reverent tones, Sister Veronica shared the following: "She cried. I cried. But that's true. And I think . . . the student who suggested giving the [Elder Program clients] something that they could give [to others] had understood that. . . . I thought what I was hearing . . . was that one of the hardest things about being poor is not being able to give."

Corporate Catholic charity encourages partnerships between actors who give, donate, support, and love others in need. Although power differentials exist throughout such charitable networks, the cultivation of vulnerability, humility, and solidarity creates a caring economy, one in which emotion and moral sentiments fuel practices. Sister Veronica fully retired in 2003. As the Center did not have staff members with the bandwidth or expertise to oversee the volunteer program and to complete the supervisory documentation required for university students seeking placement, the formal volunteer program ended. The Center did not have the funds to hire someone to replace her. But under Pierre Imbert, the staff members continued to solicit gifts for clients to their professional capacity.

Given the staff reorganization efforts underway in fall 2006, the new director did not renew the Christmas gift donation drive. I do not know if the Greater Boston Catholic Charities program offered gift assistance at the Yawkey Center subsequently. This lapse deeply distressed the Sante Manman program manager and case managers, who typically brought items to new mothers and their children. The suspension of the gift practice seemed to counter the spirit of the holiday season and indicated a shift toward less compassion and empathy for clients. The discontinuation may have been benign in intention, but it fit a cumulative pattern of acts that weakened the intimate social networks Center staff members (and particularly the case managers) had built with donors and the clients under their charge.

WITHHOLDING KNOWLEDGE

The new managerial policies restricted other connections between staff members and clients regarding document production and informal aid. By September 2006, Director Brutus had prohibited Center staff members from completing any external applications or administrative paperwork on their clients' behalf. Three instances of such assistance provoked reprimands and censure. In the first, staff assisted prospective Initial Response clients with the certifications of housing insecurity and other causes of need, drawing them to the Center because the language of the forms was often inaccessible to clients. For example, a Sante Manman staff person described how women in the program sometimes became homeless. Given the emergency that housing insecurity posed to both maternal and child health, the staff member might draft a form letter verifying housing loss or rent arrears for the landlord to sign. The staff might even drive the clients to obtain the verification or help with completion of the forms. In a second case, the Sante Manman program scope of work explicitly obligated staff to accompany clients to appointments to improve patient adherence to prenatal and postnatal care. Director Brutus preferred the funder shift to offering vouchers for clients to use taxis or other independent transportation services instead of the staff member accompaniment the program mandated. The director expressed openly his concern that such accompaniment encouraged dependency rather than self-sufficiency. But the case managers viewed the transportation they provided as necessary. Many clients still lacked linguistic fluency to communicate during appointments. Some had other children needing supervision, which complicated leaving a residence to see a healthcare provider. Furthermore, for clients lacking English language fluency and familiarity with Greater Boston, being required to navigate what many described as a deficient public transportation system to reach appointments posed an additional burden discouraging access to and compliance with care.[6]

A third constraint on staff and client communication, as well as on efforts to strengthen client social capital, was the suspension of the Center's on-site immigration services. Although the rationale was that the Charity wanted to centralize such services in its headquarters, the removal inadvertently disempowered clients seeking to regularize their legal status. Some Center staff members routinely aided clients to complete their applications for permanent residence and citizenship. Director Brutus prohibited such assistance—whether completed at the Center or on a staff member's personal time off-site—saying the Charity would be liable for any errors and face legal problems if such documentation was improperly prepared. Bernadette Hilaire, an HIV/AIDS Program case manager who lost her position in 2006, shared her exasperation with the prohibition against aiding clients to complete immigration forms. She viewed this suspension as manifesting the Center management's lack of mercy. One day, an elderly Haitian man came to ask Dr. Calixte to certify his inability to pass a citizenship exam (because of illness). The doctor was off-site, so the gentleman spoke with Bernadette. She said the man could not read and had paid someone five hundred dollars to help him complete the form, but the person had done so improperly. Bernadette read through the form and explained the contents to the client:

> Dr. Calixte, he was not there. . . . I took the papers and I looked at them. I asked [the client], and [knew] that guy could not take the test to pass the citizenship [test], especially [because] he was about sixty-seven, sixty-eight years old, ok? So, when they charged the guy five hundred dollars to fill out the form, I figured this is wrong, this is not fair. . . . And I was looking at the form . . . and I said [to myself], "Do you see

what they did to the guy?" And I did not think that was fair, they should not do that to the guy, because he's an old guy—like sixty-seven, sixty-eight years old.

Bernadette was visibly angry and upset because the client's nonliteracy had been exploited financially and because he was elderly and ill. His impairment and social vulnerability were precisely the characteristics the AIDS program had been established to remedy through mercy, social solidarity, and justice.

Although advocacy on clients' behalf has been an integral component of the Catholic charitable brand (Kammer 2009: 5), Center staff members were newly prohibited from fulfilling off-script tasks. When Director Brutus learned about Bernadette's interaction with the elderly man, he reprimanded her. She continued as follows:

> So . . . the next day . . . I went there for the meeting, and [the director] told me I had no right to be working with immigration papers. I [said], "What did I do with immigration papers? I did not fill out the form, I did not finish the form." He said, "No, you have no right. You know what happens—some programs . . . close . . . because of [dealings with] immigration. He [said], "That form you touched, is it for immigration?" I said, "Yes, it's for immigration, but did I fill out the form? I just went over it with the client. He's sixty or seventy years old. He doesn't know how to read. If he came with the form, what do you want me to do?!" So, he said, "Don't be smart!" I said, "I'm not trying to be smart." I wasn't trying to be smart.

Bernadette recognized the difficult obstacles immigrant clients faced in everyday life and their vulnerability to exploitation—especially elders with poor health. She sought to rectify an injustice by placing herself in the vulnerable position of challenging a workspace rule. She was chastised for what the director felt was noncompliance with the new regulations. Her tone conveyed indignation on the client's behalf as well as her own, having been charged with "being smart" in the way one would rebuke an errant child. I wondered if there were implicit gender undertones in this interaction. The director's reported words displayed disrespect to and admonishment of a woman employee. But I already knew the director's communications could be abrasive toward anyone who was a subordinate or defied his wishes.

When I began interviewing staff about the history of their work and programs, I learned about their personal faith, their trust in the Charity (and Church) as benevolent institutions, and how much each employee was vested in their professional program. Many expressed vociferously their belief that Catholic institutions would always sustain Center programs facing financial shortfalls—such as the period between the end of a grant cycle and a potential renewal—and also protect their individual employment. They had faith in and practiced the corporal works of mercy—aiding the stranger, the poor, and other defenseless populations. Nonetheless, the unanticipated fiscal challenges the move to the

Yawkey Center engendered intensified administrative pressures to change or reform routine practices. The rapidity of the expected professional transformation produced shock, hurt feelings, anger, and disbelief. The new environment was funded in large part by finite, secular, public and private grants, but still required a moral, affective, and spiritual investment in and performance of care for "the least of these." The dependence on impermanent secular aid provoked uncharitable behaviors toward employees like Bernadette and other stakeholders—the very embodiments of advocacy and charity whose labor built the Center in the first place.

. . .

Molé's analysis of mobbing in Italy is especially informative for characterizing how the changes in care practices among the Charity, Center, and the latter's clients devastated many long-standing staff and advisory board members. She describes late twentieth-century, postindustrial "immaterial" labor regimes as requiring the worker to "place our very souls at its disposal: intelligence, sensibility, creativity and language" (2013: 31–32). The requirement of an investment of one's affect and soul in labor under uncertain and precarious conditions are factors that precisely characterize nonprofit human services work. I suggest here the dependence on uncertain grant funding can generate mobbing and other kinds of uncharitable practices:

> Mobbing became the symbolic site at which late capitalist labor was visible at its worst: the worker-subject betrayed and harmed despite her totalizing, soul-filled investment. . . . When labor regimes became soul burdening, mobbing became the vehicle of erasure for not just employment, but personhood. (Molé 2013: 32)

Negative personal workspace conditions existed for staff who felt the new rules hampered their efforts to care for and teach clients in and beyond the Center. The disputes about how to labor and serve others charitably produced manager bullying and mobbing behavior, negative affect and poor health in some staff, and decisions to withdraw support among advisory board members—all the while staff attempted to serve their clients and meet funder reporting requirements.

Before continuing to analyze how mobbing practices can manifest between the tensions of neoliberalism, the privatization of social welfare, and the flexibilization of labor in the grant economy, it is important to note that not everyone shared this sensibility of negativity or the perception something fundamental to the Center's own charism was being lost. Among the staff, there were individuals who felt the new direction in which the Center was moving was positive, creating a rigorous and regulated environment in which their work could be more effective overall. A few Adult Ed staff members—both Haitian and non-Haitian—expressed appreciation for the new building's spaciousness and cleanliness, managerial attempts to inculcate new routines, and the resulting sense of potential to expand their work. Among those was Saul Augustin, whose classroom and teaching appeared in the documentary film *Doing Anthropology: Thoughts on Fieldwork from Three Research Sites* (Boebel 2008).[7]

As depicted in Saul Augustin's classroom, English instruction accompanied lessons on the benefits employment can yield. Many students aspired to fulfill the obligations of full-time, authorized labor and to receive the security a position with benefits could offer, especially in an increasingly hostile sociopolitical climate. Saul's efforts to provide contextual understanding of the vocabulary words also offered students the social and cultural capital to overcome growing anti-immigrant and lingering anti-Haitian sentiment in Greater Boston.

Behind these positive documentary scenes were intense, escalating struggles over the Center's mission and future vision. Such struggles further frayed the Center's ties to the Haitian community and failed to craft new bonds with the surrounding neighborhood. In addition to the Adult Education Program scenes, *Doing Anthropology* captures (in background) an Elder Program citizenship training and several clips of the annual health fair, a public health outreach event only sparsely attended and considered a failure despite the dynamism depicted onscreen. Did this poor outcome result from the health program restructuring, growing dissatisfaction with Center changes, or other factors?

HEALTH LITERACY AND COMMUNITY OUTREACH

The restructuring of the former Health Enhancement Program limited the scope and depth of the Center's health disparities work from 2006 to 2007 (and beyond). In the fall of 2006, I did not expect Director Brutus would ask for my participation in hiring new staff for the reorganized health programs' new manager, community health educators, and community outreach worker—especially after my witnessing his shaming of Dr. Calixte in the September general staff meeting. I regret that I initially said nothing to challenge Brutus. Perhaps my silence was perceived as an implicit agreement and my invitation to serve on the search committee a means to provide the director additional support. Given what I now know about the executive director's challenges with other hiring processes, however, it is possible the Charity requested a board member's involvement or the HMSC Advisory Board's executive committee requested one of its board members participate. Regardless of the reason, I agreed to join the health promotion program manager and staff search processes.

Becoming directly involved in the search altered my relationships with staff and managers. As the process was already underway, I asked to see all the candidate files. The director shared dossiers already sorted into short and long lists. I was surprised that two Haitian candidates possessing medical, public health, and even international management expertise were excluded. When I asked if there had been an oversight, the director, somewhat taken aback, said the two individuals could be considered. But he shared a disinclination to hire Haitians in managerial roles. I wasn't sure if this was a personal preference or if he'd received instructions from the Charity not to fill positions like these with Haitian professionals. (That the Charity hired a Haitian medical professional for the position after Brutus's pick, a non-Haitian, left after less than a year suggests the choice of a non-Haitian was his own preference.) The two initially rejected Haitian medical professionals were ultimately interviewed by staff and Center management. One—an individual with global health and management experience who generated broad enthusiasm and hope for the evolution of the future program—was selected by consensus to earn the position. The director told the hiring committee he would make the offer, but in the following week nothing more was communicated. When asked for an update, the director said he had asked the candidate to submit a writing sample in English by a certain deadline and that the candidate had not responded. The committee was perplexed about why the requirement was made—especially considering the candidate's fluent English communication skills—and why the candidate may not have fulfilled the request. My own expressed concern about the lack of transparency opened new lines of communication with some staff about their challenging experiences in the Yawkey Center. New lines of communication foreclosed others, with the director and other managerial staff and, perhaps, with the Charity.

Director Brutus ultimately hired an African American woman with community health, fundraising, and organizational management experience, but little expertise with Haitian culture, history, or language. In February 2007, "Roberta Johnson" started as the Health Prevention and Promotion (HPP) manager with an expectation to produce immediate "deliverables" (as she termed them), anticipating future external audits of the Center's public health work. It was vital the HPP division achieve benchmarks demonstrating progress toward its health outreach goals by June 30, 2007, the close of the fiscal year. During that window the health promotion team would offer education seminars to clients in the adult education and elder programs and at external community locations. Themes ranged from HIV/AIDS prevention to breast and prostate cancer awareness.

The primary event intended to introduce the restructured HPP to the community and demonstrate the (Yawkey) Center's leadership in reducing health disparities in Greater Boston was the annual health fair. I volunteered to help organize it alongside the HPP staff in order to learn about its role in promoting public health literacy and to offer support to the new HPP manager. The two team members I came to know well were long-standing Center employees rehired in February 2007 for new HPP positions. Dr. Oscar Fils-Aimé (see Chapter 7) earned a new position as one of the community health educators. Murielle Estimé(see Chapter 4) became a health educator. Then in her fifties, Murielle had offered breast cancer awareness education through Sante Manman in the 1990s and had worked with the Elder Program. She provided new immigrant arrivals instruction regarding

HIV/AIDS prevention as part of the Center's REACH 2010 subcontract. I had found her to be a rare kind of teacher, one enthusiastic about any subject matter, creative in conveying concepts, joyful in demeanor, and generous toward her students. But, despite the comprehensive, caring instruction I witnessed both Dr. Oscar and Murielle provide to clients both on- and off-site, the director reduced both individuals' financial compensation drastically after the June 16, 2007, health fair, and with no explanation.

THE HEALTH FAIR

Health fairs are designed to reduce health disparities by offering medical information to the public in order to aid them in preventing the spread of illness. In these festive, celebratory events, participants receive gifts of free medical screenings and health provider access, and they participate in other informational activities. Such fairs enable vendors of health-related goods and services to connect with potential consumers. Mabel Ezeonwu and Bobbie Berkowitz describe health fairs as community-based interventions to build connections between health providers and a population. Such fairs "improve community members' access to health care" by means of "a voluntary community-based, cost-effective event used to detect health problems, identify risk factors, and provide educational information and supportive resources to promote healthy lifestyles of its participants" (Ezeonwu and Berkowitz 2014: 119). Literature analyzing fairs of this kind (see, for example, Ezeonwu and Berkowitz 2014; Keaveny 1974; Murray et al. 2014; Richie 1976; and Werch, Schroder, and Matthews 1986), especially those occurring in faith-based settings (Wilson 2000), is relatively limited.

Since the early 1990s at St. Leo's, the Haitian Center staff joyously organized annual health fairs for the community. Sante Manman staff members described these events as personal and intimate—more like a family reunion than an informational gathering open to an anonymous public. At least since 1996, Nurse Pascale said, the whole stakeholder community funded the fair through sale of raffle tickets. The business office collected the funds and reserved them to pay for the event's food and other expenses. One case manager said the Center's staff members *konn fè manje* (prepared the food) and the event was sheltered under a large tent on the parish grounds. A repast of Haitian cuisine was offered, including soups, legumes simmered with crab or conch, stewed beef, or fried marinated pork (*griyo*); roasted sweet corn, *mirliton* (chayote squash), and other side dishes, either for free or for the modest price of three to five dollars. The Center offered free T-shirts, water, *kola lakay* (Haitian soft drinks), ice cream, and other items generating a carnivalesque feeling.

At the Yawkey site, the cultivation and strengthening of cultural intimacy and existing bonds with Center stakeholders was not the primary focus; rather, producing an impactful "deliverable" successfully through outreach to new publics was the primary goal. Early in February 2007, Nurse Pascale said Dr. Brutus had urged the health staff to begin planning the event, without the new HPP director's input. "Why wait," he was reported to have said, since there was donor pressure to showcase the Center's restructured health education and direct services work to a new population and potential client base.

The Yawkey health fair aimed to expand the Center's catchment area and client base through outreach to the general neighborhood, a building open house, and presenters and vendors offering informational gifts, material goods, and services. Although health fairs at St. Leo's were typically scheduled in late summer or early fall to align with the parish "Jou Kongrè" (feast days, religious convention), the date selected—Saturday, June 16, 2007—conflicted with the conclusion of the Boston public schools academic year and many Center staff members' summer vacations.

Furthermore, another similarly themed health festival might have affected the Center fair's success. In early April 2007, Roberta Johnson shared that other Haitian community-based organizations partnered with Haitian nursing students from Boston College and Dana-Farber Cancer Institute health advocates to offer a community health festival in May 2007 called "United for Health." To avoid duplication, she had arranged for the Center and Dana Farber and Boston College groups to cosponsor both planned health events. The United for Health festival would be held at the Voice of the Gospel Tabernacle Church in Mattapan, and it would offer health screenings, job placement services, and mainstream medical services. The Yawkey Center's fair, themed "The Art of Healthy Living," would offer entertainment and food, and it would present Haitian cultural traditions, such as folkloric dance and music, while vendors showcased nontraditional and complementary healing modalities like herbal medicine, massage, and Reiki. Both events were advertised jointly by flyer. The *Doing Anthropology* health fair footage inadvertently depicts the growing dissonance between Center programming and the communities traditionally served (Boebel 2008).

. . .

Saturday, June 16, 2007, was a beautiful day for a health fair, sunny and warm but not overly humid. Resembling the September 25, 2003, groundbreaking ceremony, the formerly abandoned space—now the modern Yawkey building and adjacent large parking lot—temporarily housed several tents under which community activists and public health service providers offered informational gifts to the public. Organizational vendors included a community financial sponsor (Mount Washington Bank), program funders (the Boston Healthy Start Initiative and Boston Public Health Commission), and the Center's own program representatives (Adult Education, Day Care, and the Teen Program). Community-based organizations, such as the Association of Haitian Women, CCHER, and La Alianza Hispana also offered information. External nonprofit health institutions provided testing for cholesterol, HIV/AIDS, and other chronic health conditions (i.e., the

FIGURE 22. Health fair. Photo credit: Erica Caple James.

Arthritis Foundation, Carney Hospital, Dana Farber, Harbor Health Services, and the nearby Corner Health Center). Other health-related vendors gifting service brochures and pamphlets included Bradshaw Children's Learning Center, Curves (the national women's health and fitness chain), the local Sportsmen's Tennis Club, and the Boston branch of the Young Women's Christian Association (YWCA).

Individual health practitioners gave presentations and information on complementary and alternative medicine, stress reduction, cardiovascular health, nutrition, and general fitness (see Figure 22). To empower participants, city representatives discussed voter registration and demonstrated the use of voting machines. A local Voice of the Gospel pastor offered job placement activities. The daycare program was available to entertain children on the playground and Boston College nurses were scheduled to offer face painting. A disc jockey offered festive music in between formal entertainment and an advisory board member with the Boston Fire Department arranged a fire truck to be on-site. The Picasso Creole Cuisine restaurant, which offered traditional Haitian food, catered the event. The site was well organized. Hopes were high that the health fair would bring new constituents into the building, provide underserved populations access to health screenings and information, and encourage the celebration of the Center's achievements.

Despite appearances in the *Doing Anthropology* film, the event was sparsely attended. On the exercise parade around the block, marchers asked, "Where are the people?" They contrasted how over a thousand people celebrated together in prior fairs and the event typically raised thousands of dollars for the Center. The Center's van driver had brought several elder clients to the fair, but few staff members attended. Even fewer neighborhood residents came to investigate. Almost none of the Center's 12 Bicknell Road neighbors made the one-mile journey to reunite with former neighbors. A few leaders of Haitian organizations dropped by, but they did not stay long. From a festival it had become a deliverable.

. . .

When HPP staff assessed the fair's achievements later that month, some pointedly attributed the low turnout to the Center's changed mission. Although the HPP manager thought curiosity might draw local residents, few ventured on-site. Logistical factors affecting participation involved the poor choice of date for Center students and Adult Education instructors. Dr. Oscar noted the absence of lawyers to address immigration concerns and the lack of familiar Haitian physicians to do health screenings. Furthermore, the loss of Center staff members with regular radio shows prevented widespread publicity for the event: Center staff members used to advertise the fair and announce that health providers and lawyers would be present. Representatives from Greater Boston Legal Services, Irish Immigrant Services, and Haitian community attorneys had previously attended in order to address individuals' private questions. In contrast to Center tradition, the Charity's immigration representatives had offered a group presentation to Center clients on-site earlier that year. The facilitation of legal access on familiar and safe spatial grounds would have been attractive for prospective undocumented clients who might fear seeking legal assistance in other venues. A similar dynamic likely inhibited the attendance of prospective clients who would have sought healthcare from the fair's Haitian health providers.

In 1996, the *Boston Globe* described an early Center health fair as a successful cultural festival with more than two hundred people attending.[8] In intervening years, Nurse Pascale affirmed, health fair attendees included African American neighborhood residents and, Dr. Oscar asserted, the fair typically earned six to eight thousand dollars for Center programs. Unfortunately, the 2007 event had fewer visitors than the 1996 fair. Although both of these health professionals had previously described the meaning and history of the fair to Director Brutus and HPP manager Johnson—stressing the role of Center staff in preparing food, selling raffle tickets, and offering personal talents or gifts for the event—the managers had rejected most suggestions. Other stakeholders were nostalgic for the sense of community the health fair had evoked and said it would never be recreated at the Yawkey Center. According to one, "the needs of the Haitian community are not being met in the way that the Center is currently configured." To the best of my knowledge, the Center's annual health fair tradition discontinued after 2007.

Like the suspension of the gift program described previously, the inhibition of stakeholder participation in the health fair—whether because of the choice of date, the composition of vendors, the location, the activities, or other reasons—appears to have been another effort to contain or diminish the historical communication network and the roles of staff members. Then, around the same time as the disappointing health fair postmortem assessment, Nurse Pascale, health educator Murielle, and Dr. Oscar learned that their work hours and compensation were being reduced. No explanation was given. Just as in the example of mobbing, the change appeared to be "abruptly reassigned work responsibilities" (Molé 2013: 25). Nurse Pascale interpreted the change as a form of retribution and stated that the arbitrary change to her employment made the Center noncompliant with the BHSI grant to Sante Manman. By November 2007, the new health promotion program director had resigned. The Charity next hired a male social worker who formerly practiced medicine in Haiti and who was integral to the development of CCHER's AIDS program.

Nurse Pascale resigned by the summer of 2008. Her resignation letter, which I cite at length here, testifies to the impact of the changed mood and charitable sensibilities at the Center.[9]

> I started work at Catholic Charities' Haitian Multi-Service Center in November 1994 as an agency nurse in Sante Mamman [*sic*], funded by the Visiting Nurse Association's Staff Builders Program. In January 1995, the Department of Public Health restructured the Sante Manman Program and directed that the program be overseen by a nurse/manager. On July 27, 2007, Dr. Brutus reduced my time from 30 to 15 hours, removing any responsibility for managing Sante Mamman, and restricting my duties to include only nursing. As the former manager and proposal author, I knew the Sante Mamman contract required a .5 FTE or 20/week nurse. I informed Dr. Brutus about this key program requirement, and he indicated he would confirm that requirement with Boston Healthy Start Initiative (BHSI). Since that discussion, however, there has been no communication from Dr. Brutus regarding the 20 hour nursing requirement. I believe HMSC is now-non-compliant with the BHSI contract requirements, and as such, could damage future contract awards. It is my hope that SMSP [Sante Manman se Sante Pitit] continues its past success as the most generously funded and highly regarded in the BHSI network. I wish you and the SMSP staff the very best luck with the 2009 renewal proposal effort. It is my belief that the services rendered are critical to large Haitian and minority populations in Dorchester and the surrounding communities. I depart, leaving with you Maya Angelou's philosophy: "I've learned that no matter what happens, or how bad it seems today, life does go on, and it will be better tomorrow." My career as a maternal child nurse was challenging and an extraordinary experience, as I have been privileged to touch over five thousand lives through my work.
>
> *Always in Christ,*
>
> —————·

Despite its positive reputation and successes, when the Sante Manman contract was renewed, the project lost the nursing position. The Center had to find private financing to bridge the funding gap and to support another nurse. The dance of financial improvisation met with limited success—the United Way provided temporary support to compensate a new nurse. According to a Yawkey Center administrator whom I interviewed in 2016, however, the Center lost the entire Sante Manman program in 2014. To resolve disparities in infant and maternal mortality for women of African descent, the City's public health department shifted its focus to tracking clinical rather than social work outcomes. No longer was a model centering accompaniment in a nonclinical setting sufficient to produce the desired biometrical outcomes.

PETITIONING GIFTS

A final narrative about the production of the Center's thirtieth-anniversary gala celebration further demonstrates the tensions many stakeholders felt with the Yawkey era managerial routines. These practices alienated several advisory board members and created ambivalence in others. Changes in the ethnobiographer's life altered my capacity to continue as an observant participant. The birth of my second son (in August 2007) and my return to MIT full-time (in January 2008) meant that from late 2007 to 2009 I tracked the Center's evolution primarily from monthly advisory board meetings, annual retreats, and the updates staff members still gave. From fall 2007 to November 2009, as the Charity continued restructuring organizational practices and compensating for unanticipated financial shortfalls, the attrition of stakeholders, particularly of long-standing advisory board members, continued.

Much like the historical annual summer health fairs, the November galas were celebratory events intended to reunite and expand the stakeholder network, acknowledge individual and institutional accomplishments, and raise funds for hourly staff and operating expenses not covered by public and private grants. Inaugurated in 1995, the galas resembled formal wedding receptions or cheerful holiday gatherings occurring at many corporations and nonprofits. Stakeholders sponsored tables and donated funds at levels offering the donor inclusion in stratified groups publicized in the gala programs. A former advisory board chairman shared how, under his tenure, the events would net nearly one hundred thousand dollars—a figure I was not able to confirm but that seemed possible. In 1999, with levels descending from platinum to crystal and "friend," platinum sponsors gave ten thousand dollars for a table of ten and had their name or institution listed in the evening program. With a $250 gift, a crystal donor received one ticket and was named in the program. A one hundred dollar gift included a donor's name with others in the "friend" category, but friends had to purchase their fifty dollar seat ticket separately. By way of contrast, the 2005 fundraiser honored named donors (without listed dollar amounts) under other prestigious categories, such as the Yawkey Center Circle, Freedom Circle, Founder's Circle, Toussaint Louverture's Circle, Patron, and Donor. In 2006, these same categories were enumerated, ranging from a Yawkey Center Circle ten thousand dollar gift down to listed "donors" giving $100 to $249. In 2006, however, the Toussaint Louverture Circle—the only category indexing Haitian history, sovereignty, and culture—was not included. Another change the same year, which likely influenced the success of fundraising efforts, was the advisory board doubling the price of tickets to one hundred dollars per person. The justification was funding unanticipated expenses in the new building, especially since the Center's fiscal gap was widening. While the changes in category names and levels of financing may have been coincidental, it seems likely the shift also indexed the reduction in explicit Haitian-centered focus—another sign of future programmatic consolidation to come.

. . .

Gala fundraisers commemorate organizational and community histories by honoring the accomplishments of specific members of a social network. On November 16, 2002, the Center awarded the Monsignor Leandre Jeannot Humanitarian Award to former Charity president Dr. Joseph Doolin and his wife Mary Doolin for their service to the Haitian community. At that gala, Dr. Roger Jean-Charles, the advisory board chairman at that time, introduced Cardinal Bernard Law as the "first Haitian Cardinal" and lauded his contributions to the immigrant community. As recounted in the *Boston Haitian Reporter*, Law spoke in strong terms of support for Haitians and against US immigration policies toward Haiti:

> "Our faith tells us to do it," said the Cardinal as he ardently spoke of the injustices that plagued communities and the need for people's involvement with those communities. His Eminence addressed the imprisonment of the recent 200 plus Haitian refugees and the Bush administration's INS policy. "That is wrong! That is wrong," said the frustrated Cardinal. "This policy must be changed so that all people coming to our shore are treated equally."[10]

In much the same way as had occurred in 1994, when Law emphasized the plight of detained Haitians held in Guantánamo at nearly the same time revelations were unfolding about his role in shielding predator priests, Cardinal Law spoke vociferously about the need to reform unequal racial and ethnic immigration policies. Law's statement at a gala fundraiser for a new Haitian Multi-Service Center building can be analyzed in multiple ways. His physical presence and vocal statement of solidarity can be interpreted as a charitable reward to the loyal parishioners, a defensive means of reminding stakeholders of his good works for immigrants, as well as his public spiritual correction of unjust government practices (see Chapter 3). As I have suggested in this book, his public presentation of self and words of justice for Haitians might also arise from a penitential motive to redress his failings in mishandling clergy sexual abuse cases. Indeed, Law would later express remorse publicly in his resignation letter: "'It is my fervent prayer that this action may help the Archdiocese of Boston to experience the healing, reconciliation and unity which are so desperately needed,' he said. 'To all those who have suffered from my shortcomings and mistakes I both apologize and from them beg forgiveness.'"[11]On December 13, 2002, Pope John Paul II accepted Law's resignation for his role in the unfolding clergy sex abuse crisis; he soon left permanently for Rome.[12]

In 2005, I attended a Center gala for the first time at a formal event facility in Randolph, Massachusetts—a suburb of Boston where many wealthier Haitians resided. Guests dressed in finery chatted over drinks while a slide show depicted life at the Center. Tables of ten were tastefully set. A preset, multicourse meal was paced by a prayerful invocation, some uplifting and congratulatory speeches, an award ceremony, and later, entertainment and dancing. Honorary gala chairs were State Representative Linda Dorcena Forry, the second Haitian American to hold public office at that level, and her husband William P. Forry, a Dorchester native and managing editor of the family-owned and operated *Reporter* community newspapers. With entertainment provided by the renowned Haitian band Zenglen, the gala also celebrated former executive director Pierre Imbert as keynote speaker and recipient of the 2005 Monsignor Leandre Jeannot Humanitarian Award. Although I did not know many of the attendees at the elegant event, I was struck by their diversity and their warm camaraderie.

Galas also offer opportunities to communicate, visualize, and (re)shape an institution's brand through messaging about future transitions. The 2006 gala, held at Lombardo's—another Randolph, Massachusetts, event space—honored long-standing advisory board member, Robert L. Powell, with the Monsignor Leandre Jeannot Humanitarian Award. Mr. Powell, the pioneering African American firefighter and devoted Catholic who spoke at the groundbreaking ceremony in 2003, embodied selfless dedication to Haitians and their Center from its conception. The program statement about Powell highlights how giving—through steadfast service, volunteer labor, and care—was the Center's and, by extension, the Charity's, brand:

> Bob was present for the very beginnings of the Center, when ESL and child care were the only services offered to Haitians who had immigrated to Boston.... In 1978, only five children were cared for in the Center. From 1978 to 2005, Bob watched over the Center's growth, prosperity, problems and challenges, and finally the relocation for 12 Bicknell Street and into the Yawkey Center, a beautiful new site at 185 Columbia Road.

Although Mr. Powell was retired and living modestly, his generosity in accompanying the burgeoning Haitian community was boundless. His attention to the detailed architectural renderings and construction of the new Yawkey building was displayed through faithful progress reports at advisory board meetings. Inadvertently, I also learned about his personal gift giving. In spring 2007, I witnessed him excitedly bringing one thousand dollars in cash to Director Brutus. His gift enabled ten staff members to attend that year's gala at no cost. By the time of his death on November 25, 2008, Mr. Powell had given time, structural engineering expertise, money, and care not only to the material spaces housing the Center and its programs but also to its staff, including St. Leo's Monsignor Jeannot.

Gala fundraisers cultivate and reinforce ties between nonprofits like the Center and its stakeholders. Each year's gala had an honorary event committee comprising public dignitaries and prominent members of the archdiocese. The 2007 gala committee was composed of the following persons: State Representative Linda Dorcena Forry; John Forbush, vice president of community affairs and public relations at Mount Washington Bank; Carole M. Berotte Joseph, president of Mass Bay Community College; State Representative Marie St. Fleur; State Representative Elizabeth Malia; and Mr. Powell. In previous years, the gala committee also sought to honor and seek the attendance of other public figures, such as Mayor Menino. Although honorary committee members might not always attend in person, their names lent prestige to the event and Center and maintained awareness of its service to the City.

Fundraising galas provide additional opportunities for giving among an organization's stakeholders and they can deepen ties with private institutions. To strengthen connections between the Center and UMass Boston, the 2007 gala was held in the new Campus Center, a gorgeous, windowed waterfront space adjacent to the John F. Kennedy Presidential Library. That year's event showcased Haitian art for auction, traditional dancers, and a Haitian troubadour who performed an extended set. All advisory board members were responsible for sponsoring guests, like Mr. Powell's table for staff. Those on the board's event committee were tasked with petitioning long-standing Center stakeholders to sponsor a table or donate funds for programming. The committee also contacted individual entrepreneurs and businesses to purchase advertisements or to offer congratulatory messages in the gala program booklet.

As an indicator of institutional transformations contrasting with previous years, the 2007 gala program had not inscribed textually any individual selected for the Monsignor Jeannot humanitarian award or a public list of donors. Whether these omissions were oversights or intentional is unclear. Featured speakers were the Charity president Tiziana Dearing and the Center executive director Brutus. The gala pamphlet's first pages included a letter of appreciation from Dearing and detailed letters from Chelinde M. Édouard—chair of the HMSC Advisory Board and former Blue Cross Blue Shield of Massachusetts executive—and Director Brutus. Both individuals noted the change in Center services and programming. Édouard's statement acknowledged Haitian culture and traditions but emphasized the expanded mission of serving beyond the Haitian community: "This year we are celebrating Haitian culture via the live auction of Haitian paintings, sale of Haitian artifacts, performances by the acclaimed dance troupe from the Roxbury Center for the Performing Arts and Haitian music. We are pleased to have all the artists, artisans and dancers with us to help us celebrate 29 years of service by the Center." The statement continued with a theme of transformation: "While remaining true to its core mission, within the past year, the HMSC has reached out to a broader constituency." The theme of change and expansion of mission beyond the core Haitian-centric focus resumed in Dr. Brutus's letter: "As you may already know, change is not easy. In this anti-immigrant environment in which we now live, funding for ethnic specific populations is not easy to find. . . . We are living in a new era and your Center has to move with the changing time. . . . Your continuous support will allow us to provide services that the community would otherwise not receive due to funding restrictions." From the perspective of these stakeholders, a shift beyond a Haitian-centered service focus was a pragmatic matter of political economy.

The statement that funding climates were limited and less available to ethnic-specific populations further justified broadening the Center's focus and underscored even greater need for private donations to cover gaps from funding restrictions. In contrast with previous Center executive directors, however, Dr. Brutus shared only limited budget and financial information with the advisory board. It was not clear whether restrictions in funding resulted from the Center being embedded in a Catholic social service network, one increasingly criticized for the faith-linked way it implemented human service programs. Perhaps the deteriorating financial climate resulted from the lingering reluctance of stakeholders to give to Catholic organizations because of the clergy sex abuse scandal. It is also possible that decreases in giving related to the cumulating frustration with life at the Center as it was forced to change administrative routines. After discharging expenses, the 2007 gala netted only $25,621, an amount significantly less than hoped, but still notable given the volatile financial times.

. . .

When the 2007 gala yielded less funding, the practice of administrative blame against individuals for perceived failures, and an accusatory communication style, was directed next against long-standing volunteers. At subsequent board meetings, the Center advisory board and executive director reviewed the gala outcome. Mobbing behavior resurfaced during this process. Despite a 2007 performance review—at Brutus's request—intended to dissipate friction between staff, program managers, and other stakeholders, Dr. Brutus blamed the advisory board development and event committee members (erroneously) for failing to complete tasks to encourage a successful fundraiser.

By spring 2008, the director and board had lost confidence in each other's support. A long-standing advisory board executive committee member gave me a February 2008 document disputing Brutus's accusations of board failure, which charged the director with neglecting community outreach (I have used pseudonyms for all named persons in this excerpt):

In planning for the gala, Bernard [Brutus] took little initiative and carried out few tasks. Most of the organizational work was carried out by the members of the Development Committee [a sub-committee of the Board] and especially by volunteer Lily Sinclair. All the tasks on the check-list set up the year before were not only completed, but exceeded. One exception was Bernard's not doing any fundraising with larger businesses—a goal he had repeatedly insisted over the prior year that he could and would carry out.

A precipitating event was an email Brutus had circulated disparaging "Lily Sinclair" in much the same manner as his public castigation of Dr. Calixte. Aware of his toxic communication toward employees, the executive committee statement sought to refute a disparaging depiction of their advocacy for the Center, even though staff members did not have the same ability to contest Brutus's critiques. Although, in 2007, a staff member wrote a letter to the Charity human resources office to protest the Center's deteriorating workspace environment, there was, to the best of my knowledge, no formal response. The executive committee statement next summarized a hostile exchange occurring after President Dearing visited the Center advisory board in December 2007. The excerpt suggested efforts were underway to attack the board's "communication networks, social relations, image, professional level and tasks, and well-being and health" (Molé 2013: 24).

> At the December Board meeting (after Tiziana had left), during the debriefing about the event, Bernard expressed his dissatisfaction with the gala's outcome, and informed those present that he had begun to organize a group (including former board members) to begin planning the next gala. He did not propose that this group . . . work with the Board's Development Committee, [and] gave the impression that he was now taking charge. Dr. Smith . . . acknowledged that he had had frustrations with the Board, and that the Board had had frustrations with him, and thought that this could be avoided. . . . Bernard responded as he often does when questioned or challenged: he shut down and conveyed stony, silent anger. There was no room for discussion or dialogue.

Dr. Taylor Smith, a New Englander with colonial Protestant roots, had recruited me to join the board; she honored her mother's example of welcoming immigrants of color to the United States through hospitality, advocacy, and civil rights work. Lily Sinclair, whose ancestors were prominent families in major colonial American cities, had retired from corporate management and she sought fulfilling volunteer work. Each had joined the advisory board from 1997 to 1998 after fortuitous meetings with Pierre Imbert. Both had served the Center through periods of upheaval, including moments of heightened tension with the Charity, and they were not vulnerable to its administrative, economic, or pastoral power. In the late 1990s to early 2000s, both had argued strenuously to retain the Center's organizational and spatial independence when the Charity sought to transfer

Imbert to headquarters and to consolidate the Center with another program. In 2008, however, these post-gala disputes further accomplished the Charity's long-standing plans of centralization and consolidation. The planning group Brutus selected to organize the thirtieth anniversary gala disconnected the board from its advocacy, advisory, and fundraising mission.

Other factors distancing long-standing board members from continued service occurred when Director Brutus sent Lily Sinclair the disparaging email referenced in the February 2008 executive committee statement: "Bernard's email to Lily was an example of his treatment of staff, where he would humiliate one in front of the others, look to lay blame, exaggerate their failings, and try to split and divide the targeted individual from the rest of the staff." The description mirrors the definition of mobbing—use of public shaming, humiliation, blame, and ostracism to erode social networks and employee unity in neoliberal workspaces. By the summer of 2008, both Lily Sinclair and Dr. Smith had resigned from the advisory board. The increasing tension between the board and Director Brutus produced additional attrition when other Haitian members resigned. The February 2008 statement explained the mood in this disheartening manner: "It has become increasingly difficult . . . to attend board meetings, despite warm and long-standing regard among the members, because interactions with the director have become so consistently unpleasant and unproductive."

These workspace challenges remained and the Center's thirtieth-anniversary gala, held belatedly in 2009, lost more money than it earned. Although there were disastrous hurricanes in Haiti in August and September 2008, which necessarily directed Haitian philanthropy toward the homeland, it is likely the unraveling ties binding the Center to its stakeholder network also contributed to reduced stakeholder involvement with the Center. On October 15, 2008, Director Brutus announced the postponement of the gala until spring 2009. But another unexpected administrative change also influenced these distancing processes. On October 21, 2008, Director Brutus announced his impending resignation, effective December 19, 2008, to lead a university in Haiti: "For years I have been dreaming of returning to Haiti to give back and contribute to the development of the next generation of Haitians. An opportunity has presented itself that offered me just that. . . . To me it is a call to serve, and I must report to duty."

After disconnecting the Center from its territorial parish community, expanding its mission beyond its Haitian client population, restricting its engagement with and accompaniment of clients by discontinuing several customary traditions of gift exchange, the Center's management—implementing administrative routines on the Charity's behalf—succeeded in diminishing, but not fully destroying, the solidarity among Center stakeholders.

· · ·

In his classic work *The Varieties of Religious Experience*, the pragmatic philosopher William James (1997) talks about the process of conversion. When a person is attracted to a belief system or way of being in the world that becomes persuasive or compelling internally—at emotional, intellectual, and sensory levels—a new perception comes to be rooted in soma and psyche, as if anchored in the self. Tanya Luhrmann (1989), in her study of Wiccans in the United Kingdom, undergoes what could be described as a conversion process by which she came to see or perceive the world through the worldview of contemporary witches. Rather than the abrupt process of instantaneous transformation that James describes, Luhrmann talks about "interpretive drift," a more gradual alteration of her perception and interpretation of the world through the meaning system of Wicca. Such experiences of inclusion, adoption, or incorporation into principled or mission-driven institutions and organizations resemble what I have previously interpreted as the benevolent side of pastoral power enacted through multiple forms of charity.

I have recounted in this chapter what could be interpreted as the opposite of incorporation—a process of exclusion, suspicion, accusations, and disputes in a competitive compassion or grant economy that can produce the malevolent side of bureaucraft (James 2010, 2012). Such negative practices and processes unfolded at the Center while staff members were pressured to adopt increasingly impersonal styles of charitable work while subjected to arbitrary changes in everyday routines.

Although it is possible to view these processes as the result of deliberate sabotage, intended harm, or even "evil," the cumulative mobbing practices and resistance to them generated what I term "negative charisma." Whereas charisma emerges in enchanted environments, I've shown how negative charismatic sensibilities and practices cultivate disenchantment—in both the religious and rational bureaucratic senses Max Weber offered in his sociological studies of religion and institutions.

. . .

On July 25, 2017, Haitians demonstrated outside the Yawkey Center against the closure of the elder psychosocial support program (see Figure 23). One woman protestor lamented:

> As of now, the name of the Haitian Multi-Service Center is still on the building, but these programs have been shut down one by one. . . . There was a daycare downstairs that was named Konbit Kreyol, now that's gone, and now it's a daycare center that's no longer for Haitians. We had Sante Manman, it was closed down. We had HIV programs, these are shut down. They're taking away everything that the Haitians had in this building. So now we're fighting, we're asking the community to stand with us, so that we can get this program back and then we can get what the Haitians worked hard for to get in this building.[13]

. . .

By way of an open-ended conclusion, this ethnographic biography—or postmortem assessment—has attempted to tell the story of an American community rooted in,

FIGURE 23. Ireland Plancher protests Catholic Charities outside the Haitian Multi-Service Center, July 25, 2017. Staff photo by Faith Ninivaggi. From MediaNews Group/*Boston Herald* via Getty Images.

but also extended beyond, Haitians—whether newly arrived or well-established. The Center's stakeholder community included supporters from multiple racial, religious, ethnic, and national backgrounds, and a range of economic classes. Although charitable laborers facilitating migrant incorporation benefitted from operating within a faith-based organizational framework, such an institutional location posed many challenges. From the perspective of Greater Boston's nested Catholic institutions, aiding Haitians was not solely a compassionate or virtuous act. Providing institutional charity to vulnerable persons of color who were negatively stereotyped as diseased, superstitious, and even untouchable exemplified the benevolent side of a Catholic moral economy, especially at a time of institutional crisis. Such largesse also revealed the utility of public works of mercy.

In constructing this memory palace, it has been difficult to reconcile the intense emotions shared by many of the Center's stakeholders—confusion, anger, disbelief, and frustration, still expressed with intensity even decades later—alongside reminiscences of love, joy, laughter, and care in rendering service to Haitians and others in need. I witnessed and experienced many of these same feelings during my own time volunteering on-site and when collecting life histories and vignettes of advocacy work.

I have tried to capture, however imperfectly, how fulfillment of a mission is never solely about single acts of individuals, but rather the communal striving toward aiding, educating, empowering, and instilling hope in others. These charitable acts arise from and reproduce pastoral power and a power of care, and they may also be resisted. Caring encompasses discipline, education, and correction, comforting and consoling, sustaining and accompanying the other, and establishing connection through sensory means. Many of the so-called corporal works of mercy address bodily needs. They are also conveyed sensorially. Caring through touch takes the form of a physical embrace or presence during life's struggles as a witness or advocate. Care for the bodily health of all ages is conveyed through education, supplying food to those receiving services, and through shared meals. The mouthwatering rituals of commensality among stakeholders at meetings, gatherings, and other events enlivens the sense of solidarity.

Seeing or recognizing the humanity and worth of "strangers" is conveyed by listening to the suffering, symptoms, needs and aspirations of clients, and translating them into forms engendering action—components of what I have called a scriptural economy. In this economy, salvation comes not through espousing faith and belief in Catholic theology and social teachings. Rather, scriptural economic salvation is achieved by coproducing human services to improve clients' chances of being incorporated into a commodity economy as educated laborers, and healthy parents and children. Embedded in all these activities is an understanding that each person participating in Center activities, whether as a provider or recipient of care, is human, and equally endowed with a soul—spiritual or secular—sustaining the larger mission of life.

The documentary practices I have characterized as composing a scriptural economy make visible, legible, and, perhaps, valid, these charitable activities, which can be enumerated as evidence of grants fulfilled. For a time, they also bring into being the secular soul—a representation of individual clients, but also, in aggregate across programs, the mission or charitable brand of the Center, Charity, and Church. But missing from inscriptions describing the educational goals, professional outcomes, and developmental milestones, and health information shared and received, households fed, and material support distributed, is the palpable spirit of the Center—a place and space of security, sanctuary, and transformation, one sustained despite the efforts of some to curtail the tangible ways its stakeholders cared for each other. For those who perceive their Center, its programs, and their lives have been used and even abused by Catholic institutions, corporate Catholicism has produced the death of the Center. For others, the Center has been transformed, transubstantiated, and fully incorporated into the body of the Charity, Church, and City, attaining new life.

1. LIFE AT THE CENTER

Douglas epigraph: See Douglas 1990.

1. In this ethnographic history, most public figures, institutions, and places are named. Some public figures, and other individuals whose identification might put them at risk, are given pseudonyms. Pseudonyms are designated by use of quotation marks on first usage or in other ways (i.e., whom I call . . .). There are also persons in the text who agreed to be identified by name and title, and quoted directly, whose identities I have chosen to conceal out of an abundance of caution. Much of the documentation contributing to this book was accessed from publicly available reports on organizational websites that I downloaded or printed. With the passage of time, many of the original hyperlinks are no longer functional and are not even maintained on the Internet Archive "wayback machine" (https://archive .org/). Wherever possible I cite current webpages or the physical and digital copies of documents in my possession.

2. I have seen one statement Frantz Monestime made about the Center in a news article, but I have not found a full interview about his time as executive director.

3. In this book I will capitalize Black, White, and other terms describing so-called racial or ethnic groups. I will also use African American and European American (and similar iterations) in the text. I recognize there is debate about whether and when to capitalize and use such terms. I am following Nell Irvin Painter's (2020) assertion that "in terms of racial identity, white Americans have had the choice of being something vague, something unraced and separate from race. A capitalized 'White' challenges that freedom, by unmasking 'Whiteness' as an American racial identity as historically important as 'Blackness'—which it certainly is."

4. See Yawkey Foundation, accessed September 20, 2023, http://yawkeyfoundation.org/.

5. Archbishop O'Malley was elevated to the rank of Cardinal in 2006. He would later join a group advising Pope Francis how to redress the sex abuse crisis in the Church.

6. A "diocese" is an administrative territory or group of churches under the governance of a bishop. Parishes are administrative territorial units within a diocese that usually possess a church and are under the care of a pastor.

7. See "Boston Archdiocese Launches 'Catholics Come Home' Campaign," CBS News Boston, March 9, 2011, https://www.cbsnews.com/boston/news/boston-archdiocese-launches -catholics-come-home-campaign/.

8. See "Boston Archdiocese Launches 'Catholics Come Home' Campaign," CBS News Boston, March 9, 2011, https://www.cbsnews.com/boston/news/boston-archdiocese-launches -catholics-come-home-campaign/.

9. These statistics are from CCUSA 2009. For additional assertions about the breadth and depth of Catholic Charities agencies in the United States, see Kammer 2004: 70–75. For current information on member agencies see Catholic Charities USA, accessed September 25, 2023, https://www.catholiccharitiesusa.org/.

10. See the 2011 figures in the *Caritas Internationalis Annual Report 2011*, accessed September 23, 2023, https://www.caritas.org/wordpress/wp-content/uploads/2017/07/Annual Report11.pdf. Current figures for 160 member nations are available at Caritas, "Who We Are," accessed July 19, 2023, https://www.caritas.org/who-we-are/.

11. See "The Catholic Charitable Bureau of The Archdiocese of Boston, Inc. And Affiliates Report, Combined Financial Statements June 30, 2008 and 2007," (p. 24). The same report states (p. 6) the Yawkey Center was purchased through the CCAB's "Columbia Road Development Corporation, Inc.," a "not-for-profit" corporation established during fiscal year 2005 that commenced operating in July 2004 to own real estate for the organization's Yawkey Center.

12. Brown and McKeown (1997: 1) state that "By the 1990s the umbrella organization, Catholic Charities, U.S.A., represented the largest system of private social provision in the nation." According to a CCUSA staff member I interviewed, the national network of Catholic social service agencies forms, after the federal government, the largest provider of human services in the United States. At the time of my research eighty-six percent was from the Department of Health and Human Services, 6 percent from Agriculture, 6 percent from Housing and Urban Development, 1 percent from Labor, 1 percent from FEMA, 0.4 percent from Justice, and 0.2 percent from the Veterans Administration. See Catholic Charities USA, accessed October 23, 2022, http://www.catholiccharitiesusa.org /page.aspx?pid=291.

13. The legal status of Haitian immigrants as "political refugees" or as "economic migrants" has been particularly contested over time and will be discussed in subsequent chapters.

14. Stakeholders are actors invested in an organization or corporation who are committed to ensuring it fulfills a particular mission or "principled issue" (Keck and Sikkink 1998). I use the term "stakeholder" rather than "shareholder" because stakeholders accept risks and make sacrifices on an institution's behalf regardless of whether they have a binding fiduciary or financial relationship with it or not. Supporting an institution provokes emotion and reflection on whether the entity continually upholds values, ideologies, or principles to which stakeholders remain committed.

15. See Catholic Charities of Boston, accessed July 19, 2023, https://www.ccab.org /?s=haitian&submit=Search.

16. See Shannon Lyons, "A Look at Catholic Charities Haitian Multi-Service Center," *Boston Pilot*, May 13, 2022, https://thebostonpilot.com/Opinion/article.asp?ID=192356.

17. Alexis De Tocqueville's *Democracy in America* was published in 1835.

18. I requested an interview with Cardinal Law in 2007. His then secretary responded on his behalf: "His Eminence Cardinal Law read your request and wanted me to repond [*sic*] in his name. The Cardinal does not think that he would be able to add any significant details to your project, especially regards [*sic*] the day to day [*sic*] running of the Center. He suggests that the folk who know the intimate details of decisions made about the Haitian Center are the former and present staff and the former and present staff of the Catholic Charitable Bureau of Boston. The Cardinal's continuing lover [*sic*] for and compassion with the good people of Haiti is well remembered by the Haitian Community. He wishes you well in your work . . ."

19. See also the *Catechism of the Catholic Church* (Catholic Church 1995: 648).

20. For a literature review of charity, philanthropy, and faith-based giving see *Governing Gifts: Faith, Charity, and the Security State*, ed. Erica Caple James, School for Advanced Research Advanced Seminar Series (Albuquerque: University of New Mexico Press, 2019), 1–20.

21. Shannen Dee Williams (2022: xiii) distinguishes the terms "sister" and "nun": "A Roman Catholic nun is a woman who has professed the vows and lives in a cloistered setting with minimal contact with the secular world. A sister, in contrast, is a woman who has professed the vows but engages in public works such as teaching, nursing, and other social service ministries."

22. See Michael Rezendes, "Doubts in Memo Slowed '87 case," *Boston Globe*, June 13, 2002, A 24.

23. *Ensekirite* refers to the "the seemingly random political and criminal violence that ebbed and flowed in waves amid ongoing economic, social, and environmental decline" that produces "embodied uncertainty" and "spiritual ruptures" in those who experience it (James 2010: 8).

24. This quotation comes from Norget, Napolitano, and Mayblin's (2017) introduction to the Pitt-Rivers excerpt. The editors add (2017: 62), "*Mana* is a major concept in Polynesian cultures, denoting an energy of life force of supernatural origin. *Hau*, a Maori term denoting a form of energy or spirit that binds givers and receivers, was made popular by Marcell [*sic*] Mauss ([1954] 1990) in his famous book *The Gift*."

25. In such cases, I have noted my requests for information and the negative response (or even total lack of one) and have sought public statements made by such persons to fill in some of the gaps in this narrative.

26. The revelations of clerical abuse, cultural genocide, and clandestine burials of aboriginal, indigenous, and First Nations children in colonial contexts is another emerging scandal, as are ongoing revelations of clerical sexual abuse throughout Europe and globally. Attention to these issues is beyond the scope of this book.

2. BUILDING THE BRAND: MIGRANTS AND ROMAN CATHOLIC CHARITY

1. CCAB, "Agency-wide marketing campaign is ready to launch," http://intranet.ccab.org/intranet/news/, posted 02/21/07.

2. CCAB, "Ad in Thursday's Boston Globe," http://intranet.ccab.org/intranet/news/, posted 03/07/07.

3. CCAB, "Ad in Wednesday's Boston Globe," http://intranet.ccab.org/intranet/news/, posted 03/20/07.

4. CCAB, "Ad in Thursday's Boston Globe," http://intranet.ccab.org/intranet/news/, posted 04/05/07.

5. See Rev. Robert A. Sirico, "Taking the 'Catholic' out of Catholic Charities: He Who Pays the Piper Calls the Tune," and Rev. Fred Kammer, S.J. "The 'Catholic' is in the Charity: Bringing Christ's Love to 12.7 Million People Each Year," *Philanthropy* (Winter 1998). Kammer cites the code of Canon Law.

6. Ryall (2001: 53) refers to conservative organizations like the "Neo-Catechumenate, Focolare, Opus Dei and Communion and Life (C&L)," along with "established apostolic religious [orders] such as the Jesuits," that are mobile, commit to community life, and hold property communally.

7. For these same reasons, cataloging the breadth and depth of Catholic charity over the course of its history is beyond the scope of this chapter.

8. See Benedict XVI 2005.

9. Peter Steinfels, "Cardinal Is Seen as Kind, if Firm, Monitor of Faith," *New York Times*, February 1, 1988, Section A, p. 20, col. 3.

10. See John Paul II, Pastor Bonus (apostolic constitution), Vatican, accessed October 23, 2022, http://www.vatican.va/holy_father/john_paul_ii/apost_constitutions/documents /hf_jp-ii_apc_19880628_pastor-bonus-roman-curia_en.html.

11. See the Congregation for the Doctrine of the Faith declaration, "Instruction on Respect for Human Life in its Origin and on the Dignity of Procreation: Replies to Certain Questions of the Day," Vatican, accessed October 23, 2022, http://www.vatican.va/roman _curia/congregations/cfaith/documents/rc_con_cfaith_doc_19870222_respect-for-human -life_en.html.

12. Alan Riding, "New Catechism for Catholics Defines Sins of Modern World," *New York Times*, November 17, 1992, Section A, page 1, col. 1. See "Biography of His Holiness, Pope Benedict XVI," Vatican, accessed September 27, 2023, https://www.vatican.va/content /benedict-xvi/en/biography/documents/hf_ben-xvi_bio_20050419_short-biography-old .html.

13. See the Congregation for the Doctrine of the Faith declaration, "Dominus Iesus," Vatican, accessed October 23, 2022, http://www.vatican.va/roman_curia/congregations /cfaith/documents/rc_con_cfaith_doc_20000806_dominus-iesus_en.html.

14. Compare this with the CDF's reprimand of American nuns, the Leadership Conference of Women Religious, for challenging "church teaching on homosexuality and the male-only priesthood, and promot[ing] 'radical feminist themes incompatible with the Catholic faith.'" See Laurie Goodstein, "Vatican Reprimands a Group of U.S. Nuns and Plans Changes," *New York Times*, April 18, 2012, http://www.nytimes.com/2012/04/19/us /vatican-reprimands-us-nuns-group.html?_r=1. See also the CDF's June 5, 2012, condemnation of Sister of Mercy, Margaret Farley's book, *Just Love: A Framework for Christian Sexual Ethics* (London: Continuum, 2006), for its positions justifying "divorce and remarriage, homosexuality, and . . . masturbation." See Lisa Cahill, "Vatican Dogma vs Margaret Farley's Just Love," *Guardian*, June 18, 2012, http://www.guardian.co.uk/commentisfree /2012/jun/18/vatican-dogma-v-magaret-farley-just-love.

15. Although acknowledging calls for economic justice and political liberty, John Paul II retorted that depictions of Jesus as an activist involved in class struggle against Roman

authorities "do . . . not tally with the church's catechesis." See Pope John Paul II, "Opening Address at the Puebla Conference" (delivered in Seminario Palafoxiano, Puebla de los Angeles, Mexico, January 28, 1979), Catholic Culture, accessed October 23, 2022, https:// www.catholicculture.org/culture/library/view.cfm?recnum=5529.

16. See the Congregation's declaration, "Instruction on Certain Aspects of the Theology of Liberation," Vatican, accessed October 23, 2022, http://www.vatican.va/roman_curia /congregations/cfaith/documents/rc_con_cfaith_doc_19840806_theology-liberation _en.html.

17. See Charles E. Curran, "My Turn: Celibacy, the Pope, and Sex Abuse," *Newsweek*, June 4, 2010, http://www.newsweek.com/2010/06/04/banned-by-the-pope.html.

18. The Magisterium is the teaching authority of the Church and is composed of the pope and the bishops. See the Congregation's Letter to Father Charles Curran, Vatican, accessed October 23, 2022, http://www.vatican.va/roman_curia/congregations/cfaith/documents /rc_con_cfaith_doc_19860725_carlo-curran_en.html.

19. Ian Fisher, "Benedict's First Encyclical Shuns Strictures of Orthodoxy," *New York Times*, January 26, 2006, Section A, Column 1, p. 8.

20. A presentation of the controversial historical acts and theological positions that the Church has taken, and the numerous critiques and elaborations in response, is beyond the scope of this book.

21. I discuss individuals who inspired religious orders in a subsequent section on the Center's staff members and volunteers.

22. King Louis XIV signed the Code in March 1685 (Gisler 1981: 20), just prior to the establishment of Saint-Domingue as a French territory. For an analysis of the Code Noir and its employment, even by enslaved persons, see Ghachem 2012.

23. The clergy replacing the Jesuits were said to lack "apostolic passion." Several had been sent to the colony "as punishment for misdemeanors at home" (Greene 1993: 78).

24. According to Albert J. Raboteau (1978: 112), "Catholic efforts to convert slaves were debilitated by some of the same difficulties, such as the lack of clergy and the attitudes of slaveholders, faced by the Protestants." Cyprian Davis (1990: 35–39) notes that, from the eighteenth to the nineteenth century, several men's and women's religious orders—including the suppressed Society of Jesus in Louisiana and Maryland, the Vincentians in Missouri, and the Ursuline order in New Orleans—enslaved people of African descent. The first American bishop, John Carroll, also enslaved others (C. Davis 1990: 40). See also Swarns 2023.

25. A comprehensive presentation of the history of Catholic charity in the United States is beyond the scope of this book. Several authors have outlined detailed milestones in this history. See Dorothy M. Brown and Elizabeth McKeown, *The Poor Belong to Us: Catholic Charities and American Welfare* (Cambridge, MA: Harvard University Press, 1997); Mary J. Oates, *The Catholic Philanthropic Tradition in America* (Bloomington: Indiana University Press, 1995); John O'Grady, *Catholic Charities in the United States: History and Problems* (Washington, DC: Ransdell, 1930), and Rev. J. Bryan Hehir, ed., *Catholic Charities USA: 100 Years at the Intersection of Charity and Justice*, (Collegeville, MN: Liturgical Press, 2010).

26. The Louisiana territory was French; thus, the statement shows how contemporary Catholic institutions trace their institutional lineage and religious identity to the transnational authority of another state, the Vatican.

27. Toussaint is a candidate for canonization.

28. See also C. Davis 1990: 98–105; Laguerre 1998: 31–74; Morrow 2002.

29. The SOC was founded in the tradition of the Daughters of Charity (DOC)—the French religious order established in the seventeenth century by Saint Vincent de Paul and Saint Louise de Marillac. See "Our History," Sisters of Charity of Saint Elizabeth, Convent Station, New Jersey, accessed October 23, 2022, https://www.scnj.org/about.

30. Oates 1995: 24–25, citing "Who Shall Take Care of Our Sick?" *Catholic World* 2 (February/March 1869): 734–35.

31. Davis cites *The Original Diary of the Oblate Sisters of Providence, 1827–42*, Oblate Sisters of Providence, Baltimore, p. 17. The diary is a document handwritten by Father Joubert.

32. See "Ursuline Convent Destruction," Celebrate Boston, accessed October 12, 2022, http://www.celebrateboston.com/crime/ursuline-convent-destruction.htm.

33. Contemporary efforts made by the Church hierarchy to discipline women religious provide more recent examples that women's pastoral power poses to the Magisterium. See Laurie Goodstein, "Vatican Reprimands a Group of U.S. Nuns and Plans Changes," *New York Times*, April 18, 2012, http://www.nytimes.com/2012/04/19/us/vatican-reprimands-us-nuns-group.html.

34. Walton 1993: 90, citing "A Study of Local Charities," For the Catholic Truth Committee of the Catholic Union, February 16, 1892, Thomas F. Ring Scrapbook, archives, Society of St. Vincent de Paul, Boston, MA.

35. Skok cites "An Appeal for Your Charity By the Society of St. Vincent de Paul. St. Peter's Conference," n.d., 5, 3245, RSVP.

36. Established in 1874, the National Conference of Charities and Corrections changed its name to the National Conference of Social Work in 1917 (Conrad and Joseph 2010: 52).

37. In his dissertation, "A History of the Catholic Charitable Bureau of the Archdiocese of Boston" (University of Notre Dame), Daniel McLellan (1984: vii), identified three major organizational and structural shifts: From 1908 to 1946, the Charity was unincorporated as the "Catholic Charitable Bureau of Boston, Inc." with headquarters in Boston; from 1946 to 1971, the incorporated agency bore the same name. On the Charity's current webpage, the founding year is listed as 1903 and the incorporation year is listed as 1945. See "About Us," Catholic Charities Boston, accessed October 23, 2022, https://www.ccab.org/about-us/. In 1971, the Charity was reorganized and titled the Catholic Charitable Bureau of the Archdiocese of Boston, Inc. (CCBAB). In the mid-1980s, the agency was reorganized again under Cardinal Law to adopt a "six region management model." In the late 1980s, the Charity "became responsible for four community-based agencies that had previously functioned independently under the umbrella of the Chancery office. The Labouré Center, El Centro Del Cardenal, The Haitian Multi-Service Center, and Emmanuel House were placed under the administration of Catholic Charities and Incorporated into the agency" (CCBAB 1995: 19). As will be discussed later, this version of the relationship between the Church, the Charity, and the Center is in dispute.

38. McLellan cites "Report of Reverend Frederic Gigault, O.M.I., to Archbishop John Williams," March 19, 1892, Thomas Ring Papers, 5, Society of Saint Vincent de Paul, Boston.

39. McLellan cites Bishop Regis Canevin, "Charity," *Proceedings of the 1912 Convention of the National Conference of Catholic Charities*, 25, and *Pilot*, January 18, 1908, February 4, 1911, March 8, 1930.

40. McLellan cites Reverend Michael J. Scanlan, "Our Catholic Charities and How They are Related," *Catholic Charities Review* 6 (January 1922): 68.

3. LIFE IN PURGATORIAL SPACES: HAITIAN MIGRANTS
BETWEEN CHURCH, STATE, AND LAW

Certeau epigraph: See Certeau 1984.

Conroy epigraph: Martin Conroy, personal communication, May 10, 2007.

1. A "refugee" is someone who, from a "well-founded fear of being persecuted for reasons of race, religion, nationality, membership of a particular social group or political opinion, is outside the country of his nationality and is unable or, owing to such fear, is unwilling to avail himself of the protection of that country; or who, not having a nationality and being outside the country of his former habitual residence as a result of such events, is unable or, owing to such fear, is unwilling to return to it." See UNHCR 1979: 11, 81. The questions of who constitutes a refugee, and why Haitians have rarely been granted this status, will be discussed below.

2. Although the migration stories of a few Boston Haitians with greater social and political capital appear in this book, their journeys did not, for the most part, include passages through the spaces described here.

3. Catholic theology once proposed the notion that limbo was a region existing on the border of hell that became the destiny of unbaptized infants.

4. The purgatorial spaces described are both physical and conceptual, and they inculcate externally imposed forms of "mortification" (practices of asceticism and self-denial, like fasting) in order to expiate past "sins" prior to a migrant's incorporation into, or exclusion from, the body politic. See the entry for "Mortification" in *The Catholic Encyclopedia* (New York: Robert Appleton, 1911), available online via *New Advent* (blog), accessed November 22, 2022, www.newadvent.org/cathen/10578b.htm.

5. World Bank, *World Tables: The Second Edition* (Baltimore: Johns Hopkins University Press, 1980), 444. This work is cited in Conway and Buchanan 1985: 100.

6. Conway and Buchanan 1985: 100. They cite James W. Wilkie and Stephen Haber 1983: 6–7, 12.

7. According to Richard Gullage, former deputy district director in the INS Miami office, the number of backlogs by June of 1978 amounted to approximately six or seven thousand cases. See *Haitian Refugee Center v. Civiletti*, 503 F. Supp. 442 (1980), 511.

8. Stepick and Swartz 1986: 12.

9. Ong cites Carol A. Mortland 1987: 380, 384.

10. Chierici 1991: 43–44. Chierici cites Alex Stepick, "The Roots of Haitian Migration," in *Haiti—Today and Tomorrow: An Interdisciplinary Study*, ed. Charles R. Foster and Albert Valdman (New York: University Press of America, 1984).

11. Dr. Paul Farmer asserts the image of Haitians as "disease carriers" can also be traced to colonial discourses repeated and expanded during the 1915–34 American occupation. See Farmer 1992: 235–39.

12. Nachman cites Clifford Cole, "Tuberculosis among Haitian Refugees," Community Tuberculosis Control Services Report (August 10) to Florida Department of Health and Rehabilitative Services, 1981, and Arthur E. Pitchenik et. al., "The Prevalence of Tuberculosis and Drug Resistance among Haitians," *New England Journal of Medicine* 307 (1982): 162–65.

See LCHR 1990: 4, 10. The LCHR report cites Presidential Proclamation 4865 of Sept. 29, 1981, FR28829, 46 Fed. Reg. 48, 107, reprinted in 8 U.S.C. 1182 app. at 820 (Supp. V. 1981) (hereafter "Proclamation 4865").

13. The LCHR cites Executive Order 12324 of Sept. 29, 1981, FR Doc. 81–28829, 46 fed. Reg. 48, 109, reprinted in 8 U.S.C. 1182 app. at 819–20 (Supp. V. 1981).

14. The LCHR cites Presidential Proclamation 4865 of Sept. 29, 1981, FR28829, 46 Fed. Reg. 48, 107, reprinted in 8 U.S.C. 1182 app. at 820 (Supp. V. 1981).

15. The style of violence reached new heights of depravity and vengeance when the de facto regime knew the international community would not recognize its legitimacy and the elected government of Aristide would be restored. See James 2010.

16. U.S. Coast Guard, U.S. Department of Homeland Security, "Alien Migrant Interdiction," accessed October 23, 2022, http://www.uscg.mil/hq/cg5/cg531/AMIO/amio.asp.

17. The GEO Group, Inc.'s current brand is to provide "evidence-based rehabilitation programs" through "educational and vocational programs, cognitive behavioral and substance abuse treatment, and faith-based services." See GEO Group, Inc., accessed October 23, 2022, http://www.geogroup.com/. See also "Justice Department Sues to Alter Conditions at a Prison," *New York Times*, March 31, 2000, A16.

18. See re D-J-, I&N Dec. 572, March 13, 2003, cited in Florida Immigrant Advocacy Center 2004, n. 229.

19. See Jacqueline Charles, "U.S. Expels Haitian Trying To Stay," *Miami Herald*, November 30, 2004, http://www.latinamericanstudies.org/haiti/joseph.htm.

20. See "Pedro Pan," Catholic Charities of the Archdiocese of Miami, Inc., accessed October 23, 2022, https://www.ccadm.org/adoptees-and-pedro-pan/pedro-pan/. For accusations that the Catholic Church's role was sinister, see Candiss Shumate, "Saving Children from Leftist Agendas: The Susurrant Role of the Catholic Church," Council on Hemispheric Affairs, December 16, 2011, http://www.coha.org/saving-children-from-leftist-agendas-the-susurrant-role-of-the-catholic-church/.

21. See "Monsignor Bryan O. Walsh," Operacion Pedro Pan, accessed October 23, 2022, https://www.pedropan.org/history.

22. Office of Refugee Resettlement, Report to Congress FY 1993: Refugee Resettlement Program, (Washington, DC: U.S. Department of Health and Human Services, 1993), C-21.

23. See "Resettlement Services," United States Conference of Catholic Bishops, accessed October 16, 2023, https://www.usccb.org/committees/migration/resettlement-services; Office of Refugee Resettlement, Report to Congress FY 1993: Refugee Resettlement Program, (Washington, DC: U.S. Department of Health and Human Services, 1993), C-21.

24. See "Unaccompanied Refugee Minors," Office of Refugee Resettlement, accessed October 23, 2022, http://www.acf.hhs.gov/programs/orr/resource/unaccompanied-refugee-minors.

25. See "The Founding of the Bureau of Immigration," American Catholic History Classroom, accessed October 23, 2022, https://cuomeka.wrlc.org/exhibits/show/immigration/background/immigration-intro.

26. This text was originally available on the internet at the following address: "USCCB Migration and Refugee Services," CLINIC, accessed September 29, 2023, http://cliniclegal.org/usccb-migration-refugee-services. Although, the text can no longer be accessed, I retain a copy of the original posted quotation.

27. See "Migration," United States Conference of Catholic Bishops, accessed October 16, 2023, https://www.usccb.org/committees/migration.

28. See "Welcoming the Stranger Among Us: Unity in Diversity," United States Conference of Catholic Bishops, November 15, 2000, http://www.usccb.org/issues-and-action/cultural-diversity/pastoral-care-of-migrants-refugees-and-travelers/resources/welcoming-the-stranger-among-us-unity-in-diversity.cfm.

29. Among its activities, the United States Conference of Catholic Bishops (USCCB) issues pastoral statements to promote a Catholic vision of social welfare and social justice based on scriptural sources, formal doctrinal statements, and religious practices, known as "Catholic social teaching" founded on the "life and words of Jesus Christ." See "Catholic Social Teaching," United States Conference of Catholic Bishops, accessed September 29, 2023, https://www.usccb.org/offices/justice-peace-human-development/catholic-social -teaching. For the history of the USCCB see "We Promote the Common Good Which the Church Offers Humankind," United States Conference of Catholic Bishops, accessed October 23, 2022, http://www.usccb.org/about/index.cfm.

30. See "Welcoming the Stranger Among Us: Unity in Diversity," United States Conference of Catholic Bishops, November 15, 2000, https://www.usccb.org/committees /pastoral-care-migrants-refugees-travelers/welcoming-stranger-among-us-unity-diversity.

31. In one interview with a Center staff person, the program was called Sove Lavi, "save life."

32. An article in the *Boston Globe* gave the date of termination as November 1, 1992. Interviewees gave 1994 as the end date.

33. See "DMH Young Adult Resource Guide Information about EOHHS and Other State Agencies," Mass.gov, accessed October 23, 2022, https://www.mass.gov/info-details /dmh-young-adult-resource-guide-information-about-eohhs-and-other-state-agencies.

34. Karen McCarthy Brown's ethnography *Mama Lola: A Vodou Priestess in Brooklyn* (2001: 252–53) describes how Haitian unaccompanied minors held in the custody of the ORR at a similar pastoral detention facility felt "alone and afraid" (252). Some of these children attempted to invoke the Vodou spirits and became possessed—a spiritual state that is rare among children (McCarthy Brown 2001: 252) and indicates a state of crisis (Mars 1977). The ORR facility called Brown for help, and she visited the institution with her main informant, the Vodou priestess Alourdes (Brown, personal communication). Although I do not know for certain, it is unlikely that such ritual adepts were invited to counsel Haitian children in distress at Pwojè Lavi, a facility under Cardinal Law's care.

35. See Coutin 1993; Rose 2012.

36. In the interview with Rénald St. Jacques, he indicated that the strike occurred in 1989. He also mentioned receiving assistance from lawyer Cheryl Little, who debriefed our delegation, and local Haitian activist, Marleine Bastien, a member of the delegation, both of whom were active during the hunger strikes. Because of their prominence in the media in November 1988, and other details of his story, it seems likely that this event occurred in 1988, rather than in 1989. That the dates are uncertain, however, is a testament to the extent that marking time itself may have been difficult in this purgatorial space.

37. See, for example, Haitian Refugee Center v. Civiletti. 503 F. Supp. 442. 1980. United States District Courts. 11th Circuit. United States District Courts. 11th Circuit. Southern District of Florida.

4. MEMORY PALACE I: THE BIRTH OF THE CENTER

Bachelard epigraph: See Bachelard (1958) 1969.

1. See Michael Paulson, "Archdiocese to Sell Brighton Site to BC—$65m Price Tag for 18 Acres; Offices to Move to Braintree," *Boston Globe*, May 25, 2007, https://www.proquest .com/newspapers/archdiocese-sell-brighton-site-bc-65m-price-tag/docview/405070446 /se-2?accountid=12492.

2. Lally and I had previously corresponded about my records search for the Center and St. Leo Parish, as well as the Center's merger with the Charity. He told me he had not found much—only a few items pertaining to the St. Leo Parish physical plant and various CCAB records between 1907 and 1961. Since the Charity was technically a separate corporation, he said, the archdiocese did not always receive its written materials.

3. See "Oath against Modernism," Catholic Culture, accessed October 12, 2022, https://www.catholicculture.org/culture/library/dictionary/index.cfm?id=35192&randomterm=false; Bokenkotter 2004: 345–54.

4. See "IRS Warns of 'Corporation Sole' Tax Scam," *IRS News Release*, March 29, 2004, https://www.irs.gov/pub/irs-news/ir-04-042.pdf.

5. These complex dimensions of Catholic institutions, agencies, and organizations as both secular and sacred mirror a conception of the person as both material and spiritual, as well as conceptions that Catholics compose the physical and mystical corporate body of the Church. Thus, one can say that, as a spiritual leader, the Cardinal of Boston possesses at least "two bodies" (Kantorowicz [1957] 1997). As a pastor or shepherd to his flock, he is responsible for the corporate body of souls in the archdiocese and his "powers and responsibilities are established by Canon Law" (RCAB 2011: 12). As a representative of the Holy See, the Cardinal has a second role or body as a temporal leader, and includes the secular legal, economic, political, and other roles of governance.

6. See RCAB 2011: 91–98. The recently sold Caritas Christi network of Catholic hospitals and healthcare institutions was formerly under the Corporation Sole governance structure. Corporation Sole governs parishes, the central fund, the insurance fund, and the endowment funds of the archdiocese. Corporation Sole also governs the following: pastoral operations (i.e., parish operations, multicultural ministries, ethnic apostolates, health care ministries, youth ministries, family life, etc.); educational operations, such as parish schools and college campus ministry programs; ministerial support for the formation of priests, deacons, lay ministers, and seminaries; and the Delegate for Religious (the liaison to the religious orders of priests and nuns in the archdiocese, such as the Daughters of Charity or Jesuits who report to the superior general of the particular "province" of their order). Corporation Sole governs social support for the pro-life office, youth centers, and social service programs and agencies. Corporation Sole also interfaces with regional, central, and national offices of the Roman Catholic Church (i.e., the Cardinals Office, Offices of the Regional Bishops, US Catholic Conference, etc.). Finally, Corporation Sole oversees community relations operations, including the office of public and media relations, and auxiliary service operations serving the Catholic *Pilot* newspaper, the Boston Catholic Directory, and Radio Apostolate.

7. See, for example, Scott C. Allan, "The Portal of Rouen Cathedral in Morning Light," *Scholarly Essays: Deeper Dives into Objects from the J. Paul Getty Museum Collection*, Los Angeles: J. Paul Getty Trust, 2019, https://museum-essays.getty.edu/paintings/sallan-monet-rouen/.

8. Although Evelyn's surname ordinarily would be spelled "Prophète" in French, she did not place a diacritical mark over the first 'e' in her consent form, so I leave it out here. Similarly, Father Jeannot's first name, Leandre, could be spelled Léandre, and Perard Monestime's given name could be spelled Pérard. I have opted to use the spellings that these individuals used themselves or that I saw in print.

9. See *2008 Catholic Charities Report, Crossings*, November 30, 2009, issuu, accessed October 12, 2022, https://issuu.com/ccab2008/docs/2008_catholic_charities_of_boston _annual_report.

10. I have not been able to access St. Leo's parish records to determine whether the numbers of African American, Haitian, Cape Verdean, or other Black Catholics at St. Leo's can be enumerated.

11. See "Fighting for Economic Justice and Power," OIC of America, accessed October 12, 2022, http://oicofamerica.org/.

12. Rev. Sullivan is reported as having founded OIC during the Civil Rights era as "a self-help program" focused on African Americans because "There were skills that our people never had . . . and I realized that integration without preparation is frustration." Although OIC later received federal funding, Sullivan began without public assistance and trained "inner-city minority residents in such fields as carpentry, bricklaying, auto mechanics, and secretarial skills." See Kidder 1993.

13. I did not ask the history of his father's military service or whether that service was undertaken to provide security for the Monestime family.

14. See "About Us," OIC Philadelphia, accessed October 12, 2023, https://www.philaoic .org/about.

15. The evaluation system was originally developed by JEVS from its work with Jewish immigrants and refugees during WWII. The system later provided other ethnic minority populations, federal prison parolees, high school and college students, people with disabilities, and other vulnerable groups vocational and rehabilitation services. See "Mission & History," JEVS Human Services, accessed October 12, 2022, https://www.jevshumanservices .org/about/mission-history/.

16. See "About Teradyne," Teradyne, accessed October 12, 2022, https://www.teradyne .com/company/about-us/.

17. See "We Are RTX," RTX, accessed October 12, 2022, https://www.rtx.com/who-we -are/we-are-rtx .

18. None of the founders I interviewed was certain of the exact spelling of Esther's last name and I have not been able to locate her.

19. Daily has also been controversial for his role in transferring predatory priests and for his lack of support for victims of clergy sexual abuse. See Roberts 2017.

20. See Executive Order No. 257: Refugee Policy, Mass.gov, accessed October 5, 2022, https://www.mass.gov/executive-orders/no-257-refugee-policy.

21. In 1985, Pope John Paul II elevated Law to the rank of cardinal, a member of the College of Cardinals.

22. "Aliens" who had entered the United States after January 1, 1982, were eligible to apply until May 4, 1988. See Andrew Blake, "Amnesty Deadline Extension Urged Law, Flynn Join Coalition in Making Appeal for Immigrants," *Boston Globe*, November 6, 1987, 48. In brief, the 1986 Immigration Reform and Control Act (IRCA) sought to "close the back door" through which migrants entered the United States unlawfully in search of employment with relative impunity. The act had two provisions to "stop the illegal flow of undocumented immigrants . . . through imposing sanctions in the form of fines or imprisonment on those who hire the undocumented, and an amnesty program to wipe the slate clean of undocumented immigrants already living in the country" (Hayes 2001: 4). Although

referred to as a "generous and compassionate bill," it "resulted instead in placing a highly vulnerable, silent subclass in deeper jeopardy as a result of public policy" because "barriers in the legislation prevented the majority of undocumented persons from applying" (Hayes 2002: 4–5). Undocumented persons had to provide extensive documentation to prove they had resided in the United States "continuously" (absences of forty-five days or less) over the entire period of eligibility. Those who came before January 1, 1982, the cutoff date, were eligible to apply, but they had to prove continuous residence between this date and the implementation of the act—nearly five years of residence. Furthermore, each member of a family had to meet these same criteria individually. Those who came after the January 1, 1982, were ineligible for legalization (*ibid.*: 6–7).

23. See the editorial "Boston Plans Help for Illegal Aliens," *New York Times*, October 11, 1987.

24. Although I tried repeatedly (and through a variety of means), I was never able to reach Dr. Doolin to request an interview to receive his version of this history.

25. See "We Are RTX," RTX, accessed October 12, 2022, https://www.rtx.com/who-we -are/we-are-rtx.

5. CORPORATE SECRETS

Hirschman epigraph: See Hirschman 1970.

1. See *Oxford English Dictionary*, s.v. "economy" (noun) for these and other meanings.

2. In our interview Sister Margaret asserted that by 1985 the Center was already coming under the management of Catholic Charities because its director asked her directly to assist Monestime with its administration; the executive director from ca.1987 to 1990 disputes this account, saying that the Charity's direct involvement did not truly occur until after he left.

3. I am not sure if Sister Margaret is referring to a director of the childcare service or to some other person.

4. Although the identity of the person(s) with whom Father Michel was allegedly involved has not been made public, a June 21, 2010, story by the controversial Yves A. Isidor on an equally controversial Haitian webzine, wehaitians.com, claims the pastor was engaged in sexual relationships with a few adult female parishioners. See Yves A. Isidor, "Roman Catholic Priest Allegedly Caught Having Sex," wehaitians.com, accessed October 23, 2022, http:// www.wehaitians.com/roman%20catholic%20priest%20caught%20having%20sex.html. See also, "Archdiocese Revokes Faculties of Rev. Gabriel Michel," Archdiocese of Boston, June 20, 2010, https://www.bostoncatholic.org/press-release/2010/06/june-20-archdiocese -boston-revokes-faculties-rev-gabriel-michel-priest.

5. It was not clear whether Léon was referring to the crisis at St. Leo's (on which more below) or in the Church as a whole.

6. See the allegations reported in the following article: "500 Women in Secret Affairs with Priests: Support Group," *Sydney Morning Herald*, May 22, 2009, http://www.smh .com.au/world/500-women-in-secret-affairs-with-priests-support-group-20090521-bh82 .html#ixzz21e9jiyEA.

7. See Chris Hedges, "Documents Alleged Abuse of Nuns by Priests," *New York Times*, March 21, 2001, http://www.nytimes.com/2001/03/21/world/documents-allege -abuse-of-nuns-by-priests.html?pagewanted=all&src=pm.

8. According to the Migration Policy Institute, one in four Haitian women in the United States works in a healthcare setting. See Aaron Terrazas, "Haitian Immigrants in the United States," Migration Policy Institute, January 2010, https://www.migrationpolicy.org /article/haitian-immigrants-united-states-2008.

9. See RCAB, "Minutes," Presbyteral Council Meeting, March 12, 1999.

6. CORPORATE SCHISMS: LIFE AND DEATH
BETWEEN CHURCH, STATE, AND LAW

Epigraph: See Nealon 1996.

1. See Barr Foundation, accessed October 12, 2022, https://www.barrfoundation.org.

2. Among the organizations represented were the Association of Haitian Women in Boston (Asosiyasyon Fanm Ayisyèn nan Boston, AFAB), staff members of which would conduct seminars on domestic violence prevention at the Center; the Boston Medical Center/ Children's AIDS Program (BMC/CAP); the Haitian Health Outreach Program in the Cambridge Health Alliance (CHA/HHOP), the health system spanning Cambridge, Somerville, and metro-north Boston (and teaching affiliate of Harvard Medical School); Caribbean U-Turn (CUT), a faith-based community organization affiliated with Boston University's School of Social Work assisting Caribbean youth struggling with substance abuse problems, HIV/AIDS, and other health issues; the Dorchester Nazarene Compassionate Center, Inc. (now called the Greater Boston Nazarene Compassionate Center, Inc.), a faith-based voluntary ministry affiliated with the Church of the Nazarene; the Massachusetts Coalition for Health Services/Brockton CHASE AIDS (MCHS), an organization providing violence and substance abuse prevention initiatives, and health awareness programs, including HIV prevention services; and finally, the University of Massachusetts Boston (UMASS).

3. The CDC selected forty communities to receive funding and technical assistance to inaugurate health disparities programs among American "minority" populations: African Americans, American Indians and Alaskan Natives, Asian Americans, Native Hawaiians and Pacific Islanders, and Hispanics and Latinos. See "Reach," National Center for Chronic Disease Prevention and Health Promotion (NCCDPHP), Centers for Disease Control, accessed October 23, 2022, https://www.cdc.gov/chronicdisease/resources/publications /factsheets/reach.htm#reaching.

4. Jean-Baptiste was the public face of the Center, but my understanding is that David Johnson overlapped with him and remained behind the scenes in an administrative capacity.

5. Although I have made periodic efforts to reach these program directors, I have not been able to interview Dr. Jean-Louis, Dr. Raphaël, or Jean-Marc Jean-Baptiste for this project.

6. See Daniel Golden, "The Cardinal's Ambitions: Does Cardinal Bernard Law Serve the Pope or the President? Is He Prelate or Politician—or Both?" *Boston Globe*, April 22, 1990, http://www.boston.com/globe/spotlight/abuse/archives/042290_magazine.htm.

7. The encyclical argues, furthermore, that artificial birth control methods would lead to lower moral standards and increase the potential for infidelity (sec. 17). See Paul VI, *Humanae Vitae*, July 25, 1968, http://www.vatican.va/holy_father/paul_vi/encyclicals/documents /hf_p-vi_enc_25071968_humanae-vitae_en.html.

8. Unfortunately, the Center's fiscal woes were so great that he requested (and received permission) to be able to allocate some funds to maintain the physical plant of the building and to meet the payroll costs.

9. For a biography of David Mulligan, see "Friends of David Mulligan," KCVisuals, uploaded April 10, 2015, YouTube video, 13:39, https://youtu.be/9OjMIUfAog4?si =9wooOnrwBhU_8_h3. See also Eileen McNamara, "Troubles on the Doorstep," *Boston Globe*, April 28, 2022, https://archive.boston.com/globe/spotlight/abuse/stories/042802 _mcnamara.htm.

10. As discussed in the introduction to this book, in 2003 the Center would resist the Charity's efforts to merge the two programs into one building before the Yawkey Center move.

11. See "About Project Bread: Change over Charity," Project Bread, accessed October 8, 2023, https://projectbread.org/about-us.

12. See "What We Do," The Boston Foundation, accessed October 12, 2022, https://www .tbf.org/what-we-do.

13. See "Our Mission and Vision," The Hyams Foundation, accessed October 12, 2022, http://www.hyamsfoundation.org/.

14. At the same time the archdiocese attempted to place the Haitian unaccompanied minors in the Pwojè Lavi program discussed in Chapter 3.

15. There are rumors hinting at staff administrative malfeasance. Rather than personal misappropriation, I was told there was frustration in being prevented from using the Center's limited funding beyond activities falling under a prescribed scope of work or line item in the budget.

16. The original intent was to complete seven focus groups, but two groups were not completed. Some participants resided in other cities.

17. In these sections in Haitian Creole, I have reproduced the exact text of the publicly presented PowerPoint presentation on the focus groups without correcting the orthography. The English translations are my own.

18. Indeed, for many Haitians coming from middle and upper-class backgrounds in Haiti to Boston in the 1970s, racial and linguistic differences between Haitians and European American Bostonians were more prevalent markers of distinction and cause for prejudice than class differences. Furthermore, the history of racial prejudice against African Americans in the United States had led many Haitians to distinguish themselves from "generational" Black Americans after their arrival in the United States. Although, language differences between the two groups accounted for some of these antagonisms, in regions of the United States like South Florida, where African Americans and Haitians competed for the same jobs, the friction between the two groups was more pronounced. See Portes and Stepick 1993: 55–56.

19. See Future Search Network, accessed October 13, 2022, https://futuresearch.net.

20. Mission Civile Internationale en Haïti, OEA/ONU, the UN/OAS International Civilian Mission.

7. MEMORY PALACE II: EVERYDAY LIFE AND DEATH AT THE CENTER

Epigraph: hooks 1990 (384).

1. See "About Us," FEMA, accessed October 23, 2022, https://www.fema.gov/about-agency.

2. See "FEMA Announces $153M in Homeless Prevention Aid Awards for 2008," FEMA, February 26, 2008, https://web.archive.org/web/20161117022124/https://www.fema.gov /news-release/2008/02/26/fema-announces-153m-homeless-prevention-aid-awards-2008.

3. See USDA, "The Emergency Food Assistance Program (TEFAP)," https://www
.benefits.gov/benefit/681.

4. See USDA, "When and Why Did the Emergency Food Assistance Program Start?,"
https://ask.usda.gov/s/article/when-and-why-did-the-emergency-food-assistance
-program-start. See also USDA Food and Nutrition Service, "Food and Nutrition Service
Nutrition Program Fact Sheet," https://fns-prod.azureedge.us/sites/default/files/resource
-files/FNS-101-Factsheets-All.pdf#page=14.

5. See Gordon W. Gunderson, "History of the National School Lunch Program," USDA
Food and Nutrition Service, last updated January 17, 2008, https://www.fns.usda.gov/nslp
/program-history.

6.   See the entry for "Mortification" in *The Catholic Encyclopedia* (New York: Robert
Appleton, 1911), available online via *New Advent* (blog), accessed November 22, 2022,
www.newadvent.org/cathen/10578b.htm.

7. See Boebel 2008.

8. INSCRIBING AND INCORPORATING LIFE

Epigraph: Certeau 1984 (134).

1. At this writing, Catholic Charities Archdiocese of Boston has more than seventy programs across twenty-three program locations. See "Providing Help and Hope to All Those
in Need," Catholic Charities Boston, accessed September 17, 2022, https://www.ccab.org/.

2. See "LACES Student Data Management System Information," Massachussetts Department of Elementary and Secondary Education, accessed October 23, 2022, https://www
.doe.mass.edu/acls/laces/.

3. I have copies of the DOE "Adult and Community Learning Services" documents for
these years, but the information is no longer available electronically.

4. As the city of Boston then participated in the controversial federal Secure Communities program (Sacchetti 2010: 1, 7), it pledged to automatically check the immigration
status of anyone arrested in order to identify and remand criminals to the US Bureau of
Immigration and Customs Enforcement for eventual deportation. One wonders if educational programs like those at the Haitian Multi-Service Center will eventually be obligated
to participate in such law enforcement practices as a precondition for receipt of federal and
state funding.

5. Pierre Imbert described the program in a 2002 interview with Jay Fadiman, the mod-
erator of the Boston Catholic Television program, *Hope for All*.

6. These statements were accessed on September 12, 2007, from the US Department of
Health and Human Services, Health Resources and Services Administration Maternal and
Child Health Bureau website entry for the Boston Healthy Start Initiative (BHSI Eliminat-
ing Disparities), Grant Number: H49MC00128. The website is no longer active.

7. These statements were accessed on September 12, 2007, from the US Department of
Health and Human Services, Health Resources and Services Administration Maternal and
Child Health Bureau website entry for the Boston Healthy Start Initiative (BHSI Eliminat-
ing Disparities), Grant Number: H49MC00128. The website is no longer active.

8. This statement is the Lamaze philosophy of birth.

9. While on leave he was offered a post directing the Massachusetts Office for Refugees
and Immigrants (MORI).

10. I suspect the Sante Manman grant was under consideration for renewal with a close of the fiscal year at the end of June, but I have not been able to confirm this.

11. For the full bibliographic reference, see the Healthy Start National Resource Center [HSNRC] at the National Center for Education in Maternal and Child Health 1997.

12. See Boston Catholic Men's and Women's Conferences, accessed September 25, 2022, http://catholicboston.com/index.php?content=recapbcwc2007.

13. See Donis Tracy, "Women Exhorted to 'Discover the Treasure within,'" *Boston Pilot*, March 23, 2007, http://catholicboston.com/pdfs/pilotbcwc20070323.pdf.

14. See May Bliss Dickinson, "Mothercraft Instruction for School Girls," *American Journal of Public Health* (1920): 199–202.

15. See "Reducing Infant Mortality," National Healthy Start Association, accessed September 28, 2022, https://www.nationalhealthystart.org/infant-mortality/.

16. See "Housing Instability," Healthy People 2030, accessed September 22, 2022, https://health.gov/healthypeople/priority-areas/social-determinants-health/literature-summaries/housing-instability.

17. Aid to Families with Dependent Children. In Massachusetts, the current program is called the Transitional Aid to Families with Dependent Children (TAFDC). See "Apply for TAFDC," Mass.gov, accessed September 25, 2022, https://www.mass.gov/how-to/apply-for-tafdc.

18. It was not clear whether the temporary limitation was national, simply placed on the Boston project sites, or limited to Sante Manman. If just limited to Sante Manman, it is likely the restriction related to the sexual abuse scandal in the Church.

19. I have written elsewhere extensively about conceptions of blood, heat, and cold in traditional Haitian medicine. See James 2008 and 2010.

9. BUREAUCRATIC DISENCHANTMENTS AND WOUNDS OF CHARITY

Douglas epigraph: See Douglas 1990.

1. See "HIV/AIDS Bureau," HRSA, accessed July 13, 2022, https://www.hrsa.gov/about/organization/bureaus/hab/index.html.

2. See Wendy Davis, "Church Will End AIDS Ministry," *Boston Globe*, May 22, 2003, https://graphics.boston.com/globe/spotlight/abuse/stories4/052203_aids.htm.

3. See Joseph Delany, "Fraternal Connection," New Advent, accessed October 12, 2023, https://www.newadvent.org/cathen/04394a.htm.

4. When I asked Sister Veronica about the significance of the program name, she told me that "pulse," rather than an acronym, was the name of a program that provided Boston College students opportunities to serve others in need in the Boston area.

5. See "The PULSE Program for Service Learning," Boston College Morrissey College of Arts and Science, accessed January 12, 2022, https://www.bc.edu/bc-web/schools/mcas/sites/PULSE.html.

6. See Karilyn Crockett, as told to Miles Howard, "We Can Help People Make New Connections," *Boston Globe*, June 21, 2022, https://www.bostonglobe.com/2022/06/21/opinion/we-can-help-people-make-new-connections/.

7. After protracted negotiations with Center program managers in spring 2007, the Charity agreed to MIT filming the health fair (and other regular Center activities), as well

as program activities and interviews with willing staff members, for the short documentary *Doing Anthropology*. In exchange for the opportunity to film ethnographic practices onsite and with consent of all depicted, MIT filmmakers offered the Charity all footage and assistance with editing to create promotional videos for the Center. (The Charity never pursued this offer, despite repeated overtures to its administrators.)

8. See Francie Latour, "Haitians Get All-in-One Checkup," *Boston Globe*, August 25, 1996, section B6, 25.

9. I have anonymized the executive director's name.

10. See M. Jean-Charles, "Law, Doolin Family Honored at Multi-Service Center Gala," *Boston Haitian Reporter*, December 31, 2002, https://www.proquest.com/newspapers /law-doolin-family-honored-at-multi-service-center/docview/368859708/se-2?accountid =12492.

11. See Belluck and Bruni 2002.

12. See Michael Paulson, "A Church Seeks Healing: Pope Accepts Law's Resignation in Rome," *Boston Globe*, December 14, 2002, https://www.bostonglobe.com/news/special -reports/2002/12/14/church-seeks-healing/WJSotI6gQP8zQAHjAHVhmL/story.html.

13. See Innocent 2017.

REFERENCES

Abel, David. 2002. "$500,000 Yawkey Gift to Catholic Charities." *Boston Globe*, April 27, 2002, B2.

———. 2003. "Charity Head Announces Resignation." *Boston Globe*, June 13, 2003, B3.

Agamben, Giorgio. (1995) 1998. *Homo Sacer: Sovereign Power and Bare Life*. Translated by Daniel Heller-Roazen. Stanford, CA: Stanford University Press.

———. 2005. *State of Exception*. Translated by Kevin Attell. Chicago: University of Chicago Press.

Agier, Michel. 2011. *Managing the Undesirables: Refugee Camps and Humanitarian Government*. Malden, MA: Polity.

Alba, Richard, Albert J. Raboteau, and Josh DeWind. 2009. *Immigration and Religion in America: Comparative and Historical Perspectives*. New York: New York University Press.

Albahari, Mauritzio. 2015. *Crimes of Peace: Mediterranean Migrations at the World's Deadliest Border*. Philadelphia: University of Pennsylvania Press.

———. 2019. "'We haven't risked our life for food and shelter': Mediterranean Migrations, Contentious Charity, and Justice." In *Governing Gifts: Faith, Charity, and the Security State*, edited by Erica Caple James, 99–120. School for Advanced Research Advanced Seminar Series. Albuquerque: University of New Mexico Press.

Allahyari, Rebecca Anne. 2000. *Visions of Charity: Volunteer Workers and Moral Community*. Berkeley: University of California Press.

Allen, John L., Jr. 1999. "The Vatican's Enforcer: A Profile of Cardinal Joseph Ratzinger." *National Catholic Reporter*, April 16, 1999. https://natcath.org/NCR_Online/archives2/1999b/041699/041699a.htm.

Allman, Jean. 1994. "Making Mothers: Missionaries, Medical Officers and Women's Work in Colonial Asante, 1924–1945." *History Workshop* 38: 23–47.

Anderson, Benedict. 2006. *Imagined Communities: Reflections on the Origin and Spread of Nationalism*. London: Verso.

Angrosino, Michael. 1994. "The Culture Concept and the Mission of the Roman Catholic Church." *American Anthropologist* 96 (4): 824–32.

Aretxaga, Begoña. 1993. "Striking with Hunger: Cultural Meanings of Political Violence in Northern Ireland." In *The Violence Within: Cultural and Political Opposition in Divided Nations*, edited by Kay Warren, 219–53. Boulder, CO: Westview Press.

———. 1995. "Dirty Protest: Symbolic Overdetermination and Gender in Northern Ireland Ethnic Violence." *Ethos* 23 (2): 123–48.

Aristide, Jean-Bertrand. 2004. "President Aristide in His Own Words: DN!'s Exclusive Interview, Part 1." In *Getting Haiti Right the First Time: The U.S. and the Coup*, edited by Noam Chomsky, Paul Farmer, and Amy Goodman, 165–69. Monroe, ME: Common Courage Press.

Aristide, Marx V., and Laurie Richardson. 1994. "The Popular Movement: Haiti's Popular Resistance." In *The Haiti Files: Decoding the Crisis*, edited by James Ridgeway, 64–71. Washington, DC: Essential Books.

Arthur, Charles, J., and Michael Dash. 1999. *A Haiti Anthology: Libète*. Princeton, NJ: Markus Wiener.

Asad, Talal. 1993. *Genealogies of Religion: Discipline and Reasons of Power and Christianity and Islam*. Baltimore: Johns Hopkins University Press.

———. 2003. *Formations of the Secular: Christianity, Islam, Modernity*. Stanford, CA: Stanford University Press.

Bachelard, Gaston. (1958) 1969. *The Poetics of Space*. Boston: Beacon Press. Originally published as *La poétique de l'espace* (Paris: Presses Universitaires de France).

Beaumont, Justin, and Chris Baker, eds. 2011. *Postsecular Cities: Space, Theory and Practice*. London: Continuum.

Bellegarde-Smith, Patrick. 2004. *Haiti: The Breached Citadel*. Rev. and updated ed. Toronto: Canadian Scholars' Press.

Belluck, Pam, and Frank Bruni. 2002. "Scandals in the Church: The Overview; Law, Citing Abuse Scandal, Quits as Boston Archbishop and Asks for Forgiveness." *New York Times*, December 14, 2002. https://www.nytimes.com/2002/12/14/us/scandals-church -overview-law-citing-abuse-scandal-quits-boston-archbishop-asks.html.

Benedict XVI (Ratzinger, Joseph). 2005. *Deus Caritas Est*. https://www.vatican.va/content /benedict-xvi/en/encyclicals/documents/hf_ben-xvi_enc_20051225_deus-caritas-est .html.

Bennett, Philip. 1992a. "A New Land at Last: Arriving for Resettlement, Haitians Recall Escape, Internment." *Boston Globe*, January 7, 1992, 15.

———. 1992b. "Haitians Prepare to Greet Aristide." *Boston Globe*, April 28, 1992, 21.

———. 1992c. "Young Haitians Find Waltham Refuge." *Boston Globe*, July 7, 1992, 1.

Benson, Peter, and Stuart Kirsch. 2010. "Capitalism and the Politics of Resignation." *Current Anthropology* 51 (4): 459–86.

Benton, Adia. 2016. "Risky Business: Race, Nonequivalence and the Humanitarian Politics of Life." *Visual Anthropology* 29: 187–203.

Berger, Peter L., ed. 1999. *The Desecularization of the World: Resurgent Religion and World Politics*. Grand Rapids, MI: William B. Eerdmans.

Besteman, Catherine. 2016. *Making Refuge: Somali Bantu Refugees and Lewiston, Maine*. Durham, NC: Duke University Press.

———. 2019. "Hostile Charity: Somali Refugees and Risk in a New Security Age." In *Governing Gifts: Faith, Charity, and the Security State*, edited by Erica Caple James, 121–40. School for Advanced Research Advanced Seminar Series. Albuquerque: University of New Mexico Press.

Bigo, Didier. 2002. "Security and Immigration: Toward a Critique of the Governmentality of Unease." Supplement, *Alternatives* 27: 63–92.

Blake, Andrew. 1987. "Officials Back Immigration Bill." *Boston Globe*, October 24, 1987, 17.

Boebel, Chris, dir. 2008. *Doing Anthropology*. 8 min documentary. MIT Anthropology Program. https://techtv.mit.edu/videos/315-span-classhighlightdoingspan-anthropology.

Bogdanich, Walter, and Jenny Nordberg. 2006. "Mixed US Signals Helped Tilt Haiti Toward Chaos." *New York Times*, January 29, 2006. https://www.nytimes.com/2006/01/29/world/americas/mixed-us-signals-helped-tilt-haiti-toward-chaos.html.

Bokenkotter, Thomas. 2004. *A Concise History of the Catholic Church*. New York: Doubleday.

Bolster, W. Jeffrey. 1998. *Black Jacks: African American Seamen in the Age of Sail*. Cambridge, MA: Harvard University Press.

Bornstein, Erica. 2005. *The Spirit of Development: Protestant NGOs, Morality, and Economics in Zimbabwe*. Stanford, CA: Stanford University Press.

———. 2012. *Disquieting Gifts: Humanitarianism in New Delhi*. Stanford, CA: Stanford University Press.

Bornstein, Erica, and Peter Redfield, eds. 2010. *Forces of Compassion: Humanitarianism Between Ethics and Politics*. School for Advanced Research Advanced Seminar Series. Sante Fe, NM: School for Advanced Research Press.

Boston Healthy Start Initiative (BHSI). 2005. *Phase III Impact Report: 2001–2004*. Boston, MA.

Bourdieu, Pierre. 1977. *Outline of a Theory of Practice*. Cambridge: Cambridge University Press.

Branson, Susan, and Leslie Patrick. 2001. "Étrangers dans un Pays Étrange: Saint-Domingan Refugees of Color in Philadelphia." In *The Impact of the Haitian Revolution in the Atlantic World*, edited by David P. Geggus, 193–208. Columbia: University of South Carolina.

Breathett, George. 1962. Catholic Missionary Activity and the Negro Slave in Haiti. *Phylon* 23 (3): 278–85.

Brodwin, Paul. 1996. *Medicine and Morality in Haiti: The Contest for Healing Power*. Cambridge: Cambridge University Press.

———. 2003. "Pentecostalism in Translation: Religion and the Production of Community in the Haitian Diaspora." *American Ethnologist* 30 (1): 85–101.

Brown, Dorothy M., and Elizabeth McKeown. 1997. *The Poor Belong to Us: Catholic Charities and American Welfare*. Cambridge, MA: Harvard University Press.

Brown, Karen McCarthy. 2001. *Mama Lola: A Vodou Priestess in Brooklyn*. Berkeley: University of California Press.

Butchart, Alexander. 1998. *The Anatomy of Power: European Constructions of the African Body*. London: Zed.

Butler, Judith. 2004. *Precarious Life: The Powers of Mourning and Violence*. London: Verso.

———. 2012. "Precarious Life, Vulnerability, and the Ethics of Cohabitation." *Journal of Speculative Philosophy* 26 (2): 134–51.

Butt, Leslie. 2002. "The Suffering Stranger: Medical Anthropology and International Morality." *Medical Anthropology* 21 (1): 1–24.

Cabot, Heath. 2012. "The Governance of Things: Documenting Limbo in Greek Asylum Procedure." *Political and Legal Anthropology Review* 35 (1): 11–29.

Çağlar, Ayşe, and Nina Glick Schiller. 2018. *Migrants and City-Making: Dispossession, Displacement, and Urban Regeneration.* Durham, NC: Duke University Press.

Caldwell, Melissa L. 2004. *Not by Bread Alone: Social Support in the New Russia.* Berkeley: University of California Press.

———. 2017. *Living Faithfully in an Unjust World: Compassionate Care in Russia.* Oakland: University of California Press.

Calhoun, Craig, Mark Juergensmeyer, and Jonathan VanAntwerpen. 2011. *Rethinking Secularism.* New York: Oxford University Press.

Canellos, Peter S. 1991. "Firing Brings up Thorny Issues of Church and State." *Boston Globe,* November 19, 1991, 1.

Cannell, Fenella, ed. 2006. *The Anthropology of Christianity.* Durham, NC: Duke University Press.

Catholic Church. (1994) 1995. *Catechism of the Catholic Church: With Modifications from the Editio Typica.* New York: Bantam Doubleday Dell.

CCAB (also CCB; Catholic Charitable Bureau of the Archdiocese of Boston). 1904. *Report of the Catholic Charitable Bureau for the Year 1904.* Boston.

———. 1908. *First Annual Report of the Director of Catholic Charities of the Archdiocese of Boston.* Boston: Working Boys' Home Press.

———. 1946. *Annual Report.*

———. 1995. *Strategic Plan.*

CCUSA (Catholic Charities USA). 2009. *At a Glance.* Alexandria, VA: Catholic Charities USA.

———. 2010. *Catholic Charities USA: 100 Years at the Intersection of Charity and Justice.* Edited by Rev. J. Bryan Hehir. Collegeville, MN: Liturgical Press.

———. 2011. *Catholic Charities USA 2010 Annual Survey Final Report.* Prepared by Mary L. Gautier and C. Joseph O'Hara. Washington, DC: Georgetown University Center for Applied Research in the Apostolate.

Certeau, Michel de. 1984. *The Practice of Everyday Life.* Berkeley: University of California Press.

Chibnall, John T., Ann Wolf, and Paul N. Duckro, 1998. "A National Survey of the Sexual Trauma Experiences of Catholic Nuns." *Review of Religious Research* 40 (2): 142–67.

Chierici, Rose-Marie Cassagnol. 1991. *Demele, "Making It"—Migration and Adaptation Among Haitian Boat People in the United States.* New York: AMS Press.

Chomsky, Noam, Paul Farmer, and Amy Goodman. 2004. *Getting Haiti Right This Time: The U.S. and the Coup.* Monroe, ME: Common Courage Press.

Clark, Emily. 2007. *Masterless Mistress: The New Orleans Ursulines and the Development of a New World Society, 1727–1834.* Chapel Hill: University of North Carolina Press.

Clark, Janine A. 2004. *Islam, Charity, and Activism: Middle-Class Networks and Social Welfare in Egypt, Jordan, and Yemen.* Bloomington: Indiana University Press.

Clemens, Elisabeth S. 2019. "A Believing and Benevolent Nation: Religious Mobilization as Infrastructural Power in American Political Development." In *Governing Gifts: Faith, Charity, and the Security State,* edited by Erica Caple James, 21–38. School for Advanced Research Advanced Seminar Series. Albuquerque: University of New Mexico Press.

Cloke, Paul, and Andrew Williams. 2018. "Re-imagining Religion and Belief." In *Geographical Landscapes of Religion*, edited by Christopher Baker, Beth R. Crisp, and Adam Dinham, 33–54. Bristol: Bristol University Press.

Cloke, Paul, Jon May, and Andrew Williams. 2017. "The Geographies of Food Banks in the Meantime." *Progress in Human Geography* 41 (6): 703–26.

Comaroff, Jean. 2007. "Beyond Bare Life: AIDS, (Bio)Politics, and the Neoliberal Order." *Public Culture* 19 (1): 197–219.

Conrad, Ann Patrick, and M. Vincentia Joseph. 2010. "The Rise of Professionalization: Catholic Charities and Social Work." In *CCUSA. 2010. Catholic Charities USA: 100 Years at the Intersection of Charity and Justice*, edited by Rev. J. Bryan Hehir, 47–64. Collegeville, MN: Liturgical Press.

Constable, Pamela. 1987. "Suicide Called Testimony to Haitians' Plight." *Boston Globe*, September 2, 1987, 1, 15.

Conway, Frederick J. 1978. "Pentecostalism in the Context of Haitian Religion and Health Practice." PhD diss., American University.

Conway, Frederick J., and Susan Huelsebusch Buchanan. 1985. "Haitians." In *Refugees in the United States: A Reference Handbook*, edited by David W. Haines, 95–110. Westport, CT: Greenwood Press.

Coutin, Susan Bibler. 1993. *The Culture of Protest: Religious Activism and the US Sanctuary Movement*. San Francisco: Westview Press.

———. 1995. "Smugglers or Samaritans in Tucson, Arizona: Producing and Contesting Legal Truth." *American Ethnologist* 22 (3): 549–71.

Csordas, Thomas J. 1994. *The Sacred Self: A Cultural Phenomenology of Charismatic Healing*. Berkeley: University of California Press.

Cushing, Richard. 1956. "Cushing to Mathews, November 3." St. Richard's Parish Files, Archives of the Archdiocese of Boston.

Daly, Lew. 2009. *God's Economy*. Chicago: University of Chicago Press.

Daniels, Roger. 2004. *Guarding the Golden Door: American Immigration Policy and Immigrants since 1882*. New York: Hill and Wang.

Das, Veena. 2010. "Engaging the Life of the Other: Love and Everyday Life." In *Ordinary Ethics: Anthropology, Language, and Action*, edited by Michael Lambek, 376–99. New York: Fordham University Press.

Das, Veena, and Deborah Poole. 2004. *Anthropology in the Margins of the State. School of American Research Advanced Seminar Series*. Sante Fe, NM: School of American Research Press.

Davin, Anna. 1978. "Imperialism and Motherhood." *History Workshop* 5 (Spring): 9–65.

Davis, Cyprian. 1990. *The History of Black Catholics in the United States*. New York: Crossroad.

Davis, Wendy. 2003. "Church Will End AIDS Ministry." *Boston Globe*, May 22, 2003, B7.

Delany, Joseph. 1911. "Corporal and Spiritual Works of Mercy." In *The Catholic Encyclopedia*. New York: Robert Appleton. Available online via *New Advent* (blog), accessed October 16, 2022. http://www.newadvent.org/cathen/10198d.htm.

Deleuze, Giles. 1988. *Foucault*. Translated by Sean Hand. Minneapolis: University of Minneapolis Press. Originally published as *Foucault* (Paris: Les Éditions de Minuit, 1986).

Deren, Maya. (1953) 1970. *Divine Horsemen: The Voodoo Gods of Haiti*. New York: Documentext.

Derrida, Jacques, and Anne Dufourmantelle. 2000. *Of Hospitality*, translated by Rachel Bowlby. Palo Alto, CA: Stanford University Press.

Desjarlais, Robert. 1997. *Shelter Blues: Sanity and Selfhood Among the Homeless*. Philadelphia: University of Pennsylvania Press.

Desmangles, Leslie G. 1992. *The Faces of the Gods: Vodou and Roman Catholicism in Haiti*. Chapel Hill: University of North Carolina Press.

Douglas, Mary. 1990. Foreword to *The Gift: The Form and Reason for Exchange in Archaic Societies*, by Marcel Mauss, vii–xviii. Translated by W. D. Halls. New York: W. W. Norton.

Dow, Mark. 2004. *American Gulag: Inside U.S. Immigration Prisons*. Berkeley: University of California Press.

Dowdy, Zachary R. 1994. "Locals Planning Storm Aid for Haiti." *Boston Globe*, November 20, 1994, 29.

Dubois, Laurent. 2004. *Avengers of the New World: The Story of the Haitian Revolution*. Cambridge, MA: Belknap Press.

Due, Tananarive. 1989. "Haitians Backed on INS Case Transfers." *Miami Herald*, May 20, 1989. https://miamiherald.newspapers.com/search/?query=%22Haitians%20Backed%20on%20INS%20Case%20Transfers%22&sort=paper-date-asc.

Duffield, Mark. 2001. *Global Governance and the New Wars: The Merging of Development and Security*. London: Zed Books.

Dupuy, Alex. 2007. *The Prophet and Power: Jean-Bertrand Aristide, the International Community, and Haiti*. Lanham, MD: Rowland & Littlefield.

Ebaugh, Helen Rose, and Janet Saltzman Chafetz. 2002. *Religion Across Borders: Transnational Immigrant Networks*. Walnut Creek, CA: AltaMira Press.

Elisha, Omri. 2011. *Moral Ambition: Mobilization and Social Outreach in Evangelical Megachurches*. Berkeley: University of California Press.

Eze, Emmanuel Chukwudi, ed. 1997. *Race and the Enlightenment: A Reader*. Malden, MA: Blackwell.

Ezeonwu, Mabel, and Bobbie Berkowitz. 2014. "A Collaborative Communitywide Health Fair: The Process and Impacts on the Community." *Journal of Community Health Nursing* 31 (2): 118–29.

Fabian, Johannes. 1983. *Time and the Other: How Anthropology Makes Its Object*. New York: Columbia University Press.

Farmer, Paul. 1992. *AIDS and Accusation: Haiti and the Geography of Blame*. Berkeley: University of California Press.

———. 1994. *The Uses of Haiti*. Monroe, ME: Common Courage Press. Malden, MA: Blackwell.

———. 2003. *Pathologies of Power: Health, Human Rights, and the New War on the Poor*. Berkeley: University of California Press.

———. 2013. "Accompaniment as Policy Harvard Kennedy School of Government, Commencement May 25, 2011." In *To Repair the World: Paul Farmer Speaks to the Next Generation*, edited by Jonathan Weigel, 233–48. Oakland: University of California Press.

Farmer, Paul, and Jim Yong Kim. 1991. "Anthropology, Accountability, and the Prevention of AIDS." *Journal of Sex Research* 28 (2): 203–21.

Farmer, Paul, and David Walton. 2000. "Condoms, Coups, and the Ideology of Prevention: Facing Failure in Rural Haiti." In *Catholic Ethicists on HIV/AIDS Prevention*, edited by

James F. Keenan, SJ, Jon D. Fuller, SJ, MD, Lisa Sowle Cahill, and Kevin Kelly, 108–19. New York: Continuum.

Farrelly, Maura Jane. 2018. *Anti-Catholicism in America, 1620–1860*. Cambridge: Cambridge University Press.

Fassin, Didier. 2001. "The Biopolitics of Otherness: Undocumented Immigrants and Racial Discrimination in the French Public Debate." *Anthropology Today* 17 (1): 3–7.

———. 2005. "Compassion and Repression: The Moral Economy of Immigration Policies in France." *Cultural Anthropology* 20 (3): 362–87.

———. 2007. "Humanitarianism as a Politics of Life." *Public Culture* 19 (3): 499–520.

———. 2018. *Life: A Critical User's Manual*. Medford, MA: Polity.

Fassin, Didier, and Mariella Pandolfi, eds. 2010. *Contemporary States of Emergency: The Politics of Military and Humanitarian Interventions*. Brooklyn: Zone Books.

Fatton, Robert, Jr. 2002. *Haiti's Predatory Republic: The Unending Transition to Democracy*. Boulder, CO: Lynne Rienner.

Feldman, Ilana, and Miriam Ticktin, eds. 2010. *In the Name of Humanity: The Government of Threat and Care*. Durham, NC: Duke University Press.

Fernández-Gutiérrez, M., P. Bas-Sarmiento, M. J. Albar-Marin, O. Paloma-Castro, and J. M. Romero-Sanchez. 2018. "Health Literacy Interventions for Immigrant Populations: A Systematic Review." *International Nursing Review* 65: 54–64.

Fick, Carolyn E. 1990. *The Making of Haiti: The Saint Domingue Revolution from Below*. Knoxville: University of Tennessee Press.

Florida Immigrant Advocacy Center. 2004. *Haitian Refugees: A People In Search of Hope*. Prepared by Cheryl Little and Charu Newhouse al-Sahli. Miami: FIAC.

Forry, Bill. 2003. "Catholic Charities to Build New Facility on Columbia Road." *Dorchester Reporter*, October 1, 2003. http://www.dotnews.com/2003/catholic-charities-build-new -facility-columbia-road.

———. 2006. "St. Leo's Was Spiritual Home for Waves of Dorchester Families." *Dorchester Reporter*, March 9, 2006.

Foucault, Michel. (1978) 1990. *The History of Sexuality*. Vol. 1, *An Introduction*. Translated by Robert Hurley. Vintage Books ed. New York: Random House. Originally published as *La Volonté de savoir* (Paris: Éditions Gallimard, 1976).

———. 1979. *Discipline and Punish: The Birth of the Prison*. Vintage Books ed. New York: Random House. Translated by Alan Sheridan. Originally published as *Surveiller et Punir: Naissance de la prison* (Paris: Éditions Gallimard, 1975).

———. 1982. "The Subject and Power." *Critical Inquiry* 8 (4): 777–95.

———. 1988. *Politics, Philosophy, Culture: Interviews and Other Writings, 1977–1984*. New York: Routledge.

———. 1991. *Governmentality*. In *The Foucault Effect: Studies in Governmentality*, edited by Graham Burchell, Colin Gordon, and Peter Miller, 87–104. Chicago: University of Chicago Press.

———. 1997. *Ethics: Subjectivity and Truth; Essential Works of Foucault, 1954–1984*. Edited by Paul Rabinow. Translated by Robert Hurley and others. New York: New Press. Originally published as *Dits et Écrits, 1954–1988* (Paris: Éditions Gallimard, 1994).

———. 2006. *History of Madness*. Edited by Jean Khalfa. Translated by Jonathan Murphy. Milton Park: Routledge. Originally published as *Folie et Deraison: Histoire de la folie a l'age classique* (Paris: Librairie Plon, 1961).

———. 2007. *Security, Territory, Population: Lectures at the Collège de France, 1977–1978*. Edited by Michel Senellart. New York: Palgrave Macmillan.

Frank, Jerome D., and Julia B. Frank. 1991. *Persuasion and Healing: A Comparative Study*. 3rd ed. Baltimore: Johns Hopkins University Press.

Franklin, James L. 1989. "Newton Man Is First Layperson to Head Catholic Charities Agency." *Boston Globe*, May 7, 1989.

———. 1992. "The Cardinal and the News Media." *Boston Globe*, May 27, 1992.

"Friends of David Mulligan." 2015. KCVisuals. Uploaded April 10, 2015. YouTube video, 13:39. https://youtu.be/9OjMIUfAog4?si=9wooOnrwBhU_8_h3.

Gamm, Gerald H. 1999. *Urban Exodus: Why the Jews Left Boston and the Catholics Stayed*. Cambridge, MA: Harvard University Press.

Garcia, Angela. 2010. *The Pastoral Clinic: Addiction and Dispossession along the Rio Grande*. Berkeley: University of California Press.

Ghachem, Malick W. 2010. "Of 'Scalpels' and 'Sledgehammers': Religious Liberty and the Policing of Muslim Charities in Britain and America since 9/11." *UCLA Journal of Near Eastern and Islamic Law* 9 (1): 25–68.

———. 2012. *The Old Regime and the Haitian Revolution*. Cambridge: Cambridge University Press.

Ghodsee, Kristen. 2010. *Muslim Lives in Eastern Europe: Gender, Ethnicity, and the Transformation of Islam in Postsocialist Bulgaria*. Princeton, NJ: Princeton University Press.

Giffin, Mary F., B. Scott Curry, and Julie Sullivan. 1999. *Telling the Healthy Start Story: A Report on the Impact of the 22 Demonstration Projects*. Arlington, VA: National Center for Education in Maternal and Child Health.

Gilmore, Ruth Wilson. 2007. *Golden Gulag: Prisons, Surplus, Crisis, and Opposition in Globalizing California*. Berkeley: University of California Press.

Gisler, Antoine. *L'esclavage aux Antilles françaises (XVIIe–XIXe siècle)*. Rev. ed. Paris: Éditions Karthala, 1981.

Glendon, Mary Ann. 2002. "Biographical Introduction: Bernard Cardinal Law, Gatherer of Peoples." In *Boston's Cardinal: Bernard Law, the Man and His Witness*, edited by Romanus Cessario, OP, xv–xxxvi. Lanham, MD: Lexington Books.

Glick Schiller, Nina, Ayşe Çaglar, and Thaddeus C. Guldbrandsen. 2006. "Beyond the Ethnic Lens: Locality, Globality, and Born-Again Incorporation." *American Ethnologist* 33 (4): 612–33.

Glick Schiller, Nina, and Georges Eugene Fouron. 2001. *Georges Woke Up Laughing: Long-Distance Nationalism and the Search for Home*. Durham, NC: Duke University Press.

Goffman, Erving. 1959. *The Presentation of Self in Everyday Life*. New York: Anchor Books, Doubleday.

———. 1961. *Asylums: Essays on the Social Situation of Mental Patients and Other Inmates*. New York: Anchor Books.

Golden, Daniel. 1990. "The Cardinal's Ambitions: Does Cardinal Bernard Law Serve the Pope or the President? Is He Prelate or Politician—or Both?" *Boston Globe*, April 22, 1990. http://www.boston.com/globe/spotlight/abuse/archives/042290_magazine.htm.

Graham, Renee. 1989. "Easter Celebrations Are Varied." *Boston Globe*, March 26, 1989, 1.

Greed, Clara. 2020. "Introduction: Interactions between Gender, Urban Space, and Religion." In *Gender and Religion in the City: Women, Urban Planning and Spirituality*, edited by Clara Greed, 3–15. New York: Routledge.

Greene, Anne. 1993. *The Catholic Church in Haiti*. East Lansing: Michigan State University Press.

Gribble, Richard. 2008. "Roman Catholicism and U.S. Foreign Policy—1919–1935: A Clash of Policies." *Journal of Church and State* 50 (1): 73–99.

Han, Clara. 2018. "Precarity, Precariousness, and Vulnerability." *Annual Review of Anthropology* 47: 331–43.

Hanna, E. 1911. "Purgatory." In *The Catholic Encyclopedia*. New York: Robert Appleton. Available online via *New Advent* (blog), accessed October 23, 2023. http://www.newadvent.org/cathen/12575a.htm.

Hansen, Jonathan M. 2011. *Guantánamo: An American History*. New York: Hill and Wang.

Hanson, Eric O. 1987. *The Catholic Church in World Politics*. Princeton, NJ: Princeton University Press.

Harding, Chris. 2009. "Pressure Grows on Local Food Pantries: Yawkey Center Cutback Has Widespread Impact." *Dorchester Reporter*, January 8, 2009. https://www.dotnews.com/2009/pressure-grows-local-food-pantries-yawkey-center-cutback-has-widesprea.

Healthy Start National Resource Center (HSNRC) at the National Center for Education in Maternal and Child Health. 1997. *Proceedings of Winning the Fight Against Infant Mortality: A National Summit on Community and Corporate Initiatives*. Arlington, VA: National Center for Education in Maternal and Child Health.

Hehir, J. Bryan. 2000. "Religious Ideas and Social Policy: Subsidiarity and Catholic Style of Ministry." In *Who Will Provide? The Changing Role of Religion in American Social Welfare*, edited by Mary Jo Bane, Brent Coffin, and Ronald Thiemann, 97–120. Boulder, CO: Westview.

Herzfeld, Michael. 1992. *The Social Production of Indifference: Exploring the Symbolic Roots of Western Bureaucracy*. Chicago: University of Chicago Press.

———. 1997. *Cultural Intimacy: Social Poetics in the Nation-State*. New York: Routledge.

Hewitt, Nancy P. 1940. "History of the Catholic Charitable Bureau." Master's thesis, Boston University.

Hirschkind, Charles. 2011. "Is There a Secular Body?" *Cultural Anthropology* 26 (4): 633–47.

Hirschkind, Charles, and Matthew Scherer. 2011. Introduction. *Cultural Anthropology* 26(4): 620.

Hirschman, Albert O. 1970. *Exit, Voice, Loyalty: Responses to Decline in Firms, Organizations, and States*. Cambridge: Harvard University Press.

HMSC (Haitian Multi-Service Center). 1996–97. *AIDS Program Draft Proposal*.

———. 2003. *Grant Proposal*.

hooks, bell. 1990. "Homeplace (a Site of Resistance)." In *Yearning Race, Gender, and Cultural Politics*, 41–49. Boston: South End Press.

Hopgood, Stephen. 2006. *Keepers of the Flame: Understanding Amnesty International*. Ithaca, NY: Cornell University Press.

Howell, Embry M., Barbara Devaney, Barbara Foot, Mary Harrington, Melissa Schettini, Marie C. McCormick, Ian Hill, Renee Schwalberg, and Beth Zimmerman. 1997. *The Implementation of Healthy Start: Lessons for the Future*. Washington, DC: U.S. Department of Health and Human Services Health Resources and Services Administration.

Huang, C. Julia. 2009. *Charisma and Compassion: Cheng Yen and the Buddhist Tzu Chi Movement*. Cambridge, MA: Harvard University Press.

———. 2019. "The End(s) of Compassion? Buddhist Charity and the State in Taiwan." In *Governing Gifts: Faith, Charity, and the Security State*, edited by Erica Caple James, 39–58. School for Advanced Research Advanced Seminar Series. Albuquerque: University of New Mexico Press.

Human Rights Watch/Americas, Jesuit Refugee Service/USA, and National Coalition for Haitian Refugees 1994. *Fugitives from Injustice: The Crisis of Internal Displacement in Haiti*. Vol. 6, no. 10 (Aug.).

Hunt, Nancy Rose. 1999. *A Colonial Lexicon of Birth Ritual, Medicalization, and Mobility in the Congo*. Durham, NC: Duke University Press.

Ilchman, Warren F., Stanley N. Katz, and Edward L. Queen II. 1998. *Philanthropy in the World's Traditions*. Bloomington: Indiana University Press.

Isidor, Yves A. 2001. "In Memory of Léandre Jeannot, First Boston's Haitian Monsignor and 'Man of the People.'" Wehaitians.com. July 11, 2001. http://www.wehaitians.com/in%20 memory%20of%20leandre%20jeannot.html.

Jackson, Régine O. 2007. "After the Exodus: The New Catholics in Boston's Old Ethnic Neighborhoods." *Religions and American Culture: A Journal of Interpretation* 17 (2): 191–212.

———. 2011. *Geographies of the Haitian Diaspora*. New York: Routledge.

James, Erica Caple. 2004. "The Political Economy of 'Trauma' in Haiti in the Democratic Era of Insecurity." *Culture, Medicine and Psychiatry* 28: 127–49.

———. 2008. "Haunting Ghosts: Madness, Gender, and Ensekirite in Haiti in the Democratic Era." In *Postcolonial Disorders*, edited by Mary-Jo DelVecchio Good, Sandra Teresa Hyde, Sarah Pinto, and Byron J. Good, 132–56. Berkeley: University of California Press.

———. 2010. *Democratic Insecurities: Violence Trauma and Intervention in Haiti*. Berkeley: University of California Press.

———. 2011. "Haiti, Insecurity, and the Politics of Asylum." *Medical Anthropology Quarterly* 25 (3): 357–76.

———. 2012. "Witchcraft, Bureaucraft, and the Social Life of (US)AID in Haiti." *Cultural Anthropology* 27 (1): 50–75.

———, ed. 2019. *Governing Gifts: Faith, Charity, and the Security State*. School for Advanced Research advanced seminar series. Albuquerque: University of New Mexico Press.

James, William. 1997. *The Varieties of Religious Experience: A Study in Human Nature*. New York: Simon & Schuster.

Jean-Charles, Melissa. 2002. "Women's Group Tackles Domestic Violence at RCC Conference in August." *Boston Haitian Reporter*, August 31, 2002. https://www.proquest.com /newspapers/womens-group-tackles-domestic-violence-at-rcc/docview/368761157/se-2.

Jordan, Winthrop D. 1968. *White Over Black: American Attitudes Toward the Negro, 1550–1812*. Chapel Hill: University of North Carolina Press.

Kammer, Fred. 2004. *Doing Faithjustice: An Introduction to Catholic Social Thought*. Mahwah, NJ: Paulist Press.

———. 2009. *Faith. Works. Wonders.*: *An Insider's Guide to Catholic Charities*. Eugene, OR: Wipf and Stock.

Kantorowicz, Ernst. (1957) 1997. *The King's Two Bodies: A Study in Mediaeval Political Theology*. Princeton, NJ: Princeton University Press.

Keaveny, Mary E. 1974. "A Community Health Fair." *American Journal of Nursing* 74 (2): 270–71.

Keck, Margaret E., and Kathryn Sikkink. 1998. *Activists beyond Borders: Advocacy Networks in International Politics*. Ithaca, NY: Cornell University Press.

Keenan, James F. 2008. *The Works of Mercy: The Heart of Catholicism*. 2nd ed. Lanham, MD: Rowman & Littlefield.

Kevles, Daniel J. (1985) 1995. *In the Name of Eugenics: Genetics and the Uses of Human Heredity*. Cambridge, MA: Harvard University Press.

Kidder, Rushworth M. 1983. "Boston's OIC: Training Inner-City Residents for High-Tech Jobs." *Christian Science Monitor*, February 8, 1983, 14.

Klaus, Alisa. 1993. *Every Child a Lion: The Origins of Maternal and Infant Health Policy in the United States and France, 1890–1920*. Ithaca, NY: Cornell University Press.

Kleinman, Arthur. 1988. *The Illness Narratives: Suffering, Healing, and the Human Condition*. New York: Basic Books.

———. 2006. *What Really Matters: Living a Moral Life amidst Uncertainty and Danger*. Oxford: Oxford University Press.

———. 2009. "Caregiving: The Art of Becoming More Human." *Lancet* 373 (9660): 292–93.

Kleinman, Arthur, and Joan Kleinman. 1991. "Suffering and Its Professional Transformation: Toward an Ethnography of Interpersonal Experience." *Culture, Medicine and Psychiatry* 15 (3): 275–301.

Kong, Dolores. 1990. "Race, Economics Drive Boston Rates." *Boston Globe*, September 9, 1990, 38.

Labbe, Mark. "Cardinal, Prominent Bostonians Ask City to Keep Yawkey Way Name." *Boston Pilot*, March 23, 2018. https://www.thebostonpilot.com/article.asp?ID=181867.

Lachance, Paul F. 1988. "The 1809 Immigration of Saint-Domingue Refugees to New Orleans: Reception, Integration and Impact." *Louisiana History: Journal of the Louisiana Historical Association* 29 (2): 109–41.

Laguerre, Michel Saturnin. 1973. "The Place of Voodoo in the Social Structure of Haiti." *Caribbean Quarterly* 19 (3): 36–50.

———. 1984. *American Odyssey: Haitians in New York City*. Ithaca, NY: Cornell University Press.

———. 1989. *Voodoo and Politics in Haiti*. New York: St. Martin's Press.

———. 1998. *Diasporic Citizenship: Haitian Americans in Transnational America*. New York: St. Martin's Press.

———. 2011. *Network Governance of Global Religions: Jerusalem, Rome, and Mecca*. New York: Routledge.

Latour, Francie. 1999. "Fired Director Alleges Charity Falsified Papers Sent to Auditor." *Boston Globe*, December 18, 1999, B 1:1.

Law, Bernard Francis. 1992a. "An Appeal on Behalf of Haitian Refugees: A Letter to President George Bush, 22 May 1992." In *Boston's Cardinal: Bernard Law, the Man and His Witness*, edited by Romanus Cessario, O.P., 121–22. Lanham, MD: Lexington Books.

———. 1992b. "Introduction." In *AIDS and Adolescents*, edited by Linda Thayer, 7–9. Boston: St. Paul Books and Media.

Lawler, Philip F. 2010. *The Faithful Departed: The Collapse of Boston's Catholic Culture*. New York: Encounter Books.

Lawless, Robert. 1992. *Haiti's Bad Press*. Rochester, VT: Schenkman Books.

LCHR (Lawyers Committee for Human Rights). 1990. *Refugee Refoulement: The Forced Return of Haitians under the U.S.-Haitian Interdiction Agreement*. New York: Lawyers Committee for Human Rights.

Lazo, Rodrigo. 1988. "Haitians on Strike at Krome." *Miami Herald*, November 25, 1988, 1C.

Leger, J. N. 1907. *Haiti: Her History and Her Detractors*. Westport, CT: Negro Universities Press.

Leonard, William C. 2009. "People of Faith, People of Color: Two Hundred Years of Diversity in the Archdiocese of Boston." In *Two Centuries of Faith: The Influence of Catholicism on Boston, 1808–2008*, edited by Thomas H. O'Connor, 145–69. New York: Crossroad.

Locke, John. 1689. *A Letter Concerning Toleration*. Translated by William Popple. Constitution.org. Accessed October 23, 2023. http://www.constitution.org/jl/tolerati.htm.

Low, Setha. 2003. *Behind the Gates: Life, Security, and the Pursuit of Happiness in Fortress America*. London: Routledge.

———. 2017. *Spatializing Culture: The Ethnography of Space and Place*. London: Routledge.

Lowenthal, Ira. 1987. "Marriage is 20, Children Are 21: The Cultural Construction of Conjugality and the Family in Rural Haiti." PhD diss., Johns Hopkins University.

Louis, Bertin M., Jr. 2014. *My Soul is in Haiti: Protestantism and the Haitian Diaspora of the Bahamas*. New York: New York University Press.

Luhrmann, Tanya M. 1989. *Persuasions of the Witch's Craft: Ritual Magic in Contemporary England*. Cambridge, MA.: Harvard University Press.

Maguire, Robert. 1999. "Grassroots Organising: The Peasantry and Political Change in Haiti." In *Libète: A Haiti Anthology*, edited by Charles Arthur and Michael Dash, 152–53. Princeton, NJ: Markus Weiner.

———. 2004. Statement of Robert Maguire. Committee on International Relations. United States House of Representatives, Subcommittee on the Western Hemisphere. March 3, 2004.

Malkki, Liisa. 1995. *Purity and Exile: Violence, Memory, and National Cosmology among Hutu Refugees in Tanzania*. Chicago: University of Chicago Press.

———. 1996. "Speechless Emissaries: Refugees, Humanitarianism, and Dehistoricization." *Cultural Anthropology* 11 (3): 377–404.

———. 2010. "Children, Humanity, and the Infantilization of Peace." In *In the Name of Humanity: The Government of Threat and Care*, edited by Ilana Feldman and Miriam Ticktin, 58–85. Durham, NC: Duke University Press.

Mallia, Joseph. 1994. "Hub Cardinal Blasts U.S. Policy on Haiti." *Boston Globe*, April 29, 1994, 4.

Mandler, Peter. 1990. *The Uses of Charity: The Poor on Relief in the Nineteenth-Century Metropolis*. Philadelphia: University of Pennsylvania Press.

Manly, Howard. 1994. "At St. Leo's, Immigrant Haitians Find Island of Refuge. To Community, Church Offers Blend of Salvation, Survival." *Boston Globe*, December 25, 1994, 1.

Mars, Louis. (1946) 1977. *The Crisis of Possession in Voodoo*. Translated by Kathleen Collins. Port-au-Prince: Reed, Cannon and Johnson.

Martinez, Samuel. 1995. *Peripheral Migrants: Haitians and Dominican Republican Sugar Plantations*. Knoxville: University of Tennessee Press.

Massa, Mark, SJ, and Catherine Osborne. 2017. *American Catholic History: A Documentary Reader*. 2nd ed. New York: New York University Press.

Maternowska, M. Catherine. 2006. *Reproducing Inequities: Poverty and the Politics of Population in Haiti*. New Brunswick, NJ: Rutgers University Press.

Matory, James Lorand. 2004. "Sexual Secrets: Candomblé, Brazil, and the Multiple Intimacies of the African Diaspora." In *Off Stage/On Display: Intimacy and Ethnography in the Age of Public Culture*, edited by Andrew Shryock, 157–90. Stanford, CA: Stanford University Press.

Maurutto, Paula. 2003. *Governing Charities: Church and State in Toronto's Catholic Archdiocese, 1850–1950*. Montreal: McGill-Queen's University Press.

Mauss, Marcel. 1950. *The Gift: The Form and Reason for Exchange in Archaic Societies*. Translated by W. D. Halls. New York: W. W. Norton.

McAlister, Elizabeth. 2013. "Humanitarian Adhocracy, Transnational New Apostolic Missions, and Evangelical Anti-Dependency in a Haitian Refugee Camp." *Nova Religion: Journal of Alternative and Emergent Religions* 16 (4): 11–34.

McCabe, Katharine. 2016. "Mothercraft: Birth Work and the Making of Neoliberal Mothers." *Social Science and Medicine* (162): 177–84.

McLellan, Daniel. 1984. "A History of the Catholic Charitable Bureau of the Archdiocese of Boston." PhD diss., University of Notre Dame.

Miller, Jake C. 1984. *The Plight of Haitian Refugees*. Westport: Praeger.

Mitchell, Jon P. 2017. "A Catholic Body? Miracles, Secularity, and the Porous Self in Malta." In *The Anthropology of Catholicism: A Reader*, edited by Kristin Norget, Valentina Napolitano, and Maya Mayblin, 211–26. Oakland: University of California Press.

Molé, Noelle J. 2008. "Living It on the Skin: Italian States, Working Illness." *American Ethnologist* 35 (2): 189–210.

———. 2013. "Existential Damages: The Injury of Precarity Goes to Court." *Cultural Anthropology* 28 (1): 22–43.

Mooney, Margarita A. 2009. *Faith Makes Us Live: Surviving and Thriving in the Haitian Diaspora*. Berkeley: University of California Press.

Moreau de Saint-Méry, Médéric-Louis-Elie. (1958) 1978. *Description topographique, physique, civile, politique et historique de la partie française de l'isle Saint Domingue*. Paris: Société de l'histoire des colonies françaises.

———. 1985. *A Civilization that Perished: The Last Years of White Colonial Rule in Haiti*. Edited and translated by Ivor D. Spencer. Lanham, MD: University Press of America.

Morgan, Lynn M., and Elisabeth F. S. Roberts. 2012. "Reproductive Governance in Latin America." *Anthropology & Medicine* 19 (2): 241–54.

Morrow, Diane Batts. 2002. *Persons of Color and Religious at the Same Time: The Oblate Sisters of Providence, 1828–1860*. Chapel Hill: University of North Carolina Press.

Mortland, Carol A. 1987. "Transforming Refugees in Refugee Camps." *Urban Anthropology and Studies of Cultural Systems and World Economic Development* 16, nos. 3/4 (Fall–Winter 1987): 375–404.

Muehlebach, Andrea. 2012. *The Moral Neoliberal: Welfare and Citizenship in Italy*. Chicago: University of Chicago Press.

———. 2013. "The Catholicization of Neoliberalism: On Love and Welfare in Lombardy, Italy." *American Anthropologist* 115 (3): 452–65.

Murray, Kate, Annie Liang, Jessica Barnack-Tavlaris, and Ana M. Navarro. 2014. "The Reach and Rationale for Community Health Fairs." *Journal of Cancer Education* 29: 19–24.

Nachman, Steven R. 1993. "Wasted Lives: Tuberculosis and Other Health Risks of Being Haitian in a U.S. Detention Camp." *Medical Anthropological Quarterly* 7 (3): 227–59.

Napolitano, Valentina. 2016. *Migrant Hearts and the Atlantic Return: Transnationalism and the Roman Catholic Church.* New York: Fordham University Press.

———. 2017. "On a Political Economy of Political Theology: *El Señor de los Milagros.*" In *The Anthropology of Catholicism: A Reader*, edited by Kristin Norget, Valentina Napolitano, and Maya Mayblin, 243–55. Oakland: University of California Press.

NCCB/USCC (National Conference of Catholic Bishops/United States Catholic Conference). 2000. *Welcoming the Stranger among Us: Unity in Diversity.* November 15, 2000. https://www.usccb.org/committees/pastoral-care-migrants-refugees-travelers/welcoming-stranger-among-us-unity-diversity.

Nealon, Patricia. 1996. "Haitian Services Center in Turmoil: Officials Quit amid Struggle over Catholic Charities' Policies." *Boston Globe*, June 8, 1996, 13.

Negri, Gloria. 1992. "Deportations Anger Haitian Community: Activists Blast US Policy, Urge Temporary Protective Status for Refugees." *Boston Globe*, February 4, 1992, 15.

———. 1993. "HIV 'Prison' Refugee Haitian Man, 22, Comes to Boston to Resume His Life." *Boston Globe*, June 17, 1993, 1.

Nemser, Daniel. 2017. *Infrastructures of Race: Concentration and Biopolitics in Colonial Mexico.* Austin: University of Texas Press.

Neuffer, Elizabeth. 1991. "Shelter Told Not to Offer Condoms." *Boston Globe*, November 13, 1991, 29.

Nicholls, David. 1996. *From Dessalines to Duvalier: Race, Colour and National Independence in Haiti.* Rev. ed. New Brunswick, NJ: Rutgers University Press.

Niezen, Ronald. 2010. *Public Justice and the Anthropology of Law.* Cambridge: Cambridge University Press.

Nordstrom, Carolyn. 1997. *A Different Kind of War Story.* Philadelphia: University of Pennsylvania Press.

Norget, Kristin, Valentina Napolitano, and Maya Mayblin, eds. 2017. *The Anthropology of Catholicism: A Reader.* Oakland: University of California Press.

Normén, Lena, Keith Chan, Paula Braitstein, Aranka Anema, Greg Bondy, Julio S. G. Montaner, and Robert S. Hogg. 2005. "Food Insecurity and Hunger Are Prevalent among HIV-Positive Individuals in British Columbia, Canada." *Journal of Nutrition* 135 (4): 820–25.

Norris, Pippa, and Ronald Inglehart. 2004. *Sacred and Secular: Religion and Politics Worldwide.* New York: Cambridge University Press.

Oates, Mary J. 1995. *The Catholic Philanthropic Tradition in America.* Bloomington and Indianapolis: Indiana University Press.

———. 1999. *Catholic Philanthropy in America.* New York: Center for the Study of Philanthropy.

O'Connor, Thomas H. 1998. *Boston Catholics: A History of the Church and Its People.* Boston: Northeastern University Press.

ORR (US DHHS Office of Refugee Resettlement). 1981. *Refugee Resettlement Program. Report to Congress. FY1980.* January 31.

O'Grady, John. 1930. *Catholic Charities in the United States.* Washington, DC: Ransdell.

O'Neill, Kevin Lewis. 2010. *City of God: Christian Citizenship in Postwar Guatemala.* Berkeley: University of California Press.

Ong, Aihwa. 1996. "Cultural Citizenship as Subject-Making: Immigrants Negotiate Racial and Cultural Boundaries in the United States." *Current Anthropology* 37 (5): 737–62.

———. 1999. *Flexible Citizenship: The Cultural Logistics of Transnationality*. United States of America: Duke University Press.

———. 2003. *Buddha is Hiding: Refugees, Citizenship, the New America*. Berkeley: University of California Press.

Ong, Aihwa, and Stephen J. Collier, eds. 2005. *Global Assemblages: Technology, Politics, and Ethics as Anthropological Problems*. Oxford: Blackwell.

O'Toole, James M. 2008. *The Faithful: A History of Catholics in America*. Cambridge, MA: President and Fellows of Harvard College.

Paige, Connie. "Relocation Jitters—Community Center Plans Draw Many Raves, But Haitians Worry." *Boston Globe*, September 28, 2003, 1.

Painter, Nell Irvin. 2020. "Why 'White' Should Be Capitalized, Too." *Washington Post*, July 22, 2020. https://www.washingtonpost.com/opinions/2020/07/22/why-white-should-be-capitalized/.

Pandolfi, Mariella. 2003. "Contract of Mutual (In)Difference: Governance and Humanitarian Apparatus in Contemporary Albania and Kosovo." *Indiana Journal of Global Legal Studies* 10 (1): 369–81.

Paulson, Michael. 2007. "Archdiocese to Sell Brighton Site to BC - $65m Price Tag for 18 Acres; Offices to Move to Braintree: [3 Edition]." *Boston Globe*, May 25, 2007, B1.

Peabody, Sue. 2002. "'A Dangerous Zeal': Catholic Missions to Slaves in the French Antilles, 1635–1800." *French Historical Studies* 25 (1): 53–90.

Physicians for Human Rights and the Bellevue/NYU Program for Survivors of Torture 2003. *From Persecution to Prison: The Health Consequences for Asylum Seekers*. Boston and New York: Physicians for Human Rights and The Bellevue/NYU Program for Survivors of Torture, June.

Pierre-Louis, François. 2006. *Haitians in New York City: Transnationalism and Hometown Associations*. Gainesville: University Press of Florida.

Pitt-Rivers, Julian A. 2017. "Excerpt from 'The Place of Grace in Anthropology.'" In *The Anthropology of Catholicism: A Reader*, edited by Kristin Norget, Valentina Napolitano, and Maya Mayblin, 52–62. Oakland: University of California Press.

Plough, Alonzo, and Freya Olafson. 1994. "Implementing the Boston Healthy Start Initiative: A Case Study of Community Empowerment and Public Health." *Health Education Quarterly* 21 (2): 221–34.

Poppendieck, Janet. 1998. *Sweet Charity: Emergency Food and the End of Entitlement*. New York: Penguin Books.

Portes, Alejandro, and Alex Stepick. 1993. *City on the Edge: The Transformation of Miami*. Berkeley: University of California Press.

Povinelli, Elizabeth A. 2006. *The Empire of Love: Toward a Theory of Intimacy, Genealogy, and Carnality*. Durham, NC: Duke University Press.

———. 2011. *Economies of Abandonment: Social Belonging and Endurance in Late Liberalism*. Durham, NC: Duke University Press.

Rabinow, Paul. 1999. *French DNA: Trouble in Purgatory*. Chicago: University of Chicago Press.

Raboteau, Albert J. 1978. *Slave Religion: The "Invisible Institution" in the Antebellum South*. Oxford: Oxford University Press.

Radin, Charles A. 1996. "From Haiti to Boston." *Boston Globe*, December 15, 1996, 18.

Ragan, Mark. 2004. *Faith-Based vs. Secular: Using Administrative Data to Compare the Performance of Faith-Affiliated and Other Social Service Providers*. Data Analysis by Craig Abbey. The Roundtable on Religion and Social Welfare Policy. Albany: Rockefeller Institute of Government, State University of New York.

Ramsey, Kate. 2011. *The Spirits and the Law: Vodou and Power in Haiti*. Chicago: University of Chicago Press.

Ramusack, Barbara. 1992. "Cultural Missionaries, Maternal Imperialists and Feminist Allies: British Women Activists in India, 1865–1945." In *Western Women and Imperialism: Complicity and Resistance*, edited by Nupur Chaudhuri and Margaret Strobel, 119–36. Bloomington: Indiana University Press.

Ray, Elaine. 1992. "In Another Country: Haitian Immigrants in Greater Boston Face a Daunting Array of Problems, from Health Care to Housing to Financial Responsibility for Family Members Back Home." *Boston Globe*, July 26, 1992, 14.

RCAB (Roman Catholic Archdiocese of Boston). 2011. *Financial Report for the Archdiocese of Boston 2010*. Boston, MA: Archdiocese of Boston.

Reese, Thomas. 1996. *Inside the Vatican: The Politics and Organization of the Catholic Church*. Georgetown: Woodstock Theological Center.

Reidy, Chris. 2007. "Catholic Charities Starts Marketing Push." *Boston Globe*, March 2, 2007, https://web.archive.org/web/20070305164745/http://www.boston.com/business/ticker/2007/03/catholic_charit.html.

Renda, Mary A. 2001. *Taking Haiti: Military Occupation and the Culture of U.S. Imperialism, 1915–1940*. Chapel Hill: University of North Carolina Press.

Rey, Terry, and Alex Stepick. 2009. "Refugee Catholicism and Little Haiti: Miami's Notre Dame d'Haiti Catholic Church." In *Churches and Charity in the Immigrant City: Religion, Immigration, and Civic Engagement in Miami*, edited by Alex Stepick, Terry Rey, and Sarah J. Mahler, 72–91. New Brunswick, NJ: Rutgers University Press.

Ribadeneira, Diego. 1990. "Mothers March in Streets to Seek Help in Curbing Black Infant Mortality Rate." *Boston Globe*, November 4, 1990, 29.

Richie, Nicholas D. 1976. "Some Guidelines for Conducting a Health Fair." *Public Health Reports* 91 (3): 261–64.

Richman, Karen. 2005. *Migration and Vodou*. Gainesville: University Press of Florida.

Robert, Paul. 1952. *Difficultés et ressources*. Gonaïves: n.p.

———. 1955. *Positions et proposition*. Gonaïves: n.p.

Roberts, Sam. 2017. "Thomas V. Daily, Bishop With Legacy Tarnished by Response to Abuse, Dies at 89." *New York Times*, May 15, 2017. https://www.nytimes.com/2017/05/15/nyregion/archbishop-thomas-v-daily-of-brooklyn-dead.html.

Robinson, Walter V., and Stephen Kurkjian. 2002. "Catholic Charities Plans to Cut Services, Consolidate." *Boston Globe*, September 29, 2002, A1.

Rosaldo, Renato. 1994. "Cultural Citizenship and Educational Democracy." *Cultural Anthropology* 9 (3): 402–11.

Rose, Ananda. 2012. *Showdown in the Sonoran Desert: Religion, Law, and the Immigration Controversy*. New York: Oxford University Press.

Rose, Nikolas. 1999. *Governing the Soul: The Shaping of the Private Self*. 2nd ed. London: Free Association Books.

———. 2007. *The Politics of Life Itself: Biomedicine, Power, and Subjectivity in the Twenty-First Century*. Princeton, NJ: Princeton University Press.

Rotberg, Robert I. 1971. *Haiti: The Politics of Squalor*. Boston: Houghton Mifflin.

Ryall, David. 2001. "The Catholic Church as a Transnational Actor." In *Non-State Actors in World Politics*, edited by Daphné Josselin and William Wallace, 41–58. New York: Palgrave Macmillan.

Ryden, David K., and Jeffery Polet. 2005. *Sanctioning Religion?: Politics, Law, and Faith-Based Public Services*. Boulder: Lynne Rienner.

Sabatier, Renee. 1988. *Blaming Others: Prejudice, Race and Worldwide AIDS*. Philadelphia: New Society.

Sante Manman Se Sante Pitit (SMSSP). 1997. "Breast Cancer Prevention Program Report."

———. 2003. "Program Abstract."

Sayad, Abdelmalek. 2004. *The Suffering of the Immigrant*. Translated by David Macey. Malden, MA: Polity Press.

Scheper-Hughes, Nancy. 1998. "Institutionalized Sex Abuse and the Catholic Church." In *Small Wars: The Cultural Politics of Childhood*, edited by Nancy Scheper-Hughes and Carolyn Sargent, 295–317. Berkeley: University of California Press.

Scheper-Hughes, Nancy, and Carolyn Sargent, eds. 1998. *Small Wars: The Cultural Politics of Childhood*. Berkeley: University of California Press.

Scheper-Hughes, Nancy, and John Devine. 2003. "Priestly Celibacy and Child Sexual Abuse." *Sexualities* 6 (1): 15–40.

Scherer, Matthew. 2011. "Landmarks in the Critical Study of Secularism." *Cultural Anthropology* 26 (4): 621–32.

Schneider, Eric C. 1980. "In the Web of Class: Youth, Class, and Culture in Boston, 1840–1940." PhD diss., Boston University.

Schwartz, T. T. 2000. "Children Are the Wealth of the Poor: High Fertility and the Organization of Labor in the Rural Economy of Jean Ravel, Haiti." PhD diss., University of Florida.

Seitz, John C. 2011. *No Closure: Catholic Practice and Boston's Parish Shutdowns*. Cambridge, MA: Harvard University Press.

Shoemaker, Karl. 2011. *Sanctuary and Crime in the Middle Ages*. Bronx: Fordham University Press.

Shryock, Andrew. 2004. *Off Stage/On Display: Intimacy and Ethnography in the Age of Public Culture*. Stanford, CA: Stanford University Press.

Singer, Merrill, and Scott Clair. 2015. "Syndemics and Public Health: Reconceptualizing Disease in Bio-Social Context." *Medical Anthropology Quarterly* 17 (4): 423–41.

Skok, Deborah S. 1998. "Organized Almsgiving: Scientific Charity and the Society of St. Vincent de Paul in Chicago, 1871–1918." *U.S. Catholic Historian* 16 (4): 19–35.

Smedley, Brian D., Adrienne Y. Stith, and Alan R. Nelson, eds. 2003. *Unequal Treatment: Confronting Racial and Ethnic Disparities in Health Care*. Washington, DC: National Academies Press.

Smith, Jennie M. 2001. *When the Hands Are Many: Community Organization and Social Change in Rural Haiti*. Ithaca, NY: Cornell University Press.

Smith, Tony. 2000. *The Power of Ethnic Groups in the Making Of American Foreign Policy*. Cambridge, MA: President and Fellows of Harvard College.

Smith, Tovia. 2018. "Boston Changes 'Yawkey Way' to 'Jersey Street' after Concerns over Racist Legacy." National Public Radio. April 26, 2018. https://www.npr.org/2018/04/26/605851052/boston-red-sox-want-to-strike-former-owners-name-off-street-sign.

Snyder, Larry J. 2010. "Introduction." In *Catholic Charities USA: 100 Years at the Intersection of Charity and Justice*, edited by Rev. J. Bryan Hehir, 11–26. Collegeville, MN: Liturgical Press.

Spence, Jonathan D. (1983) 1988. *The Memory Palace of Matteo Ricci*. New York: Penguin Books.

Spencer, Ivor D. 1985. "Preface." In *Médéric-Louis-Élie Moreau de Saint-Méry, A Civilization that Perished: The Last Years of White Colonial Rule in Haiti*, translated and edited by Ivor D. Spencer, iii–v. Lanham, MD: University Press of America.

St. John, Sir Spenser. 1884. *Hayti or The Black Republic*. London: Smith, Elder.

Stepick, Alex. 1998. *Pride against Prejudice: Haitians in the United States*. Boston: Allyn and Bacon.

Stepick, Alex, and Dale Frederick Swartz. 1986. *Haitian Refugees in the U.S.* London: Minority Rights Group.

Stepick, Alex, Terry Rey, and Sarah J. Mahler. 2009. *Churches and Charity in the Immigrant City: Religion, Immigration, and Civic Engagement in Miami*. United States of America: Rutgers University Press.

Stockman, Farah. 2003. "A Center of Division: Haitians Spar with Catholic Charities over a Place of Their Own." *Boston Globe*, November 26, 2003, B1.

Swarns, Rachel L. 2023. *The 272: The Families Who Were Enslaved and Sold to Build the American Catholic Church*. New York: Random House.

Taussig, Michael. 1999. *Defacement: Public Secrecy and the Labor of the Negative*. Stanford, CA: Stanford University Press.

Taylor, Charles. 2007. *A Secular Age*. Cambridge, MA: Harvard University Press.

Tench, Megan. 2001. "Haitians Remember Monsignor." *Boston Globe*, July 14, 2001, B1.

Ticktin, Miriam. 2006. "Where Ethics and Politics Meet: The Violence of Humanitarianism in France." *American Ethnologist* 33 (1): 33–49.

———. 2011. *Casualties of Care: Immigration and the Politics of Humanitarianism in France*. Berkeley: University of California Press.

TransAfrica Forum. 2004. *Deter, Detain, and Return: The U.S. Immigration Policy for Haitian Refugees*. A TransAfrica Forum Report.

Trouillot, Michel-Rolph. 1990. *Haiti—State against Nation: Origins and Legacy of Duvalierism*. New York: Monthly Review Press.

———. 1995. *Silencing the Past: Power and the Production of History*. Boston: Beacon Press.

Turner, Edith. 2012. *Communitas: The Anthropology of Collective Joy*. New York: Palgrave Macmillan.

UNHCR (United Nations High Commissioner for Refugees). 1979. *Handbook on Procedures and Criteria for Determining Refugee Status: Under the 1951 Convention and the 1967 Protocol Relating to the Status of Refugees*. Geneva: UNHCR.

USCCB (United States Conference of Catholic Bishops). 2000. *Welcoming the Stranger among Us: Unity in Diversity*. November 15, 2000. https://www.usccb.org/committees/pastoral-care-migrants-refugees-travelers/welcoming-stranger-among-us-unity-diversity.

USDA. 2006. "The Emergency Food Assistance Program." Food and Nutrition Service Food Distribution Fact Sheet. March 1–3, 2006. https://web.archive.org/web/20060929161359 /http://www.mypyramidforkids.gov/fdd/programs/tefap/pfs-tefap.pdf.

Vaccaro, Adam. 2019. "MBTA's Yawkey Station Will Be Renamed Landsdowne." *Boston Globe*, March 28, 2019. https://www.bostonglobe.com/metro/2019/03/28/mbta-yawkey -station-will-renamed-landsdowne/tDGrTTxjfM75vYx7JXGNtN/story.html.

Van Der Veer, Peter. 1996. *Conversion to Modernities*. New York: Routledge.

Van Ham, Lane. 2009. "Sanctuary Revisited: Central American Refugee Assistance in the History of Church-Based Immigrant Advocacy." *Political Theology* 10 (4): 621–45.

Wacquant, Loïc. (2004) 2009. *Punishing the Poor: The Neoliberal Government of Social Insecurity*. Durham, NC: Duke University Press.

Walton, Susan S. 1993. *To Preserve the Faith: Catholic Charities in Boston: 1870–1930*. New York: Garland.

Watkins, Mary. 2015. "Psychosocial Accompaniment." *Journal of Social and Political Psychology*. 3 (1): 324–41.

Weber, Max. 1930. *The Protestant Ethic and the Spirit of Capitalism*. Translated by Talcott Parsons. London: G. Allen & Unwin.

———. 1946. *From Max Weber: Essays in Sociology*. Translated and edited by H. H. Gerth and C. Wright Mills. New York: Oxford University Press.

Weiser, Sheri D., David M. Tuller, Edward A. Frongillo, Jude Senkungu, Nozmu Mukiibi, David R. Bangsberg. 2010. "Food Insecurity as a Barrier to Sustained Antiretroviral Therapy Adherence in Uganda." *PLoS One* 5 (4): 1–8.

Weld, Elizabeth New. 1992. "Haitians in Boston Blast Bush on Refugee Return." *Boston Globe*, May 26, 1992, 14.

Wen, Patricia. 2005. "Archdiocesan Agency Aids in Adoptions by Gays." *Boston Globe*, October 22, 2005, 1.

———. 2006a. "Seven Quit Charity over Policy of Bishops." *Boston Globe*, March 2, 2006, A1.

Wen, Patricia. 2006b. "Charity Stuns State, Ends Adoptions." *Boston Globe*, March 11, 2006, A1.

Werch, Chudley E., David A. Schroeder, and Linda L. Matthews. 1986. "The Health Fair as a Health Promotion Strategy: Effects on Health Risk Behaviors and the Utility of Specific Health Fair Activities." *Journal of American College Health* 35 (2): 74–79.

White, Ashli. 2010. *Encountering Revolution: Haiti and the Making of the Early Republic*. Baltimore: Johns Hopkins University Press.

Whitman, James Q. 2008. "Separating Church and State: The Atlantic Divide." *Historical Reflections* 34 (3): 86–104.

Wilentz, Amy. 1989. *The Rainy Season: Haiti since Duvalier*. New York: Simon & Schuster.

Wilkie, James W., and Stephen Haber. 1983. *Statistical Abstract of Latin America*. 22. Los Angeles: UCLA Latin America Center.

Williams, Eric. (1970) 1984. *From Columbus to Castro: The History of the Caribbean*. Reprint, New York: Random House.

Williams, Shannen Dee. 2022. *Subversive Habits: Black Catholic Nuns in the Long African American Freedom Struggle*. Durham: Duke University Press.

Wilson, Linette C. 2000. "Implementation and Evaluation of Church-Based Health Fairs." *Journal of Community Health Nursing* 17 (1): 39–48.

Women's Commission for Refugee Women and Children. 2001. *Innocents in Jail: INS Moves Refugee Women from Krome to Turner Guilford Knight Correctional Center*. New York: Women's Commission for Refugee Women and Children.

World Health Organization. 1998. *Health Promotion Glossary*. Geneva: World Health Organization.

Wosh, Peter J. 2005. *Covenant House: Journey of a Faith-Based Charity*. Philadelphia: University of Pennsylvania Press.

Wright, David J. 2009. *Taking Stock: The Bush Faith-Based Initiative and What Lies Ahead*. The Roundtable on Religion and Social Welfare Policy. Albany: Rockefeller Institute of Government, State University of New York.

Yankowski, Linda. 2010. "Common Ground for the Common Good: A Case Study of Church-State Partnership." In *Catholic Charities USA: 100 Years at the Intersection of Charity and Justice*, edited by Rev. J. Bryan Hehir, 85–109. Collegeville, MN: Liturgical Press.

Yawkey Foundation. 2018. "A Letter to the Boston Public Improvement Commission from Supporters of the Yawkey Foundations." March 15, 2018. https://yawkeyfoundation.org/boston-public-improvement-commission-from-yawkey/.

Zéphir, Flore. 2004. *The Haitian Americans*. Westport, CT: Greenwood Press.

Zigon, Jarrett. 2011. *"HIV is God's Blessing": Rehabilitating Morality in Neoliberal Russia*. Berkeley: University of California Press.

Founded in 1893,
UNIVERSITY OF CALIFORNIA PRESS
publishes bold, progressive books and journals
on topics in the arts, humanities, social sciences,
and natural sciences—with a focus on social
justice issues—that inspire thought and action
among readers worldwide.

The UC PRESS FOUNDATION
raises funds to uphold the press's vital role
as an independent, nonprofit publisher, and
receives philanthropic support from a wide
range of individuals and institutions—and from
committed readers like you. To learn more, visit
ucpress.edu/supportus.